CALIFORNIA REAL ESTATE

EXAM GUIDE

MINNIE LUSH, BA, GRI

Dearborn™
Real Estate Education

President: Roy Lipner
Vice-President of Product Development and Publishing: Evan M. Butterfield
Associate Publisher: Louise Benzer
Associate Development Editor: Elizabeth Austin
Managing Editor, Production: Daniel Frey
Quality Assurance Editor: David Shaw
Creative Director: Lucy Jenkins

Published by Dearborn™ Real Estate Education
a Division of Dearborn Financial Publishing, Inc.®
a Kaplan Professional Company®
30 South Wacker Drive
Chicago, Illinois 60606-7481
312-836-4400
www.dearbornRE.com

Printed in the United States of America.

05   06   07   10   9   8   7   6   5   4   3   2

To Nicole, Gabrielle, Gregory, Norman,
Joseph Sr., Amelia, and Joseph Jr.

M.L.

CONTENTS

ACKNOWLEDGMENTS

The author extends her sincere appreciation to the staff of Dearborn™ Real Estate Education for making their outstanding services so readily available. Special recognition goes to Liz Austin, Associate Development Editor, for her insight, encouragement, and valuable guidance in the format and direction of the manuscript.

Special thanks to the California Department of Real Estate for permission to use excerpts from DRE's *Reference Book*.

My thanks to Duane Gomer, President, Duane Gomer Seminars, for his reviews and suggestions. Very special thanks to Gregory Nassir, whose able assistance greatly helped with the flow of work. To family, friends, and former students go heartfelt gratitude for the patience and support shown for this project.

INSTRUCTIONS TO THE READER

This book is designed to be studied thoroughly after completing the required real estate qualifying courses and before taking the California real estate salesperson or broker examination. There is an assumption that the reader has a basic understanding of principles of real estate.

You will find the use of the Hot Notes to be extremely helpful as they are based on topics whose questions are often missed on licensing exams. By studying the Hot Notes well, along with the practice questions, and reviewing them again a few days before your actual examination, you will increase greatly your chances of success.

An estimated breakdown of the topics presented on the state examination follows. Of the percentages listed, under 10 percent of the questions on the actual exam will be presented in math form. The practice tests in this book have been patterned after the exam.

Examination Content

Subject:	Salesperson Exam:	Broker Exam:
Practice of Real Estate and Mandated Disclosures	24%	27%
Laws of Agency	12	12
Financing	13	13
Valuation and Market Analysis	12	11
Property Ownership and Land Use Controls and Regulations	18	15
Transfer of Property	9	10
Contracts	12	12

TIPS FOR SUCCESSFUL TEST TAKING

1. Congratulations on completing your required course work for the real estate license exam! Please study the Hot Notes thoroughly on a regular basis.

2. You are now ready to begin practice testing. The average score for the salesperson applicant the first time around on the practice tests is approximately 45 percent; for broker applicants the average is 55 percent, so don't be discouraged. Continue taking the practice test until you are scoring 90 percent or better before taking the actual state examination.

3. Select a quiet and undisturbed environment for practice testing. Attempt to simulate actual examination conditions, such as distribution of the test booklet (which you are asked not to mark), the score sheet, a pencil with an eraser, and a piece of scratch paper. You may erase if you wish, but usually your first selection is correct.

4. Now begin practice testing. Read each question over carefully, along with its four answer choices. Watch for qualifying words, such as *never, except, most correct,* or *least correct.* Be certain you understand exactly what the question is asking.

5. If you are struggling with a particular question, pass it up, mark the question number in column fashion on your scratch paper, and continue on. Often, the later questions will give you some insight on the questions you passed. Complete the test to the best of your ability, but be sure to go back and work on the questions you skipped on the first try.

6. You are allotted 3¼ hours to complete the 150-question California salesperson exam. This breaks down to approximately one and one-third minutes per question. The state's broker exam allows for five hours of actual testing time with a 45-minute break between test periods. Each test period for brokers covers 100 questions or 200 questions in total. This time allotment breaks down to approximately one and one-half minutes per question. Therefore, you cannot spend a disproportionate amount of time on any one question. Remember, if stuck on a question, move along to the next, keeping a running list on scratch paper so you can return to these later. You also might consider this process for math problems. Most math problems involve properly solving a number of steps, which can be time-consuming. Save them for the end, if this idea appeals to you.

7. When practice testing at home, attempt to complete each test in less time than you will be allowed for the actual state examinations.

8. You may use a programmable, battery-operated, handheld, non-printing calculator for the actual state examination. Your calculator must be quiet, and you will want to check the batteries before sitting for the exam. Calculators with alphabetic keyboards are not allowed. Palm devices are not allowed. Consider taking two calculators with you to the exam just in case one does not work well.

9. Continue to take the practice tests and reread the Hot Notes up to the day before your actual exam. **The broker applicant should study the basic 10 practice exams and its Hot Notes plus the Broker Appendix practice exams and its Hot Notes.**

10. The California Department of Real Estate publishes a *Reference Book*. If you wish for more in-depth study material and would like to purchase it, or for information on testing locations and available testing dates, please go online at *www.dre.ca.gov* or contact the DRE office in Sacramento, Los Angeles, Oakland, San Diego, or Fresno.

HOT NOTES

◼ REAL PROPERTY LAW

1. A *grant deed* transfers title. Do not confuse with a *trust deed* (financing), which is a security device.
2. A *notary public* is the party who witnesses the acknowledgment. The *grantor* acknowledges by signing in the presence of the notary.
3. To *alienate* means to transfer (or convey) title.
4. *Riparian rights* refer to those by a watercourse (river or stream).
5. The three degrees of flood hazard are *inundation*, *sheet overflow*, and *ponding*. Inundation is the first degree.
6. Stock in a mutual water company is real property.
7. *Fee simple* is the greatest interest one can have in the land.
8. An *estate of inheritance* is an *estate in fee*.
9. *Fee simple defeasible* is also known as a *determinable fee* and has conditions of ownership.
10. When a life estate terminates and the interest is to pass to one other than the original grantor, it is known as an *estate in remainder*. If interest reverts back to the original owner, it is an *estate in reversion*.
11. Less-than-freehold is known as *leasehold*.
12. An *estate for years* is a lease agreement (for a definite amount of time).
13. The lessee has the covenant of *quiet enjoyment* and *possession*, which goes with every lease agreement.
14. A lease for one year or less may be by oral agreement; more than one year must be in writing.

15. A *triple-net lease* is one wherein the tenant pays a stated rent plus property taxes, insurance, and maintenance of the property.

16. A *percentage lease* is usually based on a percentage of monthly gross income.

17. A lessee can grant an easement over the property leased, but only for the term of the lease.

18. *Rent* is consideration paid for the use of the property and is legally due at the end of the term.

19. To sublease is less than an assignment of a lease.

20. The security deposit for an unfurnished residential unit is two months' rent maximum; for furnished, the deposit maximum is three months' rent.

21. The legal action for removal of a defaulting tenant is an *unlawful detainer* action.

22. A grant deed must be signed by the grantor, not the grantee.

23. A grant deed requires only an adequate description for its validity.

24. A grant deed is presumed delivered when it is recorded or the grantee has possession of the document.

25. First to record a grant deed is *first in right,* with the exception of possession of property.

26. A witnessed will requires three signatures.

27. Customarily, the court confirms a probate sale and sets the broker's commission.

28. An administrator is not a party to a will.

29. Separate property without a will is divided one-third to the surviving spouse and two-thirds to the two or more children.

30. *Pur autre vie* means "for another's life." This expression is sometimes used in a life estate.

31. The minimum number of days for an eviction is 15. Eviction can occur after the fifteenth day by court order.

32. Neither an *estate for years* nor an *estate at sufferance* requires a notice to terminate.

33. An example of avulsion would be 150 feet of beachfront property being torn away by a flood.

34. The opposite of *avulsion* is *accretion.*

35. The opposite of *alienation* is *retention.*

36. Be alert to the correct spelling of the term "encumbrance."

37. A *lien* is a money encumbrance.

38. All liens are encumbrances, but not all encumbrances are liens.

39. A *judgment* is an example of a general lien.

40. A general lien affects all property of the debtor.

41. Mechanics' liens take priority over all other liens except taxes and special assessments but are on parity with each other.

42. The date that a mechanic's lien takes is the date the project began because of parity (equal basis).

43. An architect and drayman (truck driver) can file a mechanic's lien if unpaid.

44. When a completion bond is posted, the insurance company has ultimate responsibility for completing the job if the contractor cannot.

45. A Notice of Nonresponsibility is to be recorded and posted by an owner within 10 days of notice of work performed.

46. An *attachment* is a prejudgment action, is good for three years, and does not terminate on the death of the property owner.

47. A judgment is good for 10 years in the county where it is recorded.

48. A lis pendens action tells of a pending lawsuit affecting the title to land and clouds the title until a final judgment is rendered or until the matter is dismissed or removed.

49. Private restrictions on the use of land are usually created by the original subdivider but may be created by written agreement or general plan restrictions in subdivisions as well.

50. Covenants, conditions, and restrictions are usually found and recorded on a document called the *declaration of restrictions*.

51. Violation of a covenant can be stopped by an injunction.

52. Not all covenants "run with the land" (only some do), whereas all conditions "run with the land."

53. Violation of a condition can bring loss of title (*defeasance clause*, meaning title may be defeated or lost). Courts abhor conditions and often interpret conditions as covenants.

54. If a zoning change of a single lot is being requested, such action is a variance when it is for the owner's benefit.

55. If public restrictions (zoning) and private restrictions (CC&Rs) differ, the more stringent or rigid will prevail.

56. An *appurtenant easement* goes with the land, whereas an *easement in gross* goes to a person (e.g., Mark gives John the right to cross over his property, but John does not own any property; he has been given an easement in gross).

57. Typically, a utility company holds an easement in gross to service property owners.

58. A license allows one to use the property of another but only for the periods or conditions set by owner, and such permission can be revoked by the owner at any time.

59. Easement by prescription establishes use, whereas adverse possession may establish title claim.

60. A spouse can file a homestead declaration on the separate property of the other, if all other requirements are met.

61. A homestead declaration is effective if recorded prior to the recording of a judgment.

62. The usual methods for termination of homestead are the sale of property or the filing of a declaration of abandonment.

63. An unlocated easement is valid (e.g., old utility company easements that are difficult to precisely locate).
64. An *encroachment* is the unlawful intrusion onto the adjacent owner's land (e.g., a fence built over the property line onto a neighbor's lot). The landowner has three years from discovery to take action for its removal.
65. A homestead declaration is not an encumbrance.

■ PROPERTY OWNERSHIP AND LAND USE CONTROLS AND REGULATIONS

1. A grant deed signed by a single person under 18 is void.
2. Commission split agreements between brokers may be by oral agreement. You can pay a commission to an out-of-state broker.
3. Infill redevelops property for mixed use.
4. Executory means something is to be performed at a later date. Executed means a document has been signed.
5. The statute of limitations on a judgment is 10 years.
6. An *exclusive agency listing* allows the owner to sell the property during the listing period and not pay a commission.
7. All exclusive listings must have a definite termination date.
8. On an open listing, only the agent who is the procuring cause earns the commission.
9. A net listing is legal, but not recommended.
10. Expansion and contraction of available spaces is influenced mainly by the elasticity of demand.
11. A *kiosk* is a small freestanding building used for information purposes that is often found in shopping centers.
12. *Demography* is the study of the population.
13. A *megalopolis* is a very large city.
14. If a zoning change of a single lot is being requested, such action is a variance when it is for the owner's benefit.
15. Installation of a septic tank must be at least five feet away from the improvements.
16. The term *setback* describes the distance between the street and the front of the improvements that must remain unimproved to comply with the ordinance. There are front, side, and rear yard setbacks in most communities.
17. The purpose of the Franchise Investment Law is to protect the franchisee.
18. Discretionary funds are used to purchase a franchise.
19. A bulk sales notice must be published by a transferee (a buyer) at least 12 business days prior to the sale. The notice only has to appear once and is designed to alert the creditors. This is under the Uniform Commercial Code.

20. A buyer should obtain a clearance receipt from the State Board of Equalization to avoid successor's liability.
21. A *bill of sale* transfers title to personal property.
22. A bill of sale requires the seller's signature.
23. The Department of Alcoholic Beverage Control regulates liquor licensing.
24. To be exempt from the permit aspect of the Franchise Investment Law, a franchisor must have a net worth of $5 million with at least 25 franchises operating continuously in the five years preceding the offering.
25. A common test for water pressure is to turn on all faucets and flush the toilets.
26. Toxic waste affects the value of property near a gasoline station.
27. Title VIII of the Civil Rights Act of 1968 (federal) also prohibits discrimination in the membership of real estate boards and the multiple-listing service. Title VIII is also called the federal Fair Housing Act.
28. "As is" refers to observable defects.
29. Under California Fair Housing, an owner of a single-family residence may take in one boarder to live with him or her and is exempt from this act.
30. The Unruh Civil Rights Act controls businesses and prohibits discrimination.
31. Under the Unruh Civil Rights Act, both actual and punitive damages are possible.
32. *Steering, panic selling,* and *blockbusting* are examples of illegal and unethical practices by a real estate licensee.
33. *Redlining* is discrimination by a financial institution.
34. The purpose of federal fair housing laws is to provide fair housing for all persons in the United States.
35. Legal action based on alleged violations of fair housing laws can be brought in both federal and state courts.
36. The United States landmark case of *Jones v. Mayer* in 1968 barred racial discrimination in property matters in the United States.
37. As of 1987, a Real Property Transfer Disclosure Statement is required of sellers or transferors of one-unit to four-unit dwellings. Even if seller sells "as is," the statement is still required. A broker cannot fill in seller's portion of the form. A broker must make a competent visual inspection of the accessible areas and disclose. This is based on *Easton v. Strassburger.*
38. A written Agency Disclosure Statement, as of 1988, is required to be given by agents to sellers and buyers of one to four dwelling units.
39. A *fiduciary relationship* refers to loyalty, integrity, and utmost care.
40. There are three base and meridian lines in California-Humboldt, Mt. Diablo, and San Bernardino.

41. Do not confuse the expression "miles square," which means shape, with "square miles," which means area or content. For example, a township is a six-mile square, containing 36 square miles. How many townships are there in a 36-mile square? The answer is 36 (36 × 36 = 1,296 ÷ 36 sections to a township = 36).

42. There are 36 sections to a township. Each section contains 640 acres. A section is a one-mile square.

43. The orientation of range lines is north and south (as a memory jogger, there are five letters each in range, north, and south).

44. The orientation of base lines (or township lines) is east and west (there are four letters each in base, east, and west).

45. There are 43,560 square feet to an acre. There are 208.71 feet on each side of a square acre. There are 4,840 square yards to one acre.

46. There are 5,280 feet to a mile.

47. There are 320 rods to a mile, 16½ feet to one rod, and four rods, or 66 feet, to one chain.

48. There are nine square feet to a square yard.

49. One board foot can be described as 6" × 2" × 12" or 12" × 12" × 1".

50. The term *side yard setback* describes the distance between the property line and the edge of the improvements. Be sure to deduct any side yard setback from both sides.

51. If "setback" dimensions are given in a problem, be sure to deduct the setbacks from the total lot area to arrive at buildable square feet.

52. The term *contiguous* indicates lots that abut each other, at any point of contact.

53. The metes-and-bounds method of land description is based on angles and directions from a north and south line.

54. The metes-and-bounds method is the most complex method of land description.

55. The recorded map, lot, block, and tract system is the most commonly used, due to its simplicity.

56. To find the *cost* of property, add percentage of profit made to 100%, then divide sales price by total percentage.

57. To find *sales price*, subtract percentage of profit to be made from 100 percent, then divide the cost by the remainder.

58. The nominal rate stated on any note (financing) is the interest rate stated in the note itself.

59. To change a fraction to a percentage, divide the top number by the bottom number and then convert to the percentage form (e.g., 1/8 = 12.5%).

60. Convert any monthly or quarterly returns on investment to the annual figure before proceeding with calculating the problems.

61. The reciprocal of an 8 percent capitalization rate is 12.5. This tells us we have to receive our 8 percent return 12.5 times to equal our initial investment.

62. There are 66 feet to one chain. One hundred chains equal 6,600 feet and is longer than one mile (5,280 feet).

63. Non-conforming use is allowed to continue because it was legal before a zone change, and comes under a Grandfather clause.

64. A square parcel of one-half mile by one-half mile describes 160 acres, or a quarter of a section.

65. Avulsion describes a sudden violent action, such as a dam that breaks and washes the land away.

66. Frequent flooding occurs twice in 10 years.

67. An estate has two uses: fee simple and leasehold.

68. Escheat is not a way for an individual to receive title to property. It refers to the way the state might receive title.

69. Eminent domain is a form of involuntary conversion.

70. The county recorder is required to maintain index books.

71. An owner of property cannot be prohibited from placing a "for sale" sign on property.

72. Developers are mainly concerned with the purchasing power of the surrounding population.

73. Section 7 has 80 acres valued at $500 per acre for a total of $40,000. Section 6 has 40 acres valued at $800 per acre for a total of $32,000. The difference in value of these two sections is $8,000.

74. A parcel that has 3,960 linear feet at its frontage with 1,980 feet on one side and 3,960 feet on the other side because the parcel is bisected by a river contains 270 acres.

75. A mechanic's lien takes priority over all other liens, except taxes and special assessments, such as the 1911 Street Improvement Bond. It also takes priority over a trust deed that is recorded after the mechanic's lien.

76. R-3 zoning is used for three or more units.

77. Flood hazard zones are based on a 100 year history.

78. The footing is the base or bottom of a foundation wall, pier, or column.

79. If the interior side of an exterior wall feels the same as the outside temperature, then heat and air are being lost through wall outlets.

80. If the interior side of a partition wall feels the same as the room temperature, then the insulation in the building is sufficient.

81. Wallboard is nailed to studs.

82. If there is no Notice of Completion of work filed (done by the owner of property), then there are ninety days to file a mechanic's lien (there are three *n*'s—no, notice, and ninety, making it easy to remember ninety days to file a mechanic's lien when no Notice of Completion is filed).

83. Police power includes the government's right to enforce land use controls, such as zoning, municipal codes, rent control, and subdivision codes, without compensation to property owners. Remember it is eminent domain that requires compensation, not police power.

84. A joint tenancy may be severed by conveying it to another party (by sale or gift). The most distinguishing characteristic of joint tenancy is its right of survivorship.

85. The Federal Emergency Management Agency (FEMA) provides maps delineating areas of special flood zones where flooding occurs at least once every 100 years.

■ VALUATION AND MARKET ANALYSIS

1. An appraisal may be by oral or written means.

2. According to the Appraisal Institute's Code of Ethics, members cannot base their fee on a percentage of the final estimate of value and must disclose any interest in the property being appraised.

3. The first step in the appraisal process is to define the problem. The last step is to state the *estimated value*.

4. Amenity-type properties are single-family residences.

5. The market data or comparison approach is used on residential property and vacant land.

6. Land is always appraised separately as if vacant and available for highest and best use.

7. The methods used to appraise land are market data (comparison), land residual, development method, or allocation, not equity.

8. Location is the most important factor influencing value.

9. The south and west sides of the street are preferred for retail business.

10. Depth tables are used to appraise vacant lots. The percentage of value is estimated according to the depth of the lot.

11. Orientation refers to the placement of a structure on a lot to gain the best advantage to the elements (wind, sunlight, etc.).

12. A cul-de-sac is a dead-end street.

13. *Ad valorem* means "according to value."

14. Productivity is a direct function of use.

15. A fee appraiser is an independent contractor.

16. Economic rent refers to the going "market rate" for rent of a given unit and is used for the appraisal of income property.

17. Contract rent refers to the actual lease amount of a unit and could be above or below market rate (economic rent).

18. The average economic life of a residence is 40 years.

19. In a narrative appraisal, the type of "appraised value" being given is found in the "statement of purpose" section of the letter of transmittal. The narrative is most comprehensive.

20. In the cost approach, *replacement* means a similar building with the same utility; *reproduction* means a replica.
21. Net operating income divided by a capitalization rate equals value.
22. The higher the risk, the higher the capitalization rate and the lower the value.
23. An appraisal may be by oral or written means. A fee appraiser is an independent contractor.
24. Functional utility is a main concern of an appraiser.
25. Marketability is the ultimate test of functional utility.
26. Business opportunities are appraised on net income.
27. A commercial strip center is a string of neighborhood stores.
28. Commercial property: As the depth of the lot decreases, the front foot value decreases, and the square foot value increases.
29. Always adjust comparable properties to subject property. If a comparable sale is less than subject property, adjust it UPWARD.
30. The cost per square foot to build a two-story house is less than the cost per square foot to build a single-story house of the same square footage.
31. The major cause of depreciation is obsolescence. Depreciation is a loss in value from any cause. Accountants deal with book appreciation. Appraisers deal with actual depreciation.
32. An appraiser uses the cost approach on special properties, including a medical building. The income approach is used on a shopping center or a restaurant.
33. An investor in commercial property is interested in net income.
34. Cost equals value when the improvements are new and are of highest and best use.
35. If current highest and best use is to change, current use is called interim use.
36. A civil engineer could verify soil compaction.
37. Accrued depreciation is accumulated age depreciation with an allowance for property condition based on the property's effective age (physical condition and appearance).
38. The cost approach uses separate values to arrive at cost (value of depreciated improvements and land value).
39. Economic rent (realistic market rate) is used for the appraisal of income property.
40. The definition of value to an appraiser includes value of a commodity to be exchanged for another commodity and desirability to someone else. Value is closely related to worth.
41. The purpose of the land residual technique by an appraiser is to estimate the value of only the land (the building value is known).
42. The purpose of the building residual technique by an appraiser is to estimate the value of only the building (the land value is known).
43. The purpose of the property residual technique is to estimate the value of the total property as a single unit.

44. Use the gross rent multiplier rule: sales price divided by gross rent equals the gross rent multiplier. Property valued at $90,000 with a monthly rent of $600 ($600 times 12 months equals $7,200 annual rent) has a multiplier of 12.5 ($90,000 divided by $7,200 equals 12.5). If the monthly rent is increased to $640 ($640 times 12 months equals $7,680), then the annual rent of $7,680 times 12.5 equals the new value of $96,000.

45. An appraisal is valid for a specific date. It is usually the date of property inspection and report (or contract date).

46. In order to appraise a commercial property that's value exceeds $250,000, the appraiser must be a certified general licensee.

47. If interest rates increase, the value of property decreases. If rental income increases, the value of the property increases.

48. Effective gross income is scheduled gross income minus vacancy factor.

■ FINANCING

1. HUD, a federal agency, is the overseer of all housing matters in the United States, including fair housing, redevelopment, FHA, and so on. Discrimination complaints may be filed with HUD, and with the state and federal courts.

2. Insurance companies make large commercial loans and "participation" loans, usually charging lower interest rates due to lower servicing costs.

3. Savings associations make the bulk of home loans.

4. Commercial banks rely heavily on customer relations and past business experiences with a borrower as a consideration for granting loans.

5. Mortgage bankers "warehouse" (hold) their loans and then sell their portfolios to investors in the secondary mortgage market.

6. The largest source of junior mortgage loans is private individuals.

7. The Federal Reserve System controls the flow of money. When selling bonds from its portfolio, the Fed effectively pulls money out of the market, thereby slowing down economic activity.

8. An insurance company is the least likely source to refinance an existing home loan.

9. Fannie Mae is the largest investor in the secondary money market.

10. Fannie Mae, Ginnie Mae, Freddie Mac, mortgage companies, and private individuals deal in "passthrough" securities.

11. If a borrower chooses not to renegotiate an RRM at the end of the three-year to five-year term with the same lender, the loan balance becomes due and payable in full. The maximum interest rate fluctuation is 5 percent.

12. The *takeout loan* is the long-term loan in construction financing;

sometimes called a *standby loan*. Proceeds are used to pay off the interim (short-term) loan.

13. When a contractor secures a completion bond, the insurance company is ultimately responsible for completion of the project.

14. The purpose of the FHA insurance program is to stabilize the mortgage market by providing insured financing for loans made by approved lenders. Appraisers must also be approved by FHA.

15. There is no prepayment penalty allowed on FHA or VA loans. A prepayment penalty is allowed on Cal-Vet loans.

16. There is no down payment on VA loans unless required by lender.

17. Newer FHA and VA loans usually contain an alienation (due-on-sale) clause.

18. Cal-Vet is financed by the sale of bonds. The security device used is a real property sales contract (land contract). Cal-Vet loans are variable interest rate loans. A veteran can buy a farm on Cal-Vet.

19. In truth-in-lending, the total cost of credit must be expressed as a percentage, followed by "annual percentage rate" (fully spelled out).

20. Rescission period for truth-in-lending is until midnight of the third business day of the last of these events to occur: (A) consummation of the transaction; (B) delivery of all material truth-in-lending disclosures; or (C) delivery of the notice of the right to rescind (or after the signing of the note).

21. RESPA applies to one-family to four-family unit mortgage loans. A special information booklet and good-faith estimate must be presented on receipt of loan application or within three business days thereof. The borrower may inspect the settlement statement one business day before closing the loan transaction. No fee can be charged for this statement. HUD enforces RESPA.

22. RESPA disallows finder's fees and kickbacks for any service not actually performed. Violations of the kickback provision results in a fine of not more than $10,000 or one year in jail or both. RESPA allows the lender to collect impounds for the current installment, plus two months. A referral fee from an escrow holder to a broker is a violation of RESPA.

23. *Nominal rate* is the rate stated or named in a note.

24. Real estate loans are usually based on simple interest, not compound interest.

25. The most common form of real estate loan payment is the "level payment," indicating the same monthly payment amount with the portion of principal increasing and interest decreasing over the life of the loan (fully amortized loan).

26. A *partially amortized loan* is one that has a balloon payment remaining. A balloon payment is defined as twice the smallest installment. The loan balance is due in full at the end of the term.

27. Examples of negotiable (salable) instruments are checks, drafts, bills of exchange, and promissory notes. A trust deed or mortgage contract is not negotiable; however, this is assigned when the promissory note is sold.

28. "Without recourse" is an example of a qualified endorsement.

29. A mortgagee is a lender. Under a judicial sale of a mortgage contract, the successful bidder is given a "certificate of sale." The "sheriff's deed" is given when the redemption period is up and the mortgagor has not redeemed the property.

30. There is no deficiency judgment allowed in purchase-money transactions. Purchase money is defined as a credit extension. Hard money refers to cash in hand, such as equity loans.

31. A reconveyance deed is given by trustee to trustor, not beneficiary to trustor.

32. There is no equity of redemption on a trust deed.

33. Once a notice of default has been recorded, the trustor can reinstate the loan up to five business days before the trustee's sale.

34. A trustee's deed is given to the successful bidder at a trustee sale. Foreclosure can be by trustee sale or by judicial sale.

35. An *acceleration clause* is always found in a trust deed.

36. An *alienation* (due-on-sale) *clause* is enforceable.

37. An *or more clause* allows an early payment of the loan without penalty.

38. A *subordination clause* is often used on vacant land purchases.

39. An *assignment of rents* clause benefits a lender.

40. In a "subject to" transaction, the seller remains responsible for the loan.

41. An *open-end loan* (such as a construction loan or credit card account) allows one to borrow additional sums after the balance has been reduced without rewriting the loan agreement.

42. A *promotional note* is a short-term note of up to and including 36 months in its term.

43. A *seasoned note* is one that is 36 months and one day or longer.

44. On a real property sales contract (land contract), the vendee receives equitable title with legal title remaining with the vendor until a later agreed-upon time.

45. Under the Uniform Vendor and Purchaser Risk Act of 1947, the party in possession of the property is not relieved of the lien if the property is destroyed by some form of disaster.

46. A vendor cannot prevent prepayment by the vendee of the land contract on subdivided lots of four units or less. The vendee receives equitable title.

47. To record a land contract, the vendor's (seller's) signature on the contract must be acknowledged (notarized).

48. An acceleration clause in a note does not affect its salability (negotiability) and might enhance its desirability to the buyer of the note.
49. A conditional commitment for an FHA loan is valid for six months.
50. Real estate loans are calculated on simple interest, not compound.
51. Capital markets include bonds, short-term notes, and treasury bills.
52. Mortgage bankers must maintain a good line of credit at a bank.
53. Mortgage brokers do not lend their own money.
54. Fannie Mae only deals in the secondary mortgage market.
55. Purchase money loans are credit extensions for the purchase of one to four dwelling units. Hard money is cash.
56. In a "subject to" loan takeover, the seller remains liable.
57. A VA loan amount (federal veterans' loan program) is based on the Certificate of Reasonable Value (appraisal). The origination fee is paid to the lender.
58. An alienation clause (due on sale clause) is enforceable and is a benefit to a lender. It is a type of acceleration clause.
59. An acceleration clause is always found in a deed of trust.
60. The maximum interest rate fluctuation on a renegotiable rate mortgage is 5 percent. Its maximum annual change is ½ (one half) percent.
61. The only thing a trust deed and mortgage have in common is the security. The major difference is the title. A deed of trust may be foreclosed by trustee's sale or judicial foreclosure. A trustee's deed is given to the highest bidder at a trustee's sale. There is no right of redemption at a trustee's sale.
62. A "Request for Notice of Default" benefits any junior lien holder.
63. FHA, but not VA, provides for a duplex purchased for rental.
64. Mutual mortgage insurance is paid on an FHA loan.
65. Under a Cal-Vet loan, the California Department of Veteran's Affairs holds title to the Cal-Vet's home. A veteran can buy a farm on the Cal-Vet program. Cal-Vet prohibits the payment of points on its loans.
66. PMI (private mortgage insurance) is available through a pool of private investor insurance funds. Both FHA and PMI insure loans.
67. The Federal Reserve System does the following to stimulate the housing market: lowers interest rates, buys securities, and reduces discount rates to member banks. The effect of raising interest rates and selling securities slows down the housing market.
68. Hypothecation uses real property as security for a debt with the borrower retaining possession of the property.
69. The secondary mortgage market supplies funds to lenders in the primary mortgage market.
70. Real estate loans made or arranged by real estate brokers are exempt from the usury laws. The interest rate is unlimited.

71. A standby commitment is a pledge by a permanent lender to fund a long-term loan to take out the construction lender when the building is completed.

72. An open-end loan provides for future advances without rewriting the loan each time.

73. Under an FHA loan, the broker who contributes his or her own funds to a buyer's down payment, with no disclosure to a seller, could cause liability for both him or herself and the buyer.

74. A 100 percent loan is possible on a VA loan. Either the buyer or the seller can pay points on a VA loan. The origination fee on a VA loan is paid to the lender.

75. Completing the clause in the loan application that inquires about one's race or marital status is optional. It is not required to be completed.

■ TRANSFER OF PROPERTY

1. A *bill of sale* transfers title to personal property.

2. A security agreement is used for personal property loans.

3. The UCC-1 form (financing statement) is filed with the secretary of state.

4. FHA's minimum ceiling height is seven feet, six inches.

5. FHA's crawlspace requirement is 18 inches.

6. FHA's minimum stairwell width is three feet with one handrail.

7. A bulk sales notice must be published by a transferee (buyer) at least 12 business days prior to the sale. The notice has to appear only once and is designed to alert creditors.

8. Sales tax is a tax on only tangible personal property.

9. The maximum sales tax penalty is 35 percent for late filing of sales and use tax, due to fraud or evasion.

10. A buyer should obtain a clearance receipt from the State Board of Equalization to avoid successor's liability.

11. The maximum fee a seller can charge for an on-sale or off-sale general liquor license is $6,000, if the license is up to five years of age.

12. A bona fide club must be in existence for at least one year in order to receive a liquor license after proper application.

13. A real estate licensee may represent the sale or purchase of a mobile home. A certificate of title transfers ownership.

14. *Escrow* is a neutral third party that acts as an agent for the parties to the transaction, but cannot give legal advice.

15. Escrow instructions must be executed.

16. Escrow is considered complete when all the terms and conditions have been met.

17. Sales are not listed on a balance sheet but are shown on a profit and loss statement.

18. The terms *short rate* and *pro rata* are insurance terms. *Subrogation* means substituting one party's rights for another and is used in claims cases where the insurance company pays off the insured and then proceeds against the party who caused the problem.

19. There is only one unity in tenancy in common and it is possession.

20. There are four unities in joint tenancy and they are time, title, interest, and possession (referred to as TTIP, with a right of survivorship).

21. Joint tenancy title may be held by brother and sister, husband and wife, friends, or any relationship. Tenancy in common may also be held as such.

22. Community property is based on Spanish law and reserved for husband and wife.

23. The legal action against a buyer who defaults on a land contract is a *quiet title action*.

24. *Leasehold* is not a real property item, but describes a tenant's interest in property. Leasehold is a chattel real.

25. If the buyer's name on a contract was shown as "John Hartman and Mary Hartman" and nothing further stated, title would be assumed to be as tenants in common (they could be brother and sister). Do not assume community property unless the names are followed by husband and wife.

26. The definition of *et ux*, means *and wife*.

27. A chain of title shows a continuous record of owners of property. Without a chain, a title company fears a *wild document*.

28. A title plant contains histories of real estate transactions.

29. Corporations cannot take title as joint tenants due to their perpetual existence.

30. Title companies set their own rates.

31. Forgery would be covered on a CLTA standard title insurance policy. Such policy is most commonly obtained by homeowners and does not require on-site inspection of property.

32. Title insurance companies will not protect against known defects at the time of transfer.

■ TAX ASPECTS

1. Change of ownership statements are filed within 45 days of change. Over assessments can be appealed to the Assessment Appeals Board.

2. Sales tax applies to "tangible personal property."

3. The maximum sales tax penalty for late filing is 35 percent if due to fraud or evasion.

4. Sales are not listed on a balance sheet. They are shown on a profit and loss statement.

5. There is up to a $500,000 capital gains tax exclusion for married couples filing jointly on the sale of a principal residence in which they have lived two of the five years prior to sale. Single-filers are entitled to a $250,000 exclusion.

6. The tax exclusion described in Note 5 can be used every two years.

7. IRC 1031 exchanges require like-kind property.

8. Real estate syndications are regulated by the Corporations Commissioner.

9. A corporation cannot take title in joint tenancy because of its perpetual existence.

10. A written limited partnership is the most common form of syndication in California, and has limited liability up to the amount invested.

11. A general partnership carries "joint and several liabilities" for partnership debts.

12. A REIT is made up of 100 or more investors.

13. A condominium is the only place where one purchases a fee simple interest and an in-common interest at the same time.

14. In a community apartment project all owners are tenants in common.

15. A County Board of Supervisors sets property tax rates. The State Board of Equalization assesses public utilities.

16. The Interstate (federal) Land Sales Full Disclosure Act involves 25 or more lots with a seven-day right of rescission.

17. Tax consciousness should begin prior to the acquisition of property.

18. Income taxes are progressive taxes.

19. Property taxes are *ad valorem* taxes, which means "according to value."

20. The time frames for the first installment of property tax are November 1 and December 10; for the second installment, February 1 and April 10.

21. If property taxes remain unpaid, the county transfers the property to the state. A five-year redemption period beginning June 30 follows and the owner remains in possession.

22. Street improvement assessments are based on the front footage of property. After the assessment's due date, 30 days must pass before the unpaid balance, if any, goes to bond.

23. Boot and mortgage relief (on exchanges) are taxable in the year of sale.

24. Property taxes are calculated on 1 percent of assessed value as set by the county assessor.

25. In a "sale-leaseback," a purchaser would be least interested in the seller's book value.

26. Prepaid taxes are a credit on a seller's closing statement.

27. Exchanges are based on equity value. Equity is market value minus liens.

28. An investor of commercial or residential income property who "actively participates" in the operation of the property can deduct operating expenses from ordinary income if he owns at least a 10 percent interest and makes bona fide management decisions. The maximum annual net loss deduction against ordinary income is $25,000.

29. To avoid successor's liability in the sale of a business that collects sales tax, the buyer should be certain to include a provision in the purchase agreement that an amount for any sales tax collected and not yet paid be held in escrow until a clearance receipt is received from the State Board of Equalization.

30. The county transfer tax is easily calculated as $1.10 per $1,000 of the sales price (the actual calculation is 55 cents per each $500 of the sales price or fraction thereof). If the sales price is $90,750 with an existing loan of $30,000 which the buyer agrees to take over, then subtract the $30,000 (as it was taxed in its original sale) and tax the balance of $60,750 at $1.10 per $1,000. ($60,000 ÷ $1,000 = $60. $60 × $1.10 = $66.00. Be sure to add $1.10 for the $750). The total tax is $67.10. Improvements for streets, lights, and sewers can be paid by special assessments. Non-payment of special assessments leads to foreclosure like property taxes.

31. Impound accounts are used for recurring costs like property taxes. Title insurance is a one-time charge and is not impounded.

32. A person who buys property under a sale-leaseback agreement would be least interested in the seller's book value.

■ REAL ESTATE PRACTICE, LAWS OF AGENCY, AND MANDATED DISCLOSURES

1. Brokers must keep all records for a minimum of three years from the date of closing, or if not closed, from the date of listing.

2. If the Real Estate Commissioner needs legal advice, the commissioner goes to the state attorney general.

3. Within its own county, the district attorney's office prosecutes law violations.

4. A licensee may appeal to the court if a decision of the commissioner is deemed unfavorable to the licensee.

5. The relationship between the real estate broker and the salesperson is that of employer to employee under real estate law.

6. The Agency Relationship Disclosure Act became law on January 1, 1988, and is found in Civil Code section 2079.

7. If a mobile home has been registered with DMV or HCD, a real estate licensee can handle the transaction. A broker cannot display two or more mobile homes on the brokerage property without being a mobile-home dealer.

8. After passing the real estate exam, one has only one year from the date the exam was taken in which to mail the application for the license.

9. A foundation plan shows the piers, footing, subfloors, and columns of a building.

10. A California real estate license is good for negotiating anywhere in the state no matter where the property is located (e.g., property may be out of state).

11. A *land locator* is a broker who helps to sell government property and is required to have a real estate license because a commission is earned.

12. Failure to disclose material facts, whether in real estate or other fields, is a form of fraudulent misrepresentation.

13. Under real estate law, the salesperson is the employee of the broker. Do not confuse with the independent contractor status that most licensees choose for tax purposes. For testing purposes, select the employee-to-employer relationship.

14. An attorney-in-fact (one who has been given a power of attorney) signs the principal's name first, then his/her name followed by "attorney-in-fact." You do not have to be an attorney-at-law to be an attorney-in-fact.

15. There are 10 members, plus the commissioner, on the real estate advisory commission.

16. Real estate licenses do not have to be displayed on the wall but must be kept at the main office of the employing broker.

17. A statutory requirement calls for a written agreement between the broker and salesperson for employment; however, it does not have to be on a form approved by the commissioner. A copy of the agreement is to be kept by both the broker and the salesperson for three years.

18. A salesperson cannot act independently of the broker, and no referral fees or commissions can be received through any other source for real estate activities other than through the employing broker.

19. Under the prepaid rental listing service requirement, a prospective tenant who has paid the fee must be provided with at least three available rentals within five days of payment.

20. When a salesperson transfers a license, the new broker must advise DRE in Sacramento within five days of new employment.

21. There must be a definite termination date on all exclusive listing agreements.

22. A real estate licensee cannot make a secret profit and must disclose if he or she is buying property for his or her own account.

23. An owner (nonlicensee) may make a secret profit. Owners of property do not have to disclose what they paid for their property.

24. The term REALTOR® is owned by the National Association of REALTORS® and only those members may use the term.

25. Inducements to "panic selling" and "blockbusting" are discriminatory activities by a real estate licensee, which are violations of law.

26. Joists are supports that are parallel to the floor and ceiling.

27. An agent cannot answer a seller's question, "What is the racial background of the buyer?"

28. Mortgage (broker loan) disclosure statements must be kept for three years. It is illegal and discriminatory for a lender to charge a translation fee for a foreign language-speaking borrower.

29. Within three business days, trust funds received by a broker are to be placed into either a neutral escrow depository, the hands of the principal, or the broker's trust fund account unless written instructions from the buyer are to the contrary.

30. If a promissory note is offered as a deposit on an offer, the broker must advise the principal of this material fact.

31. In an S corporation, all profits and losses are passed through to each stockholder to calculate against ordinary income.

32. A license is required to act in real estate matters for compensation, including property management and mortgage lending.

33. An unlicensed person (e.g., secretary, bookkeeper) cannot give information regarding a real estate transaction on the telephone or in any way practice real estate for compensation.

34. Real Estate Principles is a required course before applying for a license.

35. One must be 18 years of age or older to apply for a license, once statutory requirements are completed.

36. Competing brokers agreeing to set commissions at a certain percentage are in violation of antitrust laws.

37. The maximum amount payable from the recovery account per transaction is $20,000. The maximum payable per licensee (multiple transactions) is $100,000.

38. Any further licensing information can be obtained from the following address: California Department of Real Estate, Information Section, P.O. Box 160009, Sacramento, CA 95816, or go online at *www.dre.ca.gov*.

39. If you give the Real Property Transfer Disclosure Statement after acceptance of offer, the buyer has five days if it is given by mail (or three days if given in person) to rescind the contract. The *Easton v. Strassburger* case reaffirms that both the seller and the agent must make full disclosure of material facts that may be known or unknown to a potential buyer.

40. An injured party has two years in which to file legal action on the Transfer Disclosure Statement. An amendment has a three-day right of recission.

41. "As is" sales of one to four dwelling units require a Transfer Disclosure Statement.

42. Both the buyer's agent and the seller's agent must render a competent and diligent visual inspection of the accessible areas of one to four dwelling units.

43. A Homeowner's Guide to Earthquake Safety must be given on the sale of one to four dwelling units of wood frame construction built prior to 1960. The Alquist-Priolo Special Studies Zones Act requires disclosure of property located within one-quarter of a mile of a fault line.

44. *Jones v. Mayer,* a 1968 U.S. Supreme Court landmark decision bars (stops) racial discrimination on property matters in the United States.

45. Properties of one to four dwelling units built prior to 1978 require a lead-based paint disclosure. These properties are referred to as "target housing."

46. The Agency Relationship Disclosure Act became effective in 1988. The process is to disclose, elect, and confirm. Confirmation is done in the purchase agreement (deposit receipt).

47. The Mello-Roos Tax lien disclosure is required from seller to buyer on all types of property.

48. The Natural Hazards Disclosure is required from seller to buyer.

49. The company dollar is gross income minus commissions.

50. The desk cost includes operating expenses for the office, including salaries, divided by the number of salespeople.

51. The Unruh Civil Rights Act prohibits discrimination by businesspersons. The California Fair Housing Act (Rumford Act) applies to everyone in the state. Complaints may be filed with the California Department of Fair Employment and Housing. A homeowner may bring in one roommate and be exempt from this act.

52. Advertisements that state that the offering is made only to single women or only to persons of a minority background are in violation of fair housing laws.

53. An agent cannot answer any questions about one's race.

54. A temporary 150-day real estate license may be issued to a qualified license applicant whose name appears on a delinquent child support payment list.

55. An unlicensed person who practices real estate may be fined up to $10,000. A broker who hires an unlicensed person to practice real estate also may be fined up to $10,000.

56. An unlicensed assistant who prepares an advertisement must have prior written approval by the employing broker.

57. The maximum amount of compensation the DRE will pay out of the recovery account per transaction is $20,000, even if a victim holds an uncollectible judgment for more than $20,000.

58. Construction work of less than $500 in value can be done by someone who does not have a contractor's license.

59. Worker's compensation is required for all real estate licensees, no matter whether the licensee is an independent contractor for taxation purposes.

60. Eighteen hours of the 45 hours of required continuing education must be about consumer protection.

61. The district attorney prosecutes law violations by unlicensed persons.

62. In-house sales might give rise to an undisclosed dual agency.

63. As a matter of good practice, a broker who purchases property for his own account should consider having another agent present the offer.

64. Electronic records are acceptable to the DRE as long as they are backed up for a three year period. Upon request by the DRE, a broker must provide paper copies of trust records at the broker's expense.

65. Radon gas is tested by a spectrometer.

66. A broker who shows a property in which the broker has an option to purchase must disclose anticipated profit and that he is a principal.

67. Net operating income minus debt service equals the cash flow of income property.

68. An investor of commercial property is interested in the property's net income.

69. Failure to disclose a dual agency can lead to loss of commission, suspension or revocation of the real estate license, and civil action by the injured party.

70. Illegal use of the term REALTOR® can result in loss of license. It is also a violation of California real estate law.

71. Warranty of authority states that a principal (seller-employer) is liable for the acts of the agent (employee) within the scope of authority granted. Therefore, both the seller and agent may be liable for any misrepresentations. (If the agent exceeds the authority, the agent alone may be liable for resulting damage.)

72. The lead-based paint disclosure applies to residential one to four dwelling units built prior to 1978; therefore, this would apply to a single-family residence built in 1975. This disclosure is especially concerned with small children who might ingest paint chips.

73. Home sales can be a good indication of the consumer price index because a home is the largest purchase the average consumer makes.

74. A broker who wants to use a fictitious business name must file a fictitious business name statement with the county clerk, have the notice published in a newspaper of general circulation once a week for four weeks and apply to the real estate commissioner for approval of the use of the name.

75. A real estate license can be restricted as to term, employment to a particular broker, limitation to a certain type of activity, and the requirement of the posting of a surety bond.

76. In addition to the "Homeowner's Guide to Earthquake Safety" being provided to buyers of residential property built prior to January 1, 1960, it is also required on a masonry building built prior to January 1, 1975, containing portions of wood frame construction.

77. The property manager is responsible for routine maintenance and is to be employed under a written management agreement. The issue of property management should be decided upon before one buys investment property.

78. An unlicensed person who practices real estate is subject to a fine of up to $10,000, along with other possible actions by the district attorney.

79. The Department of Real Estate recovery account fund may pay only a maximum of $20,000 per transaction to a person who holds an uncollectible court judgment against a real estate licensee, even if the person holds a judgment for $25,000. The maximum payable in behalf of one licensee is $100,000.

80. A real estate broker can legally offer gifts as an inducement for business, whether for sales or loans, providing the conditions for earning the gifts are in any advertisements.

81. Mello-Roos tax funds may be used to finance the cost of subdivisions.

82. The Natural Hazards Disclosure states whether or not a property is in an earthquake zone.

83. If a buyer hands a deposit check to an escrow clerk, then a broker should reflect it in his files, and does not have to keep a trust record of that check.

84. Unstable real estate values tend to occur in areas of mixed home values.

85. There is a two-year grace period after expiration of the real estate license in which the license can be renewed without taking the real estate examination again. In this period, one may renew simply by paying the renewal fee and late fees. However, one cannot practice real estate during that time. After the two-year grace period expires, the real estate license examination would have to be passed again in order to apply for the license.

86. A fictitious business name refers to "doing business as."

87. A seller of property in an earthquake fault zone, or the seller's agent, must disclose to the buyer that the property is situated in an earthquake fault zone. This can be done in the Real Estate Transfer Disclosure Statement or in the Purchase Agreement.

88. A seller of one to four dwelling units must disclose if there is a Mello-Roos Tax lien against the property. Mello-Roos municipal bonds may be used to finance the improvements of streets, gutters, and sidewalks.

89. The Americans with Disabilities Act provides for the disabled. This act could require the removal of barriers from commercial properties.

90. A property manager is responsible for routine maintenance, is employed under a written agreement, and must have a broker's license.

91. Misuse of the trade names REALTOR® or REALTIST® is both unlawful and unethical.

92. The laws of agency are found in the Civil Code.

93. A blind ad is where the broker does not indicate his or her license status or company name in an ad.

94. A broker's failure to make a required disclosure is not excused, even if the buyer has a right of rescission.

95. Even though a salesperson works for a broker as an independent contractor, the broker should still provide workers' compensation coverage.

96. A Buyer-Broker Representation Agreement must be in writing.

97. The agent acts without the authority of the principal. Later, the principal accepts the acts of the agent. This becomes agency by ratification.

■ CONTRACTS

1. A contract must have *capacity*, *mutuality*, *lawful object*, and *sufficient consideration* to be valid. If it is a real estate contract, it also must be in writing.

2. There is no minimum age for a married person to be able to contract.

3. A deposit receipt is only a receipt for deposit and an offer to purchase. It contains the clause *time is of the essence*.

4. A real estate licensee must have been licensed at the time the real estate transaction occurred to be able to collect a commission.

5. The listing agreement belongs to the broker even though the salesperson takes the listing. The agency relationship is established between the principal and the broker.

6. A listing agreement authorizes a broker to accept a deposit; it contains the safety clause.

7. A copy of a contract must be given to each party who signs it at the time of obtaining signatures.

8. In an option agreement, consideration (deposit) must be paid and can be in any amount. The seller may keep the consideration whether or not the buyer exercises the option to purchase.

9. Contract law states that there is no minimum age for a married person to enter into a contract.

10. A listing agreement for the sale of personal property may be by oral agreement (in limited instances).

11. The maximum term of an agricultural lease is 51 years.

12. A real property sales contract must include the number of years to complete the contract and the basis for a tax estimate. The five essentials of a land contract are *capacity*, *mutuality* (*offer* and *acceptance*), *lawful object*, *sufficient consideration*, and a *proper writing* (the same as any other real estate contract).

13. The legal action against a buyer who defaults on a land contract is the quiet title action.

14. A land contract is also called a real property sales contract, installment sales contract, and agreement for purchase or sale. The vendor (seller) is the one who must acknowledge (notarize) the land contract in order for the vendee (buyer) to have it recorded. The vendee receives only equitable title, not legal title. A quiet title action may be used to enforce a forfeited recorded land contract.

15. If there is fire damage to property, a landlord may choose to abate (forgive or lower) the rent.

16. An exclusive authorization to locate property, in addition to being a type of buyer-broker representation agreement, could lead to a dual agency with the informed consent of all parties.

17. Tenant improvements are provided by a tenant improvement allowance.

18. If title and possession do not occur at the same time, an interim occupancy agreement should be created.

19. Estate at sufferance describes a tenant who occupies property after his rights have expired.

20. Illusory refers to uncertain terms.

21. If a tenant is forced to sign a contract for tenant improvements, the contract may be voidable.

22. The consumer price index includes home prices. A reference to HVAC (heating, ventilation, and air conditioning) is found in a commercial lease.

23. A lessee has five days in which to respond to a notice of unlawful detainer action.

24. A corporation seal authorizes an officer to sign for a corporation.

25. Title to property passes when a deed is delivered.

26. An oral agreement for the sale of real property is unenforceable. A broker is barred (stopped) from enforcing an oral agreement for real property. A listing agreement for personal property or a business opportunity may be by oral agreement.

27. The effective date of the deposit agreement is the date the parties sign it.

28. A broker who is not authorized to collect a commission (no listing agreement) must follow the instructions of the buyer regarding the deposit.

29. An exclusive-right-to-sell listing is a bilateral executory agreement.

30. Multiple offers on property must be presented to the seller at the same time, regardless of the price or terms of the offers.

31. An attorney in fact must record her authorization, and cannot sell the property to herself even if she is willing to pay full price.

32. As to covenants, conditions, and restrictions, all conditions run with the land and bind into the future. Covenants, conditions, and restrictions (CC&R's) are enforceable as long as they are legal and reasonable.

33. A seller and a broker do not have a listing agreement. The seller tells the broker that he will pay the broker a commission if the broker brings an offer that the seller accepts. The broker does bring an offer with a deposit that is everything the seller wants and it is accepted. Even if the seller wants the deposit, the broker should place the deposit in his trust account. Remember, it is in a listing agreement that a broker is authorized to accept a deposit. Without the listing agreement, the broker must follow either the buyer's instructions as to the deposit, or place the deposit into his trust account.

34. The statement on an Exclusive Authorization and Right to Sell Listing agreement, "Seller acknowledges that Seller has read and understands this Agreement, and has received a copy" is important in creating a bilateral agreement—the seller's signature and the agent's signature, i.e., two promises, create a two-sided or bilateral agreement.

35. When an agent is acting as an "agent for the buyer," that agent would not be liable for misrepresentations of the seller or the seller's agent.

36. A bill of sale transfers title to personal property. A listing of personal property (in some instances) may be by oral agreement.

37. A listing agreement must be in writing in order to enforce the payment of a commission.

38. A real estate broker who has an option to purchase property must disclose that he is acting as a principal when offering to sell such property.

39. In an option agreement, the optionee (prospective buyer) does not have to perform.

40. A seller sells corn crop land to a buyer. After the completion of the sale, the seller wants to come back and harvest the corn crops. The buyer is within his rights to say no, as the growing crops run with the land and now belong to the buyer.

41. The buyer makes an offer. The seller rejects the offer and issues a counteroffer. The buyer rejects the seller's counteroffer. The seller then wants to accept the buyer's original offer. Is there a contract? No. Remember, a counteroffer terminates the original offer.

42. The seller can revoke an exclusive authorization and right to sell listing by sending a notice and certified letter to the broker.

43. The commission to be earned as a rental agent is by written agreement between the parties.

44. An action to enforce an oral agreement for a contract, obligation, or liability must be brought within two years.

45. The statute of limitations on a written contract is four years.

46. A real estate licensee can sell a mobile home that has been registered with the Department of Housing and Community Development.

47. The maximum commission one can charge when acting as agent is negotiable between the parties.

48. An oral agreement for real estate is unenforceable. A broker is barred (stopped) from enforcing an oral agreement.

49. A notice of completion, a notice of cessation, and a notice of non-responsibility are terms that refer to a mechanic's lien.

50. If a seller directs an agent to write into an agreement, "if the buyer defaults, any deposit would be given to the seller," this likely refers to the liquidated damages clause.

REAL ESTATE MATHEMATICS

NOTE: Math will be approximately 10 percent of your exam.

■ OUTLINE OF CONCEPTS TO UNDERSTAND

I. Three-Way Formulas: When using this three-way formula system in solving a variety of math problems, one item is equal to the other two. Place one item in the top half of the circle, according to the formula. Place each of the other two items in adjacent quarters of the bottom half of the circle. Divide the upper half by one of the lower quarters and you will arrive at the solution for the adjacent quarter and vice versa. When multiplying a lower quarter times the adjacent quarter, you will arrive at the solution in the upper half of the circle.

A. Interest Formula: Interest = Rate × Principal

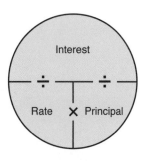

B. Income Formula: Income = Rate × Value

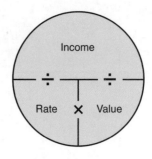

C. Area Formula: Area = Width × Length

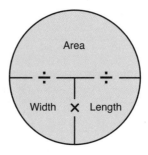

D. Commission Formula: Commission = Rate × Sales Price

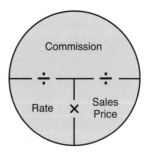

E. Appraisal Formula: Net Operating Income = Capitalization Rate ×
    Value

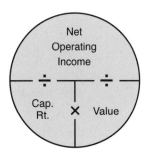

F. Made-Percent-Paid Formula: Made = Percent × Paid

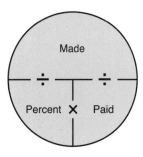

II. Selling Price Rule: To find the selling price of an item, subtract the
    percentage of profit desired from 100 percent and then divide the cost
    by the remainder. Remember that there is the letter *s* in both *selling*
    and *subtract*. This will help to recall that you should subtract from 100
    percent, then divide, when it is the selling price you are seeking.

    A. Selling price rule applied: Joe wishes to earn 10 percent profit over
        the sales price on a lot he bought for $60,000. Joe will have to pay
        closing costs of $460. What should he sell the lot for? 100% − 10%
        = 90%. Add the closing costs to the cost of $60,000 to equal
        $60,460. Divide $60,460 by 90 percent to arrive at the answer of
        $67,177.78.

B. Selling price rule applied to discounted note problems: Norman bought a note for a 4 percent discount and paid $16,800. What is the face amount of the note? 100% − 4% = 96%. Divide the cost of the note of $16,800 by 96 percent and the answer is $17,500.

III. Cost Rule: To find the cost or net of an item, add the percentage of profit desired to 100 percent and then divide the selling price by the total percentage. Remember there are three letters in the word *net*, which is for this discussion the same as cost, and three letters in the word *add*. This will help to recall that you should add to 100 percent then divide, when it is the cost you are seeking.

A. Cost rule applied: Mayme sold her property at $90,000, and made a 15 percent profit. What did the property cost? 100% + 15% = 115%. Divide $90,000 by 115 percent, and the answer is $78,260.87.

B. Cost rule applied when closing costs are included: Mike sells his vacant lot for $45,000. He makes an 18 percent profit after paying closing costs of $350. What did the lot cost? 100% + 18% = 118%. Deduct closing costs of $350 from the selling price of $45,000 to equal $44,650. Divide $44,650 by 118 percent, and the answer is $37,838.98.

IV. Principal-Interest-Rate-Time Rule: *Principal* is the loan amount; *interest* represents the cost of borrowing money; *rate* is the cost of borrowing expressed as a percentage of the loan amount paid in interest for one year; and *time* refers to the length of the loan, usually expressed in years.

A. Principal unknown: Principal = Interest ÷ (Rate × Time). What is the loan amount necessary to receive $1,200 interest at 12 percent if the money is loaned for three years? Solution:

$$P = \frac{\$1,200}{.12 \times 3} \qquad P = \frac{\$1,200}{.36} \qquad P = \$3,333.33$$

B. Interest unknown: Interest = Principal × Rate × Time. Find the interest on $3,333.33 for three years at 12 percent.

$$I = \$3,333.33 \times 3 \times .12$$
$$I = \$1,200$$

C. Rate unknown: Rate = Interest ÷ (Principal × Time). Find the rate on $3,333.33 that earns $1,200 interest for three years.

$$\text{Rate} = \frac{\$1,200}{\$3,333.33 \times 3} \qquad \text{Rate} = .12 \text{ or } 12\%$$

D. Time unknown: Time = Interest ÷ (Rate × Principal). Find the time necessary to return $1,200 on a principal amount of $3,333.33 at an annual rate of 12 percent.

$$\text{Time} = \frac{\$1,200}{.12 \times \$3,333.33} \qquad \text{Time} = 3 \text{ years}$$

PRACTICE EXAMINATION I

1. Tenants in common share in the matter of

   a. time.
   b. title.
   c. interest.
   d. possession.

2. When comparing the economic life of improved property with physical life of the property, the economic life

   a. is longer.
   b. is shorter.
   c. is the same.
   d. depends on the type of improvements.

3. The builder's plan that displays the piers, subfloors, footing, and columns within a structure is called a(n) _____ plan.

   a. floor
   b. elevation
   c. foundation
   d. plot

4. Federal law protects purchasers of subdivision properties that are located in the United States and are being offered for sale in interstate commerce. This law provides for a right of rescission within _____ days.

   a. three
   b. five
   c. seven
   d. ten

5. A mortgage company would give the least consideration to which of the following in granting a loan?

   a. Borrower's present and future income
   b. Value of the property in relation to loan
   c. Borrower's need for financial assistance
   d. Amount of down payment

6. In the event the parties to a bulk sale do not comply with the provisions of the bulk sales law as outlined in the Uniform Commercial Code, the party that would probably be injured the most would be the

   a. seller.
   b. buyer.
   c. creditor.
   d. lender.

7. In California, brokers must have an employment contract with each of the licensed employees in his or her office. This contract

   a. must be kept by the employees for five years after the term of employment.
   b. must be in writing.
   c. need not be retained by the broker.
   d. need not be retained by the salesperson.

8. Through valid contractual assignment of a lease, the assignee purchases the leasehold interest and becomes a

   a. landlord.
   b. guarantor.
   c. sublessee.
   d. tenant.

9. Which of the following is true with respect to an impound account?

   a. The lender holding the account pays the same interest rate on funds as that paid by a savings and loan on savings accounts.
   b. It benefits both the trustor and the beneficiary.
   c. The maximum amount cannot exceed 5 percent of the annual disbursements.
   d. It is required on all home loans.

10. Upon payment of a fee, information on inspection reports issued by any licensed structural pest control operator may be obtained from the Structural Pest Control Board for up to two years by

    a. the seller only.
    b. the buyer only.
    c. the seller and buyer only.
    d. anyone who requests it and pays the fee.

11. A real estate license is required by a(n)

    a. principal who sells three or more homes in one year.
    b. trustee.
    c. mortgage loan broker.
    d. appraiser.

12. An unlicensed secretary working in a real estate office may legally

    a. discuss terms for sale of a property advertised by the broker.
    b. type listing agreements for salespersons.
    c. collect rent on properties managed by the office.
    d. quote prices on listed property over the telephone.

13. To an appraiser, a definition of value is

    a. the relationship of a desirous person to the thing desired.
    b. the ability of one commodity to command other commodities in exchange.
    c. the present worth of all rights to future benefits arising out of property ownership.
    d. All of the above

14. Smith granted Williams a subsurface easement to remove the minerals from the land but never designated the place of removal, so

    a. Williams must obtain Smith's consent as to right of entry.
    b. Williams has an implied easement to enter and use the surface of land to extract the minerals.
    c. Williams has no right of entry to remove the minerals.
    d. Williams easement rights are land locked.

15. If a salesperson misinforms a buyer as to deed restrictions,

    a. there is no liability if the restrictions are a matter of record.
    b. the salesperson and broker may both be liable for damages.
    c. only the salesperson is liable.
    d. only the principal is liable.

16. A real estate broker negotiates a $7,000 second trust deed note secured by real property. The loan was to be paid in full in five years. The most the broker could charge as a commission for her services would be

    a. 3 percent.   c. 15 percent.
    b. 6 percent.   d. 10 percent.

17. The trustor under a trust deed is the party who

    a. signs the note as maker.
    b. holds the title to the property in trust.
    c. acknowledges the note for recording.
    d. lends the money.

18. The act providing for civil action against persons conducting business establishments by aggrieved persons claiming discrimination on account of sex, color, religion, ancestry, or national origin is the

    a. Civil Rights Act.   c. Unruh Act.
    b. Rumford Act.   d. Act of 1969.

19. A licensed real estate broker is accused of violating the Unruh Act for refusing to rent property to anyone other than persons of the Caucasian race. If found guilty, he or she

    a. must pay $250 to the party infringed on as punitive damages.
    b. is subject to actual damages.
    c. Both *a* and *b*
    d. Neither *a* nor *b*

20. The act that empowers the State Department of Fair Employment and Housing to act against discrimination in both publicly assisted and private housing accommodations under specified conditions is the

    a. Civil Rights Act.   c. Unruh Act.
    b. Rumford Act.   d. Act of 1969.

21. In a tight money market which of the following would be a true statement regarding conventional loans?

    a. The buyer will pay a lower origination fee.
    b. The buyer will pay more points.
    c. The seller will pay greater discount points.
    d. The seller will pay a higher origination fee.

22. Which of the following best describes a "complete" escrow?

    a. It is considered a perfect escrow.
    b. The escrow holder has ceased being an agent for both parties.
    c. All papers are properly drawn up and ready for final steps to be taken to close the escrow.
    d. All services of the escrow holder are involved.

23. When an escrow is in progress and all the conditions have been satisfied, the escrow officer becomes

    a. a counselor to both the buyer and the seller.
    b. an advocate to safeguard the interest of the principal.
    c. the independent agent for each of the parties to the escrow.
    d. None of the above

24. A *promotional note* is a promissory note secured by a trust deed executed on unimproved real property or executed after construction of an improvement of the property but before the first sale of the property as so improved, provided the note was not executed in excess of a specified period of time. A note that has been in effect _____ months would not be classified as a "promotional note."

    a. 18   c. 30
    b. 24   d. 37

25. A life insurance company that is engaged in making real estate loans would normally create these loans with the assistance of

    a. the VA or through the FHA.
    b. a federal-chartered or state-chartered savings and loan association.
    c. a mortgage banker.
    d. All of the above

26. For a homestead to be effective, it must be filed before the

    a. judgment is rendered.
    b. judgment is recorded.
    c. lawsuit is filed.
    d. lis pendens is recorded.

27. Garcia, Lewis, and Thompson are joint tenants. Garcia conveys his interest to Jackson. This changes the ownership as follows:

    a. Lewis, Thompson, and Jackson are joint tenants.
    b. Lewis, Thompson, and Jackson are each one-third tenants in common.
    c. Jackson owns one-third as a tenant in common with Lewis and Thompson, who now own two-thirds as joint tenants.
    d. None of the above

28. Salesperson Hollis, who was employed by broker Baker, was able to secure an acceptance of an offer from a buyer on a property that was listed by broker Donald. Broker Donald had agreed to cooperate with broker Baker. After escrow was opened, Hollis was in need of $100 and asked broker Donald to advance him $100 from the eventual commission. If broker Donald advances Hollis the $100,

    a. it would be acceptable, provided it is released through the escrow holder.
    b. it would be a violation of the real estate law.
    c. it would be perfectly legal as it doesn't matter from whom Hollis receives the money.
    d. it would be legal as long as it does not come out of the escrowed money.

29. Should a dispute regarding a commission arise between two sales licensees who are member of the National Association of REALTORS®, by the provisions of that organization's Code of Ethics, they will settle the matter by

    a. litigation.   c. arbitration.
    b. estoppel.   d. mandamus.

30. A liquidated damages clause in a real estate contract

    a. allows the buyer to withdraw her offer at any time before acceptance.
    b. is looked on with disfavor by the courts.
    c. determines the damages to be paid in case of fire during escrow.
    d. sets up a procedure to be followed in case of foreclosure.

31. With regard to a deed of trust and promissory note, which of the following statements is correct?

    a. The provisions of the promissory note prevail over the deed of trust.
    b. The promissory note secures the trust deed and the property.
    c. The provisions of the trust deed prevail over the promissory note.
    d. The trust deed secures the promissory note.

32. Able is leasing Blackacre for a 10-year term. Gentry owns Brownacre, which is adjacent to Blackacre. Gentry asks Able to grant him an easement over Blackacre. In these circumstances, which statement would be true?

    a. This would be illegal, as only the lessor can grant such a use.
    b. This would be legal for the term of the lease.
    c. This would be illegal because the owner must join in such a grant with the lessee.
    d. The tenant can legally grant such a right for an indefinite period.

33. Which of the following is community property?

    a. Husband's salary
    b. Income from husband's separate property earned during marriage
    c. Income from wife's separate property earned during marriage
    d. All of the above

34. A deed to a person under an assumed name is

    a. void.   c. permissible.
    b. voidable.   d. prohibited.

35. In the capitalization of net income approach in appraising, the Hoskold method differs from the Inwood method because of which of the following factors?

    a. Interest rate
    b. Sinking fund
    c. Land residual
    d. Annuity capitalization

36. The statute of limitations specifies the time limits in which lawsuits must be brought to court in the event of a breach. Under this statute, a buyer must bring legal action against a seller for failure to perform under a valid purchase contract within

    a. 90 days.   c. 2 years.
    b. 1 year.   d. 4 years.

37. The type of interest usually charged on single-family home loans is

    a. annuity.   c. compound.
    b. prepaid.   d. simple.

38. Mrs. Johnson engages broker Green to sell her home under an exclusive authorization and right-to-sell listing. Under these circumstances broker Green's authority is

    a. whatever third parties perceive it to be.
    b. whatever Green believes his authority to be, even if it extends beyond those duties agreed-on under the listing contract.
    c. that which will be necessary to sell the property, regardless of the listing terms, because that is the purpose for which he has been hired.
    d. that which has been agreed on between the principal and the agent and that which is necessary, proper, or usual in the ordinary course of business for effecting the sale of the property.

39. When reviewing the credit standing of a prospective borrower, the bank would probably grant the loan if the borrower showed that her

    a. fixed assets were 10 times her current assets.
    b. cash in the bank almost equaled her liabilities.
    c. liabilities were three times her net worth.
    d. existing loan was in default only one month.

40. A commercial acre is defined as an acre of land

    a. in a shopping center in a rural area.
    b. in an industrial development.
    c. in a new subdivision zoned for commercial use.
    d. less the streets and alleys.

41. An individual purchased a fee simple interest in airspace and an undivided interest in common in a portion of a parcel of real property that could be used for residential, commercial, or industrial use. This would be classified as a

    a. condominium.
    b. stock cooperative.
    c. planned development.
    d. None of the above

42. Filing a complaint under the federal housing law must, according to the statute of limitations, be done within _____ days from the occurrence of the alleged act.

    a. 60   c. 180
    b. 90   d. 360

43. Which of the following is necessary to legally transfer title to real property?

    a. A current beneficiary statement on any existing loan
    b. A title policy showing title vested in in the grantor
    c. The services of a licensed real estate broker
    d. None of the above

44. FHA loans can be granted only on residential properties that meet minimum building standards. In a residence approved for FHA financing, which of the following requirements for the construction of a stairwell does not have to be met?

    a. There must be two handrails.
    b. The tread of the step must have a minimum width.
    c. The riser must be a minimum height.
    d. The stairwell must allow for minimum headroom.

45. If an owner dies leaving a will, but without heirs, his property

    a. vests in the devisees, subject to administration.
    b. escheats to the State of California.
    c. escheats to the United States.
    d. None of the above

46. An investor owned a number of promissory notes secured by trust deeds. To relieve herself of the burden of keeping an account of those that paid and those that had not paid, she employed a real estate broker to handle the collections. One of the requirements imposed by the real estate law is that the broker

    a. post a bond with the commissioner.
    b. have a special endorsement on his license.
    c. have a written contract with the investor.
    d. All of the above

47. When a loan is obtained to purchase real property and a note and trust deed are executed, the party that furnishes the funds is the

    a. grantee.   c. trustor.
    b. beneficiary.   d. trustee.

48. The best appraisal method to establish the current market value of a shopping center would be the

    a. cost-income.
    b. market data-income.
    c. income-gross rent multiplier.
    d. cost-gross rent multiplier.

49. A "holder in due course" brings action to collect on the note. Which one of the following may the maker of the note use as a defense?

    a. Lack or failure of consideration
    b. Prior cancellation
    c. Fraud in the inducement
    d. Material alteration of the note

50. Which of the following would be considered an estate of indefinite duration?

    a. An estate for years
    b. An estate of inheritance
    c. A lease for 99 years
    d. Material alteration of the note

51. If the owner enters into an exclusive-agency listing and thereafter sells the property through his own efforts,

    a. no commission is payable.
    b. the broker is entitled to 50 percent of the commission.
    c. the broker is entitled to full commission.
    d. None of the above

52. If a person affixes property to the land of another by mistake

    a. he or she may remove it under prescribed conditions, including payment of damages.
    b. the property may not be removed because it has become a fixture.
    c. the landowner must pay for its cost.
    d. the landowner may destroy it.

53. Which of the following is the viewpoint of the accountant and the appraiser with respect to depreciation?

    a. The accountant is concerned with book depreciation, while the appraiser deals with actual depreciation.
    b. The appraiser is interested only in book value.
    c. The accountant is interested only in what caused the depreciation.
    d. The accountant is interested in the book value, while the appraiser is interested in the theory of depreciation.

54. If zoning prohibits a use permitted by private deed restrictions, the

    a. zoning controls.
    b. courts must be called on.
    c. deed restrictions control.
    d. zoning is invalid.

55. A prospective buyer, who was not a real estate licensee and had no ties with the seller's broker, wished to purchase a large parcel of land and made an offer on the property at a price of $600 per acre. The seller accepted the offer and escrow was opened. During the escrow period the seller discovered that the buyer had already entered into an agreement to resell the acreage at a price of $2,000 per acre to an unknown buyer. Under these circumstances the original seller's recourse is to

    a. rescind the contract.
    b. refuse to close the escrow and sue for damages.
    c. void the contract based on misrepresentation.
    d. do nothing.

56. A beneficiary statement is furnished by the _____ upon the demand of the _____.

    a. trustee, trustor
    b. beneficiary, escrow company
    c. beneficiary, trustee
    d. surveyor, beneficiary

57. An individual who has rented real property may remove which of the following on termination of the lease?

    a. Manufacturing equipment
    b. Trade fixtures
    c. Items for domestic use
    d. All of the above

58. Attachment is a(n)

a. legal seizure of property.
b. assessment.
c. lien.
d. form of tax.

59. If the U.S. government obtained a lien against a taxpayer who failed to report a certain portion of his rental income, it would be classified as

a. general.
b. specific.
c. voluntary.
d. None of the above

60. Limitations on the use of real property may be created by

a. building codes.
b. zoning regulations.
c. deed restrictions.
d. All of the above

61. For a judgment to constitute a lien, it must meet certain prerequisites. Which of the following is not a prerequisite?

a. It must be a judgment that money is owed.
b. It must be a valid judgment.
c. An abstract of judgment must be recorded in the state in which the real property is situated.
d. It must be rendered by a lawfully constituted court.

62. An owner knew the roof leaked in his house and disclosed that fact to the broker with whom he listed the property for sale. The broker would be required to

a. comply with the owner's request to keep it a secret.
b. disclose such fact to a prospective buyer.
c. protect the seller and not say anything.
d. have a new roof put on and put the bill into escrow.

63. A copy of the Real Estate Commissioner's public report that was issued on land within a land project must be given by the subdivider or his or her agents or salespersons to

a. all owners of land adjacent to the subdivision.
b. every adult prospect who wrote or telephoned requesting one or who visits the site and indicated interest in purchasing one or more of the sites.
c. every prospective buyer, but the subdivider or his or her agents can wait until just prior to signing the purchase agreement.
d. the local newspaper so it can be published in the legal section.

64. A township is

a. 6 miles square.
b. 24 miles around.
c. 36 square miles.
d. All of the above

65. A broker who has a signed listing to sell a property can refuse to submit an offer on that property

    a. in circumstances in which the broker also has obtained a backup offer.
    b. whenever the offer is for less than the listed price.
    c. if in the listing agreement the broker also has an option to purchase the property.
    d. when expressly instructed to do so by the owner.

66. Which of the following is correct with regard to an enforceable standard listing agreement that has been signed by the seller and broker?

    a. It obligates the seller to sell.
    b. It requires a meeting of the minds.
    c. It requires a seller able to deliver a marketable title and a buyer "ready, willing, and able" to buy.
    d. All of the above

67. A salesperson receives an offer from a buyer who has no cash but offers a deposit of $500 in the form of a personal note payable in 30 days. Which of the following applies?

    a. This is unacceptable because a deposit must be in cash or a check.
    b. The form of deposit is immaterial, as long as the $500 figure appears on the deposit receipt.
    c. A salesperson may accept a personal note as deposit if he or she advises the seller of this prior to acceptance.
    d. A salesperson may accept a note if made in favor of the broker to handle expenses.

68. Functional utility in a dwelling depends on

    a. the desires of its occupants.
    b. its floor plan and equipment.
    c. zoning of the area.
    d. condition of the heating system.

69. Broker Brown was taken to court by a client who was suing the broker for fraud in a real estate transaction. The client was successful and was awarded damages in the civil suit. After the judgment has been handed down, the Real Estate Commissioner can immediately

    a. revoke the broker's license.
    b. suspend the broker's license pending a hearing.
    c. file an accusation and statement of issues and proceed against the broker.
    d. hold a hearing with his or her deputies to decide if a Notice of Suspension should be mailed.

70. The taxpayer would ordinarily have to pay property taxes on all of these EXCEPT

    a. a condominium interest.
    b. intangible personal property.
    c. public tax-exempt land under a lease (e.g., an oil lease).
    d. an easement over the land of another.

71. When issuing the closing statement, escrow would debit the seller of income property for which of the following items?

    a. Prepaid taxes
    b. Prepaid rent
    c. Prepaid fire insurance premium
    d. All of the above

72. When applying the principle of substitution, the home buyer would consider

    a. use.
    b. earnings.
    c. structural design.
    d. All of the above

73. The law that requires that certain contracts be in writing is contained in the

    a. statute of limitations.
    b. Small Loan Act.
    c. statute of frauds.
    d. Fair Trade Law.

74. The legal procedure to evict a nonpaying tenant is by

    a. action by lessor through physical ejection.
    b. court action for specific performance.
    c. unlawful detainer.
    d. nonaction.

75. Which of the following statements is correct with regard to an easement and the dominant tenement?

    a. The dominant tenement receives both the benefit and the burden of the easement.
    b. The owner of the dominant tenement can retain the easement but can transfer title to the property.
    c. It can be created for ingress and egress only.
    d. The easement is transferred with the transfer of the dominant tenement.

76. Legal enforcement of the terms of a deed of trust in case of default may be

    a. either by trustee's sale or judicial foreclosure.
    b. by trustee's sale proceedings only.
    c. by judicial foreclosure only.
    d. None of the above

77. California law permits a person to file a declaration of homestead, provided that person is living in

    a. the residence on which he or she holds a 35-year lease.
    b. a cooperative apartment project in which he or she has a fee interest in the unit that he or she occupies.
    c. a 12-unit apartment building which he or she owns.
    d. All of the above

78. The person who has gained the right to act in behalf of another is known as a(n)

    a. affiant.
    b. principal.
    c. attorney-in-fact.
    d. executor.

79. The commissioner may suspend or revoke the license of any real estate licensee who

    a. demonstrated negligence or incompetence in performing any act for which he or she is required to hold a license.
    b. failed to exercise reasonable supervision over the activities of his or her salespeople.
    c. willfully disregarded or violated any of the provisions of the real estate law.
    d. All of the above

80. Which of the following is an encumbrance?

    a. Fence c. Homestead
    b. Lease d. Trade fixture

81. The fee that the appraiser charges for his appraisal is established by the

    a. agreement between the appraiser and the client.
    b. Department of Veterans Affairs.
    c. Real Estate Commissioner.
    d. American Institute of Real Estate Appraisers.

82. A broker licensee can legally claim a commission for

    a. a loan that he or she did not negotiate.
    b. the sale of a property on which he or she had an exclusive authorization to sell with a definite termination date.
    c. the sale by another of a property on which he or she had an open listing with a termination date.
    d. the sale by another on which he or she had a net listing with a termination date.

83. An appraiser in analyzing the data for a final estimate of value on a property would give least consideration to

    a. the assessed value of the property.
    b. the value of the land.
    c. comparisons of other properties.
    d. its highest and best use.

84. Airspace is a public highway, but the landowner's property line in the sky

    a. is owned by the federal government.
    b. may be owned by the surface owner.
    c. is owned by the state where the land is located.
    d. is as much as he or she can use and occupy in connection with the land.

85. A purchaser of a condominium unit recorded a homestead on her property immediately after its purchase. One year later this owner failed to pay her monthly homeowners' association fees, and the association began legal steps to enforce the collection. Under these circumstances which is true?

    a. The homestead would offer her no protection.
    b. The other owners could collect the amount due but only the excess over the amount of the homestead exemption.
    c. The homestead is invalid as it does not protect a condominium unit owner's interest.
    d. The homestead would give the unit owner full protection.

86. For demand to be effective, it must be accompanied by

    a. objectivity.
    b. inflation.
    c. purchasing power.
    d. transferability.

87. Which of the following would be the key factor in a developer's decision in choosing the best site to build a new shopping center in a suburban area?

    a. Traffic count
    b. Population
    c. Purchasing power
    d. Topography

88. The words *procuring cause* would have an important meaning in which of the following?

    a. A dispute over commission on an open listing
    b. When securing a listing
    c. The sale of government land
    d. A lawsuit against a licensee involving fraud

89. Jones owned a farmer property on which he was growing a crop of corn. Before the harvest he sold the property to Henry. Jones intended to harvest the crop after the sale, even though this was not stated in the sales agreement. The following would most likely be true regarding the corn crop.

    a. Jones would have the right to harvest the crop, as this was his intention.
    b. The crop would go with the land, as it is considered real property.
    c. Jones intent would take precedence over the sales agreement.
    d. Henry cannot claim the crop, as it would be considered personal property.

90. A purchaser obtains a property for 20 percent less than the listed price and later sells the property for the original listed price. The percentage of the profit on her original investment is

    a. 10 percent.   c. 25 percent.
    b. 20 percent.   d. 40 percent.

91. The Real Estate Commissioner may impose a fine against a real estate broker who pays an unlicensed person to negotiate real estate loans. The maximum fine would be

    a. $10,000.
    b. $50,000.
    c. $1,000.
    d. $5,000.

92. A real estate licensee, in advertising property for sale, includes the credit terms available to complete the sale. With respect to advertising, which of the following is true?

    a. Regulation Z allows exceptions.
    b. Regulation Z applies in all instances.
    c. Both *a* and *b* are true if the loan exceeds $25,000.
    d. The real estate licensee is not bound by Regulation Z, as he or she is subject to the Real Estate Commissioner.

93. An individual purchased a nine-acre parcel of unimproved property. He then subdivided the nine acres into one-acre parcels. If the subdivider plans to sell only three one-acre parcels per year over the next three years, he or she must comply with

    a. the State Subdivision Map Act.
    b. the State Subdivided Lands Act.
    c. Both *a* and *b*
    d. Neither *a* nor *b*

94. The maximum space that is permitted between wall studs under most building codes is _____ inches on center.

    a. 6
    b. 12
    c. 16
    d. 24

95. Which of the following is true with respect to riparian rights?

    a. The riparian land owner has the absolute ownership of the adjacent water.
    b. The ownership of riparian rights can be determined from the public records.
    c. Riparian land must be adjacent to the stream and in the watershed of the stream.
    d. They must be expressly stated in the deed to such land.

96. Acquisition of property by its incorporation with other property is known as

    a. accession.
    b. succession.
    c. recession.
    d. commingling.

97. A landlord and a tenant enter into a discussion relating to an extension of a lease under which the tenant had occupied the property for some length of time. Because they could not agree on the terms, it was decided between the parties that the lease would be discontinued. This decision to discontinue the lease would be considered a(n)

    a. termination.
    b. rescission.
    c. voided contract.
    d. unenforceable contract.

98. A contract signed under duress is

    a. void.
    b. voidable.
    c. illegal.
    d. enforceable.

99. Which of the following could be similar to a planned development in California?

    a. Stock cooperative
    b. Land project
    c. Condominium
    d. Community apartment project

100. An investor who is interested in purchasing a commercial property for investment purposes would be most interested in

    a. gross income.
    b. net income.
    c. topography.
    d. pedestrian traffic.

101. The issuance of a writ of execution could result in a

    a. sheriff's sale.
    b. reassessment of property taxes.
    c. mechanic's lien.
    d. tax deed.

102. When risk increases, capitalization rates

    a. increase.
    b. remain constant.
    c. decrease.
    d. None of the above

103. All of the following terms may be used to describe a construction loan *EXCEPT* a(n)

    a. interim loan.
    b. loan for future advances.
    c. open-end loan.
    d. package loan.

104. Jones has decided to take legal action against Smith. The legal procedure Jones might seek prior to a judgment being rendered is a(n)

    a. attachment.
    b. trustee's sale.
    c. judicial sale.
    d. writ of execution.

105. The substitution of a new contract for an existing one is known as a

    a. subordination.
    b. novation.
    c. rescission.
    d. pledge account.

106. A home contains massive cornices that affect the value of the property. This is an example of

    a. functional obsolescence.
    b. external obsolescence.
    c. physical deterioration.
    d. deferred maintenance.

107. The degree of an angle of a slope or roof is called the

    a. gable.   c. pitch.
    b. hip.   d. mansard.

108. Which agency oversees the Interstate Land Sales Disclosure Act?

    a. HUD
    b. IRS
    c. Department of Real Estate
    d. Federal Trade Commission

109. The purchase price of property is the starting point in calculating

    a. book value.
    b. sales price.
    c. market value.
    d. liability potential.

110. Real estate broker Able, when acting as agent for seller Baker,

    a. is obligated to render faithful service to Baker.
    b. can modify the terms of any contract that Baker enters into.
    c. can give Baker legal advice.
    d. can eliminate any offers on Baker's property that Able believes are not good enough.

111. In the event a licensee is found guilty of violating the antidiscrimination regulations of the Real Estate Commissioner, the commissioner may take which of the following legal actions against the licensee?

    a. A suit for damages for expenses incurred
    b. Collect punitive damages to insure against further discrimination in the future
    c. Revocation or suspension of the license of the individual
    d. All of the above

112. The phrase that best describes the nature of a broker's duty to keep a principal fully informed is

    a. ethical conduct.
    b. continuing responsibility.
    c. fiduciary obligation.
    d. trustworthy business principles.

113. Under the authority of a valid California real estate license, you may market

    a. residential property.
    b. agricultural property.
    c. industrial and commercial property.
    d. All of the above

114. After recording a "Notice of Default," a trustee who is foreclosing under the power of sale clause in a trust deed must wait three months before

    a. issuing a trustee's deed.
    b. filing court action.
    c. reconveying title to the beneficiary.
    d. publishing the "Notice of Sale."

115. Which of the following parties would be in violation of the real estate law if they were not licensed by the Department of Real Estate?

    a. An attorney-in-fact who signed a deed to the property owned by his or her principal
    b. An attorney operating a real estate business out of his or her law office
    c. An attorney's secretary who also performs his or her duties as a secretary in a real estate business
    d. All of the above

116. The major part of the California laws relating to real property are created by

    a. the state constitution.
    b. the legislative acts.
    c. the Real Estate Commissioner.
    d. the Business and Professions Code.

117. If a broker makes a misrepresentation, relying on information furnished by the owner, and the purchaser is consequently relieved from the contract because of the misrepresentation, the broker is entitled to

    a. a full commission.
    b. whatever compensation he or she might ask for in a court action.
    c. reimbursement for only "out-of-pocket" expenses in connection with the the unexecuted contract.
    d. no commission.

118. For the person who has qualified in an examination for a real estate license, the maximum time allowed to file the required application is

    a. one year from taking the test.
    b. one year from being notified of the results of the test.
    c. two years from taking the test.
    d. two years from being notified of the results of the test.

119. Under the law of agency a fiduciary relationship is created between the broker and the seller on execution of the listing agreement. As far as the broker's responsibility to third parties, the broker

    a. must be fair, honest, and disclose material facts.
    b. has no obligation.
    c. need disclose material facts only when asked about them.
    d. should disclose the lowest price the seller is willing to accept.

120. The law of agency is concerned with the rights and duties between and among the

    a. agent and the principal, whether disclosed or undisclosed.
    b. principal and third parties with whom the agent deals on behalf of the principal.
    c. agent and the third parties with whom the agent deals on behalf of the principal.
    d. All of the above

121. The master plan of the city or county of San Francisco typically shows its

    a. traffic patterns.
    b. street patterns.
    c. public transportation locations.
    d. All of the above

122. An agreement between two parties to do or not to do certain things is known as a(n)

    a. affidavit.
    b. contract.
    c. declaration.
    d. verification.

123. The termination of a power of attorney can occur by the

    a. death of the attorney-in-fact.
    b. revocation by the principal.
    c. incapacity of the parties to the power of attorney.
    d. All of the above

124. There are many duties and responsibilities of a property manager. Some of the duties include

    a. protecting the investor's capital.
    b. providing effective services for the owner and the tenants.
    c. attempting to increase the net income of the property.
    d. All of the above

125. During the redemption period of a loan under a judicial foreclosure who is in possession of the property?

    a. The mortgagee
    b. The mortgagor
    c. The trustee
    d. The sheriff

126. The purpose of Division 6 of the Uniform Commercial Code, which addresses the bulk transfer of inventory of a business being sold, is to alert the

    a. transferor's buyers.
    b. transferor's creditors.
    c. transferee.
    d. transferor's customer list.

127. The most logical first step for subdivider Livingston to take before going forward with plans to create a new development with all of the latest amenities is to

    a. find the best location.
    b. secure adequate financing.
    c. purchase the land.
    d. prepare a market analysis.

128. Buyer Able gives a full offer to purchase seller Smith's property. Smith rejects the offer. What recourse is available to Able?

    a. Sue Smith for specific performance
    b. Sue Smith for actual and punitive damages
    c. Both *a* and *b*
    d. None of the above

129. The personal assets of each partner may be sought by the creditors of which type of syndication?

    a. Regular corporation
    b. General partnership
    c. Limited partnership
    d. All of the above

130. For Johnson to hedge her capital against inflation, she would invest in

    a. government bonds.
    b. equity assets.
    c. savings accounts.
    d. mortgages.

131. If owner Todd did not pay broker Gonzales the earned and agreed-on commission, what action could Gonzales take?

    a. File a lis pendens
    b. File a lawsuit in civil court
    c. File a complaint with the Real Estate Commissioner
    d. Both *b* and *c*

132. All of the following are assignable *EXCEPT* a

    a. trust deed.
    b. grant deed.
    c. lease agreement.
    d. deposit receipt.

133. According to Regulation Z of the Federal Reserve System, which of the following advertisements is correct?

    a. Assume a 6 percent APR loan
    b. Assume a 6 percent annual percentage rate loan
    c. Assume a 6 percent annual mortgage loan
    d. All of the above

134. Under the cost approach to the appraisal of property, the land and improvements are valued

    a. jointly in one approach.
    b. singly, using more than one approach.
    c. singly, using one approach.
    d. None of the above.

135. The deferred maintenance of a building refers to

    a. the need for rehabilitation of the building.
    b. future repairs that are anticipated.
    c. the upgrading of appliances and fixtures for greater appeal of the building.
    d. None of the above

136. It is important to the running of a commercial bank to maintain liquidity and salability of its loans. Therefore, which type of loan would most commercial banks prefer to make?

    a. Short-term loans
    b. Junior trust deeds
    c. Real estate loans for their own portfolios
    d. Takeout loans

137. Which of the following would be considered an offer in a real estate transaction?

    a. An option
    b. A covenant
    c. A verbal agreement
    d. Tender

138. Real property of the estate of a person who died intestate is to be sold by the administrator. This property can be sold only

    a. at public auction.
    b. to the highest bidder resulting from a newspaper advertisement.
    c. after the court has approved the terms of sale and the price.
    d. for cash.

139. A lessee's interest is

    a. personal property.
    b. chattel real.
    c. a grant to use property for a period of time that reverts to the grantor at the expiration of the term.
    d. All of the above

140. When a stream tears land away from its bank, it is called

    a. accretion.   c. absorption.
    b. avulsion.   d. alluvion.

141. When a husband and wife hold title to property in joint tenancy, the wife can will

    a. one half of the husband's share.
    b. one half of the entire property.
    c. one half of her share.
    d. none of the property.

142. A joint tenancy estate

    a. is a single estate.
    b. is an estate in severalty.
    c. involves real property.
    d. involves personal property only.

143. In real estate the word *tenancy* means

    a. two or more people joined in an enterprise.
    b. a way of holding ownership.
    c. a tenacious person.
    d. a devise.

144. A man willed his property to his favorite nephew, Bill, and Bill's wife, Mary, giving them a two-thirds and one-third interest respectively with the right of survivorship. Title would be held by Bill and Mary as

    a. joint tenants.
    b. community property.
    c. tenants in common.
    d. tenancy in partnership.

145. To be effective and to transfer title, a deed must

    a. be acknowledged.
    b. be executed on a day other than Sunday.
    c. have an adequate description of the property.
    d. contain the phrase "to have and to hold."

146. Which of the following is the kind of information one might expect to find on the elevation sheets of construction plans?

    a. Construction details and arrangements of inner areas
    b. Exterior sides of a house as they will appear after structural work is complete
    c. Contour of the plot, elevations of the land in relation to the streets, boundaries, and the finished grade
    d. Thickness of slab floor, kind and size of steel wire reinforcement, and areas where slab is to be thickened for placement of load-bearing walls

147. "Tender," as used in contract law, means

 a. a promise to perform, such as to buy or sell.
 b. actual payment of money or delivery of deed.
 c. an offer of money or deed or other performance.
 d. fully executed contract.

148. When compared with a conventional contract of sale, the distinguishing characteristic of an option to purchase real estate is

 a. irrevocability.
 b. mutuality of contract.
 c. lack of mutuality in obligations.
 d. Both *b* and *c*

149. When the sale of a business also involves the bulk sale of the stock in trade (inventory), a notice of the sale must be given as provided in the

 a. California Real Estate Law.
 b. California Civil Code.
 c. Uniform Commercial Code.
 d. Article 7 of the Business and Professions Code.

150. A prudent lender would take into consideration which of the following before issuing a loan?

 a. Borrower's ability to pay
 b. The market value of property that is the security for the loan
 c. Current economic trends
 d. All of the above

■ ANSWER KEY

1. d. There is only one unity to tenancy in common. That's the matter of possession. Do not confuse with the four unities that belong to joint tenancy.

2. b. Economic life refers to the useful life of improved property, which is customarily shorter than the actual physical life of the property.

3. c. It is the foundation plan that will show the placement of the piers, subfloors, footings, and columns within the structure.

4. c. Under the Federal Interstate Land Sales Full Disclosure Act, right of recission lasts for seven days. Also recall that the number of lots in discussion under this act would be 25 or more lots being sold from state to state with a seven-day right of rescission.

5. c. The borrower's need for financial assistance is the least consideration that a mortgage company would give.

6. b. If the requirements of the bulk sales law are not met, the creditor could move to unravel the sale between the seller and the buyer. The buyer would stand to lose any deposit monies presented into the escrow to that point in time.

7. b. The employment contract between the broker and the salesperson must be in writing due to a statutory requirement. A copy of this employment contract must be kept by both the broker and the salesperson for up to three years after termination of employment.

8. d. The assignee takes over all rights and interests of the original tenant in a lease agreement. The assignee becomes a tenant, replacing the original tenant.

9. b. An impound account benefits both the trustor (borrower) and the beneficiary (lender). By impounding taxes and insurance, the lender is certain that these debts will be paid. The borrower is also certain that the payments will be made.

10. d. The Structural Pest Control Board in Sacramento retains information on pest control reports for up to two years. This information may be secured by anyone who requests it and pays a fee.

11. c. Of the four choices offered, only a mortgage loan broker is required to have a real estate license.

12. b. An unlicensed person can only type listing agreements for salespersons.

13. d. Choices *a, b,* and *c* are all good definitions of value in the opinion of an appraiser.

14. b. An implied right of entry goes along with a reservation of rights, as stated in the question.

15. b. If there is any form of misinformation or misrepresentation by a salesperson to a potential buyer, both the salesperson and the broker may be liable for damages.

16. c. Under Article 7 (Loans), with reference to a junior trust deed that is under $20,000, the maximum commission that a broker can earn if the payment of the debt is in three years or more is 15 percent.

17. a. The trustor is the borrower under a deed of trust and is the one who signs the note and the deed of trust itself.

18. c. It is the Unruh Civil Rights Act that prohibits discrimination by businesses.

19. c. Under the Unruh Civil Rights Act there is the possibility of payment of both punitive damages and actual damages for discrimination activities.

20. b. The Rumford Act, also called the California Fair Housing Act, empowers this commission to take action for discrimination violations.

21. b. In a tight money market the cost of existing dollars available would increase. Therefore, buyers would be expected to pay more points for securing a loan.

22. c. A complete escrow is one wherein all documents have been properly drawn and are prepared for final signature, allowing that escrow to close.

23. c. The escrow agent is truly an independent agent for each of the parties to the escrow and can act neither as an advocate nor as a counselor.

24. d. A promotional note is a short-term note and generally does not run beyond 36 months.

25. c. Most life insurance company loans are made through a loan correspondent that could be defined as a mortgage banker or mortgage broker.

26. b. For the homestead to be effective, the recording must occur before an ultimate judgment is recorded. Notice the difference between recorded and rendered. Recording occurs after a judgment is rendered.

27. c. Jackson becomes a one-third tenant in common with Lewis and Thompson, who remain as joint tenants.

28. b. A commission is not earned until the transaction closes. Therefore, it would be illegal to allocate funds from escrow that have not yet been earned. It is a violation for a broker to pay another broker's salesperson.

29. c. The National Association of REALTORS® encourages settlement of disputes between the parties by arbitration whenever that can be arranged.

30. b. Liquidated damage agreements have been disliked by the courts. However, often they are allowed if the amount discussed is not unusually high and perhaps it might be difficult to fix actual damages suffered by the insured party.

31. d. The promissory note is merely evidence of the debt and must be secured by another device commonly called the *trust deed*. Hence, a trust deed is a security device.

32. b. A lessee has a possessory interest in real property and is able to grant an easement but only for the term of the lease.

33. a. The husband's salary as well as the wife's salary are considered community property.

34. c. A deed to an assumed name, sometimes called a *fictitious name*, is permissible, such as a deed to property bought by a person in the name of a business.

35. b. Hoskold recommends the use of a sinking fund. He suggests, in addition to depreciating an item over its economic life, actually taking those same dollars and depositing them into an interest-bearing savings account, thus accumulating the monies necessary to replace the depreciable items.

36. d. The statute of limitations for a contract in writing is four years.

37. d. Simple interest is the form of interest customarily charged on real estate loans.

38. d. Choice *d* is a proper definition for the exclusive authorization and right-to-sell listing.

39. a. Fixed assets of 10 times current assets would indicate that the borrower was in a stronger financial condition than the other choices.

40. d. A commercial acre is defined as the remainder of an acre after the land has been subdivided to include areas devoted to streets, sidewalks, curbs and alleys, and so on.

41. a. A condominium purchase is the only transaction in which the buyer receives a fee simple interest and an in-common interest at the same time.

42. c. The time period in which to file a complaint for violation under the federal fair housing law is 180 days.

43. d. None of the choices are required to legally transfer title to real property.

44. a. Two handrails are not required for minimum building standard requirements by FHA.

45. a. When one expires leaving a will without heirs, the property transfers according to the provisions of the will and possibly to the interests of potentially existing devisees subject to the proper administration of that will.

46. c. The only item the broker must have is a written contract or written authorization with the note-holder to be able to service that note.

47. b. The beneficiary is the lender.

48. a. The preferred method for the appraisal of a shopping center would be the replacement cost approach and the capitalization of net income approach.

49. d. A hold in due course is a third party who buys up an existing note. The maker is the borrower. The borrower may refuse payment on the note if there is material alteration on the face of the note.

50. b. An estate of inheritance is another form of fee simple. A main characteristic of this interest is that the estate is of indefinite duration.

51. a. Under an exclusive-agency listing, the seller reserves the right to sell the property himself or herself and not pay anyone a commission.

52. a. If a person affixes property to the land of another by mistake, then that property may be removed, providing payment for damages is made.

53. a. Depreciation is a term with two applications. For accounting purposes, depreciation is taken off book value. For appraisal purposes, depreciation is taken off actual replacement value of a new commodity.

54. a. If deed restrictions and zoning conflict, the more rigid of the two will prevail. In this example, zoning is more rigid.

55. d. The seller has no recourse against the buyer because the buyer is fulfilling his purchase portion of the transaction. If the buyer had been a real estate licensee, then the buyer would have been obligated to disclose the intent to resell at a profit.

56. b. The escrow company writes to the lender requesting a beneficiary statement. That statement will indicate the condition of the loan, the balance due, rate of interest due to date, and so on.

57. d.   Trade fixtures are items that can be removed on termination of the tenancy if the contract provides for that, as long as the tenant makes any repairs to the premises necessitated by the removal of such trade fixtures. Choices *a* and *c* are examples of trade fixtures.

58. a.   An attachment is a legal seizure of the title to property by a court. It is a prejudgment activity, typing up that property until a hearing date is set.

59. a.   Unpaid taxes would be classified as general liens.

60. d.   Building codes, deed restrictions, and zoning regulations are all examples of public and private restrictions that may limit the use of real property.

61. c.   When recorded, an abstract of judgment becomes a lien on any property owned by the judgment debtor in the county where the abstract is recorded.

62. b.   Both the seller and broker are obligated to disclose any material facts to a prospective buyer concerning the property in question.

63. b.   Every potential buyer of land within a land project is entitled to a copy of the public report.

64. d.   A township is a six-mile square, containing 36 square miles, with a 24-mile perimeter.

65. d.   Usually, a broker is obligated to submit all offers on a listing, unless the owner has expressly instructed the broker not to do so.

66. b.   The requirement of the meeting of the minds is a requirement for a contract, and a standard listing agreement is an example of a contract.

67. c.   The salesperson is obligated to disclose to the owner of property the form of the good-faith deposit that is being presented by a potential buyer, whether it is in the form of a note or by any other method. The form of deposit must be disclosed to the seller prior to the seller's acceptance of the offer.

68. b.   The floor plan and the equipment help define functional utility.

69. c.   The commissioner would file an accusation and statement of issue, allowing the licensee to respond to such accusation. The commissioner then would proceed against the licensee as the commissioner felt appropriate.

70. b.   Intangible personal property is not subject to taxation.

71. b.   Prepaid rent is considered a charge, or debit, to the seller.

72. d.   Choices *a*, *b*, and *c* are all of concern to the homebuyer.

73. c.   The statute of frauds says certain items, including real estate transactions, must be in writing to be enforceable.

74. c.   An unlawful detainer action is the legal action an owner may take to remedy a default in rental payment.

75. d.   The easement is an easement appurtenant, meaning it will run with the land and be transferred to the buyer of the dominant tenement interest. The dominant tenement interest describes the land that is benefited by the easement; the servient tenement, interest is the land that is burdened by the easement.

76. a. The most common remedy for default of loan payment secured by a deed of trust is by the trustee sale, or public sale, even though many trust deeds contain a provision that will allow the beneficiary to go to court and seek a judicial or court foreclosure.

77. d. A declaration of homestead is allowed in all three choices.

78. c. An attorney-in-fact has been given the right to act for another.

79. d. The Real Estate Commissioner may choose to suspend or revoke the license of any real estate licensee who acts as described in choices *a*, *b*, and *c*.

80. b. A lease interest is an encumbrance on real property. It bars the owner from access to the property for the period of the lease with some minor exceptions.

81. a. The fee that the appraiser charges for his or her services is established by the agreement that the appraiser and the client ultimately reach.

82. b. A licensee can claim a commission only for the sale of property in which that licensee had an exclusive authorization to sell with a definite termination date.

83. a. In attempting to arrive at an opinion of value, an appraiser gives the least consideration to the assessed value of the property and most consideration to its current value of land, its highest and best use, and how subject property compares to other recently sold similar property.

84. d. Airspace is considered real property for the amount of airspace the property owner can reasonably use in connection with his or her own parcel.

85. a. A declaration of homestead offers only a limited amount of protection against actions by unsecured creditors. In this example, the homeowners' association fees would be considered a secured debt.

86. c. Demand is a necessary ingredient in creating value, but demand must be backed up by purchasing power to create "effective demand."

87. c. Before a developer chooses a shopping center site, the developer is concerned with the neighborhood residents' ability to pay.

88. a. In an open listing, the broker who is the procuring cause will be the broker who earns a commission. Hence, a dispute over commission in an open listing could be settled only by determining which broker was the procuring cause—the one who brought the buyer whose offer was accepted.

89. b. Unless stated in a contract to the contrary, crops not yet harvested would go with the sale of the property.

90. c. To calculate the answer of 25 percent, take 80 percent of the listed price, divide by the 20 percent deduction; hence, 80 percent divided by 20 percent would equal 25 percent made.

91. a. Statement of fact.

92. a. Regulation Z allows some exception to the advertising of credit offerings. For example, simply the percentage rate cited as the annual percentage rate fully spelled out is acceptable in the advertising format without having to spell out other credit terms.

93. c. If there are five or more parcels with the intent to resell, then that project will come under both the Subdivision Map Act and the Subdivided Lands Act, whether the sale is to occur now or in the future.

94. c. California requires 16-inch-on-center stud placement. While some communities have expanded that, the majority of local ordinances will still require that the placement be 16 inches on center.

95. c. Choice *c* is a better definition with respect to riparian rights than the other choices.

96. a. Accession indicates the owner of land is entitled to all that is added or united to his or her land.

97. a. When the parties decide to terminate the lease, the expression "termination" is the appropriate one to use.

98. b. A voidable contract is one wherein the elements required for a contract are present, but there may have been an injury, and at the option of the injured party the contract may be rescinded.

99. b. A land project involves 50 or more parcels offered for residential or recreational purposes in a remote area of California. It could be considered similar to a planned development in California.

100. b. On income-producing property, the net income is important to the potential investor. The net income remains after the deduction of a vacancy factor and certain allowable expenses.

101. a. A writ of execution refers to a forced sale of property to satisfy the claims of a judgment creditor. The court orders the sheriff to sell the property at a public auction.

102. a. A capitalization rate can be described in one sense as a yield rate that is necessary to attract investors to a certain type of investment. The higher the risk to the investor, the higher the capitalization rate must be to attract the investor.

103. d. The question asks for the exception. Choice *d* is not another term for a construction loan. The other choices are often used interchangeably with "construction loan."

104. a. An attachment is a prejudgment action whereby the court seizes and holds the title to the property until the matter of the attachment is dismissed or removed or until final judgment is rendered.

105. b. The term "novation" is used when substituting a new contract for an existing contract. The term *nova* is Latin for "new."

106. a. Massive cornices are within the property and are an example of functional obsolescence.

107. c. Pitch refers to the incline, rise, or degree of the angle of a roof or slope.

108. a. The Department of Housing and Urban Development (HUD) is the agency that oversees this act through one of its divisions called the Office of Interstate Land Sales Registration.

109. a. The "book value" (or "cost basis") is the starting point for calculating gain at a future time when the property is sold. It is an important record item for accounting and subsequent taxation purposes.

110. a. The topic of the question is found in the regulations of the Real Estate Commissioner.

111. c. The commissioner may take action to revoke or suspend the license of an indi-

vidual if that individual is found guilty of violating antidiscrimination regulations. Do not confuse choices *a* and *b*, which would be court action, but not instituted by the commissioner.

112. c. The fiduciary relationship between a broker and principal is one that is of trust and confidentiality and obligates the broker to keep the principal fully informed of all matters with reference to that transaction.

113. d. A California real estate license is valid for transactions occurring in California. Although the property in question might be out of state, as long as the negotiations are occurring within California, it is a legal transaction. With a real estate license, you can also collect a fee for negotiating the sale of a note and for representing the sale of a business opportunity.

114. d. When a property is into foreclosure, the trustee must wait at least three months before beginning the publishing of the notice of sale, indicating the upcoming trustee sale or public sale of that property.

115. b. If an attorney wishes to operate a real estate business, the attorney needs to be licensed by the Department of Real Estate as well.

116. b. The majority of California laws concerning real property are created by legislative acts.

117. a. The broker did the job that the owner hired the broker to do, so the seller is not relieved from the payment of commission to the broker.

118. a. The maximum time allowed to file the required application for a real estate license is up to one year from the date of taking the test, not from the date of being notified.

119. a. While the agency relationship creates a fiduciary relationship between the broker and seller, the broker must still be "honest and fair" to third parties in the transaction and disclose material facts.

120. d. The law of agency describes a fiduciary (a position of trust and confidentiality) relationship that exists between the real estate agent and the principal (owner). Choices *a*, *b*, and *c* would all describe the rights and duties between the agent and principal.

121. d. Statement of fact.

122. b. This is a simple definition of a basic contract.

123. d. Statement of fact.

124. d. The other three choices are some of the many duties and responsibilities of a property manager.

125. b. The mortgagor (borrower) remains in possession of the property during the judicial redemption period. (A way to remember who the mortgagor and mortgagee are: two *e*'s in the word *lender* and two *e*'s in the word *mortgagee*. Therefore, the mortgagor must be the borrower.)

126. b. Statement of fact.

127. d. The market analysis is important to do first to determine if the project would be worthwhile to build.

128. d. Neither sue for damages nor specific performance, as there is no contract yet. All that has taken place is an offer that has been rejected. There is no recourse on the part of the prospective buyer.

129. b. The personal assets of each partner in a general partnership are available to creditors to satisfy the debts of the partnership.

130. b. Equity assets, such as real estate investments, generally grow in value during an inflationary period. The other investment examples usually have a fixed rate of return that normally does not keep up with inflation.

131. b. The broker can file a lawsuit in civil court against the seller. (The Real Estate Commissioner does not become involved in commission disputes of brokers.)

132. b. A grant deed is not assignable. A new grant deed is made up for each subsequent sale of a piece of property.

133. b. If the annual percentage is used in any advertising, it must be fully spelled out.

134. b. The improvements are valued by the replacement cost method. The land can be appraised by various techniques, but the sales comparison approach is commonly used for land values.

135. a. Deferred maintenance refers to wear and tear that has already taken place, thereby requiring rehabilitation of the building.

136. a. Statement of fact.

137. d. To "tender" an offer is an "offer to perform."

138. c. When a person dies intestate, no will was left. The court then appoints an administrator who will attempt to sell the property only after the court has approved the terms of the sale and the price.

139. d. Choices a, b, and c are all good definitions of the lessee's interest in real property.

140. b. The term *avulsion* describes a sudden violent action that results in loss of a portion of land.

141. d. Because of the right of survivorship in joint tenancy, there is no right to will.

142. a. A joint tenancy is made up of two or more persons but is a single estate involving real or personal property.

143. b. Tenancy in common is a way of holding title to property.

144. c. Unequal interest is a feature of tenancy in common. By willing such interest the right of survivorship is disregarded, as the right to will is a feature of tenancy in common.

145. c. To be effective, a deed must contain an adequate description of the property.

146. b. An elevation sheet is a view of the property as it would appear from the exterior or outside. It shows the upright parts of the property.

147. c. To "tender" an offer is an offer (not a promise) to perform one's part of the contract.

148. c. Under a real estate option only one party is bound by the contract. The optionee (buyer) has the right to either purchase or not purchase, and therefore, there is no mutuality of obligations.

149. c. The provisions of the Bulk Sales Law are found in the Uniform Commercial Code.

150. d. The lender would consider all aspects of possible risk as mentioned in choices a, b, and c.

PRACTICE EXAMINATION II

1. When the real estate appraiser is concerned with the "present worth of future potential benefits" in appraisal, he is concerned with

   a. market data. c. cost.
   b. income. d. financing.

2. In making an appraisal of a shopping center, the appraiser would most likely make use of the _____approach.

   a. market data
   b. income
   c. cost of reproduction
   d. cost to care

3. Real property of the estate of a person who died intestate is to be sold by the administrator. This property can only be sold

   a. at public auction.
   b. to the highest bidder resulting from a newspaper advertisement.
   c. after the court has approved the terms of sale and the price.
   d. for all cash.

4. Property owned by Adams has an easement from Baker over Baker's property. This easement would be

   a. restrictive. c. in gross.
   b. appurtenant. d. selective.

5. When a subdivider submits an application on a new proposed subdivision to the Real Estate Commissioner and requests a Final Public Report, the subdivider will be required to submit all of the following EXCEPT

   a. the condition of the title.
   b. floor plans of the proposed housing units.
   c. copies of the sales agreements.
   d. provisions for the completion of the promised utilities.

6. A licensed real estate broker had a listing on a residence at a price of $120,000. There was no stipulation in the listing contract about buyer deposits. The broker advertised the property and received an inquiry from a prospect. After showing the property, the prospective buyer told the broker that he and his wife wanted to make an offer on the property for the full listed price and terms but were not willing to give the broker a deposit with their offer. Under these circumstances the broker should

   a. accept the offer but should tell the prospective buyer that the offer is possibly void without a deposit.
   b. refuse to accept the offer, as it is not a legally binding offer without a deposit.
   c. refuse the offer, as it is a violation of the licensing laws.
   d. accept the offer and present it to the seller but advise the seller there is no deposit.

7. The VA is concerned over many aspects of housing, including the development of neighborhood tracts. As a policy-making agency the VA

   a. is prohibited by law from influencing the development of neighborhood areas.
   b. has no practical influence over such developments.
   c. has developed a policy of laissez-faire.
   d. has indirect control over the development of subdivisions where purchasers use VA financing.

8. A lessee's interest is

   a. personal property.
   b. chattel real.
   c. a grant to use property for a period of time that reverts to the grantor at the expiration of the term.
   d. All of the above

9. Who determines the amount of taxes to be paid by the individual taxpayer?

   a. County Treasurer
   b. County Board of Supervisors
   c. County Assessor
   d. State Board of Equalization

10. In performing his or her task of determining the worth of a parcel of real property for a specific reason as of a definite date, an appraiser is making a(n)

   a. evaluation.
   b. valuation.
   c. determination of highest and best use.
   d. None of the above

11. A single young man enters into a contract to sell real property he owns. After escrow closes and the deed is recorded, the title company determines that the young man is under 18 years of age. In this circumstance, the transaction is

   a. valid.   c. voidable.
   b. void.   d. illegal.

12. Before a land sales contract can be recorded, it must be acknowledged by the

   a. grantor.
   b. seller.
   c. vendor and vendee.
   d. buyer.

13. Any gain realized by a real estate broker would be taxed as ordinary income if the sale resulted from the sale of

   a. his or her residence.
   b. the building in which he or she operates a business.
   c. property purchased for his or her investment.
   d. subdivision lots he or she owns.

14. Liquidating a financial obligation on an installment basis is known as

   a. acceleration.
   b. alienation.
   c. amortization.
   d. conversion.

15. It is possible to purchase title insurance to protect a purchaser's interest in real property against which of the following risks?

   a. The validity of an unrecorded easement
   b. Loss resulting from a breach of recorded private covenants, conditions, and restrictions
   c. The validity of a lessee's interest in an unrecorded leasehold interest in real property
   d. All of the above

16. Under current federal tax law, the ownership holding for multiple investors that would both minimize the tax obligation for the individual and also limit their personal liability would be a

   a. general partnership.
   b. limited partnership.
   c. corporation.
   d. proprietorship.

17. Which of the following has the least effect on today's value of property?

   a. Utility
   b. Scarcity
   c. Demand
   d. Original cost

18. When a dam breaks and floods an area, it is called

   a. accretion.
   b. avulsion.
   c. absorption.
   d. alluvion.

19. The word *rescind* most nearly means

   a. changed.
   b. terminated.
   c. substituted.
   d. revoked.

20. Under RESPA, anyone found guilty of paying a "kickback" for services not actually performed is subject to a maximum penalty of

   a. a fine of not more than $10,000.
   b. imprisonment for not more than a year.
   c. a one-year license suspension.
   d. Both *a* and *b*

21. Any citizen injured by discrimination in housing practices may under the Civil Rights Act of 1968

   a. institute a private action in a state or federal court.
   b. file criminal charges in federal court.
   c. file criminal charges with local law enforcement authorities.
   d. bring a civil action in a state superior court for specific performance.

22. An investor would deduct which of the following from the gross income to arrive at the effective gross income of a property?

   a. Vacancy allowance and bad debts
   b. Reserve for furniture replacement
   c. Payments on principal and interest
   d. Taxes

23. During an escrow period, which of the following is not prorated?

    a. Property taxes
    b. Rent
    c. Title insurance premiums
    d. Homeowners' dues

24. When a salesperson chooses to advertise property that is listed for sale by his or her office, which one of the following would be true?

    a. The salesperson's name may not appear in an ad for the sale of real property.
    b. The salesperson's name may appear in an ad for the sale of real property if the ad includes the name of the broker.
    c. The salesperson's name may appear in an ad for the sale of real property if the ad includes the name and address of the broker.
    d. Salespersons may advertise in their name only as long as they are REALTOR-ASSOCIATES® members of the National Association of REALTORS®.

25. Which of the following would be considered a valid delivery of a deed?

    a. The escrow officer mailed the deed that was acknowledged by the seller, but the delivery was made after the seller died.
    b. The escrow company delivered the deed to the buyer prior to the buyer's meeting all the terms of the escrow.
    c. The grantee delivered the deed after the death of the grantor in accordance with the instructions left by the grantor with his attorney.
    d. The seller handed the deed to the buyer, but the buyer failed to record the deed.

26. An owner may be required to have a real estate license when selling his or her own

    a. promissory notes.
    b. lots in a California subdivision.
    c. business opportunity.
    d. four-unit apartment.

27. A subdivider and developer purchased considerable acreage and now plan to construct a tract of 50 homes. In arranging the financing for the new construction, the lender has agreed to advance part of the funds immediately and will release a set amount of additional money as each home is completed. The funds that will be forthcoming as construction progresses are known as

    a. obligatory advances.
    b. reconveyance funds.
    c. release monies.
    d. open-end mortgage payments.

28. If a borrower pays $1,650 interest per quarter on a straight note of $60,000, the interest rate is

    a. 8.5 percent.   c. 10.5 percent.
    b. 9 percent.   d. 11 percent.

29. An appraiser would most likely use a depth table when confronted with a value problem involving a

    a. capitalization rate.
    b. sinking fund.
    c. commercial property.
    d. residential property in an urban subdivision.

30. Stone looked for some subdivision property under development. The licensee with whom he dealt stated that this investment was as good as gold. She also stated that the property would more than double in value in two years. In two years time the property was worth less than the purchase price Stone paid to buy the property. Four years after the purchase, Stone wishes to take legal action. Which of the following would very likely be true?

    a. Stone may file a civil suit against the licensee for misrepresentation and punitive damages.
    b. The licensee's actions were lawful as they merely constituted "puffing," as is normal in many sales situations.
    c. The licensee would not be subject to disciplinary action by the Real Estate Commissioner.
    d. Stone cannot sue in this matter because the statute of limitations has expired.

31. The maximum amount that can be paid from the Real Estate Education, Research, and Recovery Account on behalf of a licensee as a result of judicial actions is

    a. $10,000.   c. $40,000.
    b. $20,000.   d. $100,000.

32. If a real estate broker undertakes to canvass a neighborhood area that is very near to a section into which minorities have recently moved and tells the people to whom he talks that they should sell now, as their property might suffer a loss in the future, that broker would be guilty of

    a. steering.   c. blockbusting.
    b. panic peddling.   d. Both b and c

33. A real estate broker, in one of her weekly sales meetings, made the following statements to her sales staff in order to promote greater sales activity: (1) "We are going to solicit listings from this particular neighborhood because there is a big influx of black and Asian buyers who seem to be moving into the neighborhood," and (2) "Speak only to the Caucasian owners in the neighborhood because most of the other owners are new to the neighborhood and would probably not be interested in selling at this time." Which of the following statements would be in violation of the fair housing laws?

    a. Statement 1 only
    b. Statement 2 only
    c. Statements 1 and 2
    d. Neither statement 1 nor 2

34. The principle of substitution would be used by the real estate appraiser in which of these?

    a. The cost approach
    b. The capitalization of income
    c. The comparison approach
    d. All of the above

35. A contract signed under duress, although voidable by one of the parties, is still valid until it is

    a. rescinded.   c. corrected.
    b. discovered.   d. declared illegal.

36. A real estate broker negotiated the sale of a real property and acted as agent for the seller. By agreement, the licensee can be paid commission in the form of a(n)

    a. assignment by seller of first monies due seller from buyer on a mortgage.
    b. assignment of a note.
    c. buyer's personal note.
    d. Any of the above

37. An interest in a joint tenancy holding of real property could be terminated or transferred in all of the following ways *EXCEPT* by a

    a. lease of the property.
    b. sale of the interest.
    c. devise of the property.
    d. gift of a part interest.

38. Broker Adams is listing a property of Smith's. Smith has advised Adams that he wishes to realize $37,000 cash from the sale after paying Adams a 4 percent commission and paying $600 estimated closing costs. To accomplish this and assuming that the property is free and clear, the selling price must be at least

    a. $37,856.   c. $39,110.
    b. $38,480.   d. $39,167.

39. If the inside of the exterior wall of a home is as warm as an interior partition in the home, it indicates that the

    a. heating in the house is inefficient.
    b. insulation in the house is good.
    c. windows in the structure are not sealed properly.
    d. vents and ducts for the furnace leak.

40. A homeowner hired a broker to negotiate a hard money loan for her. In this case the hard money loan would be

    a. FHA or VA financing.
    b. secondary financing.
    c. purchase money.
    d. cash.

41. When a person is purchasing property on a land contract of sale, the one who is making the payment is known as the

    a. vendor.   c. trustor.
    b. payor.   d. grantor.

42. Mr. and Mrs. Tatum purchased a home for $45,000 and later sold it for a total price of $50,000. Within a year of the sale they purchased another home for $60,000. They lived in this home for about four years and sold it for $68,000. If they do not intend to purchase a replacement residence, their gain from these transactions under the federal income tax laws, not considering closing costs, would be

    a. $2,000.   c. $5,000.
    b. $0.   d. $8,000.

43. An eligible military veteran may purchase a personal residence under the Cal-Vet program. In such a transaction the seller will execute a grant deed in favor of the

    a. California Department of Veterans' Affairs.
    b. buyer.
    c. veteran, who assigns the title to the California Department of Veterans' Affairs until the contract is paid in full.
    d. None of the above

44. A holder who takes a promissory note for value, in good faith, without notice that it is overdue or has been dishonored, and without notice of any defense against it or claim to it on the part of any person, is a(n)

    a. endorser without recourse.
    b. bona fide assignee for value.
    c. holder through a holder in due course.
    d. holder in due course.

45. Accruals for depreciation are considered under which of the following approaches to value?

    a. Market and income
    b. Cost and market
    c. Income and cost
    d. None of the above

46. An ALTA lender's policy of title insurance provides protection for

    a. lessees taking possession after the date of the policy.
    b. loss or damage from defects in the title existing on the date of the policy.
    c. easements created during the term of the policy.
    d. encroachments created during the term of the policy.

47. The main duty of the county assessor is to determine the

    a. amount of tax to be paid by a property owner.
    b. proportion of tax to be paid by a property owner.
    c. tax rate to be applied to assessed values.
    d. assignment of parcel numbers to current, secured tax roll.

48. The date by which property must be sold to the state by the county for delinquent taxes is on or before

    a. June 30.   c. March 15.
    b. July 1.   d. January 1.

49. The owner of a leasehold estate is the

    a. remainderman.   c. lessor.
    b. lessee.   d. reversioner.

50. A loan broker asks a person applying through the broker's office for a new loan to fill out a questionnaire in which the borrower's race and marital status are left blank. The applicant can

    a. refuse to disclose race or marital status.
    b. file a complaint with the Real Estate Commissioner.
    c. supply the information requested so his or her credit history can be properly checked.
    d. All of the above

51. A covenant differs from a condition because

    a. a condition can be created only by a grant of an estate.
    b. a covenant cannot be created by a grant of an estate.
    c. only conditions run with the land.
    d. only covenants can restrict the use of land by the owner.

52. Which of the following circumstances would be interpreted to mean that a person is mentally incompetent?

    a. The person goes to a psychiatrist three times a week.
    b. The person has himself or herself committed to an institution.
    c. The person is committed to a mental institution.
    d. A conservator is appointed for the person by the court.

53. A prepayment penalty clause is found in most trust deeds and notes today and provides for a penalty to be paid by the borrower in the event

    a. property taxes or assessment liens become delinquent.
    b. the loan is paid off before its maturity date.
    c. the property securing the debt is sold.
    d. the loan payments become delinquent beyond 30 days of their due date.

54. A real estate developer subdivided a large parcel of land into 25 parcels with each parcel containing several acres. If the developer wishes to offer these parcels for sale in several states, the developer would be exempt from the Interstate Lands Full Disclosure Act if each parcel contained

    a. 10 acres.
    b. 15 acres.
    c. 20 acres.
    d. None of the above

55. Which of the following statements regarding options is incorrect?

    a. The optionee who does not exercise his or her option loses the money given for the right to the option.
    b. The optionee must surrender a valuable consideration to the optionor.
    c. Should the optionee elect to buy the property within the option period, to be legally bound, he or she must enter into a written sales contract with the optionor before the expiration of the option period.
    d. An option can be used in conjunction with the right to purchase a business opportunity separate from the real estate owned by the business.

56. A broker who has a written option agreement to purchase a parcel is now dealing with a potential buyer of that property. In this situation, the broker must reveal to the buyer that he is acting as a(n)

    a. licensee.   c. fiduciary.
    b. optionor.   d. principal.

57. Should a licensed real estate salesperson advertise the sale, lease, purchase or exchange or real property for a principal as an agent, the licensee must include in the advertising the

    a. salesperson's name.
    b. employing broker's last name.
    c. employing broker's last name and address.
    d. Both *a* and *b*

58. Larry is purchasing real property from Thomas under a real property sales contract. The property is presently encumbered by an underlying first deed of trust. With regard to the payments made by Larry to Thomas under the real property sales contract, Thomas

    a. must apply Larry's payment directly toward any payment due under the first trust deed existing on the property.
    b. need not apply any part of Larry's payment toward the first trust deed existing on the property.
    c. must place the payment in a trust account to ensure that any payment that may be due on the existing first trust deed will be paid.
    d. is not required to apply Larry's payment toward the first trust deed existing on the property as long as Thomas makes his payments within 90 days of their due date.

59. The item that would normally be prorated by the escrow holder in the sale of real property would be the

    a. documentary transfer tax.
    b. recording fees.
    c. prepaid rents.
    d. title insurance premium.

60. The Equal Credit Opportunity Act, which was enacted in 1974, was created to

    a. set uniform interests on real estate loans in the country.
    b. set minimum requirements to qualify a person to make credit purchases.
    c. forbid discrimination based on sex and marital status in the extension of credit.
    d. None of the above

61. An appraiser, when evaluating the quantity and durability of a property's net income expectancy, would use the results of the valuation in

    a. the capitalization of the net income.
    b. a HUD survey.
    c. the market data approach.
    d. establishing the property's marginal utility value.

62. "Of indefinite duration" is the chief characteristic of a(n)

    a. estate for years.
    b. estate at will.
    c. estate of inheritance.
    d. periodic tenancy.

63. All of the following are essential elements of an agency agreement EXCEPT

    a. payment of consideration.
    b. fiduciary relationship of the agent to the principal.
    c. agreement by the principal.
    d. a competent principal.

64. A partial release clause would most likely be used together with which of the following?

   a. A conditional installment sales contract
   b. A single parcel of property encumbered with a first, a second, and a third lien
   c. A blanket mortgage
   d. A short-term construction loan for a single-family residence

65. An adequate legal description is one that describes with certainty a particular parcel of land. A legal description that uses monuments in describing a particular parcel would be least satisfactory and could be defective because

   a. there is a possibility of the destruction of the monuments.
   b. title companies will not insure title to parcels of land in which the legal description is based on monuments.
   c. there is no external evidence of range line designations.
   d. appurtenances may not be in proximity to the improvements.

66. Under the provisions of the Civil Rights Act of 1968 (federal fair housing law), which of the following actions would be considered discriminatory and unlawful?

   a. A broker assigning salespeople to prospects according to the race of the associates
   b. A broker assigning salespersons to certain prospects according to the race of the prospects
   c. A broker who assigns salespersons to branch offices in line with the racial composition of the neighborhood in which those offices are located
   d. All of the above

67. Upon the last payment and fulfillment of the terms and conditions of a real property sales contract, a quitclaim deed would most likely be executed and signed by the

   a. vendor.   c. trustor.
   b. vendee.   d. trustee.

68. Which of the following are never considered to be liens on real property?

   a. Mortgages
   b. Judgments
   c. Deed restrictions
   d. Property taxes

69. Of the following, which would least likely involve an on-site inspection of the property?

    a. An extended coverage policy on a residence
    b. An extended coverage policy on rural property
    c. A standard policy on a residence
    d. An ALTA lender's policy on a residence

70. The impairment or reduction of desirability or use of real property that is due to or that is caused by economic changes is known as

    a. obsolescence.
    b. an over-improvement.
    c. public restriction.
    d. incurable physical deterioration.

71. Escrow instructions generally call for prorations based on a year of

    a. 355 days.   c. 360 days.
    b. 350 days.   d. 365 days.

72. Which of the following acts would *NOT* be a violation of the California Fair Housing Law (Rumford Act)?

    a. An owner of a single-family residence refuses to sell his home to two parties because the buyers are unmarried.
    b. Owners of a single-family residence refuse to rent a room within their residence to a prospective tenant because of her religious beliefs.
    c. An owner of a duplex refuses to rent one unit to a prospective tenant because of the prospect's race.
    d. An owner of a large apartment complex refuses to lease an apartment unit to a single person because most of the other tenants are married.

73. An apartment building was purchased for $200,000 with a $50,000 down payment. One year later its market value increased by 10 percent. This is an example of

    a. escalation.   c. discounting.
    b. leverage.   d. liquidity.

74. The Department of Real Estate is precluded from issuing or renewing a full-term real estate license if the applicant is on a list of persons who have not complied with a court order to provide child support payments. A temporary license may be issued to an otherwise qualified applicant for a period of

    a. 120 days.
    b. 150 days.
    c. 180 days.
    d. 30 days.

75. The phrase that best describes the nature of a broker's duty to keep a principal fully informed is

    a. ethical conduct.
    b. continuing responsibility.
    c. fiduciary obligation.
    d. trustworthy business principles.

76. In discussing real estate appraisals, it is most important to differentiate between the fundamental purpose of an appraisal and the

    a. levels of appraisal activity.
    b. functions for which the appraisal is required.
    c. forces that affect the value of real property.
    d. procedures followed in the appraisal process.

77. Sam offered to purchase Patterson's farm for a total price of $250,000. Sam was to give a $50,000 cash down payment, assume an existing first trust deed and note of about $160,000, and execute a new trust deed and note in favor of Patterson for the balance. The new trust deed and note was to be payable at 2 percent or more per month including interest at 15 percent—all due and payable five years from the closing date of escrow or on any subsequent conveyance of title. If the sale is consummated under these terms,

    a. a prepayment penalty may be demanded by Patterson in the event that the second trust deed and note is paid off within two years.
    b. Sam can later sell the property, and the new purchaser would be permitted to assume both existing loans.
    c. if only the minimum required payments are made on the new trust deed and note held by Patterson, Sam will be required to make a balloon payment on the due date.
    d. the acceleration clause in the new trust deed and note would be unenforceable in the event of a conveyance of title, because these clauses are no longer permitted in purchase-money loans.

78. In the field of real estate, a seller's market is said to exist when

    a. competition between sellers is increasing.
    b. a multiple-listing service is functioning, collecting, and distributing information about properties for sale.
    c. sellers outnumber buyers in the market.
    d. fewer properties are offered for sale to an increasing number of prospects with the ability to buy.

79. A listing agreement to sell community real property signed by one spouse is

    a. valid.   c. unenforceable.
    b. enforceable.   d. illegal.

80. On defaulting in making scheduled payments on a trust deed note, the trustor has a period of time to reinstate the loan. During this time the rights to possession of the property belong to the

    a. mortgagee.   c. beneficiary.
    b. trustor.   d. trustee.

81. Real estate broker Barry prepared an offer by Williams to purchase Sung's residence. The offer read, "Buyer to pay $27,500 cash with balance of the purchase price to be paid from the proceeds of a new first trust deed and note in the amount of $45,000, payable $287 per month including interest at 14 percent; seller to obtain new first trust deed and note, which is to be assumed by buyer." When the offer was presented to Sung, Sung amended the terms to read "Buyer to pay $27,500 cash with the balance of the purchase price to be paid from the proceeds of a new first trust deed and note in the amount of $45,000, payable $287 per month including interest at 14 percent; buyer to obtain new first trust deed." Sung's action

   a. was minor, and it does not alter the terms of the original agreement.
   b. means that Barry is entitled to a commission because he produced a buyer that is ready, willing, and able to buy.
   c. constitutes a rejection of the offer.
   d. becomes binding on both parties unless Williams disapproves of the change within a reasonable period of time.

82. All of the following constitute a release or satisfaction of a judgment *EXCEPT* a(n)

   a. release by the plaintiff.
   b. court order.
   c. order by the levying officer.
   d. judgment in favor of the plaintiff.

83. A licensed real estate broker was successful in selling a home for a party with whom the broker had entered into an oral listing agreement. If there were no subsequent written verification of the oral agreement, the payment of a commission to the broker is

   a. prohibited under the commissioner's regulations.
   b. illegal and contrary to public policy.
   c. enforceable in a court of law.
   d. permissible if the seller elects to do so.

84. Lester sold a residence that was free and clear of all liens and received a check for $30,580. If closing costs of $430.60 had been deducted as well as the broker's 6 percent commission, the actual selling price would have been most nearly

   a. $31,590.   c. $32,885.
   b. $31,825.   d. $32,990.

85. A conveyance of real property was accomplished by a deed that stated "I, Jim Roth, a single man, grant to Mark Shay, a widower, all that real property situated in Los Angeles County, State of California, described as follows: Lot 54, Tract 6448, Recorded in Book 104 at Page 18, official maps and records of Los Angeles County. Witnessed by my hand this 15th day of May, 1986. (Signed) Jim Roth." If Roth owned an absolute estate, Shay would receive

   a. a life estate.
   b. all of Roth's interest without warranty.
   c. an estate for years.
   d. a fee simple estate.

86. An owner of an 80-acre horse ranch entered into an exclusive authorization and right-to-sell contract with a licensed real estate broker. Included in the listing contract was an agreement by the broker to advertise the property in a special catalog that the broker published on a quarterly basis. The owner gave the broker $100 at the time of the listing to pay for the cost of advertising in the catalog. According to the Real Estate Law and Regulations, this $100

    a. must be deposited in the broker's trust account and can be withdrawn only to pay for actual expenses incurred in advertising the property.
    b. may be used by the broker for any purpose, provided proper entries are made in the broker's trust account record.
    c. must be deposited in the broker's trust account but may be withdrawn and kept as liquidated damages in the event the owner cancels the listing contract.
    d. need not be deposited in the broker's trust account, but the broker must be prepared to return the money if not spent on advertising the property.

87. The owner of which of the following would normally obtain the least "return of" their investment?

    a. Residential property
    b. Agricultural property
    c. Industrial property
    d. Commercial property

88. Under the authority of a valid California real estate license, you may

    a. negotiate in California the sale of a ranch located in Nevada.
    b. negotiate the sale of a note and collect a fee.
    c. sell a business.
    d. All of the above

89. The California Subdivided Lands Act controls the sale or leasing of new subdivided land to California residents

    a. only if the property is located in California.
    b. only if the property is unimproved.
    c. regardless of the location of the property.
    d. only if the property is unimproved and located outside of California.

90. Laurel, a real estate developer, located 10 acres of unimproved land that was being offered for sale at a price of $100,000. She was very interested in purchasing the acreage but did not have the required cash. She contacted another investor named Dade and convinced Dade to purchase the property for the $100,000 price and then entered into a contract of sale for the property with Dade for a contract price of $115,000. Under these circumstances, the transaction is

    a. usurious.
    b. voidable by Dade.
    c. voidable by Laurel.
    d. a valid purchase and resale by Dade.

91. The most popular and best form of real estate syndicate that affords the least amount of liability but allows the free flow of tax advantages would be a

    a. real estate investment trust.
    b. limited partnership.
    c. corporation.
    d. joint venture.

92. Maxwell purchased a new mobile home from a mobile home dealer six months ago and had the mobile home placed on a lot that he had purchased in a mobile home park. He now wishes to sell the mobile home and has asked licensed real estate broker Smith to list and sell the mobile home and lease or sell the lot. Based on the information above, broker Smith may

    a. list the lot at this time and list or sell the mobile home.
    b. sell the mobile home and lot at this time because the mobile home is incidental to the sale of the mobile home lot.
    c. lease or sell the lot but may not sell the mobile home even if she were also a licensed mobile home dealer.
    d. not list or sell the mobile home at any time until the unit has been affixed to a permanent foundation system and the proper changes have been made in the registration.

93. Information with respect to footing, mudsill, anchor bolts, piers, and floor joists could be obtained from a review of which of the following plans?

    a. Floor   c. Foundation
    b. Elevation   d. Grading

94. Which of the following statements with regard to depreciation is NOT correct?

    a. Reserves for depreciation may be set aside for both past and future depreciation.
    b. Depreciation is the loss in value from any cause.
    c. Depreciation is the difference between the present value of the improvements and the cost to replace them on today's market.
    d. Depreciation results from only influences that are inherent in the property and not from extraneous factors.

95. Janis has fee simple title to a vacant lot on a commercial street. Her lot is rectangular in shape, contains 16,500 square feet, and each side measures 150 linear feet in depth. Janis wants to build a store building but needs more space. There are two lots of identical size and shape available for purchase. One is located adjacent to the left of Janis's lot and the other immediately to its right. Each of the lots measures 150 feet in depth and contains 4,950 square feet. If Janis acquires both of these lots and combines them with her original lot, the total square frontage in linear feet

    a. cannot be calculated from the information given.
    b. will be 176.
    c. will be 159.
    d. will be 143.

96. Real estate broker Carl presented a offer from a prospective purchaser to the sellers on Sunday morning. The sellers reviewed the offer and requested 24 hours to consider the offer. Later that day, two of the broker's salespersons received additional offers on the property. The prices on these two additional offers were much lower than the pending offer, and broker Carl felt that they would certainly be rejected by the sellers. Under these circumstances, broker Carl should

    a. present each additional offer, one at a time, in the order the offers were received by the salespersons.
    b. advise the seller of these two additional offers and present them as soon as conveniently possible.
    c. hold the two additional offers until the seller has reached a decision on the initial offer.
    d. advise the salespersons to have their prospective buyers resubmit their offers at a more realistic price, as the broker is positive that the seller will not accept the offers as presently written.

97. A lender grants a loan to Lee for 80 percent of the value of property as shown on the appraisal. The interest rate is at 11 percent. The total interest amount for the first year is $7,040. What is the appraised value of Lee's property?

    a. $76,000
    b. $89,000
    c. $80,000
    d. $64,000

98. Which of the following statements is incorrect with respect to the ownership of real property that includes riparian rights?

    a. The riparian rights may not be severed from the land by prescription or condemnation.
    b. An owner may sell any part of the land without transferring the riparian rights, provided the part being sold is not adjacent to the watercourse.
    c. An owner of real property with riparian rights may convey title to a portion of the real property together with riparian rights.
    d. An owner of real property may transfer riparian rights together with title to the real property by express agreement, even though that portion of the real property is not adjacent to the watercourse.

99. Which of the following actions taken by the owner of a fee simple estate would cause her interest to be converted to that of less-than-freehold estate?

    a. A grant of the mineral rights therein to a third party
    b. A lease of the land for agricultural purposes to a third party for a period of five years
    c. A grant of life estate
    d. Sale-and-leaseback

100. A statement in writing that is sworn to or affirmed before a person who has authority to administer an oath or affirmation is known as a(n)

    a. acknowledgment.
    b. affidavit.
    c. verification.
    d. abstract.

101. A recorded notice of pending legal action on real property is called a(n)

   a. notice of nonresponsibility.
   b. lis pendens.
   c. homestead exemption.
   d. abstract of judgment.

102. Which of the following is used to estimate value using the market data approach?

   a. The cost to replace the improvements
   b. The capitalized income stream of the property
   c. The depreciation of the property due to its age
   d. The adjusted values of comparable properties

103. An individual can be classified as a "dealer" for income tax purposes if she sells

   a. stock-in-trade.
   b. investment property.
   c. property held for the production of income.
   d. property used in a trade or business.

104. To estimate the value of property using the cost approach, the appraiser would consider all of the following *EXCEPT* the

   a. capitalization rate.
   b. reproduction cost.
   c. market value of the land.
   d. depreciation rate.

105. An acknowledgment of a document is made by a

   a. county recorder.   c. judge.
   b. grantor.   d. notary.

106. A misplaced improvement, such as a building that is not an appropriate improvement for the site, is an example of

   a. incurable physical depreciation.
   b. curable functional obsolescence.
   c. incurable functional obsolescence.
   d. economic obsolescence.

107. Which of the following can be used to determine a capitalization rate?

   a. Replacement cost method
   b. Band of investment method
   c. Unit-in-place method
   d. Depreciation method

108. Which of the following is the best description of actual fraud?

   a. A false promise
   b. An action intending to deceive another
   c. The deliberate withholding of a material fact
   d. All of the above

109. A promissory note contains all of the following *EXCEPT* the

   a. physical description of the property being used as security for the debt.
   b. total amount for the loan.
   c. terms of payment.
   d. rate of interest.

110. The price of real property rises when

   a. supply is the same as demand.
   b. supply exceeds demand.
   c. demand is greater than supply.
   d. None of the above

111. A federal law requires that special disclosures be given to borrowers on consumer real estate loans stating approximate closing costs. These disclosures are to be supported by a special pamphlet and forms approved by HUD. This law is called

    a. Regulation Q.
    b. the Civil Code.
    c. the Truth-in-Lending Act.
    d. RESPA.

112. An appraiser wishes to determine the effective gross income of an apartment building. Which of the following would the appraiser deduct from the gross income?

    a. Principal and interest payments
    b. Depreciation
    c. The vacancy factor and loss of rent
    d. Management fees

113. The term *emblements* as used in real estate refers to

    a. fixtures that have been permanently attached.
    b. farm equipment.
    c. the right of a tenant farmer to harvest his crops.
    d. All of the above

114. In the sale of real property it is customary to specify a time period for the escrow process. If no period were stated in the escrow instructions, then the parties would have

    a. 30 days.
    b. 60 days.
    c. any amount of time that each party needed.
    d. a reasonable time period.

115. Which of the following best describes a failure to fulfill the terms of a contract?

    a. A liquidated damages agreement
    b. An agreement to arbitrate disputes
    c. A default
    d. A delinquency

116. Regarding "prior appropriation," water rights are ranked by

    a. purpose for the use of the water.
    b. priority in time of use.
    c. Both *a* and *b*
    d. None of the above

117. Sally James wants to open up her own escrow services company. She must be licensed by the

    a. Real Estate Commissioner.
    b. Corporations Commissioner.
    c. Insurance Commissioner.
    d. None of the above

118. Before the Real Estate Commissioner will issue a final public report, he or she will want to see any advertising to be used on

    a. all condominium projects.
    b. land projects.
    c. community apartment projects.
    d. all standard subdivisions.

119. All of the following require recording *EXCEPT* a

    a. notice of default.
    b. mechanic's lien.
    c. trust deed.
    d. notice of nonresponsibility.

120. Which of the following is required on a bill of sale?

    a. An acknowledgment
    b. Amount of consideration
    c. The date
    d. Description of the property

121. Under the Subdivision Map Act, a parcel map is required for two to four parcels. A tentative map is required for five or more parcels. With which of the following agencies are these maps initially filed?

    a. State government
    b. Local government
    c. The Real Estate Commissioner
    d. None of the above

122. A real estate broker's trust account checks that have been voided or canceled must be kept for

    a. five years.
    b. four years.
    c. three years.
    d. seven years.

123. Dawson sells his real property to Jones. Each party has fully performed his requirements to the escrow holder. Dawson dies before the transfer of title and recording of the deed. The escrow is

    a. void.
    b. void, and Dawson's heirs may ask for relief of any obligations to the court.
    c. valid, and Jones can demand that the deed be recorded as agreed-on in the escrow instructions.
    d. void, as the death of one of the parties to the escrow cancels the escrow.

124. What interest rate will prevail if the rate is not stated on the face of a promissory note, although it is implied that there will be interest charged?

    a. The maximum set by the law
    b. The legal rate of interest allowed
    c. The note is not enforceable without interest
    d. The rate set by court action

125. In which of the following government records would one likely find out about liens against many types of personal property?

    a. The records of the county recorder
    b. The records of the city clerk
    c. The records of the county assessor
    d. The Office of the Secretary of State

126. The maximum amount that a lender would grant for a conventional loan is normally based on

    a. the sales price or the appraised value, whichever is less.
    b. the sales price of the property.
    c. the appraised value of the property.
    d. 80 percent of the sales price.

127. The capitalization of net income approach to the estimate of property value is dependent on

    a. adjusting the sales price of comparable properties.
    b. the property's ability to generate net income.
    c. discounted cash flows.
    d. None of the above

128. The disclosure statement under RESPA is called the

    a. mortgage disclosure form.
    b. Uniform Settlement Statement.
    c. Uniform Disclosure Statement.
    d. None of the above

129. Under the statute of frauds, all contracts for the sale of real property must be in writing. The main reason for this law is to

    a. protect the broker.
    b. protect the buyer.
    c. prevent fraudulent proof of a fictitious oral agreement.
    d. protect the seller.

130. Property owned by Adams has an easement from Baker over Baker's property. This easement would be

    a. restrictive.   c. in gross.
    b. appurtenant.   d. selective.

131. Expensive homes tend to be found

    a. on high ground in urban areas.
    b. near water.
    c. near freeways.
    d. Both *a* and *b*

132. Ms. Greg employed the Mark Pool Construction Company to install a swimming pool at her home. After completion, the contractor filed a lien to obtain payment of the contract price. The encumbrance created was a

    a. general lien.
    b. voluntary lien.
    c. specific lien.
    d. None of the above

133. All of the following are examples of specific liens when properly recorded *EXCEPT*

    a. real property taxes, delinquent for two years.
    b. mechanics' liens for labor or supplies furnished on an improvement.
    c. a blanket mortgage on a subdivision without a release clause.
    d. a judgment for punitive damages.

134. Deed restrictions are placed on a subdivision development by

    a. the Federal Housing Administration.
    b. state and local ordinances.
    c. the developer.
    d. the permanent lender.

135. A property owner would have the least protection against mechanics' liens if she filed a notice

    a. to quit.
    b. of nonresponsibility.
    c. of cessation.
    d. of completion.

136. A tract developer learns that a large national cosmetics manufacturer is moving one of its plants near an area where he is building a large number of new homes and condominiums. Because a great number of employees of the cosmetics firms will be women, he decides to gear his sales promotion toward this group. He tells his advertising agency to aim all of their ads to reflect a preference for female buyers. Realizing he can't discriminate toward any one racial group, he advises his sales agent to be sure to set up a quota for Caucasian, African American, Latino, and Asian buyers. Once the quota has been reached, they should discourage further sales to that racial group by adjusting the prices. If the developer follows this plan, he violates

    a. no fair housing laws.
    b. the fair housing laws based on his ad campaign but not the quota system.
    c. the fair housing laws based on his racial quota system but not the ad campaign.
    d. the fair housing laws in both his ad campaign and racial quota system.

137. The Street Improvement Act of 1911 may be used for all of the following EXCEPT

    a. purchasing land for a subdivision.
    b. sewers.
    c. drainage.
    d. off-site improvements.

138. All of the following conditions must exist at the time of the conveyance before an easement by implied grant will be given effect EXCEPT

    a. there must be a separation of titles.
    b. the use must be visible on inspection of the surface of land.
    c. the easement must be reasonably necessary to the beneficial use of land granted.
    d. the use that gives rise to the easement must have continued so long and so obviously as to show that it was intended to be permanent.

139. Which of the following would be classified as an encumbrance?

    a. Homestead
    b. Freehold estate
    c. Lease
    d. None of the above

140. Which of the following groups of words contains an incorrectly spelled word?

    a. Tenement, forfeiture, obsolescence, encumbrace
    b. Acknowledgement, jurisdiction, judgment, hypothecate
    c. Accommodate, appurtenance, amenities, alluvium
    d. Prescription, riparian, subordinate, subrogation

141. Three of the following real estate terms are closely associated. Which term does not belong with the choices offered?

    a. Easement   c. Attachment
    b. Lien   d. Judgment

142. A restrictive covenant contained in a deed that prohibits sale of property to persons of a particular race will

    a. invalidate the conveyance.

    b. have no effect on the conveyance, but the covenant will be unenforceable.

    c. create the power in the grantee to void the conveyance.

    d. retain in the grantor the power to enforce the covenant.

143. Protective covenants that place restrictions on buyers of lots in a new subdivision would most likely be found in the

    a. original deed held by the subdivider.

    b. recorded declaration of restrictions.

    c. zoning codes.

    d. subdivision map.

144. With regard to general and specific liens, which of the following contains only specific liens?

    a. Mortgage, attachment, judgment, and corporation tax lien

    b. Attachment, mechanic's lien, mortgage, and taxes

    c. Inheritance taxes, mortgage, assessments, and mechanic's lien

    d. Judgment, trust deed, attachment, and taxes

145. A lien created by a money judgment affects the real property of a judgment debtor

    a. no matter where the property is located in the United States.

    b. in each county where the abstract of judgment is recorded.

    c. in the entire state.

    d. only in the county where the trial was held.

146. An appurtenant easement is

    a. an interest in land incapable of transfer.

    b. an interest in land capable of transfer.

    c. a possessory interest in the land of another person.

    d. personal to the holder and incapable of transfer.

147. Which of the following statements regarding deed restrictions is true?

    a. A covenant is generally more severe than a condition.

    b. To be legally enforced, a private restriction must promote public health, safety, and welfare.

    c. The term *covenant* is an all-inclusive word embracing both "restrictions" and "conditions."

    d. A violation of a condition might result in the loss of title.

148. Every lease contains an implied covenant of "quiet enjoyment and possession." This covenant directly relates to

    a. title that is free of all encumbrances.

    b. tenant's possession free of disturbances by the landlord or another who has paramount title.

    c. nuisances inflicted by adjoining neighbors.

    d. liability for damages due to tenant's negligence.

149. A broker has an option to purchase property and at the same time is employed by the owner to sell the property and obtain a commission from the sale. Before the broker can legally exercise the option he must

a. make a public notice of his intention to exercise the option.
b. put the necessary funds in escrow.
c. obtain the written consent of the seller.
d. give constructive notice to the seller.

150. A developer who is not a real estate licensee is selling tract homes and conditions each sale and home loan obtained by the buyer with an agreement whereby the buyer must pay for the title insurance from a specific title company selected by the seller. The seller gets a rebate. This is

a. a violation of the California Real Estate Law.
b. a violation of RESPA, and the seller could be liable for treble damages.
c. perfectly legal; the seller has every right to do so.
d. not a violation of RESPA but a violation of the Insurance Code.

■ ANSWER KEY

1. b. When appraising income-producing property, an appraiser needs to estimate the present worth of future potential benefits of the investment, such as the rental income.

2. b. Even though the cost approach is taken into consideration, the issue here most likely to be used would be the income approach.

3. c. When a person dies intestate, no will is left. The court appoints an administrator who will attempt to sell the property only after the court has approved the terms of the sale and the price.

4. b. When an easement is granted to a property owner for use over the property of another, the easement is an "easement appurtenant."

5. b. Under the Subdivided Lands Act, the Real Estate Commissioner is not concerned with the floor plan of the proposed project. The commissioner is more concerned with attempting to minimize fraud and misrepresentation, and is therefore concerned with the matter of the contents of the sales agreement, the title to the project, and any provisions for the completion of the utilities as promised to the buyers.

6. d. The broker is to present the offer and indicate that there is no actual deposit being presented, because the broker is obligated to present all offers.

7. d. The VA can require certain construction standards, thereby imposing an indirect control over the development of subdivisions wherein VA financing will be allowed.

8. d. Choices *a*, *b*, and *c* all define the lessee's interest in real property.

9. b. The County Board of Supervisors sets the tax rate. Do not confuse with the county assessor's office, which determines the full cash value of property.

10. b. Notice that the process of estimating value is called a *valuation process*, not an *evaluation*.

11. b. A single person under 18 years of age does not have contractual capacity. Therefore, the contract to sell the real property would be considered void.

12. b. Under a land sale contract, the seller, whom we call the *vendor*, must sign in the presence of a notary public before that contract can be recorded. The vendee's signature is not required.

13. d. Any gains realized from the sale of subdivision lots that a broker owns would be treated as ordinary income.

14. c. Amortization means to liquidate or to extinguish an obligation on an installment basis.

15. d. Choices *a*, *b*, and *c* could all be protected via the purchase of title insurance.

16. b. The limited partnership is the most common form of syndication in California because it has historically limited the liability of the individual investor and to some degree minimizes tax obligation.

17. d. In determining an estimate of value of property, original cost has no impact. The elements that create value surely would, such as demand, utility, scarcity, and transferability.

18. b. The term *avulsion* describes a sudden violent action that results in loss of a portion of land.

19. b. The term *rescind* most nearly means a termination or annulment of a contract.

20. d. The penalty for violating the kickback provision under RESPA is a fine of no more than $10,000 and imprisonment for not more than one year.

21. a. An injured party in a matter of discrimination may institute private action in either a state or federal court.

22. a. From gross scheduled income of a property, we deduct the vacancy factor and bad debts to arrive at what is called the *effective gross income* of that property.

23. c. Statement of fact.

24. b. If a salesperson wishes to advertise property, the broker's name must be included in the ad, and the salesperson's name may appear in the ad as well.

25. d. There must be an effective delivery of a deed before title is transferred. Delivery may be in the form of merely handing the deed to the buyer or the buyer's recording the deed. However, recording the deed is not a requirement, just a well-established practice.

26. a. If selling his or her own promissory note eight or more times in a calendar year, then one must have a real estate license. A real estate license is not required in choices *b, c,* and *d* as long as the owner is buying or selling for himself or herself only.

27. a. Obligatory advances represent one form of construction loan distribution, often used in subdivision financing activities.

28. d. Multiply the $1,650 of interest by four quarters of the year to equal $6,600 annual interest. Take $6,600 and divide by $60,000 to equal 11 percent.

29. c. Depth table rules are used on vacant land, usually for commercial property.

30. a. Stone has clearly been injured; he may file a civil suit for misrepresentation and may seek punitive damages.

31. d. $100,000 is the maximum amount that can be paid from the recovery account on behalf of a licensee. Had the question stated "on behalf of an individual transaction of the licensee," the maximum would have been $20,000. The recovery account provides up to $100,000 to be paid on behalf of a licensee as a result of judicial action.

32. d. The terms *panic peddling, panic selling,* and *blockbusting* could be used to describe this activity.

33. c. Both statements 1 and 2 are in clear violation of fair housing laws.

34. d. The principle of substitution appears in the cost approach when attempting to determine replacement cost. This principle also is used when we attempt to capitalize the net income of recently sold income-producing property, and it is surely used in the comparison or market data approach when comparing the subject property with similar properties that have recently sold.

35. a. If a contract is signed under duress, then the contract may be rescinded by the injured party, but it is still considered valid until that action is taken.

36. d. Choices *a, b,* and *c* could all be commission payments due the broker by the seller.

37. a. Leasing the property wherein title is held as joint tenancy would not break the joint tenancy form of title taking.

38. d. Applying the selling price rule, subtract from 100 percent and then divide. In this case, subtract the 4 percent commission from 100 percent, leaving 96 percent. Add the $600 in closing costs to the net amount of $37,000 that the seller wishes to receive. Then divide $37,600 by 96 percent and you will get $39,167.

39. b. The insulation in the subject house is apparently good to create an exterior wall that is as warm as an interior partition of the home.

40. d. Cash is considered an example of a hard money loan. Equity loans are also examples of hard money loans. The expression *purchase money* refers merely to a credit extension and not cash.

41. b. The buyer on a land contract is known as a *vendee* or *payor* of the payments on that debt.

42. b. Under current tax laws, gain up to $250,000 for a single person or up to $500,000 for a married couple is excluded from taxation on the sale of a principal residence every two years.

43. a. When the California Department of Veterans' Affairs approves a Cal-Vet's application to purchase a home, the state presents cash to the seller of the home. The seller then executes a grant deed in the favor of the California Department of Veterans' Affairs. That department will then sell the house to the approved veteran using a land sales contract. The state obtains funds for the purchase of homes under this program via the sale of bonds.

44. d. A holder in due course is a third person who buys up an existing promissory note for value and in good faith.

45. c. Accruals for depreciation occur in the cost approach when depreciating the value of the improvements due to the age of the improvements. Accruals for depreciation occur in the selection of a capitalization rate when calculating the return of the investment (depreciation recaptured).

46. b. The protection afforded relates directly to any defects existing on the date the policy was issued.

47. b. One of the duties of the county assessor is to determine the portion of tax to be paid by the property owner. Currently it is at 100 percent of full cash value.

48. a. Property is transferred to the state by the county for delinquent property taxes not later than June 30 of that tax year.

49. b. The owner of a leasehold estate is the lessee, more commonly called the *tenant*.

50. a. With reference to a loan application, the borrower is not obligated to disclose either race or marital status.

51. a. A condition is a qualification of ownership and can be imposed only in conveyances.

52. d. If a person is judicially declared mentally incompetent, a conservator is appointed to act in behalf of that person by the court.

53. b.   A prepayment penalty is often charged if a loan is paid off before its due date.

54. d.   The Interstate Land Sales Full Disclosure Act controls offerings of 25 or more parcels of any size being sold interstate.

55. c.   In an option, the buyer has already entered into a contract to purchase at the time of entering into the option agreement. Choice *c* is the incorrect statement.

56. d.   The broker has an option agreement for his or her own account and must now reveal to the potential buyer of the property that the broker will be acting as a principal.

57. b.   If a salesperson advertises real property, the licensee must also include the employing broker's last name in the ad.

58. a.   It is a statutory requirement that a seller under a land contract continue to make payments on any existing underlying loan on subject property.

59. c.   Of the choices given, prepaid rents would be prorated and treated as a debit to the seller and a credit to the buyer.

60. c.   The Equal Credit Opportunity Act of 1974 prohibits discrimination based on sex and marital status with reference to application for credit.

61. a.   With reference to quantity and durability of net income, the appraiser is looking at the amount of any existing leases and the terms of such leases in attempting to arrive at a property capitalization of the net income.

62. c.   An *estate of inheritance* is another expression for *fee simple*. A main characteristic of this interest is that the ownership is of indefinite duration.

63. a.   Choices *b, c,* and *d* are essential elements for an agency relationship. The payment of consideration is not a legal requirement for an agency agreement.

64. c.   A blanket mortgage is a single mortgage that covers more than one piece of property. If it contains a release clause, then on payment for an individual property, for example, a home in a subdivision, such property can be released from the lien of a mortgage and transferred to the buyer.

65. a.   The use of monuments is found in the metes-and-bounds method of land description. It is not a satisfactory method of land description because the monuments might shift or move over the years or could possibly be destroyed.

66. d.   Choices *a, b,* and *c* are all examples of actions that would be considered discriminatory and unlawful.

67. a.   Another expression for a real property sales contract is a *land contract*. When the terms of the land contract have been met, it is the vendor's (seller's) obligation to execute a document that relinquishes any interest the vendor has in the property, thereby allowing the vendee (buyer) full right and claim to title of the property.

68. c.   Deed restrictions place certain limitations on the use of property but are not considered liens.

69. c.   A standard policy of title insurance for a resident does not require an on-site inspection of the property.

70. a.   Obsolescence causes a loss in value. In this example, economic changes are contributing to the property's obsolescence.

71. c. 360 days is the figure used for escrow proration purposes and is sometimes referred to as either an *escrow* or a *banker's year*.

72. b. An owner of a single-family dwelling is exempt from the provision of California fair housing, provided that the owner is renting to only one person and is bringing that person into the house to reside with the owner.

73. b. The question reflects a good example of leverage.

74. b. Statement of fact.

75. c. The fiduciary relationship between a broker and principal is one of trust and confidentiality and obligates the broker to keep the principal fully informed of all matters about that transaction.

76. b. An appraiser needs to know the purpose and the function of the appraisal. For example, an appraisal might be required for a new loan, or it might be required for a company merger or dissolution. Hence, different methods would be applied, depending on the function the appraisal will serve.

77. c. The or-more clause, as stated in the question, allows the buyer to pay the debt off early without being charged a prepayment penalty. If the buyer pays only the minimum payment, there will be a balloon payment remaining on the note.

78. d. A seller's market describes an advantage position of a seller. If there are fewer properties available but an increasing number of buyers, the supply and demand principle will demonstrate that prices will increase, hence, leading to a sellers' market.

79. a. A listing agreement to sell community real property signed by only one spouse is valid.

80. b. During the reinstatement and redemption period of a defaulted loan, the trustor (borrower) has the right to remain in possession of the property.

81. c. Because Sung did not accept the terms of the original offer, Sung's action would be deemed a rejection of the offer. Sung may wish to prepare a counteroffer to be presented to the buyer, but in any event the original offer is considered to be rejected.

82. d. The question highlights the term *release* or *satisfaction*. Choice d, a judgment in favor of the plaintiff, creates another judgment, so it is not a means of releasing a judgment.

83. d. Because the contract is oral, it would be difficult to enforce. Therefore, the payment of commission to the broker is permissible if the seller chooses to do so. The statute of frauds requires that all real estate contracts be in writing to be enforceable, so the broker would have difficulty enforcing the oral agreement for payment of commission.

84. d. Add the closing costs of $430.60 to the net amount of $30,580, giving a total of $31,010.60. Apply the selling price rule that says subtract from 100 percent and then divide, then subtract the 6 percent commission from 100 percent and divide the remaining 94 percent into $31,010.60, and you will arrive at a selling price of $32,990.

85. d. The conveyance described is that of a fee simple estate, which is the greatest interest one can have in the land.

86. a. The $100 given is an example of a trust fund item; it must be deposited in the broker's trust account and can be used only to pay for the actual expenses incurred in advertising the property.

87. a. The expression *return of the investment* applies to business properties and other investment types of properties. The return of the investment refers to depreciation recapture. There is no depreciation allowed on residential property for owner-occupied use.

88. d. A California real estate license is valid for transactions occurring in California. Although the property in question might be out of state, as long as the negotiations are occurring within California, the transaction is a legal one. With a real estate license, you may collect a fee for negotiating the sale of a note and for representing the sale of a business opportunity.

89. c. Subdivisions offered for sale to Californians that are either in or outside the State of California are still under the control of the Subdivided Lands Act.

90. d. The question describes a valid purchase and resale by Dade.

91. b. A limited partnership is the most common form of syndication in California.

92. a. Smith may list the lot for sale and list or sell the mobile home, if it has been registered with the Department of Housing and Community Development.

93. c. The foundation plan would include information regarding footings, mud fill, anchor bolts, piers, and floor joists.

94. d. Depreciation can result from influences that are outside the property lines as well as from within the property lines.

95. b. Use the formula area divided by depth equals width or area divided by width equals depth; then take the first lot containing 16,500 square feet and divide by its depth of 150 to arrive at a frontage or width of 110 feet. Then take the area of the next lot, 4,950 square feet, and divide by its depth of 150 feet to equal a width of 33 feet. There are two lots of this size. Then add 33 feet twice to 110 feet, the width of the first parcel, to arrive at the combined front footage of 176 feet.

96. b. The broker is still obligated to present all offers on the property, and the decision as to which offer should be accepted is left purely up to the seller, not the broker.

97. c. $7,040 divided by 11% = $64,000. $64,000 divided by 80% = $80,000.

98. a. Choice *a* is incorrect.

99. d. A sale-and-leaseback is an example of a less-than-freehold interest. In a sale-and-leaseback, an owner of a building decides to sell and remain on the premises as a tenant. Often this is done to free up working capital.

100. b. An affidavit is a statement only, and is made before one who has the authority to administer the oath or affirmation.

101. b. A "lis pendens" is a pending lawsuit, usually regarding the title to real property.

102. d. Statement of fact.

103. a. A "dealer" in real estate is one who buys and sells real property for his or her own account as a main source of income, as a subdivider would do. The disadvantage of being labeled a "dealer" by the

Internal Revenue Service is that dealers lose many of the tax advantages of investors.

104. a. The capitalization rate is part of the income approach, not the cost approach.

105. b. The grantor acknowledges deeds; the notary witnesses (or accepts) the acknowledgment.

106. d. If an improvement is not compatible with its environment, the loss in value that is most likely to occur is called *economic obsolescence*.

107. b. The band of investment method is another way to calculate a capitalization rate.

108. d. All of the choices are examples of fraud.

109. a. The physical description of the property would be found in the security device (trust deed) and not in the note.

110. c. When there is not enough supply to meet the demand of buyers, the price of the short supply goes up.

111. d. RESPA is the federal law that requires that lenders of certain real estate loans give borrowers a good-faith estimate of settlement costs and a special information booklet by HUD.

112. c. The difference between gross income and effective gross income is the vacancy factor and loss of rent (i.e., bad checks).

113. c. Statement of fact.

114. d. A reasonable time may be defined as "a question of fact based on circumstances." A reasonable time period may be used when no specific time period is stated in the escrow instructions.

115. c. A default is a breach or breaking of the contract agreements.

116. c. Statement of fact.

117. b. Statement of fact.

118. b. The Real Estate Commissioner's Regulations require that any advertising of a land project be approved by the commissioner prior to the issuance of a final public report.

119. c. A trust deed does not require recording; however, it is customarily recorded to protect the lender's interest.

120. d. The description of the personal property being sold is a requirement on the bill of sale.

121. b. The Subdivision Map Act is under the jurisdiction of local government. The Map Act is concerned with the physical aspects of the subdivision and how it will affect the existing community. The Map Act controls begin at two or more parcels.

122. c. Real estate brokers must keep all records for at least three years. This includes trust records and checks.

123. c. Statement of fact.

124. b. Statement of fact.

125. d. Statement of fact.

126. a. The usual procedure of a lender on a conventional loan is to base the loan amount on the lesser of the sales price or the appraised value.

127. b. Regarding income-producing property, value is a function of net income.

128. b. The Uniform Settlement Statement is required under RESPA.

129. c. The written agreement minimizes the chances for a fraudulent verbal agreement.

130. b. When an easement is granted to a property owner for use over the property of another, the easement is called an *easement appurtenant*.

131. d. Choices *a* and *b* are correct. In California, most expensive homes are located on high ground (hill areas) and/or near water.

132. c. A lien filed for an unpaid contractor's fee is considered a specific lien. A specific lien ties up a particular parcel until the lien is resolved.

133. d. Choices *a*, *b*, and *c* are examples of specific liens. When recorded, judgment is an example of a general lien.

134. c. The developer creates the deed restrictions placed on a subdivision development. These are private restrictions limiting the use of the property.

135. a. A property owner would use a notice to quit when dealing with a tenant who has defaulted in rental payment. Choices *b*, *c*, and *d* do afford some protection against a mechanic's lien.

136. d. The activity in the question is a violation of fair housing laws.

137. a. Statement of fact.

138. b. The question asks for the exception. For example, underground sewer lines carry an easement by implication for use and are not visible on inspection of the surface of the land. Hence, the use for an easement does not necessarily have to be visible.

139. c. A lease is considered an encumbrance on real property. It is a possessory interest of the property. A homestead is a way to protect a certain amount of equity against unsecured creditors. A freehold estate describes the greatest interest one can have in the land. Neither the homestead or the freehold estate would be considered an encumbrance.

140. a. The term *encumbrace* is misspelled. The correct spelling is *encumbrance*.

141. a. An easement is the right to use the land of another and is not considered a lien agreement title; the other three choices are examples of liens.

142. b. Discriminatory covenants are unenforceable, but will not affect the conveyance.

143. b. Conditions, covenants, and restrictions are usually found on the recorded declaration of restrictions.

144. b. The choices given are all examples of specific liens.

145. b. A judgment becomes a general lien only in each county where the abstract is recorded.

146. b. An appurtenant easement is a right to use another's land that is attached to the land. When the land is sold, this interest or easement passes to the grantee.

147. d. Conditions and covenants are considered deed restrictions. A covenant is a promise and, if violated, results in damages or an injunction to stop the violation. A violation of a condition could result in loss of title.

148. b. This covenant or promise, even if not written into the contract, exists in every lease. In the covenant the landlord promises not to disturb the tenant in any unreasonable way.

149. c.   The broker is permitted to take a listing as well as an option on the same property, but if he decides to exercise his option, he must obtain the written consent of the seller.

150. b.   RESPA prohibits the payment of kickbacks on transactions involving home loans.

PRACTICE EXAMINATION III

1. After recording a "notice of default," a trustee who is foreclosing under the power of sale clause in a trust deed must wait three months before

   a. issuing a trustee's deed.
   b. filing court action.
   c. reconveying title to the beneficiary.
   d. publishing the "notice of sale."

2. A real estate licensee offered to pay part of her commission to the buyer if the buyer would increase his offered price to a level that the agent knew would be high enough to get an acceptance from the seller. Under these circumstances,

   a. this information must be disclosed to the seller before the offer is accepted by the seller.
   b. this action is a violation of the licensing law and would lead to immediate disciplinary action by the commissioner.
   c. the licensee could be held liable for damages in a civil suit even though this information was given to the seller prior to the seller's acceptance.
   d. All of the above

3. A land developer/home builder plans to make an offer on a large parcel of unimproved land. For the transaction to be completed, it will be necessary for the seller to take back a first mortgage. Which of the following clauses would be most important to place in the mortgage for the benefit of the developer?

   a. Acceleration clause
   b. Alienation clause
   c. Exculpatory clause
   d. Subordination clause

4. A legal description in a deed that is found to be ambiguous

   a. invalidates the deed.
   b. can be corrected by legal action only.
   c. can be corrected by legal action or by mutual agreement of the parties.
   d. requires no further action as long as the title insurance company is aware of the ambiguity.

5. Harry and Moe purchased improved property while they were single and took title as joint tenants. Some years later, Harry needed cash for a business venture and borrowed money against the property without the consent of Moe. Before the loan was paid off, Harry died. Under these circumstances,

   a. Moe would hold title in severalty, free and clear of Harry's debt.
   b. Moe would be a tenant-in-common with the lender, each holding a one-half interest.
   c. Moe would hold title in severalty subject to the outstanding loan of Harry.
   d. Harry's lender becomes a joint tenant with Moe.

6. In purchasing a home, the purchaser generally gives a note secured by a first deed of trust to a lending institution. In addition, he or she may give the seller cash and a note secured by a second deed of trust on the property. A "request for notice" would be filed for the benefit of the

   a. mortgagor.
   b. holder of the second.
   c. trustor.
   d. holder of the first.

7. Property is being sold under an agreement whereby the purchase is to continue the payments of an existing amortized loan secured by a first mortgage. For the purchaser to assume the existing mortgage without penalty, the real estate agent should check to be sure the mortgage does not includes a(n)

   a. acceleration clause.
   b. release clause.
   c. subordination clause.
   d. partial release clause.

8. Of the limitations imposed by subdivision restrictions, the least effective is shown by experience to be

   a. minimum dollar cost for the improvements on each lot.
   b. minimum lot size.
   c. maximum height of the improvements.
   d. minimum area of the improvements.

9. Which of the following statements is incorrect with respect to real property tax liens?

   a. A lien for real property taxes has priority over all other liens, including special assessments, regardless of the date the other liens were created.
   b. When real property is sold by the state for delinquent taxes, the buyer receives title free and clear of all liens, including any existing trust deed.
   c. The failure of an owner to pay the property taxes on an encumbered property is usually considered a default on the loan and could lead to a foreclosure by the lender.
   d. A real property tax lien has priority over any other lien resulting from contractual obligations of the owner.

10. A licensed real estate broker who is representing the seller in a transaction becomes the gratuitous agent (no fee) of the buyer and accepts all of the fiduciary responsibilities as the buyer's agent when he or she

    a. shows property to the prospective buyer.
    b. sets up a financing package for the buyer including a purchase-money loan.
    c. gives the buyer a list of recommended real estate appraisers.
    d. writes up the offer to purchase the seller's property.

11. When a real estate broker discharges a real estate salesperson employed by the broker for a violation of the real estate law, the broker must notify the Real Estate Commissioner in writing that the salesperson is no longer employed by the broker. This must be done

    a. by certified mail.
    b. within five days of the termination.
    c. immediately together with a certified written statement of the facts.
    d. by telegram or certified mail.

12. A property has a market value of $41,000. It is encumbered with a first trust deed lien of $20,000. Several years ago, Mr. Tanner, the owner, recorded a homestead exemption protecting the property. However, his wife did not sign the declaration. Recently, a mechanic's lien was recorded against the property. The mechanic's lien is

    a. not enforceable, as homestead properties are protected from after-recorded mechanics' liens.
    b. enforceable because Mrs. Tanner did not sign the declaration of homestead.
    c. not enforceable because of insufficient equity above the exemption amount.
    d. enforceable because mechanic's liens have priority over homestead exemptions.

13. In the event the Real Estate Commissioner discovers that a subdivider is selling subdivided land unlawfully or the subdivider is not following the procedures as outlined in the Commissioner's Final Public report, the commissioner may immediately

    a. revoke the license of the subdivider's agent.
    b. revoke the Final Public Report.
    c. issue a desist and refrain order.
    d. All of the above

14. In the event a breach of contract and an award for damages to the injured party would not be considered an adequate remedy, a suit for specific performance would most likely be successful for all of the following *EXCEPT* for a suit by a

    a. principal against a real estate broker who failed to use diligence on behalf of the principal.
    b. seller of a large parcel of land against a buyer who refused to complete the transaction.
    c. purchaser of real property against a seller who negotiated the purchase through the seller's attorney-in-fact.
    d. home purchaser against the seller who refused to convey title.

15. Prospective buyer Terry signed a deposit receipt and gave the broker her personal check, made payable to an escrow company, as a deposit. She stipulated that the broker was to hold the check until her offer was accepted by the seller. The listing agreement, however, specified that any deposit money must be in the form of a cashier's check made payable to the seller. Under these circumstances, the broker should

    a. submit the offer and hold the check until the offer is accepted.
    b. submit the offer and deposit the check in escrow immediately.
    c. hold the check but need not reveal to the seller the type of check until the seller has accepted the offer.
    d. refuse to accept the deposit because it does not conform to the exact terms of the listing.

16. An agency relationship may be created by all of the following *EXCEPT*

    a. an oral agreement.
    b. necessity or emergency.
    c. subsequent ratification.
    d. subornation.

17. Len is purchasing real property under a real property sales contract. If Len wishes to sell the property to Joel, Len will be required to execute a(n)

    a. reconveyance deed.
    b. lease of at least 25 years.
    c. grant deed.
    d. assignment.

18. Diaz sells a condominium unit to Greg for $90,750. There is an existing loan of $30,000 on the property. Greg agrees to assume the $30,000 loan. There is a county transfer tax of .55 cents per each $500 or fraction thereof. The amount of the tax is

    a. $66.00.
    b. $67.10.
    c. $100.10.
    d. None of the above

19. The following are examples of specific liens when properly recorded *EXCEPT*

    a. real property taxes, delinquent for two years.
    b. mechanics' liens for labor or supplies furnished on an improvement.
    c. a blanket mortgage on a subdivision without a release clause.
    d. a judgment for punitive damages.

20. Mr. and Mrs. Jenner executed a purchase agreement through real estate broker Kurt to purchase a single-family residence in a new subdivision tract that they intended to occupy as their home. The Jenners also applied for a loan to purchase the property through a local federally chartered savings and loan association. Broker Kurt assisted the Jenners in completing the loan application and explained the various costs that were entailed in obtaining the new loan. Under these circumstances, RESPA requires that a special booklet entitled "Settlement Costs and You" be provided the Jenners by

    a. broker Kurt at the time the loan application is completed.
    b. the lender within 48 hours of receipt of the loan application.
    c. broker Kurt or the lender within 48 hours of receipt of the loan application.
    d. the lender within three business days of the receipt of the loan application.

21. A note secured by a second deed of trust with a remaining balance of $5,000 was sold for $3,500. This transaction is an example of

    a. leverage.   c. discounting.
    b. foreclosure.   d. devaluating.

22. Deed restrictions are placed on a subdivision development by

    a. the Federal Housing Administration.
    b. state and local ordinances.
    c. the developer.
    d. the permanent lender.

23. Which of the following is correct with regard to the redemption rights of an owner with respect to delinquent property taxes?

    a. Any delinquent taxes and accrued penalties may be paid in monthly installments.
    b. The sale date of the property to the state begins the redemption period but does not disturb the owner's possession of the property.
    c. The owner has only one year after the date of sale to the state in which to redeem the property.
    d. In the event the delinquent taxpayer alienates the title to the liened property, the delinquent taxes all become due and payable by the new owner and the redemption period ends.

24. Murray listed his home for sale with broker Loren. The listing was $40,000 and Murray told Loren that a quick sale was imperative. Loren showed the home to Joe and told Joe that Murray was financially insolvent and would accept $38,000 for the property. Based on Loren's statement, Joe offered to purchase Murray's home for $38,000. Murray accepted the offer. Regarding Loren's action, which of the following is true?

    a. Loren did not violate her fiduciary obligation to Murray because Murray did, in fact, accept the offer.
    b. Loren did not violate her fiduciary obligation, because she was employed to sell the property and she fulfilled her obligation.
    c. Loren violated her fiduciary obligation to Murray because she acted in excess of her authority.
    d. Loren was unethical and violated her fiduciary obligation to Murray. However, since Murray accepted the offer, no harm was done.

25. To maintain a high level of ethics in business practice, real estate licensees should avoid engaging in certain activities. Which of the following is considered to be unethical conduct?

    a. Claiming to be an expert in the area of property management or appraising when the licensee has had little or no preparation or experience in such areas
    b. Using the term *appraisal* falsely in any advertising to promote real estate business
    c. Failure to disclose any violation to a regulatory agency
    d. All of the above

26. Under the Civil Rights Act of 1968, Title VIII, persons complaining of discrimination in housing may choose which of the following remedies?

    a. File a civil action in federal court
    b. File a civil action in state or local court
    c. File a complaint with HUD
    d. Any of the above

27. Which of the following would not constitute an estate in real property?

    a. A reversion   c. A leasehold
    b. A remainder   d. An easement

28. Which of the following expenses would never be found on the Uniform Settlement Statement form issued at the closing of a RESPA-covered transaction?

    a. Appraisal fee
    b. Finder's fee
    c. Discount points
    d. Title report

29. Tim sold 640 acres of land to Len by agreement and deed that provided that the "seller retains rights to all minerals and oil under the land." Shortly thereafter, while Len was preparing his land for cultivation, Tim appeared with oil drilling equipment. Len refused to allow him on the land. Tim sued Len. The judge's decision should be that

    a. Tim has the right of entry on Len's land to drill for oil.
    b. Tim has no right of entry on Len's land because the agreement and deed did not provide for it.
    c. Tim may drill below Len's land but must do so from outside its boundaries.
    d. Tim may enter Len's land only 500 feet below the surface.

30. Presenting competing offers to purchase real property to an owner in such a manner that the owner is influenced to accept an offer favorable to the agent is deemed

    a. unethical.
    b. illegal per se.
    c. legitimate practice.
    d. Both *a* and *b*

31. When financing real property, a prepayment penalty is often

    a. demanded from a trustor who pays off a loan prematurely.
    b. charged when applying for a loan.
    c. a clause in the deed of trust that protects the trustor.
    d. charged for late payments on the loan.

32. A partnership may take title to real property in the

    a. name of the partnership.
    b. individual names of one or more partners.
    c. name of a third party as trustee for partnership.
    d. Any of the above

33. In the event a salesperson wishes to spend his or her own money on advertising a home for sale that was listed by the salesperson on behalf of the employing broker, the advertisement must include the name

    a. of the salesperson.
    b. of the employing broker.
    c. and address of the employing broker.
    d. of the salesperson and the name of the employing broker.

34. A landlord would be in a violation of the California Fair Housing Law if he or she required each prospective tenant to

    a. provide references from the past two landlords.
    b. secure a cosigner for the lease if the prospect is an unmarried individual.
    c. be gainfully employed and meet minimum credit requirements.
    d. pay the first month's rent in advance, plus an extra two months as a security deposit.

35. Title to real property can be acquired by which of the following?

    a. Accretion   c. Certiorari
    b. Hypothecation   d. Both *a* and *c*

36. The rights to minerals that lie beneath the surface of land

    a. are transferred with the sale of the real property, unless specifically reserved.
    b. cannot be leased.
    c. are retained by the grantor.
    d. cannot be conveyed apart from the surface of the land.

37. An individual who is itemizing his or her expenses for federal income tax purposes may deduct which of the following expenditures incurred with respect to an owner-occupied, single-family residence?

    a. Mortgage interest payments, property taxes, and a mortgage prepayment penalty
    b. Mortgage interest payments, property taxes, and insurance premiums
    c. Mortgage interest payments, property taxes, and late mortgage payment penalties
    d. Mortgage interest payments, property taxes, and cost of capital improvements

38. One of the purposes of the Health and Safety Code is to prevent discrimination in financing or refinancing property. A denial by a lending institution to anyone because of which of the following would be unlawful?

   a. Sex or ancestry
   b. Trends in the neighborhood
   c. Geographic area surrounding a housing accommodation
   d. All of the above

39. Which of the following parties would hold a less-than-freehold estate?

   a. A lessee
   b. A dominant tenement
   c. A beneficiary
   d. A mortgagee

40. An owner of land that does not abut a stream may gain rights to the use of excess water through the State Division of Water Resources by

   a. prescription.   c. accretion.
   b. appropriation.   d. avulsion.

41. A property owner would have the least protection against mechanics' liens if he filed a notice

   a. to quit.
   b. of nonresponsibility.
   c. of cessation.
   d. of completion.

42. Mrs. Lemay owned a residence valued conservatively at $125,000 and told a broker that she wanted to exchange it for income property and that she would be willing to add $30,000 cash if necessary. On the usual commission basis, she signed a contract employing the broker to arrange a trade for a suitable property. The broker located a small apartment house that she agreed was worth $155,000 During the negotiations, the broker himself took an option on the apartment house for $141,000. He exercised the option and proceeded with the exchange, taking title to Mrs. Lemay's house and receiving $30,000 cash in the name of a corporation, which he controlled. He collected a full selling commission from Mrs. Lemay on her house at $125,000, but collected no commission from the apartment house owner from whom he had bought the apartment house under the option contract. In your opinion is the broker

   a. in violation of the real estate law because he did not tell the apartment house owner he was receiving a commission from Mrs. Lemay?
   b. a good, sharp businessman who took advantage of an opportunity to make a profit while remaining within all legal demands of the real estate law?
   c. in violation of the real estate law and subject to disciplinary action but not in violation of the laws of agency?
   d. in violation of the real estate law and the laws of agency and subject to disciplinary action by the commissioner and to a civil suit by Mrs. Lemay for recovery of the commission paid and the broker's profit?

43. Another term for *nondisclosure* is

    a. false promise.
    b. negative fraud.
    c. Neither *a* nor *b*
    d. Both *a* and *b*

44. Upon the signing of a real property sales contract

    a. the legal title passes to the purchaser.
    b. an equitable title passes to the purchaser.
    c. title reverts back to the seller.
    d. all rights and interests of the seller pass to the purchaser.

45. The maximum allowable commission that can be paid by an owner of real property to a real estate broker for the negotiation of a lease agreement is limited by

    a. law, regardless of the lease term.
    b. agreement between the parties.
    c. law, if the lease is for a term of less than one year.
    d. the REALTORS® Code of Ethics.

46. Regarding real estate laws, which of the following lenders have policies characterized by long-term financing, make few construction loans, prefer large loans, and usually do not service their loans?

    a. Insurance companies
    b. Commercial banks
    c. Savings and loan associations
    d. Mortgage companies

47. Which of the following best defines a purchase-money mortgage?

    a. A single mortgage that covers several real estate parcels
    b. A real estate mortgage that includes chattels, such as household appliances, as additional collateral
    c. A mortgage given as part of all of the consideration for the property
    d. A mortgage that provides for additional advances to the mortgagor without the necessity of writing a new mortgage

48. During prolonged inflationary periods, the appreciation in the value of residential real property that has been owned for a period of years would be to the benefit of the

    a. beneficiary of the original loan.
    b. trustee of the original loan.
    c. trustor of the original loan.
    d. None of the above

49. Mrs. Baker, a prospective buyer, hired broker Henson to find her a home, and she promised that if it met her specifications, she would pay Henson a commission. Broker Henson located a property that seemed to meet Mrs. Baker's needs and contacted the owner. Broker Henson was able to convince the owner that it would be to the seller's advantage to consider selling the property at this time and was able to secure an exclusive authorization and right-to-sell contract from the owner. Shortly thereafter, broker Henson showed the property to Mrs. Baker, who was quite interested in it and made an offer that was accepted by the seller. Broker Henson had advised Mrs. Baker of the double commission but never disclosed to the seller that he held an employment contract from Mrs. Baker. If before or after close of escrow the seller discovered the dual position of broker Henson, Henson may be subject to

a. the denial of the payment of a commission from both the buyer and the seller.
b. disciplinary action by the Real Estate Commissioner.
c. a suit for damages by the seller.
d. All of the above

50. A broker is required to keep his or her principal informed of all material facts. A broker who holds a listing from the seller must disclose which of the following facts when presenting an offer?

a. The purchaser is not Caucasian.
b. A cooperating broker will be presenting a higher offer the following day.
c. The buyer's lender is insisting on an impound account.
d. None of the above

51. The loan-to-value ratio on real estate loans is the ratio of the loan value to

a. appraisal.
b. assessed value.
c. sales price.
d. monthly payments.

52. Broker Able is employed by a seller to sell a residence. Able is showing the home to Harry, a prospective purchaser. Able is aware that the home is in need of extensive plumbing repairs. Able has a duty to disclose this fact to Harry

a. only if seller authorizes her to do so.
b. provided the property is not sold "as is."
c. because all known material facts must be disclosed.
d. only if Harry asks specific questions about the condition of the plumbing.

53. Escrow has just closed on a sale that was extremely complicated and very time consuming for the salesperson. In addition to his normal commission from the broker, the salesperson could accept a bonus from the

a. seller.
b. buyer.
c. broker.
d. All of the above

54. Under the provisions of Title I of the National Housing Act, a purchaser may obtain FHA insurance for the purchase of a manufactured home (mobile home) that satisfies HUD construction standards for a maximum term of

a. 5 years. c. 15 years.
b. 10 years. d. 20 years.

55. The standard coverage policy of title insurance covers the following defect in its coverage:

    a. Private deed restrictions
    b. Forgery in the chain of title
    c. Undisclosed liens
    d. Defects known to the insured

56. The term *impounds* most nearly means

    a. penalties.
    b. attachments.
    c. reserves.
    d. points.

57. Rex gets to one of his barns by driving across Smith's land. He has been making the drive daily for the past six years. Smith has often asked Rex to stop this practice. Rex now says he has a legal right to continue this use of Smith's land. Rex's right, if valid, is an easement by

    a. necessity.
    b. implied grant.
    c. prescription.
    d. defeasance.

58. Under normal economic conditions and in a freely competitive market, the vacancy rate in an apartment building is primarily influenced by

    a. the supply and demand for housing in the area.
    b. the cost of financing and new construction.
    c. fluctuations of the employment market.
    d. the number of available unfurnished units in relation to furnished units.

59. A large real estate investment company that is attempting to obtain a $5 million loan to purchase a new commercial shopping center would most likely obtain the loan from

    a. private sources.
    b. the sale of bonds.
    c. an insurance company.
    d. a commercial bank.

60. The right to use, possess, enjoy, transfer, and dispose of a thing to the exclusion of others best defines

    a. an estate.
    b. real estate.
    c. ownership.
    d. equity.

61. The primary purpose of city and county building codes is to

    a. enforce mandatory standards of construction, design, and safety features on new subdivisions.
    b. guarantee that cost-effective methods are used in all construction.
    c. ensure that skilled labor is used in the construction or renovation of new or used residential and commercial property.
    d. set minimum building and construction standards on all proposed new construction or remodeling to protect the health, safety, and general welfare of the public.

62. When real property is encumbered by a deed of trust, the naked "legal title" to the property is held by the

    a. trustor.
    b. beneficiary.
    c. trustee.
    d. mortgagor.

63. Which of the following is not a requisite for creation of an enforceable leasehold agreement?

   a. Amount of rental payments
   b. Rent payments made in advance
   c. Length of time the lease will continue
   d. Description of the property

64. Once a lender commences a foreclosure under a defaulted deed of trust by trustee's sale, the lender will receive the proceeds from the foreclosure in about

   a. one month.   c. four months.
   b. three months.   d. one year.

65. A clause in a recorded trust deed that allows a subsequently recorded loan or lien to have priority over it, is known as a(n)

   a. subordination clause.
   b. acceleration clause.
   c. alienation clause.
   d. partial reconveyance clause.

66. Baker owned an apartment building that had an adjusted basis for income tax purposes of $210,000. He feels that the property is now worth about $335,000. If he were to exchange the property for another income property that is worth $345,000 but neither party to the exchange gives or receives boot or mortgage relief, the book value on the new property would be

   a. $210,000.   c. $335,000.
   b. $220,000.   d. $345,000.

67. The use of land is least affected by

   a. covenants, conditions, and restrictions.
   b. zoning ordinances.
   c. liens.
   d. easements.

68. A real estate licensee is taking a listing on a property from the owner and is using an exclusive authorization and right-to-sell listing contract. The licensee does not complete the section relating to the amount of commission to be paid to the agent and indicates in the terms of sale that the listed price will be a "price to give the owner $20,000 cash after close of escrow." Under these circumstances, it would appear that

   a. this is a net listing.
   b. the listing is unenforceable.
   c. the contract is illegal.
   d. this is a binding exclusive and authorization-to-sell listing.

69. The nominal rate of interest on a real estate loan is the

   a. legal rate.
   b. maximum rate allowed by law.
   c. rate named in the contract.
   d. discount rate.

70. All of the following are considered real-property EXCEPT

   a. immovable improvements.
   b. easements appurtenant.
   c. leaseholds.
   d. trees.

71. When applying the cost approach in the appraisal of real property, the easiest method to establish the square-foot value is the

   a. quantity survey.
   b. market comparison.
   c. unit-in-place.
   d. price index.

72. An easement held by a utility company is

    a. a possessory interest.
    b. an appurtenance.
    c. real property.
    d. personal property.

73. In searching the records at the county recorder's office, you can usually distinguish a second trust deed from the first trust deed by the

    a. heading of the recorded documents.
    b. information contained in the grant deed.
    c. information contained in the trust deed.
    d. time and date of recordation.

74. The seller in a land contract is sometimes called the

    a. vendee.   c. vendor.
    b. lessee.   d. lessor.

75. Which of the following would constitute an "estate" in real property?

    a. An easement
    b. A lease
    c. A mortgage
    d. All of the above

76. One of the essential elements for a contract that is to create a binding and enforceable principal-agency relationship for the sale of any right, title, or interest in real property is a(n)

    a. written instrument.
    b. written agreement as to the amount of commission.
    c. authorization to accept a deposit.
    d. written authorization to accept offers on the property.

77. Which of the following is incorrect? A licensee of the Department of Real Estate who wishes to sell subdivided property

    a. must show a termination date in an exclusive listing, even though it is not known how long it will take to sell all of the lots.
    b. may obtain the listing prior to the issuance of the commissioner's public report.
    c. may not sell or offer to sell lots prior to the issuance of the commissioner's final subdivision public report.
    d. may sell lots for as long as the deposit receipt is made subject to the issuance of the commissioner's final public report.

78. A residence that is being sold under a contract of sale is destroyed by an earthquake. The party who is responsible for the loss under the Uniform Vendor and Purchaser Risk Act of 1947 would be the

    a. party in possession.
    b. vendor.
    c. vendee.
    d. owner of record.

79. If the city or county authorities who enforce building codes allow an improvement to be made that is inconsistent with the construction systems or standards of the existing building code, it is known as a(n)

    a. exemption.   c. deviation.
    b. violation.   d. variance.

80. Accrued depreciation in appraising terms is best described as

    a. a book entry made to reflect the depreciation accrued over the economic life of an improvement, with allowances for later additions.
    b. an appraiser's estimate of the accumulated age depreciation with allowance for condition based on effective age.
    c. the total accrued loss of value based on replacement cost figures using the chronological age only.
    d. a projection for property residual purposes using a conservative rate of accrual based on the remaining economic life.

81. The most favorable type of lease to be entered into by the owner of an improved business property in an area which is rapidly gaining in population is a

    a. percentage lease based on gross business done with a minimum guaranteed rental and with the lessee to pay the taxes.
    b. percentage lease based on the net earnings of the business with a minimum rental and with the lessee to pay the taxes.
    c. straight long-term lease at a fixed rental that provides for the tenant to pay the taxes.
    d. year-to-year lease, the rent to be determined by annual pedestrian traffic counts.

82. Which of the following is not a characteristic of a fee simple title?

    a. It is free of encumbrances.
    b. It is of indefinite duration.
    c. It is transferable with or without consideration.
    d. It is transferable by will or intestacy.

83. There is an agreement in a lease that provides that the lessee's security deposit is nonrefundable. Such an agreement would be

    a. prohibited by statute.
    b. legal, as long as both parties have signed the lease contract.
    c. legal, as long as the deposit is less than $100.
    d. legal, as long as there is a clause in the lease contract stating that it will be used only to repair damage to the property by the lessee.

84. An investor would be allowed to take a capital gain or loss for income tax purposes under which of the following transactions? The investor had

    a. collected liquidated damages from a prospective buyer who had defaulted under a contract of sale.
    b. received less than the book value of an income property as the result of a sale.
    c. received full payment on a short-term note that had been purchased at a substantial discount.
    d. received a substantial amount of cash as a result of refinancing an existing loan on an income property.

85. Which of the following parties would be in violation of the real estate law if they were not licensed by the Department of Real Estate?

    a. An attorney-in-fact who signed a deed to the property owned by his principal
    b. An attorney operating a real estate business out of his law office
    c. An attorney's secretary who also performs her duties as a secretary in a real estate business
    d. All of the above

86. A square parcel of land measuring 1,780 feet long and 1,780 feet wide would be most nearly equal in size to

    a. 73 acres.   c. 43 acres.
    b. 65 acres.   d. 27 acres.

87. When a trust deed and note are used on a purchase-money loan secured by real property, the trustor is the party who

    a. loans the money.
    b. signs the trust deed and note.
    c. holds the trust deed and note.
    d. holds the title as security for the loan.

88. An easement acquired by prescription is similar to

    a. adverse possession.
    b. eminent domain.
    c. Both *a* and *b*
    d. Neither *a* nor *b*

89. A real estate salesperson working under a licensed real estate broker may not

    a. secure a listing for the leasing of real property.
    b. take an open listing in the broker's name that has no final or definite termination date.
    c. sell his or her own home.
    d. claim a commission through his or her broker on an exclusive listing that has no termination date.

90. An easement appurtenant exists between at least two tracts of land in separate ownerships. The dominant tenement

    a. can use easement right only for purposes of ingress and egress.
    b. is burdened by the easement.
    c. obtains the benefit of the easement.
    d. exists separate and apart from the land.

91. When taking a listing on a residence of the owners, the listing broker noted that the vesting clause in the owner's deed read "John Smith and Mary Smith, husband and wife." From this information the broker would know that the title is being held as

    a. joint tenants.
    b. tenancy in common.
    c. tenants in partnership.
    d. community property.

92. Once the court has awarded a claimant a favorable decision in the form of money damages and the judgment has been properly recorded in the county in which the judgment debtor owns real property, it becomes a(n)

    a. attachment lien.
    b. voluntary lien.
    c. involuntary lien.
    d. specific lien.

93. If a borrower fails to make the necessary payments on his or her home loan and falls two months behind schedule in making such payment, he or she

    a. has a right of redemption.
    b. has a right of reinstatement.
    c. has no right in the property.
    d. loses the property.

94. All of the following are required for a legally enforceable lease of real property for a period of more than one year *EXCEPT*

    a. a contract or other memorandum in writing.
    b. the amount of rent and the time and manner in which it is to be paid.
    c. the name of the lessor and lessee.
    d. the signatures of the lessor and lessee.

95. Certain requirements are deemed essential in a declaration of homestead. Which of the following is not a requirement?

    a. Statement that claimant is a married man
    b. Name of spouse, if any
    c. Statement that claimant is residing on the premises and claims it as a homestead
    d. A description of the property

96. Assume a brother and sister own title in a parcel of real estate as joint tenants. The sister marries and deeds half her interest to her husband. Under these circumstances, the brother now holds title to the property as

    a. a joint tenant.
    b. community property.
    c. sole owner.
    d. a tenant in common.

97. Which of these determines the annual tax rate on residential property in each county in California?

    a. Assessor
    b. Board of Supervisors
    c. Tax collector
    d. Board of Equalization

98. Owner Mel entered into a written open listing with broker Able in which Mel agreed to pay Able a commission if she was instrumental in selling Mel's property. Able then entered into a verbal agreement with a cooperating broker named Jones, promising Jones that she would split the commission if Jones located a buyer. Jones located a buyer whose offer was accepted when presented by Able. Upon close of escrow, Able received a full commission but refused to split it with broker Jones. Under these circumstances, Jones

    a. would have no recourse since his agreement with Able was not in writing.
    b. would probably be successful in enforcing the collection of his commission in a civil action.
    c. should file a written complaint with the Real Estate Commissioner and ask the commissioner to arbitrate the matter.
    d. has no legal claim for a commission because he did not have a written contract with owner Mel.

99. An assessment bond was levied against a property for street improvements just prior to the date the property taxes became a lien. Under these circumstances, the

    a. property taxes have priority over the assessment.
    b. assessment has priority over the property taxes.
    c. assessment and the property taxes are in parity with each other.
    d. assessment has the same priority as a mechanic's lien.

100. A commercial office building yields an annual net income of $174,000. If an appraiser applied a capitalization rate of 8 percent to the property, the market value of the property would most nearly be

    a. $1,392,000.   c. $1,932,000.
    b. $1,666,000.   d. $2,175,000.

101. Easements may be terminated in all of the following ways EXCEPT by

    a. express release.
    b. nonuse for a very long time.
    c. adverse possession.
    d. grant deed.

102. The term *marketable title* within the title insurance industry refers to

    a. having title that may be clouded but is covered by a CLTA policy.
    b. having title that is free from reasonable objections.
    c. an absolutely clear title.
    d. None of the above

103. The legal basis for zoning laws is taken from

    a. state legislation.
    b. local mandates.
    c. covenants.
    d. All of the above

104. The expression *reversionary interest* is best connected to the

    a. lessor.   c. mortgagor.
    b. optionor.   d. trustor.

105. In a business partnership, if one partners dies, the surviving partner

    a. becomes the sole operator of the business until the heirs of the deceased partner can step in and carry their share of the responsibilities.
    b. inherits the business free and clear of any debts of the deceased partner.
    c. becomes the exclusive operator of the business and retains title to the assets of the business until he can wind up the partnership affairs.
    d. cannot transact for the partnership alone.

106. The State Board of Equalization

    a. collects the sales tax.
    b. equalizes.
    c. assesses public utilities.
    d. All of the above

107. There is a specific questionnaire to be completed when a subdivider is seeking subdivision approval. From whom is this form obtained?

    a. The local building inspector
    b. The county building inspector
    c. The Real Estate Commissioner
    d. The Corporations Commissioner

108. The county recorder is required by law to index deeds. This is to be done by the

    a. assessor's parcel map number.
    b. street address.
    c. grantor and grantee.
    d. None of the above

109. Which of the following items could be added to the cost basis of a personal residence?

    a. The total amount of interest paid over the life of the loan
    b. The cost of painting the interior of the house
    c. Depreciation
    d. The addition of a new roof and concrete patio

110. Under RESPA, how many days does the lender have to give the good-faith estimate of settlement costs to the borrower?

    a. One day
    b. Within three business days of receipt of loan application
    c. Seven days
    d. Ten days

111. Under the Truth-in-Lending Act, if one detail of the credit offering is shown in any advertising, then which of the following must also be shown?

    a. Total loan amount
    b. Amount of the down payment
    c. Due dates of payments
    d. All of the above

112. Which of the following is normally prorated during the escrow process?

    a. Notary fees
    b. Title insurance fees
    c. Rents
    d. Recording fees

113. There is a history in chronological order of the transfer of property from the earliest record to present time. This history is called a(n)

    a. chain of title.   c. livery of seisin.
    b. allodial tenure.   d. freehold report.

114. The tax basis of real property is its

    a. profit.   c. equity.
    b. value.   d. cost.

115. A postdated check

    a. has the same value as a check dated and cashed today.
    b. is the same as a promissory note.
    c. can only be accepted as a deposit by a real estate broker if there is full disclosure to the seller.
    d. Both *b* and *c*

116. The term that describes the reversion of property to the state by legal process is

    a. eminent domain.
    b. escheat.
    c. public grant.
    d. statutory dedication.

117. An ALTA title insurance policy insures against loss by

    a. errors in the sequence of recorded deeds.
    b. existing easements and liens of record.
    c. relocation of property lines due to a formal survey.
    d. deeds issued by minors.

118. The loan documents pertinent to a real property transaction are

    a. the financing statement and the trust deed.
    b. the security agreement and the financing statement.
    c. the private mortgage insurance and the security agreement.
    d. the promissory note and the deed of trust.

119. What is required in an option agreement?

    a. A statement that the offer will be good for a specified time
    b. A statement that the optionor may retain the option money if the option is not exercised
    c. The time during which the optionee must proceed with the purchase
    d. A statement that no consideration is required because it is only an option and not an immediate purchase

120. An offer to purchase and receipt for deposit that is properly completed by a prospective buyer of real estate is a(n)

    a. offer.
    b. enforceable and binding contract.
    c. voidable contract by the seller.
    d. None of the above

121. The reason that building permits are required is to

    a. control the amount of growth in a community.
    b. evidence compliance with local building requirements.
    c. give the city control over the design of buildings.
    d. prove that building and development fees have been paid.

122. To attract investors for a syndication, a local real estate broker could form which type of syndication that would have limited liability for the investors?

    a. A real estate investment trust
    b. A limited partnership
    c. A corporation
    d. All of the above

123. Depending on the type of loan and the lender making it, loan-to-value ratios will vary. On which of the following would a lender probably offer the lowest loan-to-value ratio?

    a. Residential   c. Industrial
    b. Commercial   d. Agricultural

124. Grant deeds

    a. transfer title to real and personal property.
    b. must show the amount of consideration paid for the property.
    c. have an implied warranty that there are no encumbrances against the property.
    d. have an implied warranty by the grantor that he or she has not previously conveyed title to anyone else.

125. When title to property conveys individual ownership of a lot and a common interest in the recreational areas, the property being transferred is a(n)

    a. apartment project.
    b. planned unit development.
    c. stock cooperative.
    d. condominium.

126. Which of the following documents would not be in a printed form?

    a. Formal will
    b. Grant deed
    c. Holographic will
    d. Abstract of judgment

127. For income taxation purposes, prepaid rents are taxable to the receiver

    a. when the tenancy terminates.
    b. as prorated and received over the life of the lease or rental agreement.
    c. as divided in two years.
    d. in the year received.

128. An exchange of like-kind property

    a. can include only two properties.
    b. can include only six-properties.
    c. is only a once-in-a-lifetime tax break.
    d. can include an unlimited number of properties.

129. Owner Chan and Baker are joint tenants of a piece of property. Chan alone wishes to divide the real property; Baker does not. Chan can seek a

    a. quitclaim deed.
    b. quiet title action.
    c. lis pendens.
    d. partition action.

130. An easement can be terminated in all of the following ways *EXCEPT* by

    a. merger.
    b. destruction of the servient tenement.
    c. express written authorization from the dominant tenement.
    d. express written authorization from the servient tenement.

131. A grant deed that is not dated or recorded is

    a. unenforceable.   c. valid.
    b. voidable.   d. void.

132. Which of the following is a general lien?

    a. Mechanic's lien
    b. Attachment
    c. Judgment
    d. Real property tax

133. Mrs. Randolph enters into a contract to sell her separate property without Mr. Randolph's signature. This action creates a contract that is

    a. illegal.
    b. unenforceable.
    c. valid because she is married.
    d. valid.

134. In the banking community, the prime rate is an important rate. It refers to the

    a. rate set by the government in making nonconventional loans.
    b. most favorable interest rate charged by banks on short-term loans.
    c. lowest rate charged by savings and loan associations on all types of real estate loans.
    d. rate that banks charge each other for overnight loans.

135. Which of the following factors regarding value is most important in the decision to purchase property?

    a. Location
    b. Price asked
    c. Present and future use of the property
    d. Age of the property

136. Mr. Davis negotiates a five-year lease agreement that provides for increases in rent from year to year. This type of lease is a(n) _____ lease.

    a. percentage
    b. escalation
    c. graduated
    d. gross

137. Emily has decided to rent out her leased apartment for the summer while she is away. This would normally be handled as a(n)

    a. transfer.
    b. sublease.
    c. assignment.
    d. assumption.

138. When one loses a right in a contract due to failure to exercise that right within a timely period, it is known as a(n)

    a. cancellation.
    b. estoppel.
    c. laches.
    d. recision.

139. Which of the following types of real estate are exempt from real property taxation?

    a. State government property
    b. Nonprofit church property
    c. Grapevines of less than three years of age
    d. All of the above

140. When property is sold through the court probate sale process, offers must be at least what percentage of the court-appraised value?

    a. 65 percent
    b. 75 percent
    c. 90 percent
    d. 100 percent

141. At what point has a real estate broker technically earned a commission?

    a. When the sales contract has been signed by both parties and the seller's acceptance has been communicated back to the buyer in the manner stated in the offer
    b. When the escrow closes
    c. When the grant deed is recorded
    d. When the escrow instructions are signed

142. Salesperson Jones violates a provision of real estate law. How long does the Real Estate Commissioner have to take action in most instances?

    a   30 days
    b. 3 years for most acts
    c. 2 years for most acts
    d. By the next business day after being informed of the violation

143. The term that is used to describe the balancing of the broker's trust account records with the bank's records is

    a. trial balance.
    b. reconciliation.
    c. monthly balance check.
    d. balance sheet.

144. Salesperson Maxwell is discharged by broker Hansen for a misrepresentation of a material fact in the sale of an apartment building. How quickly must Hansen notify the Real Estate Commissioner?

    a. Within 5 business days
    b. Immediately
    c. Within 10 days
    d. Within 30 days

145. Tenant Harry remains in possession of a house after the lease has expired. Harry has not negotiated an extension or renewal of the lease and furthermore is not paying any rent. Harry has a(n)

    a. periodic tenancy.
    b. estate for years.
    c. tenancy at sufferance.
    d. tenancy at will.

146. Which of the following people is/are required to have a real estate license as a salesperson or broker?

    a. An appraiser
    b. A negotiator of real estate mortgage loans.
    c. Both *a* and *b*
    d. None of the above

147. The instrument used to remove the lien of a trust deed from record is called a

    a. satisfaction.
    b. release.
    c. deed of reconveyance.
    d. certificate of redemption.

148. The type of mortgage loan that permits borrowing additional funds at a later date is called a(n)

    a. equitable mortgage.
    b. junior mortgage.
    c. open-end mortgage.
    d. extendable mortgage.

149. Equity in real property is the

    a. cash flow value.
    b. total of all mortgage payments made to date.
    c. difference between mortgage debt and market value.
    d. appraised value.

150. A loan to be completely repaid including principal and interest by a series of regular equal installment payment is a

    a. straight loan.
    b. balloon payment loan.
    c. fully amortized loan.
    d. variable rate mortgage.

■ ANSWER KEY

1. d. When a property is into foreclosure, a trustee must wait at least three months before beginning the publishing of the notice of sale indicating the upcoming trustee sale or public sale of that property.

2. a. All information regarding that transaction must be disclosed to the seller before the offer is accepted by the seller, and that would include the arrangement of the commission payment.

3. d. A subordination clause is of benefit to a developer and is often used in vacant land transactions. The seller is asked to take back the first loan in a subordinated position, thereby making it a junior lien, to allow the developer to secure construction fund financing in the primary position. Construction lenders will not grant construction loans in other than the primary position.

4. c. A legal description that is either ambiguous or incorrect can be corrected by legal action or if the parties agree to do so.

5. a. A surviving joint tenant is not responsible for the debt of the deceased joint tenant on unforeclosed liens if the surviving joint tenant had not signed for the debt.

6. b. A request for notice of default would benefit any junior lienholder. The junior lienholder has an opportunity to cure the default on the first loan and begin the foreclosure process himself or herself.

7. a. For the buyer to take over the existing loan without the payment of a prepayment penalty by either the seller or buyer, the trust deed should be examined carefully for an acceleration clause. An aliena-tion clause or due-on-sale clause is a form of an acceleration clause and could stop the takeover.

8. a. Setting a minimum dollar cost for the improvements on each lot has not been highly successful, as most often it is fair market value that will lead to a probable selling price of the improvements.

9. a. Real property taxes and special assessments are in parity with each other.

10. b. If the broker takes on the responsibility of setting up a financing package for the buyer, then the broker becomes responsible to the buyer and acts as the buyer's agent, whether or not any fee will be earned.

11. c. The broker must immediately notify the Real Estate Commissioner if a licensee employed by the broker violates the law. The broker is to include a certified written statement of facts as well.

12. d. The mechanic's lien is enforceable because it is a secured lien and the homestead declaration protects only against unsecured liens to a certain maximum.

13. c. The first step the commissioner would probably take is to issue a desist and refrain order and then proceed against the subdivider. The desist and refrain order is to stop all activities in that transaction.

14. a. It would be impractical for the principal to file a suit for specific performance against a broker who is not acting adequately in the principal's behalf. More likely, the principal would sue the broker for damages.

15. a. The broker should submit the offer and follow the instructions to hold the check until the offer is either accepted or rejected.

16. d. The term *subornation* means to bribe someone to commit an illegal act.

17. d. With reference to a real property sales contract, commonly known as a *land sales contract*, the interest is to be assigned to the next party, not granted, because there is no grant deed until the land contract terms are completed.

18. b. Remember to subtract the existing $30,000 as it was taxed at its original transaction. $90,750 minus $30,000 leaves $60,750. The easy calculation is $1.10 per each $1,000. Therefore, 61 times $1.10 is $67.10.

19. d. A judgment when recorded is an example of a general lien.

20. d. Under RESPA, the lender is required to present the borrower with a good-faith estimate of closing costs and a special information booklet within three business days of receipt of the loan application.

21. c. Whenever a note is purchased for less than the face amount of the note, the process is known as *discounting*.

22. c. The developer creates the deed restrictions placed on a subdivision development. These are private restrictions limiting the use of the property.

23. b. The date that the property is sold to the state for unpaid property taxes begins a five-year redemption period. The owner remains in possession of the property during this five-year redemption period.

24. c. Loren violated the agency relationship by disclosing the weak position of the seller. The fiduciary relationship between Loren and Murray required that Loren act in Murray's best interest, yet be "honest and fair" with the buyer.

25. d. Choices *a, b,* and *c* would all be considered unethical conduct.

26. d. Choices *a, b,* and *c* are all potential remedies for violation of the Civil Rights Act of 1968.

27. d. An easement does not represent an estate in the land of another. It is merely the right to use the land of another.

28. b. RESPA prohibits the payment of a finder's fee.

29. a. With a reservation of rights there is an implied right of entry. Tim has the right to enter Len's land and drill for oil based on his reservation of rights as stated in the deed.

30. a. The question clearly discusses an unethical practice.

31. a. A prepayment penalty is charged to the borrower on a loan for paying off the loan prior to the maturity date if the trust deed contains a prepayment penalty clause.

32. d. Choices *a, b,* and *c* are all methods of taking title to real property by a partnership.

33. b. If a salesperson advertises property he or she is representing in the name of the broker, then the broker's name must appear in the advertisement as well.

34. b. Under California Fair Housing, there can be no discrimination due to marital status, in addition to the reasons more commonly found.

35. a. *Accretion* describes a process whereby soil is deposited onto the land of another through the action of either wind, water,

or glacial ice. *Accession* says the property owner is entitled to all that is added or united to his or her land.

36. a. Mineral rights customarily transfer with the sale of real property unless they are specifically reserved.

37. a. The items listed in choice *a* are items that are deductible for tax purposes with reference to an owner-occupied, single-family residence.

38. d. A denial by a lender based on choices would be considered unlawful.

39. a. A less-than-freehold estate is known as a *leasehold estate* and is one that is held by a lessee (tenant).

40. b. Under the Doctrine of Appropriation, an owner of land that is not adjacent to water may be able to access that water by applying to the State Division of Water Resources.

41. a. A property owner would use a notice to quit when dealing with a tenant who has defaulted in a rental payment.

42. d. The broker clearly is in violation of real estate law and the laws of agency and would be subject to action by the commissioner as well as to a possible suit by the principal for misrepresentation and lack of disclosure of his participation as a principal.

43. b. *Negative fraud* is another expression for nondisclosure and is a violation of law.

44. b. A real property sales contract, commonly called a *land sales contract*, delivers only equitable title to the purchaser (vendee).

45. b. The payment of commission is by agreement between the parties.

46. a. The lending activities described are those of insurance companies.

47. c. A purchase-money mortgage or trust deed is really a credit extension. A borrower arranges for a real estate loan; the loan approval is justification for the lender advancing funds to the seller on behalf of the buyer.

48. c. Any appreciation in the value of property would be to the benefit of the trustor or borrower of the original loan who is the buyer of the property.

49. d. Choices *a*, *b*, and *c* are all possible actions taken against the broker who failed to disclose the dual-agency relationship.

50. b. The broker is required to disclose that another offer will be coming in on the property.

51. a. Lenders are concerned with making a loan in accordance with the appraised value of the property, not basing that decision on the selling price. In fact, most lenders will lend a certain percentage against property based on the appraised value or selling price, whichever is lower.

52. c. The broker is legally required to disclose all material facts concerning a property the broker is representing. Including a statement of selling property "as is" does not relieve the broker from disclosing all material facts.

53. c. The salesperson cannot accept monies for work done in a real estate transaction from any source other than the employing broker.

54. d. Twenty years is the maximum term for FHA insurance on the purchase of a mobile home.

55. b. The matter of forgery in the chain of title is covered under the standard coverage policy title insurance.

56. c. Reserves for the payment of property taxes and insurance premiums are often referred to as *impounds*, because the lender will impound these amounts on some loans as a requirement of the loan.

57. c. The activity in the question possibly describes an easement by prescription, which requires open and continuous use of the land of another for at least five years in a manner hostile to the owner.

58. a. The vacancy rate in an apartment building is directly influenced by the supply of apartment buildings and the demand for housing in that area.

59. c. An insurance company would prefer to make large commercial loans much like that described in the question.

60. c. Ownership refers to the right to use, possess, enjoy, transfer, and dispose of an item to the exclusion of others. This interest in real property ownership would be referred to as a *bundle of rights*.

61. d. The city and county building codes are created to protect the general welfare and benefit of the public by setting minimum building and construction requirements for all new proposed projects.

62. c. The trustee acts as a neutral middle party between the trustor (borrower) and the beneficiary (lender) and holds the legal title to property during the period of the loan.

63. b. Choices *a*, *b*, and *c* are all requirements for an enforceable leasehold agreement. Choice *b* is customary but not a legal requirement for the contract.

64. c. Once a lender decides to foreclose, a "Notice of Default" is recorded by the trustee. Then a three-month period begins followed by a three-week advertising period. The trustor (borrower) can invade the three-week advertising period and reinstate the loan (bring it up to date) up to five business days before the trustee's sale is held. If there is not reinstatement or redemption (loan paid in full) before the trustee's sale, the property is sold to the highest bidder. Therefore, consider that the three-month period, followed by the three-week advertising period, is approximately a four-month period before the lender receives any proceeds.

65. a. A subordination clause indicates that the loan will remain in a junior or subordinated position. A subordination clause is often used in vacant land purchases to allow the borrower to arrange a construction loan recorded in the primary position. Most lenders will not grant a construction loan, unless it is recorded in the primary position.

66. a. When properties are being exchanged, the old basis is carried over to the new property and sets the basis for the newly acquired property.

67. c. Choices *a*, *b*, and *d* would strongly affect the use of land. They are examples of private and public restrictions. A lien could be an example of a loan against the property and would have the least effect on the use of land.

68. a. The question does not clearly indicate what commission would be paid to the broker, but merely that the seller will receive a certain amount of cash after close of escrow. This would be an example of a net listing where the broker earns as

commission anything in excess of what the seller wishes to receive after close of escrow.

69. c. The expression *nominal rate* refers to the rate named or stated in the contract.

70. c. Leaseholds are personal property.

71. b. Market comparison, or market data approach, is the easiest method used in establishing the square-foot value of property based on what similar properties have sold for recently.

72. c. An easement held by a utility company is known as an *easement in gross*. This kind of easement is not appurtenant to the land, and it is not a possessory interest in land. However, it is an example of a real property item.

73. d. The significant difference between priority of trust deeds is the time and date of recordation. Also, the county recorder's office will affix a number to each document to further clarify the earliest date of recording.

74. c. The seller under a land contract has not granted legal title and is, therefore, called a *vendor*.

75. b. A lease describes a leasehold interest in the land of another for a specified period of time. It is a possessory interest.

76. a. Under the statute of frauds is the requirement that real estate transactions be reduced to writing so as to create an enforceable agreement.

77. d. The question asks for the incorrect choice.

78. a. The Uniform Vendor and Purchaser's Risk Act of 1947 decides who is responsible for a lien created on property when that property is destroyed, for example, by an earthquake. Choice *a* is the best answer and indicates the party in possession, as that could be either vendor, vendee, or owner of record.

79. d. Whenever one seeks to be given permission to use a lot for a purpose that is inconsistent with zoning requirements in an area, the request is known as a *variance*.

80. b. Accrued depreciation for appraising purposes refers to the appraiser's estimate of the accumulated age appreciation with allowance for the property condition based on its effective age. The term *effective age* refers to the property's physical condition.

81. a. A percentage lease is often a favorable type of lease for an owner of improved property to enter into; it requires payment of a percentage, usually of monthly gross income, with a minimum guaranteed rental that the owner can depend on receiving each month.

82. a. The characteristics of a fee simple interest in property, which is the greatest interest one can have in the land, is that it is of indefinite duration. It's freely transferable, either by will or intestate succession. The fact that the title may or may not be free of encumbrances is not a characteristic or an issue of fee simple.

83. d. In a lease agreement, the security deposit is to be used only for repairs that become necessary to the property due to damages created by the lessee, cleaning, back rents, or any costs of a default. With reference to a residential property, unused security deposits are to be returned to the tenant within 21 days after termination of tenancy, along with a statement indicating any monies withheld for damages created by that tenant.

84. b. The investor has received less than the book value or purchase price of the income property as a result of the sale, thereby indicating a loss on the sale of that property, and to some extent that loss may become a deduction to the investor.

85. b. The issue in the question is concerned with one who is practicing real estate without a license. If any attorney wishes to operate a real estate business, the attorney would need to be licensed by the Department of Real Estate as well.

86. a. Take 1,780 feet times 1,780 feet, and that equals 3,168,400 square feet. Divide by 43,560 square feet to an acre, and your answer will be 72.74 acres, or approximately 73 acres.

87. b. The trustor is the party who signs the trust deed and the note. The trustor is the borrower, the trust deed is the security device, and the note is the evidence of the debt.

88. a. An easement by prescription is similar to adverse possession with a major difference being that the property taxes on subject property be paid by an adverse possessor for five continuous years in order to establish an adverse claim to the title of property. Otherwise, the basic ingredients for both easement by prescription and adverse possession are the same.

89. d. An exclusive listing agreement must have a definite termination date. Hence, the salesperson could not claim a commission from the broker on an exclusive listing that had no definite termination date.

90. c. The dominant tenement interest refers to the property that is benefited by the use of the easement.

91. d. If there is a vesting clause in an owner's deed that simply reads "John Smith and Mary Smith, husband and wife," then there is a presumption that title is being held as community property. If husband and wife wish title to be held as other than community property, they would specifically have to indicate it on the document.

92. c. A judgment when recorded becomes a general lien in the county where recorded and is an example of what is called an *involuntary lien*.

93. b. When a real property loan is in default, there is a three-month right of reinstatement following the filing of a notice of default. Recent California law allows a reinstatement of the loan to continue right up until five business days before a trustee sale is held.

94. d. The signatures of both the lessor and lessee are not required. The signature of the lessor, which is required, and possession of the property by the lessee is deemed a valid lease agreement.

95. a. In filing a declaration of homestead, a statement that a claimant is a married person is not a requirement for filing such declaration.

96. d. In a joint tenancy interest, a joint tenant can deed a portion of the interest to another, thereby creating a tenancy in common relationship with the newly brought-in party.

97. b. The Board of Supervisors sets or determines the annual tax rate on residential property in each county in California.

98. b. Jones, the injured party, would probably be successful in taking legal action to enforce the collection of the commission that is due Jones by the verbal agreement between brokers.

99. c. The assessment and the property taxes are in parity, that is, an equal basis, with each other. One cannot take priority over the other for payment purposes.

100. d. The formula for estimating value of income-producing property is to take the net income and divide it by the capitalization rate. Take $174,000 and divide it by 8 percent capitalization rate to equal a fair market value of the property at $2,175,000.

101. b. An easement by prescription requires continuous use of another's property for five years. It would require nonuse for a continuous period of five years to terminate it. "For a very long time" is not the proper wording.

102. b. Statement of fact.

103. a. Statement of fact.

104. a. The lessor has a reversionary interest in the property. This means that when the lease expires, the control of the property usage reverts to the lessor (owner).

105. c. When one partner dies, the title to the business vests in the surviving partner, who controls the business and winds up partnership affairs. The heirs of the deceased partner do not have the right to step in and run the business with the surviving partner.

106. d. Statement of fact.

107. c. The questionnaire is obtained from the office of the Real Estate Commissioner. The commissioner is very actively involved in subdivision matters.

108. c. Deeds are indexed by the grantor and grantee.

109. d. The cost of capital improvements to property (improvements of a permanent nature) is added to the cost basis of the property. For taxation purposes, the higher the cost basis of the property, the lower the amount of gain on the sale.

110. b. The good-faith estimate and special information booklet must be given upon receipt of loan application or within three business days thereof.

111. d. Statement of fact.

112. c. Any rents collected will be prorated between the seller and the buyer of rental property according to the date that escrow closes.

113. a. A chain of title is a continuous history of all conveyances and encumbrances against a piece of property from the earliest record to the present time.

114. d. The tax basis of property refers to its acquisition cost.

115. d. Statement of fact.

116. b. The term *escheat* means to revert. In California, property escheats to the state when a property owner dies intestate (without a will) and has apparently left no heirs. There is a five-year waiting period by the state before the property is sold. During this time, the state advertises information on unclaimed properties giving any possible heirs a chance to come forth and place a claim on the property.

117. c. Statement of fact. The other items are covered in a CLTA standard policy.

118. d. The documents used for real estate loans include the promissory note, which is the evidence of the debt, and the trust deed, which is the security device.

119. c. The time in which the optionee (prospective buyer) must purchase if he or she is going to do so is a requirement of the option agreement.

120. a. At the point of drawing up a deposit receipt by the prospective purchaser, there is only an offer to purchase. There is no contract formed until the offer is accepted and the acceptance is communicated back to the buyer.

121. b. Statement of fact.

122. d. In all of the choices offered, buyers would have limited liability to the extent of their investment.

123. c. Lenders take a greater risk when making industrial property loans; therefore, they offer a lower loan-to-value ratio than they would on other types of properties. The risk lies in that industrial property is generally for a special usage and is not as easily resold if the lender has to take the property back due to a borrower's default.

124. d. The two implied warranties of a grant deed state that the property has not been previously conveyed and that any existing encumbrances have been disclosed to the buyer. Grant deeds are used to transfer title to real property. The consideration paid for the property is not required to appear on the grant deed.

125. b. In a planned unit development, the buyer receives an interest in the common area and individual ownership in the townhouse and the lot beneath it.

126. c. A holographic will is one that is written entirely in one's own handwriting.

127. d. Prepaid rents are taxable to the receiver in the year received.

128. d. An exchange of property (IRC 1031) can involve any number of like-kind properties.

129. d. A partition action is a court action to divide land physically or divide its proceeds on sale among disputing co-owners.

130. d. The servient tenement refers to the land that is burdened by the easement. The servient interest alone cannot terminate the easement.

131. c. The deed does not require a date. Although the grant deed does not require recording, it is certainly a good idea for the buyer to record it, which publicly discloses the buyer's claim to the property.

132. c. A judgment is a general lien that affects all property of a debtor.

133. d. The contract is valid. The sale of a spouse's separate property does not require the signature of the other spouse.

134. b. Statement of fact.

135. a. Location is the most important factor regarding the value of subject property.

136. c. Statement of fact.

137. b. In subletting, the original tenant remains responsible for the lease agreement.

138. c. Laches refer to the law that refuses to protect those who do not go after their legal rights in the proper time period allotted by the law.

139. d. Statement of fact.

140. c. Statement of fact.

141. a. The broker earns the commission at the time the contract is formed between

the buyer and the seller (when the seller's acceptance is communicated to the buyer). However, the commission is not paid until the escrow closes.

142. b.   Statement of fact.

143. b.   Brokers must reconcile their trust records with the bank's accounting at least once a month. This process is known as *reconciliation*.

144. b.   The broker must notify the commissioner immediately. "Immediately" is usually defined within the real estate industry as being "by the next business day."

145. c.   When a tenant remains in possession of the property without the consent of the landlord, it is at the sufferance of the landlord.

146. b.   California requires that loan brokers be licensed as real estate licensees.

147. c.   A deed of reconveyance acts like a receipt for the payment of a loan secured by a trust deed.

148. c.   An open-ended mortgage loan allows additional funds to be borrowed without having to rewrite the original loan contract.

149. c.   Equity is defined as the difference between what is owed on the property and its market value.

150. c.   A fully amortized loan is one that is reduced to nothing by a series of equal installment payments over a given time period.

PRACTICE EXAMINATION IV

1. The major part of the California laws relating to real property are created by

   a. the California Constitution.
   b. legislative acts.
   c. the Real Estate Commissioner.
   d. the Business and Professions Code.

2. If there is an increase in the property taxes on an income property and all the other expenses and income remain the same, the property value, when applying the capitalization of net income approach, will

   a. increase by an amount equal to the property tax increase.
   b. increase by an amount greater than the property tax increase.
   c. decrease by an amount equal to the property tax increase.
   d. decrease by an amount greater than the property tax increase.

3. Riparian waters applies to waters in a

   a. river.
   b. stream.
   c. water course.
   d. All of the above

4. If a broker, relying on information furnished by the owner, makes a misrepresentation and the purchaser is consequently relieved from the contract because of the misrepresentation, the broker is entitled to

   a. a full commission.
   b. whatever compensation he might ask for in a court action.
   c. reimbursement for "out-of-pocket" expenses only in connection with the unexecuted contract.
   d. no commission.

5. A final value estimate is the correlation of the value indications obtained from which of the following approaches?

   a. Cost, development, and income
   b. Cost, residual, and income
   c. Cost, income, and comparative
   d. Income, land residual, and market data

6. A buyer who invests in the purchase of a condominium, receives

   a. a divided interest in all land.
   b. fee title to airspace.
   c. a contract.
   d. None of the above

7. Which of the following forms of ownership is the most widely used and protects the investor against personal liability?

   a. REIT
   b. Limited partnership
   c. Cooperative
   d. General partnership

8. Which of the following is not an accelerated method for calculating depreciation for income tax purposes?

   a. 200 percent declining balance for personal property
   b. Straight line
   c. 150 percent declining balance for personal property
   d. 175 percent declining balance

9. When Adams transfers an interest in trade fixtures to a purchaser, which of the following instruments will she use to convey title?

   a. Chattel real
   b. Warranty deed
   c. Bill of sale
   d. None of the above

10. When a trust deed is foreclosed by court action,

    a. the procedure is the same as for a trustee's sale.
    b. the trustor has a one-year redemption period.
    c. a deficiency judgment is not possible.
    d. the trustor has a three-month reinstatement right.

11. An escrow for the sale of real property may be terminated by

    a. unilateral rescission of either party.
    b. revocation of the instructions by the seller's agent.
    c. death or incapacity of either party.
    d. mutual consent of the parties to the escrow.

12. Which of the following would be related to intestate succession?

    a. A holographic will
    b. Dying without a will
    c. A will that does not specify all possible heirs
    d. None of the above

13. The Feldmans own a three-bedroom house with a fair market value of $39,000 that they rent for $300 per month. A neighbor of the Feldmans owns a four-bedroom home in the same neighborhood that can be rented for $345 per month. By applying the same ratio of increased rent of the neighbor's home as compared with the rent of the Feldmans' home, the fair market value of the neighbor's home would be

    a. $44,200.   c. $43,000.
    b. $42,930.   d. $44,850.

14. When an individual is buying property under a real property sales contract and is paying pro-rata taxes and insurance to the seller, which of the following is correct?

    a. The seller can deposit the funds in his personal bank account.
    b. The seller must keep the funds in a separate account.
    c. The seller can apply the funds to the principal of the loan.
    d. The seller can use the funds until the taxes and insurance are due.

15. Which of the following would not constitute an estate in real property?

    a. A reversion   c. A leasehold
    b. A remainder   d. An easement

16. An oral agreement for the sale of real estate may be enforced where

    a. the consideration is less than $2,500.
    b. the purchasers have taken possession, have paid part of the purchase price, and have made improvements.
    c. the broker guarantees performance.
    d. two neutral witnesses will testify.

17. A minor can do which of the following without court approval?

    a. Convey title of real property to another
    b. Receive title to real property by a gift or inheritance
    c. Convey real property to another through a guardian
    d. Delegate another to act as agent in his or her behalf

18. The one characteristic that is always present in both a joint tenancy holding and a community property holding is

    a. each party's interest is equal.
    b. each party has the right of survivorship.
    c. all parties must enter into a conveyance of any part of the interest.
    d. the party's interest may not be willed.

19. Mr. and Mrs. Barrett, who had been shopping for a new home, found one that they liked very much but, because of the high asking price, they decided not to buy it. Their reason for not buying was probably based upon the principle of

    a. conformity.
    b. highest and best use.
    c. substitution.
    d. anticipation.

20. A valid bill of sale need not contain

    a. a date.
    b. an acknowledgment.
    c. a description of the property.
    d. mention of consideration.

21. A principal using an open listing may employ several brokers who will

    a. share the commission if the owner sells the property.
    b. share the commission if any of them sells the property.
    c. each have an opportunity to earn the entire commission.
    d. each have the option to buy the property himself or herself during the time of the listing period.

22. Once real property is sold to the state by operation of law following the fiscal year in which the real property taxes were unpaid and had become delinquent, the owner-occupant

    a. must pay rent to the state.
    b. must vacate the property.
    c. may remain in undisturbed possession.
    d. is free of liability for taxes accruing thereafter.

23. Anyone offering to sell parcels of land to residents of California when the land is located in the state of Arizona must file with the

    a. Secretary of State.
    b. Department of Real Estate.
    c. Federal Trade Commission.
    d. Department of Corporations.

24. A lender who (1) prefers loans secured by property in close proximity to the lender, (2) prefers to have had a prior relationship with the borrower, and (3) prefers to make short-term loans would most likely be a

    a. mortgage company.
    b. life insurance company.
    c. commercial bank.
    d. savings and loan association.

25. All of the following are necessary for a valid contract *EXCEPT*

    a. payment of money.
    b. genuine assent.
    c. lawful object.
    d. mental capacity of contracting parties.

26. In the terms of a deed of trust, the power of sale is granted by

    a. trustor to beneficiary.
    b. trustor to trustee.
    c. beneficiary to trustee.
    d. None of the above

27. An owner of a liquor store received an original off-sale general license from the state two years ago and now wants to sell the business. The maximum the owner can charge for the license is

    a. $2,000.
    b. $4,000.
    c. $6,000.
    d. not limited by law.

28. When showing properties listed by his office, broker Sheehan makes it a policy for his sales staff not to show properties located in areas to which minorities have moved recently. Such a practice is known as

    a. redlining.
    b. steering.
    c. blockbusting.
    d. None of the above

29. Zoning protects

    a. property rights.
    b. riparian rights.
    c. title, interests, and property rights.
    d. None of the above

30. Normally a deed deposited in escrow may be delivered to the grantee

    a. immediately.
    b. on payment of equity to the seller.
    c. only on the performance of all conditions of the escrow.
    d. on the request of the real estate broker.

31. Which of the following state agencies is empowered to prevent acts of discrimination in housing accommodations in California because of race, color, religion, national origin, or ancestry?

    a. Real Estate Commission
    b. Labor Commission
    c. Department of Fair Employment and Housing
    d. Division of Housing

32. When a business venture involving the use of a liquor license is transferred, the Department of Alcoholic Beverage Control can

    a. transfer an on-sale general license into any county that has a population of 35,000 or less.
    b. issue a license to any legally organized club after the club is formed and immediately applies for an on-sale general license.
    c. issue an on-sale general license to a business located in the same area and doing business on a seasonal basis.
    d. issue an off-sale general license for the same location for which an on-sale beer and wine license had been issued previously.

33. An attachment lien placed on real property can be released by all of the following EXCEPT

    a. court order.
    b. death of the defendant.
    c. written release by the plaintiff.
    d. a satisfaction of judgment, provided it is in favor of the plaintiff.

34. Under the bulk sale provisions of Division 6 of the Uniform Commercial Code, the publishing and recording requirements are intended to alert which of the following about the intended transfer?

    a. Broker   c. Vendor
    b. Creditor   d. Vendee

35. A tenant notices the release of hazardous substances on the property. What is the tenant's obligation in this matter?

    a. The tenant must send a written notice to the landlord advising of the matter.
    b. The tenant has no obligation.
    c. It is up to the landlord to notice these matters.
    d. None of the above

36. A builder/contractor owns a parcel of real property on which he is about to complete a building. He is forced to use some backfill. This would be to

    a. fill in the space around the foundation, a retaining wall, or other excavations.
    b. remove excess soil from the site caused by earlier excavations.
    c. assist in landscaping the property.
    d. None of the above

37. The initials SBB&M, HB&M, and MDB&M refer to

    a. certified benchmark locations.
    b. approval by a surveyor as to the accuracy of a survey.
    c. starting points in a metes-and-bounds description as used in a survey.
    d. points in the U.S. Government Survey System.

38. Which of the following would least likely affect the business cycle?

    a. Erratic spending by government, public, and business people
    b. The government creating new loans for low income housing in a major metropolitan area
    c. New innovations in industrial production
    d. Fluctuations in interest rates and changes in lending policies by the major lending institutions

39. The real estate law permits a licensee to act as an agent on behalf of an owner of a mobile home under certain conditions. When acting as an agent, the licensee must comply with the real estate law and commissioner's regulations. All of the following acts as an agent on behalf of a seller would be in violation of the law and could lead to the revocation or suspension of a license EXCEPT

    a. failure to provide for the delivery of the certificate of ownership or certificate of title to the buyer.
    b. selling a mobile home that has been registered with the Department of Housing and Community Development and is greater than 8 feet wide and 32 feet long.
    c. submitting a check to the Department of Housing and Community Development for fees that are due if the check is dishonored by the bank on presentation.
    d. advertising or implying that the mobile home is "new."

40. If the borrower is unable to make payments and falls two months behind in making required trust deed loan payments, he or she

    a. has a right of redemption.
    b. has a right of reinstatement.
    c. has no rights.
    d. loses the property.

41. A borrower was denied credit because of a poor report from a credit agency. The agency refused the borrower access to the information in the report. Under those circumstances, California law gives the borrower the right to

    a. recover actual damages.
    b. recover punitive damages of $5,000.
    c. recover attorney's fees.
    d. All of the above

42. Which of the following forms of real estate syndicate require 100 or more investors?

    a. Limited partnership
    b. Corporation
    c. General partnership
    d. Real estate investment trust

43. A licensed real estate broker negotiated a sale of real property and was instrumental in having both parties sign escrow instructions. The initial deposit had been held by the broker and was in the broker's trust account. Before the sale was consummated, one of the parties refused to complete the sale and demanded that the broker release the deposit to her. The other party claimed the deposit was rightfully his and demanded that the deposit be given to him. Since the broker was unsure who had legal right to the money, he turned the money over to the court and asked the court to hold the money and have the disputing parties file their claim with the court. This action by the broker is known as a(n)

    a. injunction.
    b. unlawful detainer.
    c. interpleader.
    d. partition action.

44. Which of the following is the most common type of easement on residential property?

    a. Prescriptive
    b. In gross
    c. Adverse possession
    d. Open end

45. Economic rent can best be described as the

    a. amount paid by the lessee as specified in the lease.
    b. amount remaining from the gross rent after deducting vacancies and bad debt.
    c. current rent being paid by other tenants for comparable space and property.
    d. amount received by the landlord under an oral agreement.

46. All of the following statements are correct with respect to title held by cotenants *EXCEPT*

    a. cotenants can partition the property into separate parcels by mutual agreement.
    b. due to the confidential relationship among cotenants, one cotenant can create an easement without the consent or knowledge of the other cotenants, provided the easement is beneficial to all cotenants.
    c. a cotenant's interest may be transferred involuntarily by operation of law.
    d. title is deemed to be held as tenancy in common when title is not specifically held in joint tenancy, community property, or partnership.

47. An owner of an older apartment building is considering whether to enter into an extensive modernization and remodeling program for the property. The key factor in making a decision to proceed will be the

    a. potential increase in rents.
    b. resulting increase or decrease in net income.
    c. total cost of the program.
    d. amount of reduction in vacancies.

48. Under the law of agency, a fiduciary relationship is created between the broker and the seller on execution of the listing agreement. As far as the broker's responsibility to the third parties, the broker

    a. must be fair and honest.
    b. has no obligation.
    c. need only disclose material facts when asked about them.
    d. should disclose the lowest price the seller is willing to accept.

49. All of the following may be assigned, EXCEPT a

    a. broker's right to a commission.
    b. grant deed.
    c. mortgage.
    d. real property sales contract.

50. A 74-year-old man sold his personal residence after living in it for the past 18 years. The gross selling price was $121,000 and the expense of sale was $12,000. If the cost of the home was only $60,000 and he did not purchase another home, his capital gain for income tax purposes could be as little as

    a. $19,600.   c. $49,000.
    b. $61,000.   d. nothing.

51. Which of the following is correct regarding postdated checks?

    a. A postdated check is a form of promissory note.
    b. A broker must obtain the approval of the seller before accepting the postdated check as a deposit.
    c. The value of a postdated check is the same as a check of proper dating.
    d. Both a and b

52. Unpaid real property taxes constitute a lien

    a. prior to a mortgage lien.
    b. concurrent with a mortgage lien.
    c. after a mortgage lien.
    d. None of the above

53. The easiest way to check the water pressure in a home would be to turn on

    a. all the faucets and flush a toilet.
    b. the shower and flush a toilet.
    c. all the faucets to see if the flow is even.
    d. the outside faucet closest to the water source.

54. A licensee was listing homes for sale by cautioning owners that minority groups were moving into the area and would decrease property values, the quality of the schools would suffer, and crime rates would increase. Under these circumstances

    a. there has been no violation of the REALTOR®'s Code of Ethics.
    b. the Real Estate Commissioner cannot discipline the licensee because he or she has no jurisdiction even though the licensee is acting unethically.
    c. the Real Estate Commissioner can discipline the licensee.
    d. if the facts are true, the licensee cannot be disciplined.

55. When a husband and wife hold title to property in joint tenancy, the wife can will

    a. one half of the husband's share.
    b. one half of the entire property.
    c. one half of her share.
    d. none of the property.

56. When a document is signed by officers acting on behalf of their corporation, a seal is attached that

    a. makes it eligible for recording.
    b. shows that consideration has been paid.
    c. implies authority of the person signing.
    d. All of the above

57. When using the market-data approach in the appraisal of improved real property, the final estimate of value is

    a. determined by capitalizing the annual net income.
    b. inferred from the selling prices of recently sold comparable properties.
    c. based on today's cost to duplicate the same improvements less any depreciation plus the value of the land.
    d. computed on factual data that is based on the income yield of the property.

58. The columns of townships that are numbered to the north or south of the baseline and run parallel to the principal meridian are called

    a. ranges.   c. tracts.
    b. tiers.   d. parallels.

59. Which of the following statements is incorrect with regard to the recordation of a deed?

    a. It preserves the evidence of a deed.
    b. It prevents the creation of a "wild" document.
    c. It gives constructive notice to subsequent purchasers and encumbrances.
    d. It allows a subsequent purchaser to examine the public records to ascertain the owner of record.

60. A person selling a personal residence may receive a tax exemption of up to $250,000 of gain if single and up to $500,000 of gain for a married couple, once every _____ years.

    a. five   c. three
    b. two   d. four

61. Three of the following real estate terms are closely associated. Which term does not belong with the group?

    a. Heir   c. Sale
    b. Executor   d. Will

62. Able, who owns Greenacres Ranch, leases the property to Taylor for a 10-year term. Able had signed a will that stated that all his interest in Greenacres Ranch would go to his friend Barnhill. Shortly after executing the lease, Able died. During the probate proceedings, the will was held to be invalid and void. It also was discovered that Able had no living heirs. Under these circumstances, Greenacres Ranch

    a. passes to Barnhill.
    b. passes to the county after five years.
    c. passes to Taylor.
    d. escheats to the state subject to the lease.

63. Insurance companies use which of the following to channel their funds for availability to buyers who wish to obtain mortgage financing and once these loans are made, use the same party to handle their loan servicing?

    a. Savings and loan associations
    b. Federal Housing Administration and Department of Veteran's Affairs
    c. Mortgage companies
    d. Institutional lenders

64. A joint tenancy estate

    a. is a single estate.
    b. is an estate in severalty.
    c. involves real property only.
    d. involves personal property only.

65. The quickest method that an appraiser could use to establish the value of a building using the cost approach is the

    a. quantity survey.
    b. unit in place.
    c. market comparison.
    d. assemblage.

66. If the antidiscrimination law, which prohibits various types of discrimination by an operator of a real estate business, is violated, a court of law may do all of the following EXCEPT

    a. award punitive damages.
    b. award actual costs and expenses to the plaintiff.
    c. award money damages because of humiliation and embarrassment.
    d. cause the broker to have his or her license suspended or revoked.

67. The liquidation of a financial obligation on the installment plan is known as

    a. conveyance.   c. amortization.
    b. acceleration.   d. conversion.

68. The Real Estate Settlement Procedures Act of 1974 requires that certain lenders provide the borrower with loan expense information when the borrower is applying for a first trust deed loan and the borrower is using an owner-occupied residence of four units or less as the security for the loan. This law applies to a

    a. seller of a single-family residence who takes back the first trust deed and note as part of the purchase price of the property.
    b. lender whose deposits are insured by the Savings Association Insurance Fund or the Federal Deposit Insurance Corporation.
    c. private individual who advances the funds and whose loan is arranged through a licensed real estate broker.
    d. All of the above

69. "No person acting under the real estate law shall accept any purchase or loan funds or other consideration from a prospective purchaser or lender, or directly or indirectly cause such funds or other consideration to be deposited in an escrow except as to a specific loan or a specific real property sales contract or promissory note secured directly or collaterally by a lien on real property on which loan, contract, or note the person has a bona fide authorization to negotiate or to sell." In the preceding quotation taken from the real estate law, the term *collaterally* means a

    a. hard money note.
    b. note secured by another note.
    c. purchase-money loan.
    d. real property security.

70. The maximum amount that can be charged and held by the landlord as a security deposit on a furnished apartment is

    a. one month's rent.
    b. two months' rent.
    c. three months' rent.
    d. four months' rent.

71. A licensed real estate broker, who owned a large real estate firm operating under the name of XYZ Realty Company, listed a property for a total price of $90,000. The broker and many of her salespersons were all principals in an investment company operating under the name of ABC Realty Investment Company. The investment company decided to purchase the property, so the broker presented an all-cash offer to the owner for the full price but did not disclose to the seller who the purchasers were. The seller accepted the offer and opened escrow. Under these circumstances the

    a. broker's actions were perfectly legal because she offered the full cash price.
    b. broker's offer would be legal; provided she added to the escrow instructions the fact that the purchasing firm was composed of brokers and salespersons.
    c. broker acted properly, provided she had agreed to waive any commission.
    d. broker's action was improper because she did not reveal the true identity of the purchaser.

72. A gift of real property by a valid will is known as a

    a. devise.
    b. legacy.
    c. bequest.
    d. None of the above

73. Under the Uniform Commercial Code, the document that is most often filed with the Secretary of State on the sale of a business is the

    a. security agreement.
    b. bill of sale.
    c. notice of intention to sell.
    d. financing statement.

74. Tyrone owns a commercial store property which he leases to Crow for six years. Crow's estate in the store is

    a. personal property.
    b. an estate for years.
    c. a chattel real.
    d. All of the above

75. The extent of a real estate agent's authority to act on behalf of a principal is

    a. the authority that third-party principals interpret the agent as possessing.
    b. that which the principal confers on the agent, whether actual or otherwise.
    c. any authority the agent chooses to accept, regardless of restrictions placed upon that authority.
    d. the authority to sell and convey real property and modify or cancel purchase agreements after they have been made.

76. An attorney-in-fact can best be described as a(n)

    a. duly authorized person who has been granted both actual and implied powers to act as a principal for another.
    b. properly authorized party who is acting as a dual agent.
    c. attorney appointed by the court to administer an estate of a deceased person.
    d. legally competent person who has been given the power of attorney by another competent person.

77. Which of the following parties would be involved in a search of a title at the time of sale?

    a. Broker and escrow official
    b. Escrow officer and title company employees
    c. Attorney and title company employees
    d. Attorney and escrow officer

78. A standard title insurance policy insures against

    a. a recorded deed in the chain of title that was not properly delivered.
    b. claims of persons in possession of the property.
    c. easements by prescription.
    d. losses sustained by improved property only.

79. Which of the following is responsible for ensuring that the off-site improvements such as streets, sewers, curbs, gutters, and so on, in a new subdivision are complete?

    a. A bonding company
    b. Planning commission
    c. Developer-builder
    d. Property owner

80. Which of the following is covered under an extended coverage form of title insurance that is not covered under a standard policy of title insurance?

    a. Trust deed of record
    b. Tax lien
    c. Encroachment
    d. Homestead exemption

81. When making an appraisal in an urban area, a neighborhood analysis is an important part of the appraisal process because

    a. of the immobility of real estate.
    b. employment trends in the surrounding area may affect the final value estimate.
    c. available or proposed transportation facilities would affect the market value.
    d. All of the above

82. Which of the following statements is incorrect with regard to a life estate?

    a. The holder of the life estate does not have fee title.
    b. It is a freehold estate.
    c. It must be created by an instrument in writing.
    d. It can only be based on the life of the tenant.

83. Which of the following items can currently be deducted for federal income tax purposes on real property owned and used by the taxpayer for his or her personal residence?

    a. Annual depreciation
    b. Expenses of maintenance, repair, and care
    c. Property taxes and mortgage interest
    d. Losses that might be deferred if the property is sold

84. Robinson gives a quitclaim deed to Anderson for a parcel of real property, but Anderson does not record the deed. In this situation, which of the following is true? The deed is

    a. invalid as between Robinson and Anderson.
    b. invalid as between Robinson and Anderson but valid to subsequent recorded interests.
    c. valid as between Robinson and Anderson but invalid as to subsequent recorded interests without notice.
    d. valid as between Robinson and Anderson and valid as to subsequent recorded interest without notice.

85. James, a 16-year-old emancipated minor, desired to sell real estate he owned and has presented evidence of his emancipation to the listing broker. When the broker discovers a buyer for the property he or she will submit the proof of emancipation to the

    a. title insurer.
    b. escrow company.
    c. buyer's lender.
    d. buyer.

86. Which of the following is classified as personal property?

    a. A dwelling
    b. A mortgage
    c. An easement
    d. Riparian rights

87. The statement "The value of the best property in a neighborhood will be adversely affected by the presence of comparatively substandard property" relates to one of the basic principles of value known as the principle of

    a. balance.
    b. contribution.
    c. regression.
    d. anticipation.

88. Broker Baker secured a 90-day non-exclusive listing contract from owner Stanley. Broker Baker located a prospective buyer named Able who made an offer on the property. The offer was rejected by Stanley, as Stanley believed the offer was too low. After the listing expired, owner Stanley listed the property with another broker named Fox. Broker Fox was contacted by prospective buyer Able and Able made another offer on the property that was accepted by Stanley. When Baker received word of the sale, she immediately contacted the owner and demanded a commission. Under these circumstances, broker Baker is entitled to

    a. a full commission.
    b. one-half of the commission.
    c. no commission.
    d. the same amount of commission paid to Fox.

89. When real property is subleased, the interest held by the sublessor is commonly called a(n)

    a. double lease.
    b. freehold lease.
    c. assignment.
    d. sandwich lease.

90. In some areas of California where wood-frame structures are very susceptible to wood-destroying pests, a structural pest control report will be required

    a. in all sales of wood-frame structures.
    b. when an FHA or a VA loan is being used to finance the purchase.
    c. if requested by the buyer regardless of whether the seller had or had not agreed to permit such an inspection.
    d. All of the above

91. The interest rate on a straight note in the amount of $25,000 that calls for interest payments of $593.75 each quarter would most nearly be

    a. 8.4 percent.   c. 8.5 percent.
    b. 7.2 percent.   d. 9.5 percent.

92. A farmer had 150 acres of agricultural land that he decided to subdivide into five parcels of equal size and sell them for agricultural use. He contacted a real estate broker regarding the need of a final public report. The broker should advise the party that

    a. there is no need for a public report because the resulting parcels are not small enough to come under the law.
    b. this is a subdivision under the law, and he must follow the Subdivided Lands Act public report procedures.
    c. this is not a subdivision under Subdivided Lands Act, as the law excludes agricultural land subdivisions of 40 acres or more.
    d. this is not a subdivision, as all agricultural land subdivisions are excluded under the law.

93. With regard to general and specific liens, which of the following groups of words represent specific liens?

    a. Mortgage, attachment, judgment, corporation tax lien
    b. Attachment, mechanic's lien, mortgage, taxes
    c. Inheritance taxes, mortgages, assessment, mechanic's lien
    d. Judgment, trust deed, attachment, taxes

94. The rate or amount of commission that is paid to a broker on the sale of real property that is part of the estate of a deceased person is determined by the

    a. administrator or executor of the estate.
    b. local real estate board.
    c. Real Estate Commissioner's regulations.
    d. court.

95. Under the terms of most trust deeds used in California today, the trustor is considered to have defaulted on the loan if the

    a. trustor becomes delinquent on the loan payments.
    b. property is used for illegal purposes.
    c. trustor fails to keep the property in good condition and repair.
    d. All of the above

96. Under some loans covered under the federal Truth-in-Lending Act, the borrower has a right to rescind the loan. The right to rescind is

    a. 3 days.   c. 10 days.
    b. 5 days.   d. 14 days.

97. A licensed real estate broker may legally refuse to take a listing from a seller of a minority race without fear of violating the law

    a. if the seller has insisted on a price that the broker believes to be too high.
    b. when the property is located in a racially mixed area that the broker does not wish to work in.
    c. provided he refers the listing to another broker who is the same race as the seller.
    d. All of the above

98. "Market value" of real property most nearly means the

    a. valuation that has been determined by a well-qualified fee appraiser or experienced real estate broker.
    b. estimated value that was determined by considering the exact current prices of materials and labor that would be needed to build the improvements at the present time.
    c. expected price if a reasonable amount of time is allowed to find a buyer and if both the prospective buyer and seller are substantially familiar with market conditions.
    d. present value of the net revenue that is expected to be received during the remainder of the property's productive life.

99. Which of the following would be appurtenant to land?

    a. Anything acquired by legal right that is to be used with the land for its benefit
    b. A right-of-way over another owner's adjoining land
    c. Stock in a mutual water company
    d. All of the above

100. A real estate broker would most commonly receive a commission from more than one party when

    a. selling a business opportunity.
    b. holding an open listing.
    c. negotiating a long-term lease.
    d. negotiating an exchange.

101. A federal law is designed to protect purchasers of subdivision properties that are located in the United States and are being offered for sale in interstate commerce. This law provides for right of rescission within

    a. three days.   c. seven days.
    b. five days.   d. ten days.

102. The act that provides for civil action against persons conducting business establishments by aggrieved persons claiming discrimination on account of sex, color, religion, ancestry, or national origin is the

    a. Civil Rights Act.   c. Rumford Act.
    b. Unruh Act.   d. Act of 1969.

103. A licensed real estate broker is accused of violating the Unruh Act for refusing to rent property to anyone other than Caucasians. If the broker is found guilty, she

    a. must pay $250 to the party infringed on as punitive damages.
    b. is subject to actual damages.
    c. Both *a* and *b*
    d. Neither *a* nor *b*

104. The act empowering the State Department of Fair Housing and Employment to act against discrimination in both publicly assisted and private housing accommodations under specified conditions is the

    a. Civil Rights Act.   c. Rumford Act.
    b. Uhruh Act.   d. Act of 1969.

105. If the U.S. government obtained a lien against a taxpayer who failed to report a certain portion of his rental income, it would be classified as

    a. general.
    b. voluntary.
    c. specific.
    d. None of the above

106. A copy of the Real Estate Commissioner's public report that was issued on land within a land project must be given by the subdivider and his agents or salespersons to

    a. all owners of land adjacent to the subdivision.
    b. every adult prospect who wrote or telephoned requesting one or who visits the site and states that he or she is interested in purchasing one or more of the sites.
    c. every prospective buyer, but the subdivider or agent can wait until just prior to signing the purchase agreement.
    d. the local newspaper so it can be published in the legal section.

107. An individual purchased a nine-acre parcel of unimproved property. She then subdivided the nine acres into one-acre parcels. If the subdivider plans to sell only three one-acre parcels per year over the next three years, he must comply with the state

    a. Subdivision Map Act.
    b. Subdivided Lands Act.
    c. Both *a* and *b*
    d. Neither *a* nor *b*

108. Which of the following could be similar to a planned development in California?

    a. A stock cooperative
    b. A land project
    c. A condominium
    d. A community apartment project

109. When a subdivider submits an application on a new proposed subdivision to the Real Estate Commissioner and requests a final public report, the subdivider will be required to submit all of the following *EXCEPT*

    a. the condition of the title.
    b. floor plans of the proposed housing units.
    c. copies of the sales agreements.
    d. None of the above

110. Under the current federal tax law, the ownership holding for multiple investors that would both minimize the tax obligations and limit an individual's personal liability would be a

    a. general partnership.
    b. limited partnership.
    c. corporation.
    d. proprietorship.

111. Any citizen injured by discrimination in housing practices may under the Civil Rights Act of 1968

    a. institute a private action in a state or federal court.
    b. file criminal charges in federal court.
    c. file charges with local law enforcement authorities.
    d. bring a civil action in a state superior court for specific performance.

112. If a real estate broker undertakes to canvass a neighborhood area that is very near to a section into which minorities have recently moved telling the people that they should sell now because their property might suffer a loss in the future, that broker would be guilty of

    a. steering.   c. blockbusting.
    b. panic peddling.   d. Both *b* and *c*

113. The date by which property must be sold to the state by the county for delinquent taxes is on or before

    a. June 30.   c. March 15.
    b. July 1.   d. January 1.

114. Under the provisions of the Civil Rights Act of 1968 (federal fair housing law), which of the following actions would be considered discriminatory and unlawful?

    a. A broker assigning salespeople to prospects according to the race of the associates
    b. A broker assigning salespersons to certain prospects according to the race of the prospects
    c. A broker who assigns salespersons to branch offices in line with the racial composition of the neighborhood in which those offices are located
    d. All of the above

115. All of the following acts would be a violation of the California Fair Housing Law (Rumford Act) *EXCEPT* refusal by

    a. an owner of a single-family residence to sell his or her home to two parties because the buyers are unmarried.
    b. owners of a single-family residence to rent a room within their residence to a prospective tenant because of his or her religious beliefs.
    c. an owner of a duplex to rent one unit to a prospective tenant because of the prospect's race.
    d. an owner of a large apartment complex to lease an apartment unit to a single person because most of the other tenants are married.

116. Of the limitations imposed by subdivision restrictions, the least effective is shown by experience to be

    a. minimum dollar cost for the improvements on each lot.
    b. minimum lot size.
    c. maximum height of the improvements.
    d. minimum area of the improvements.

117. Which of the following statements is incorrect with respect to real property tax liens?

    a. A lien for real property taxes has priority over all other liens, including special assessments, regardless of the date the other liens were created.
    b. When real property is sold by the state for delinquent taxes, the buyer receives title free and clear of all liens, including any existing trust deed.
    c. The failure of an owner to pay the property taxes on an encumbered property is usually considered a default on the loan and could lead to foreclosure by the lender.
    d. A real property tax lien has priority over any other lien resulting from contractual obligations of the owner.

118. If the Real Estate Commissioner discovers that a subdivider is selling subdivided land unlawfully or the subdivider is not following procedures as outlined in the commissioner's final report, the commissioner may immediately

    a. revoke the license of the subdivider's agent.
    b. revoke the final public report.
    c. issue a desist and refrain order.
    d. All of the above

119. Superior Loan Company charges borrower Tom one discount point for a loan. One point is equal to 1 percent of the

    a. sale price.
    b. loan amount.
    c. appraised value.
    d. None of the above

120. Discount points in FHA and VA loans may be paid by the

    a. seller only.
    b. buyer only.
    c. seller and/or the buyer.
    d. broker only.

121. The borrower is the

    a. mortgagee.   c. mortgagor.
    b. trustee.   d. beneficiary.

122. Real estate taxes become a lien on the property

    a. on July 1 of each tax year.
    b. the first Tuesday of November of the fiscal tax year.
    c. if not paid by December 10 of the tax year.
    d. on January 1 of each year.

123. If borrower Tim decides to cancel the loan for the refinancing of an existing home loan within the three-day period for the right of rescission, he will owe the lender a

    a. 1 percent finance charge.
    b. processing fee normally charged for preparation of documents.
    c. 10 percent fee.
    d. None of the above

124. The successful licensee should possess characteristics of honesty, sincerity, and a desire to serve people. What primary attitude should the licensee maintain in dealing with prospective clients?

    a. One that is "color-blind" and free from bias
    b. One that treats minorities with respect but advises them to contact other brokers who deal in minority areas
    c. One that accepts all clients willingly, even though the licensee may prefer not to work with such clients
    d. One that allows the licensee to use his or her best judgment in deciding which clients to handle

125. The Subdivision Map Act requires

    a. delivery of a copy of the Real Estate Commissioner's public report to all prospective buyers.
    b. the subdivider to prepare a tentative map and file it with the city or county.
    c. insertion of release clauses in all blanket mortgages.
    d. submission of proposed sales contracts for subdivision lots that a local agency has approved.

126. A three-bedroom house sells for $124,000 and the broker's total commission is 6 percent of the selling price. The commission is

    a. $6,000.
    b. $20,667.
    c. $7,440.
    d. $744.

127. On a $78,000 sale of a house, the rate of commission is 6 percent. The salesperson gets 40 percent of the commission and the broker gets the remainder. How much does the broker get?

    a. $40,000
    b. $2,808
    c. $1,872
    d. $4,680

128. The commission on a house that sells for $96,000 is $4,800. What was the rate of commission?

    a. 20 percent
    b. 2 percent
    c. 50 percent
    d. 5 percent

129. A salesperson received $2,880 for selling a house. This was 40 percent of the total commission on the sale of a $120,000 house. What was the commission rate on the sale?

    a. 6 percent
    b. 12 percent
    c. 4 percent
    d. 3 percent

130. A house sold for $110,000 and the rate of commission was 6 percent. If the salesperson got $1,980, what percentage of the commission did the salesperson get?

    a. 70 percent
    b. 30 percent
    c. 66 percent
    d. 3 percent

131. A broker charges a rental management fee of one-third of the first month's rent, and 2 percent of each month's rent thereafter. He must pay a $100 "finder's fee" to an agent. If the house rents for $600 per month, how much does the licensed broker make in one year?

    a. $232
    b. $432
    c. $332
    d. $100

132. A broker gets 6 percent of the first $100,000 and 3 percent of any amount over $100,000. What would be the loss to the broker if a house listed for $180,000 has to be reduced by 20 percent?

    a. $8,400
    b. $7,320
    c. $15,720
    d. $1,080

133. Broker Nicole has taken a listing on a lot owned by seller Diane. The seller advises Nicole that she wishes to realize $45,000 cash from the sale after paying a 7 percent commission and paying the approximate closing costs of $1,200. The lot is free and clear. What should the selling price be?

    a. $39,677
    b. $49,832
    c. $43,177
    d. $49,677

134. Find the interest on $32,000 at 12¼ percent per annum (year) for six months.

    a. $2,640
    b. $1,960
    c. $1,320
    d. $326

135. If the interest on a loan at 13 percent per annum for eight months was $5,400, what was the amount of the loan?

    a. $72,900
    b. $81,000
    c. $62,300
    d. $67,500

136. If the interest for nine months on a loan of $80,000 was $7,200, what was the rate of interest per annum?

    a. 13.5 percent
    b. 12 percent
    c. 9.6 percent
    d. 10.5 percent

137. A purchase-money mortgage carried back by seller for $60,000 at 10¾ percent was made February 1 and paid November 1. What was the total outstanding amount due at the time of payment?

    a. $64,837.50
    b. $48,375
    c. $55,162.50
    d. $66,450

138. A loan is made for 90 percent of the $96,000 appraised value of a house. The annual rate of interest is 12 percent. What is the bimonthly (every two months) interest payment?

    a. $864
    b. $8,208
    c. $684
    d. $1,728

139. On a simple interest loan of $15,000 that has an interest rate of 13 percent per annum, what is the total interest payment for two years, six months, and ten days?

    a. $3,033.33
    b. $2,403.30
    c. $2,433.30
    d. $4,929.20

140. A woman receives a purchase-money $30,000 loan from the seller at a reduced rate of 9 percent. Assuming the loan interest is calculated on a declining balance, if her payment is $250 per month, including interest, what is her balance after three payments?

    a. $29,975
    b. $29,949.81
    c. $29,924.43
    d. $29,898.86

141. A property valued at $120,000 is earning an 8 percent return. What is the monthly return?

    a. $9,600
    b. $4,800
    c. $800
    d. $80

142. A property valued at $150,000 earns $750 per month. What is the annual percentage return?

    a. 7.5 percent
    b. 6 percent
    c. 9 percent
    d. 12 percent

143. A business shows a monthly profit of $1,050. If this is a 9 percent return, what is the value of the property?

 a. $140,000   c. $14,000
 b. $94,500   d. $9,450

144. A man owns a building with six apartments. Three of the apartments net him $200 each per month and the other three net him $150 each per month. For what amount should he sell the building to net the same profit if he invests the money at 9 percent?

 a. $126,000   c. $12,600
 b. $105,000   d. $140,000

145. A woman rents each of her five apartments for $600 per month and has a total amount of expenses of $1,000 per month. She has an investment of $50,000 at 8 percent a year in the bank. She decides to use the bank interest to pay for better and more frequent property maintenance. What percent increase in rent per apartment must she obtain to offset this additional expense?

 a. 33.33 percent   c. 11.11 percent
 b. 66.67 percent   d. 20 percent

146. A store in a shopping center under a percentage lease pays a monthly rent of $600 plus 4 percent of the annual gross over $150,000. The gross yearly income was $250,000. If the lessor's interest in the store is valued at $150,000, what is the percentage return to the lessor?

 a. 7.5 percent   c. 15 percent
 b. 11.2 percent   d. 14 percent

147. A property is valued at $180,000 and is making an 8 percent net return on the investment. By what percentage must the monthly profit be increased to make a 10 percent annual return?

 a. 15 percent   c. 30 percent
 b. 20 percent   d. 25 percent

148. What percentage profit is made on a sale, if the selling price is $90,000 and the purchase price is $75,000?

 a. 15 percent   c. 120 percent
 b. 20 percent   d. 12 percent

149. If the purchase price of a property was $50,000, what should the selling price be to realize a 5 percent profit?

 a. $47,500   c. $52,500
 b. $53,750   d. $51,500

150. A man buys a house for $50,000. He sells it for $60,000 with a 6 percent broker's fee and closing costs of $400. What was his percentage profit?

 a. 11.2 percent   c. 5.6 percent
 b. 1.12 percent   d. 12 percent

■ ANSWER KEY

1. b. The majority of California laws concerning real property are created by legislative acts.

2. d. If there is an increase in property taxes on income property, then the net operating income of that property will decrease. When we capitalize net income to arrive at value of property, we find that the value will decrease by a much larger amount than that property tax increase.

3. d. The term *riparian* means river bank and refers to waters found in a river or stream—a watercourse of some type. Riparian waters would not be found in a lake or ocean; those waters or rights would be known as *littoral* rights.

4. a. The broker did the job that the owner hired the broker to do, which was to secure a purchase whose offer was accepted by the owner. There was misrepresentation by the owner of which the broker was not aware. The seller is not relieved from the payment of commission to the broker.

5. c. In the appraisal process, a final value estimate is based on the correlation of the value indications obtained by the cost, income, and comparative or comparison approach.

6. b. When one purchases a condominium, one receives a fee title to the airspace therein.

7. b. A limited partnership is the most common form of syndication in California because the investor's liability is limited to the amount of the investment made.

8. b. The straight-line method for depreciation is not an accelerated form of depre-

ciation. Under straight line, the same percentage is used for depreciation each year.

9. c. A bill of sale is used to transfer title to personal property items.

10. b. If a trust deed is foreclosed by court action, then the redemption period of up to one year is allowed to the borrower (trustor) as though the provisions of a mortgage contract prevailed. A mortgage contract calls commonly for a court foreclosure rather than a public sale. If a trust deed is being foreclosed as though it were a mortgage by using the court action, then all provisions of a mortgage would prevail, to include the one-year maximum redemption period.

11. d. An escrow with reference to real property may be terminated by the mutual consent of the parties to the escrow.

12. b. If one expires without having left a will, the expression *intestate succession* applies.

13. d. To solve this problem, apply the gross rent multiplier rule. Take the sales price of $39,000 for the Feldmans' house and divide $39,000 by the $300 monthly rent to equal 130 as a monthly gross rent multiplier. Multiply the gross rent multiplier of 130 times $345 monthly rental for the neighbor's home to equal a fair market value of the neighbor's home of $44,850. The gross rent multiplier rule is as follows: selling price divided by gross rent equals gross rent multiplier. This rule can be used for either annual or monthly gross rent.

14. b. The question is describing a land sales contract wherein the seller is collecting impounds for property taxes and insurance premium payments and must keep these funds in a separate trust account.

15. d. An easement is a nonpossessory interest in the use of land of another.

16. b. It may be possible when a purchaser has taken possession of property, having paid part of the purchase price and subsequently having made improvements, to enforce that purchase of real property made by oral agreement.

17. b. A minor can receive title to real property by gift or inheritance without court approval but cannot convey title without court approval.

18. a. One of the four unities of joint tenancy is the matter of equal interest, and this same characteristic is present in a community property form of title taking.

19. c. The principle of substitution indicates that when two or more commodities with about the same features and benefits are available, usually the one with the lowest price will receive the greatest demand. Mr. and Mrs. Barrett probably found another home that they liked equally for a lower price.

20. b. A valid bill of sale need not contain an acknowledgment, which indicates the signature has been notarized. While the signature of the seller is the most important feature on a valid bill of sale, it does not have to be signed in the presence of a notary.

21. c. In an open listing, many brokers can be employed to attempt to sell the property, but it is only the broker who is the "procuring cause" who will earn the entire commission.

22. c. An owner-occupant of real property does remain in possession of the property, even when the property has been sold to the state for nonpayment of property

taxes. The owner is given five years to redeem the property from the state by paying back due property taxes and any interest and penalty that may accrue.

23. b. Whenever out-of-state land is being offered to California residents, the offering must first be approved by the Department of Real Estate.

24. c. The lending characteristics described in the question are those of a commercial bank.

25. a. While the payment of money is usual in a contractual relationship, it is not a requirement for validity of the contract. A contract requires consideration; however, consideration may be in forms other than money.

26. b. When a trustor signs a deed of trust, the trustor is giving the power of sale to the trustee. It is the power of sale that authorizes the trustee to conduct a foreclosure sale if necessary.

27. c. The maximum the owner can charge for a general liquor license up to and including five years of age is $6,000.

28. b. Steering is an illegal activity by the real estate licensee.

29. d. Zoning is a form of land use control and is an example of local government's exercise of police power.

30. c. A deed is delivered to the grantee when all terms and conditions of the contract have been met in the escrow period.

31. c. The Department of Fair Employment and Housing enforces requirements of California Fair Housing laws.

32. c. The Department of Alcoholic Beverage Control can issue an on-sale general

license to a business located in the same area and doing business on a seasonal basis. The license is referred to as a *seasonal license*.

33. b. An attachment lien is not released due to the death of the defendant (property owner).

34. b. The creditor is intended to be protected by the publishing requirement of the Uniform Commercial Code bulk sale provisions.

35. a. It is the tenant's obligation to notify the landlord of this matter.

36. a. For backfill purposes, filling in a space around the foundation or retaining wall might be a requirement.

37. d. The initials refer to the three main intersections found in California under the U.S. government survey and township system.

38. b. The government's creation of new loans aimed at low-income housing would have the least effect on the business cycle, because it's aiming at a smaller percentage of the population.

39. b. A real estate licensee is allowed to sell a mobile home that has been registered with either DMV or HCD.

40. b. There is a right to reinstate a loan that is into default under a trustee for up to five days before a trustee's sale.

41. d. Choices *a, b,* and *c* are all available to a borrower.

42. d. A real estate investment trust is a form of syndication requiring 100 or more investors to participate.

43. c. An interpleader action is available to a broker or to an escrow company that may be handling an escrow transaction involving disputing parties.

44. b. An easement in gross is most common on residential property. That form of easement allows the utility company access to residential properties to service them as it normally does.

45. c. Economic rent refers to what's called *market rent* or *the going market rate* for income-producing properties. Economic rent is used to appraise income-producing properties.

46. b. The question is asking for the exception. All tenants in common would have to agree on the decision to create an easement over subject property.

47. b. Most owners of income-producing property are mainly interested in the resulting net income of property. While remodeling would surely make the units more desirable, the resulting increase in rental income may not offset the cost of remodeling.

48. a. While the agency relationship creates a fiduciary relationship between broker and seller, the broker must still be "honest and fair" to third parties in the transaction.

49. b. Choices *a, b,* and *d* may be assigned, but a new grant deed would be required in each subsequent transfer to title to property.

50. d. Statement of fact.

51. d. Both *a* and *b* are correct.

52. a. Property tax liens and assessment liens take priority over all other liens.

53. a. Choice *a* is the easiest and simplest way to check the water pressure in a home.

54. c. The activities of the licensee in the question are discriminatory and illegal. The Real Estate Commissioner could take action to discipline the licensee. This kind of activity by the licensee is known as *panic selling* or *blockbusting*.

55. d. Under the joint tenancy form of title holding, a joint tenant cannot will interest to another because of the right of survivorship, which is the most distinguishing characteristic of joint tenancy.

56. c. A seal appearing on a corporation document indicates that the person who signed the document on behalf of the corporation has the authority to do so.

57. b. The market data or comparison approach in the appraisal of improved real property incorporates the use of selling prices of recently sold comparable property to help arrive at a final estimate of value.

58. a. The column of townships that are numbered to the north or south of the baseline and run parallel to the principal meridian are called *ranges*.

59. b. A wild document exists but has not been recorded with reference to the transfer or real property.

60. b. Statement of fact.

61. c. The three terms that are closely related are choices *a*, *b*, and *d*, which all have to do with a will.

62. d. Because Able had no living heirs, the property would escheat (revert) to the state subject to the lease on the property.

63. c. Mortgage companies act as loan correspondents.

64. a. A joint tenancy form of title taking may be for either real or personal property transactions. It is a single estate in which two or more persons take title with a right of survivorship.

65. c. The fastest method used by an appraiser to establish the value of a building using the cost approach is to determine what the cost today would be to replace that building. The arrival at cost is based on comparing the cost of labor, materials, and installation, and what's done in the market comparison of the cost of these items.

66. d. Only the Real Estate Commissioner, not the court, can cause the broker to have his or her license suspended or revoked.

67. c. The term *amortization* means to liquidate or extinguish a financial obligation on an installment plan.

68. b. RESPA refers to one-unit to four-unit owner-occupied dwellings wherein a federally related mortgage loan is involved. A lender whose deposits are insured by the Savings Association Insurance Fund or the Federal Deposit Insurance Corporation would, of course, be federally related.

69. b. Collateralization of a note allows a holder to borrow against an existing note, thus using a note secured by another note as a way to borrow money.

70. c. With reference to residential property, in addition to the first month's rent, the maximum security deposit on a furnished apartment is the equivalency of three months' rent. The maximum security on an unfurnished apartment is two months' rent.

71. d. The broker is to disclose the true identity of the purchaser and all true facts concerning the transaction. In this instance, the broker acted improperly.

72. a. A gift of real property by will is known as a *devise*. A gift of personal property by will is known as a *legacy* or a bequest.

73. d. In a personal property loan transaction involving the sale of a business, a financing statement (do not confuse with financial statement) is filed with the Secretary of State in Sacramento. This document is used to give notice to whomever may inquire as to who the true extender of credit is on that loan transaction. It is used to perfect the security agreement between the lender and the borrower.

74. d. Statement of fact.

75. b. The extent to which a real estate agent may act on behalf of the principal is that which the principal (owner) extends to the agent, whether it is by actual agency or other means. The most common form in creating this agency relationship is through the creation of an exclusive-right-to-sell listing agreement, which is an example of actual agency.

76. d. An attorney-in-fact is the title given to a legally competent person who has been given the power of attorney by another to act in his or her behalf.

77. c. Customarily, it is the title company that would search the condition of title at the time of the sale of real property; attorneys involved in that transaction might also participate in the search.

78. a. One of the many items included in coverage under a standard title insurance policy would be a recorded deed in the chain of title that was not properly delivered.

79. a. The ultimate responsibility for ensuring that the off-site improvements are completed in a new subdivision would rest with the bonding (insurance) company.

80. c. An item of encroachment is covered under an extended coverage form of title insurance and is not covered under a standard policy.

81. d. In the appraisal process within a city environment, a neighborhood analysis is extremely important and would influence an estimate of value because of choices *a*, *b*, and *c*.

82. d. Choice *d* is incorrect, as the life estate can be based on anyone's life as designated in the instrument.

83. c. With reference to one's personal residence, the cost of property taxes and mortgage interest remain as a deduction for federal income tax purposes.

84. c. The unrecorded quitclaim deed is valid between parties Robinson and Anderson, but will be considered invalid as to any subsequent recorded interests that have no notice of the quitclaim action.

85. b. Whenever party to the transaction is in a position of having to prove competency in order to participate in the transaction, such evidence must be submitted to the entity that is conducting the escrow process.

86. b. A mortgage contract or any piece of paper is considered a personal property item.

87. c. The quotation in the question is a definition of the principle of regression.

88. c. The question states a 90-day non-exclusive listing contract from owner Stanley. In a nonexclusive listing contract, commonly called an *open listing*, only the broker who is the "procuring cause" is entitled to commission. In this case, broker Baker was not the one who brought in the offer and therefore is not entitled to a commission.

89. d. When real property is subleased, the interest held by the sublessor is referred to as a *sandwich lease*.

90. b. In most FHA and VA loans a structural pest control report is required.

91. d. Multiply quarterly payment of $593.75 by four to equal annual interest of $2,375. Divide $2,375 by the face amount of the note, which is $25,000 and that will equal 9½ percent.

92. b. A subdivision is a division of land into five or more parcels for the purpose of sale, lease, or financing, whether now or in the future, excluding divided parcels of 160 acres or more.

93. b. The terms shown in choice *b* are all examples of specific liens.

94. d. The rate of commission that is to be paid to a broker on a probate transaction is determined by the court.

95. d. If any of the activities shown in choices *a, b,* and *c* occur, then such activity would be deemed a default on a real estate loan secured by a trust deed.

96. a. On most transactions covered by the Federal Truth-in-Lending Act, there is a three-day right of rescission.

97. a. A broker has the right to refuse to take a listing from any seller of real property if the broker believes that the price requested on the listing is unrealistically high.

98. c. The explanation offered in choice *c* is a good definition of the expression *market value*.

99. d. Choices *a, b,* and *c* are definitions of items that would be appurtenant to the land. The term *appurtenant* means "that which runs with the land" or that which is hooked onto the land.

100. d. In an exchange transaction the broker would probably receive a commission from more than one party to the transaction, because an exchange transaction generally has two or more sales involved.

101. c. Under the federal Interstate Land Sales Full Disclosure Act, there is a right of rescission that lasts for seven days. Also recall that the number of lots under this act is 25 or more lots being sold from state to state with a seven-day right of rescission.

102. b. The Unruh Civil Rights Act prohibits discrimination by businesses.

103. c. Under the Unruh Civil Rights Act, there is the possibility of both punitive and actual damages for discrimination activities.

104. c. The Rumford Act, also called the California Fair Housing Act, empowers this department to take action for discrimination violations.

105. a. Unpaid taxes would be classified as general liens.

106. b. Every potential buyer of land within a land project is entitled to a copy of the public report.

107. c. If there are five or more parcels with the intent to resell, then that project will

come under the Subdivision Map Act and the Subdivided Lands Act, whether the sale is to occur now or in the future.

108. b. A land project involves 50 or more parcels offered for residential or recreational purposes in a remote area of California. It is considered similar to a planned development in California.

109. b. Under the Subdivided Lands Act, the Real Estate Commissioner is not concerned with the floor plan of the proposed project. The commissioner is more concerned with attempting to minimize fraud and misrepresentation.

110. b. The limited partnership is the most common form of syndication in California in that it has historically limited the liability of the individual investor and to some degree minimizes tax obligation.

111. a. An injured party in a matter of discrimination may institute private action in either a state or federal court.

112. d. The terms *panic peddling, panic selling,* and *blockbusting* could be used to describe the activity in this question.

113. a. Property is transferred to the state by the county for delinquent property taxes no later than June 30 of that tax year.

114. d. Choices *a, b,* and *c* are all examples of actions that would be considered discriminatory and unlawful.

115. b. An owner of a single-family dwelling is exempt from the provision of California fair housing, provided that owner is renting to only one person and is bringing that person into the house to reside with the owner.

116. a. The most commonly found restrictions within a subdivision have to do with choices *b, c,* and *d.* Setting a minimum

dollar cost for the improvements on each lot has not been highly successful, as frequently fair market value will lead to a probable selling price of the improvement.

117. a. The question is asking for the incorrect choice. Real property taxes and special assessments are on a parity with each other.

118. c. The first step the commissioner would probably take is to issue a desist and refrain order and then proceed against the subdivider. This desist and refrain order is to stop all activities in that transaction.

119. b. Discount points are charged to increase the lender's yield. They are based on 1 percent of the loan amount.

120. c. Currently, on both FHA and VA loans, either the seller or the buyer or both can pay any discount points.

121. c. The borrower is called the *mortgagor* (or trustor).

122. d. Real property taxes become a lien on January 1 prior to the tax year.

123. d. Under the Truth-in-Lending Act, there is a three-day right of rescission available to borrowers on certain types of consumer loans, such as a refinance of an existing home loan. This allows the borrower to change his or her mind without any penalty on a loan to purchase a personal residence.

124. a. The licensee is to act in a "color-blind" fashion and is to be absolutely free from bias.

125. b. The Subdivision Map Act is under the control of local governing agencies and is concerned with the physical aspects of the subdivision. This act requires that a tentative map be filled with the local governing agency.

126. c. Solution:

$$\begin{array}{r} \$124{,}000 \\ \times\ .06 \\ \hline \$7{,}440.00 \end{array}$$

127. b. Solution:

$$\begin{array}{r} 78{,}000 \\ \times\ .06 \\ \hline \$4{,}680.00 \end{array}$$
The commission is $4,680.
Because the salesperson gets 40 percent, the broker gets 60 percent.

$$\$4{,}680 \times .60 = \$2{,}808$$

128. d. Solution:

$$\begin{array}{r} \$96{,}000 \\ \times\ ? \\ \hline \$\ 4{,}800 \end{array}$$
$$.05 = 5\%$$
$$96{,}000\ \overline{)4{,}800.00}$$

129. a. Solution:

First determine the total commission: $2,880 is 40 percent of what?

$$\begin{array}{r} ? \\ \times\ .40 \\ \hline \$2{,}880 \end{array}$$
$$\begin{array}{r} 7{,}200 \\ 4.0\ \overline{)28{,}000} \end{array}$$
The total commission was $7,200.

$$\begin{array}{r} \$120{,}000 \\ \times\ ? \\ \hline \$7{,}200 \end{array}$$
$$.06 = 6\%$$
$$120{,}000\ \overline{)\ 7{,}200.00}$$

130. b. Solution:

First determine the total commission:

$$\begin{array}{r} \$\ 110{,}000 \\ \times\quad .06 \\ \hline \$6{,}600.00 \end{array}$$
$6,600 is the total commission.

Then the salesperson's commission was what percent of $6,600?

$$\begin{array}{r} \$6{,}600 \\ \times\quad ? \\ \hline \$1{,}980 \end{array}$$
$$.30 = 30\%$$
$$6{,}600\ \overline{)\ 1{,}980.00}$$

131. a. Solution:

1st month
$$\begin{array}{r} 200 \\ 3\ \overline{)\ 600} \end{array}$$

each month after
$$\begin{array}{r} \$\ 600 \\ \times\ .02 \\ \hline \$\ 12.00 \end{array}$$

$200.00 for the first month
$132.00 for 11 months ($12 × 11)

The total commission is: $332.00
Less $100 "finder's fee":   −100.00
        $232.00

132. d. Solution:

Old commission: $ 100,000 $ 80,000
                   ×   .06   plus   ×   .03
                   $6,000.00 $2,400.00

Total $6,000 + $2,400 = $8,400

New sales price: Old price $ 180,000   New price $180,000
                                     ×   .20   − 36,000
                                     $36,000.00 $144,000

New commission: $ 100,000   44,000
                   ×   .06   +   ×   .03
                   $6,000.00 $ 1,320.00

Total $6,000 + $1,320 = $7,320

Difference: $8,400
               −7,320
               $1,080

133. d. Solution:

$45,000   net after expenses
+1,200   to pay closing costs
$46,200   net to seller

Seller price = Subtract from 100 percent and then divide.
100% − 7% = 93%
$46,200 ÷ .93 = $49,677.42

134. b. Solution:

32,000 $326.67 per month   326.67
× .1225   12) 3,920   ×   6 months
3,920   1,960.02

135. c. Solution: $5,400 for eight months is $675 per month and is $8,100 for the year.

$675 $ 675
8) 5,400   ×   12
                                    $8,100

Then   ? $62,307.69
                    × .13   .13) 8,100.00
                    $8,100

136. b. Solution: The interest per month is $800.   800
                                                               9) 7,200

The interest per year is $9,600. $ 800
                                                  ×   12
                                                  $9,600

Then $80,000
            ×   ?   .12 = 12%
            $ 9,600   80,000) 9,600.00

137. a. Solution:

$ 60,000
×   .1075
$6,450.00 total interest for the year

               537.50 interest per month
12) 6,450.00

$ 537.50
×   9 months
$ 4,837.50 total interest for 9 months

Balance $60,000.00
             + 4,837.50
             $64,837.50

138. d. Solution:

$ 96,000 $86,400
×   .90   ×   .12
$86,400.00 = amount of loan $10,368 = interest for the year

          864
.12) 10,368
$ 864 interest per month
×   2 months
$1,728.00

139. d. Solution:

$15,000 interest per year
×   .13
$ 1,950

        $162.50 interest per month
12) 1,950.00

         $5.42 interest per day
30) 162.50

2 years   2 × $1,950 = $3,900.00
6 months   6 × $162.50 =   975.00
10 days   10 × $5.42   =   54.20

140. c. Solution:

                         $225
          $30,000   12) 2,700
1st payment   ×   .09
         $ 2,700.00 $250 payment
                       –   225 interest
                       $ 25 to balance

$30,000 old balance
–   25 to balance
$29,275 new balance

2nd payment

$$\begin{array}{r} \$29,975 \\ \times \quad .09 \\ \hline \$ 2,697.75 \end{array}$$

$$12\overline{)2,697.25}^{\$224.81}$$

$$\begin{array}{r} \$250.00 \text{ payment} \\ -224.81 \text{ interest} \\ \hline \$ 25.19 \text{ to balance} \end{array}$$

$$\begin{array}{r} \$29,975.00 \text{ old balance} \\ - \quad 25.19 \text{ to balance} \\ \hline \$29,949.81 \text{ new balance} \end{array}$$

3rd payment

$$\begin{array}{r} \$29,949.81 \\ \times \quad .09 \\ \hline \$ 2,695.48 \end{array}$$

$$12\overline{)2,695.48}^{\$224.62}$$

$$\begin{array}{r} \$250.00 \text{ payment} \\ -224.62 \text{ interest} \\ \hline \$ 25.38 \text{ to balance} \end{array}$$

$$\begin{array}{r} \$29,949.81 \text{ old balance} \\ - \quad 25.38 \text{ to balance} \\ \hline \$29,924.43 \text{ new balance} \end{array}$$

141. c.   Solution:

$$\begin{array}{r} \$ 120,000 \\ \times \quad .08 \\ \hline \$ 9,600.00 \text{ profit per annum} \end{array}$$

$$12\overline{)9,600}^{\$\ 800 \text{ per mo.}}$$

142. b.   Solution:

$$\begin{array}{r} \$ 750 \text{ month earnings} \\ \times \quad 12 \\ \hline \$9,000 \text{ yearly earnings} \end{array}$$

$$150,000\overline{)9,000}^{.06\ =\ 6\%}$$

$$\begin{array}{r} \$115,000 \\ \times \quad ? \\ \hline \$ 9,000 \end{array}$$

143. a.   Solution:

$$\begin{array}{r} \$ 1,050 \text{ per month} \\ \times \quad 12 \\ \hline \$12,600.00 \text{ profit per year} \end{array}$$

$$\begin{array}{r} ? \\ \times \quad .09 \\ \hline \$12,600 \end{array}$$

$$.09\overline{)12,600}^{\$140,000}$$

144. d.   Solution:

$$\begin{array}{r} \$200 \\ \times \ 3 \\ \hline \$600 \end{array} \quad \begin{array}{r} \$150 \\ \times \ 3 \\ \hline \$450 \end{array} \quad \begin{array}{r} \$ 600 \\ + \ 450 \\ \hline \$1,050 \text{ per month} \end{array} \quad \begin{array}{r} \$1,050 \\ \times \quad 12 \\ \hline \$12,600 \text{ per year} \end{array}$$

$$\begin{array}{r} ? \\ \times \quad .09 \\ \hline \$12,600 \end{array} \quad .09\overline{)12,600}^{\$140,000}$$

145. c. Solution:

$\begin{array}{r} \$\ 50,000 \\ \times\quad .08 \\ \hline \$4,000.00 \text{ yearly} \end{array}$ $12\overline{)\,4,000\,}^{\$333.33}$ $5\overline{)\,333.33\,}^{\$66.67}$

Raise each rent $66.67

$\begin{array}{r} \$\ 600 \\ \times\quad ? \\ \hline \$66.67 \end{array}$ $600\overline{)\,66.67\,}^{.11\ =\ 11\%\ \text{increase}}$

146. a. Solution:

$\begin{array}{r} \$\ 600 \\ \times\quad 12 \\ \hline \$7,200 \text{ fixed rent} \end{array}$ $\begin{array}{r} \$250,000 \\ -150,000 \\ \hline \$100,000 \end{array}$ $\begin{array}{r} \$100,000 \\ \times\quad\ .04 \\ \hline \$\quad 4,000 \end{array}$

$7,200 + $4,000 = $11,200 year rent

$\begin{array}{r} \$150,000 \\ \times\quad ? \\ \hline \$\ 11,200 \end{array}$ $150,000\overline{)\,11,200.00\,}^{.074\ =\ 7.5\%}$

147. d. Solution:

$\begin{array}{r} \$\ 180,000 \\ \times\qquad .08 \text{ old rate} \\ \hline \$14,400 \text{ yearly} \end{array}$ $12\overline{)\,14,400\,}^{\$1,200 \text{ monthly profit (old)}}$

$\begin{array}{r} \$\ 180,000 \text{ yearly} \\ \times\qquad .10 \text{ new rate} \\ \hline \$18,000 \text{ yearly} \end{array}$ $12\overline{)\,18,000\,}^{\$1,500 \text{ monthly profit (new)}}$

$\begin{array}{r} \$\ 1,500 \text{ new monthly profit} \\ -1,200 \text{ old monthly profit} \\ \hline \$\quad 300 \text{ gain} \end{array}$

$\begin{array}{r} 1,200 \\ \times\quad ? \\ \hline 300 \end{array}$ $75,000\overline{)\,300.00\,}^{.25\ =\ 25\%\ \text{increase}}$

148. b. Solution:

$\begin{array}{r} \$90,000 \\ -75,000 \\ \hline \$15,000 \text{ profit} \end{array}$ $75,000\overline{)\,15,000.00\,}^{.20\ =\ 20\%\ \text{profit}}$

$\begin{array}{r} \$75,000 \\ \times\quad ? \\ \hline \$15,000 \end{array}$

or:

$\begin{array}{r} \$75,000 \\ \times\quad ? \\ \hline \$90,000 \end{array}$ $75,000\overline{)\,90,000\,}^{1.20\ =\ 120\%\ \text{return}}$

149. c. Solution:

$\begin{array}{r} \$50,000 \\ \times\quad 1.05 \\ \hline \$52,500 \end{array}$

150. d. Solution:

$$
\begin{array}{r}
\$\quad 60{,}000 \\
\times \qquad .94 \\
\hline
\$56{,}400 \\
-\qquad 400 \\
\hline
\$56{,}000 \\
\$50{,}000 \\
\times\quad ? \\
\hline
\$56{,}000
\end{array}
$$

$$
50{,}000 \overline{\smash{\big)}\ 56{,}000} \quad \underline{1.12} = 12\%\ \text{profit (112\% return)}
$$

PRACTICE EXAMINATION V

1. A lease for a three-year term that called for rent to be paid quarterly expired. If at the end of the term the landlord accepted another payment of rent, the lease would be

   a. extended another three years.
   b. a periodic tenancy.
   c. extended for a term not to exceed one year.
   d. canceled in any event.

2. The loan instrument allowing for future additional advances but using the same instrument for security is a(n)

   a. acceleration clause.
   b. reconveyance deed.
   c. exculpatory clause.
   d. open-end trust deed.

3. Tom made an offer to purchase Ron's residence subject to his being able to assume Ron's existing loan. The lender was contacted and it agreed to a substitution of liability. If the sale is consummated under these conditions

   a. Tom is primarily responsible for the loan and Ron is secondarily liable.
   b. Ron is relieved of all further liability on the loan.
   c. Ron remains primarily responsible for the loan and Tom is secondarily liable.
   d. both parties are relieved of any further liability on the loan.

4. If is common procedure to record all the following instruments *EXCEPT*

   a. a real property sales contract.
   b. a notice of completion.
   c. assignment of deed of trust or mortgage.
   d. a promissory note secured by a deed of trust or mortgage.

5. When using the cost approach to determine the value of the land and improvements of a property, the appraiser would use

   a. separate approaches to arrive at a value based on income.
   b. one approach to arrive at a different value of each.
   c. one approach to arrive at one value for both.
   d. separate approaches to arrive at a value for both after allowing for depreciation.

6. When real property is used as the security for a loan, the property is said to be

   a. pledged.
   b. hypothecated.
   c. assigned.
   d. warranted.

7. A junior lien

   a. is always barred from a deficiency judgment.
   b. is never barred from a deficiency judgment.
   c. may be effective in a foreclosure.
   d. always contains a subordination clause.

8. The Federal Reserve may take any of the following actions that will affect government and monetary policy EXCEPT

   a. adjusting the discount rate.
   b. setting the interest rate on government guaranteed or insured loans.
   c. setting minimum reserve requirements.
   d. buying or selling bonds.

9. The law of agency is concerned with the rights and duties between and among the

   a. agent and the principal, whether disclosed or undisclosed.
   b. principal and third parties with whom the agent deals on behalf of the principal.
   c. agent and the third parties with whom the agent deals on behalf of the principal.
   d. All of the above

10. Fee schedules setting forth charges for title policies and other services performed by title companies are set by

    a. the Department of Insurance.
    b. title insurance companies.
    c. the Department of Real Estate.
    d. the Department of Corporations.

11. The legal action for recovery of possession of real property by a lessor from the lessee, where the lessee is in default of the rental payments and reentry is being unlawfully withheld from the landlord, is known as

    a. adverse possession.
    b. unlawful detainer.
    c. wrongful entry.
    d. ad hoc ejection.

12. A salesperson receives a deposit together with a written offer to purchase and delivers them to the employing broker, who presents the offer to the seller. The seller signs and accepts the offer. Without the consent of the salesperson and through no fault of his, the buyer and seller instruct the salesperson's employing broker to return the deposit. Which of the following is true?

   a. The salesperson's employing broker may retain one-half of the deposit and must give one-half to the seller.
   b. The broker may sue the seller, but must return the deposit.
   c. The broker may retain one-half of the deposit and must return only one-half to the buyer.
   d. The broker may retain the deposit to compensate him for his efforts.

13. For it to become effective and to transfer title, a deed must

   a. be acknowledged.
   b. be executed on a day other than Sunday.
   c. have a proper description of the property.
   d. contain the phrase "to transfer."

14. Buyer Sims employed salesperson Pat to negotiate the purchase of vacant land owned by the U.S. government. Pat was able to effect a sale of the property for a total price of $100,000. Upon the close of escrow, Sims could pay Pat a commission of

   a. 6 percent.
   b. $10,000.
   c. $3,000.
   d. nothing.

15. Adams purchased real property and acquired a fee simple absolute estate. All of the following are characteristics of a fee simple absolute estate *EXCEPT* that it is

   a. of indefinite duration.
   b. a determinable fee.
   c. a freehold estate.
   d. inheritable.

16. It is proper business practice for real property managers to be compensated in all of the following ways *EXCEPT* by a

   a. percentage of gross receipts.
   b. commission on new leases.
   c. commission on major repairs or alterations.
   d. receipt of discounts on purchase of supplies.

17. Which of the following statements is correct with respect to the purchasing power of the individual and property value?

   a. It is only important on commercial property.
   b. It is only important on industrial property.
   c. It has an insignificant effect on the property's value.
   d. It has a significant effect on the property's value.

18. When a buyer of a residence, after signing a valid agreement of sale, asks the broker for permission to move into the property before the sale closes, the broker should

   a. deny the buyer permission.
   b. grant the buyer oral permission.
   c. have the buyer sign a temporary lease for the property.
   d. obtain written consent from the owner.

19. To alienate title to property, one

    a. secures an ALTA policy of title insurance.
    b. clouds the title.
    c. records a homestead.
    d. conveys title.

20. The Real Estate Commissioner is not required by the Business and Professions Code to approve which of the following documents that might be used by a licensed real estate broker?

    a. Real Property Security Statement
    b. Broker-salesperson's employment agreement
    c. Mortgage Loan Disclosure Statement
    d. Advance fee agreements and material

21. A licensed real estate broker obtained an exclusive authorization and right-to-sell listing from an owner of a residence. During the listing period the broker found a buyer who made an offer on the property that was accepted by the seller. Neither the offer nor the escrow instructions made any mention of the broker's being the agent or regarding the payment of a commission. Under these circumstances, the broker

    a. will have no legal right to enforce the collection of the commission.
    b. must prove that she was the "procuring cause" to collect a commission.
    c. is legally entitled to a commission.
    d. is subject to disciplinary action by the commissioner for negligence.

22. A legal order directing a designated official to satisfy a judgment out of property of the debtor is a

    a. writ of foreclosure.
    b. writ of execution.
    c. writ of attachment.
    d. quiet title action.

23. All California counties collect a documentary transfer tax when most transfers of title are recorded. The rate is $.55 of each $500 of consideration paid or any part thereof. If a property sold for $150,000 and the buyer assumed an existing loan of $25,000, the amount of tax would most nearly be

    a. $28.   c. $165.
    b. $138.   d. $113.

24. All of the following conditions must exist at the time of the conveyance before an easement by implied grant will be given effect EXCEPT

    a. there must be a separation of titles.
    b. the use must be visible on inspection of the surface of the land.
    c. the easement must be reasonably necessary to the beneficial use of the land granted.
    d. the use that gives rise to the easement must have been so long continued and so obvious as to show that it was intended to be permanent.

25. A real estate broker who speaks of "tax shelter" could be referring to

    a. depreciation.
    b. interest income.
    c. financing.
    d. real property taxes.

26. If a court proceeding is entered into between two licensed real estate brokers over a commission split, it is not necessary for the brokers to show the court a written contract between the brokers regarding the commission split because

    a. this type of agreement is not covered under the Statute of Frauds.
    b. it is judicial recognition that this is a common practice between cooperating brokers.
    c. the real estate law specifically exempts these contracts.
    d. no listing agreement or commission agreement need be in writing to be enforceable in court.

27. Mr. Frank Adams grants an option to Mr. Aaron James to purchase the former's ranch. This option most clearly constitutes a(n)

    a. voluntary lien on Adam's ranch.
    b. contract to keep an offer open.
    c. fiduciary agreement.
    d. offer to enter into a contract.

28. A brother and sister received title to a house through the death of their father and held title in joint tenancy. Aside from the house, both conducted their other affairs separately and owned no other property together. Some years later, the brother died and left substantial unpaid debts. Under these circumstances, the sister would take title to the house

    a. free and clear of the debts of her brother.
    b. after the brother's estate cleared probate.
    c. together with any heirs the brother may have had.
    d. subject to liens of her brother's unpaid creditors.

29. The maximum interest rate that can be charged on a broker-made or arranged loan is

    a. 5 percent.
    b. 12 percent.
    c. unlimited.
    d. 10 percent.

30. An appraiser using the cost method may use the unit cost per square foot or cost per cubic foot in her computations. On a unit cost basis

    a. a small house would cost less than a large house.
    b. a large house would cost more than a small house.
    c. a small house would cost more than a large house.
    d. the cost of a small house and a large house would be the same.

31. The seller of a parcel of land accepted a purchase-money first trust deed that contained a subordination clause. This clause would

    a. permit additional liens to be placed against the property without the buyer's consent.
    b. permit the buyer to place a future loan on the property that would have priority.
    c. preclude the buyer's placing of construction loans on the property.
    d. guarantee priority of the first trust deed.

32. A tenant is justified in abandoning a leased property if the landlord demonstrates constructive eviction. Of the following, which is considered to be constructive eviction?

    a. The property has been shown to another party who has entered into negotiations with the landlord.
    b. The landlord has failed to make needed repairs and maintain the property in the agreed manner.
    c. The landlord has altered the building to an extent that it is no longer usable for its original purpose.
    d. All of the above

33. If the Federal Reserve wants to increase the amount of money available to member banks to ease a tight money market, it could

    a. raise the discount rate to its member banks.
    b. lower the minimum reserves required by its member banks.
    c. raise the minimum reserves required by its member banks.
    d. sell government bonds.

34. Which of the following would be an example of the exercise of police power?

    a. Zoning restrictions
    b. Rent control laws
    c. Subdivision codes
    d. All of the above

35. The owner-operator of a small retail store sold the building housing his business and immediately leased back the property from the new owner on a long-term basis. Several advantage are offered to the business operator in such a leaseback arrangement, the most important of which is

    a. relief from the problems of property management.
    b. increased working capital.
    c. rental payments are deductible as a business expense.
    d. the hazard of increased property taxes is lessened.

36. A group of neighbors who had pleaded with their neighbor Charles to stop burning garbage on his property finally obtained a court order to stop him from continuing to do so. This court order would be known as

    a. a judgment.
    b. an injunction.
    c. inverse condemnation.
    d. an indenture.

37. An alienation clause is not permitted under which of the following types of financing?

    a. Conventional
    b. Cal-Vet
    c. FHA
    d. Private loan

38. A developer purchased four lots in 1992. Then years later each lot was sold for $10,000 apiece. The tax basis for each lot was $2,000. For federal income tax purposes, the capital gain recognized in this sale would be

   a. $8,000.
   b. $32,000.
   c. $40,000.
   d. not determinable from information given.

39. As a general rule concerning land value units, it is recognized that as the depth of a lot increases beyond the typical lot depth, the

   a. value per front foot increases.
   b. square foot unit value increases.
   c. value of the lot decreases.
   d. front foot and the square foot units' value decreases.

40. Prior to the issuance of a title policy, the title company will investigate and review any and all documents and records that are available. Which of the following will be given the greatest weight in deciding whether to issue a policy on a given property?

   a. The title search
   b. No cloud in the chain of title
   c. A previous guarantee of title
   d. A preliminary title report

41. Lenders are more inclined recently to make 95 percent loans on single-family residential properties because of

   a. Freddie Mac's activity in the marketplace.
   b. credit life insurance.
   c. private mortgage insurance.
   d. the activity of Ginnie Mae.

42. The ultimate recipient of the 0.005 mutual mortgage insurance premium paid on older FHA loans is the

   a. FHA.   c. mortagee.
   b. trustor.   d. beneficiary.

43. Lani sold a 640-acre parcel of agricultural land to Jack but included the following in the deed: "Excepting and reserving all mineral, oil, and gas substances under and on said land." Jack commenced farming the land, but three years later Lani moved drilling equipment onto the property and started to drill for oil. Jack then instigated court action against Lani to stop the drilling and have him remove his equipment. Under these circumstances Lani

   a. had a legal right to enter the land and can proceed to drill.
   b. can be stopped from proceeding with the drilling.
   c. cannot drill from Jack's land and must slant the drill from the adjacent land.
   d. can drill on Jack's property but can only remove minerals below 500 feet.

44. In California, the minimum required crawlspace in a structure as required by the building codes is

   a. 16 inches.   c. 20 inches.
   b. 18 inches.   d. 24 inches.

45. Fannie Mae (the Federal National Mortgage Association) was created for the primary purpose of

   a. advancing funds to mass production builders in our near urbanized areas.
   b. lending money on FHA Title II loans when banks, savings and loan associations, or private lenders are unwilling to do so.
   c. increasing the amount of housing credit available to the economy.
   d. supervising public lending agency associations.

46. The section number that is due west of Section 18 is section number

   a. 13.
   b. 17.
   c. 19.
   d. 24.

47. The expansion-contraction of demand for residential housing is largely dependent on

   a. prices.
   b. availability and terms of financing.
   c. obsolescence.
   d. elasticity of demand.

48. All of the following would have an effect on the final estimate of value when making an appraisal of an old family residence *EXCEPT* the

   a. purpose of the appraisal.
   b. suitability of the residence to the site.
   c. physical condition of the building.
   d. original cost of the residence.

49. A and B hold title to farmland as tenants in common. A occupies and farms the land. A could be liable to B for all of the following *EXCEPT*

   a. principal payments under a trust deed.
   b. rental value for renting a portion of the land to a third party.
   c. value of extracted oil and minerals.
   d. rental payments for use of the land.

50. California's sales tax due on the fixtures in the sale of a business opportunity is

   a. paid by the buyer to the seller together with the purchase price.
   b. remitted by the seller to the State Board of Equalization.
   c. paid before the certificate of clearance is issued.
   d. All of the above

51. Riparian rights extend to an owner of land that borders on

   a. a watercourse.
   b. a lake.
   c. the seashore.
   d. All of the above

52. Under most circumstances it is unlawful for anyone to act as an escrow holder unless he or she has been licensed by the Commissioner of Corporations. Which of the following would be in violation of the law?

   a. The real estate broker who holds an escrow for a buyer and seller whom he or she had represented in the sale
   b. The real estate broker who solicits escrows from fellow brokers and agrees to make no charge for the work
   c. The attorney-at-law who handles an escrow for a fee on behalf of clients
   d. The licensed escrow company that is incorporated and advertises for escrows for a fee

53. Most of the junior loans that are available today are secured through

    a. savings and loan associations.
    b. private investors.
    c. commercial banks.
    d. mortgage bankers.

54. A CLTA standard policy of title insurance involves three processes. Which of the following is not one of these processes?

    a. Search and examination of title
    b. Determination of the amount of insurance required
    c. Protection of the insured for potential losses
    d. A survey of the property to determine the correct property lines

55. Licensed real estate broker Marsh takes an exclusive authorization and right-to-sell listing on a residential property. In the listing contract the owner specifies that Security Escrow Company is to be used if an agreement to sell the property is signed. Broker Allen brings an offer to the owner that calls for escrow to be handled through Alliance Escrow Co. If the seller accepts the offer submitted by broker Allen, the

    a. seller's escrow company will be used because it was so indicated in the listing.
    b. selling broker must select another escrow company because the buyer and seller have each requested different companies.
    c. buyer's preference in the choice of the escrow company is given first priority.
    d. escrow should be held at Alliance Escrow Company, as both the buyer and the seller agreed to this when signing the purchase contract.

56. Because of the long-term nature of their assets, amortized real estate loans make particularly suitable investments for

    a. national banks.
    b. credit unions.
    c. life insurance companies.
    d. individuals.

57. Two parties owned a square parcel of land that was 1,980 feet by 1,980 feet. If they divided the parcel by cutting it diagonally in a straight line from the northwest corner to the southeast corner, the total number of acres in each parcel would most nearly be

    a. 22½ acres.   c. 45 acres.
    b. 30 acres.   d. 90 acres.

58. The Subdivision Map Act in California is administered by the

    a. Real Estate Commissioner.
    b. local planning commission.
    c. State Registrar of Contractors.
    d. State Department of Housing Community Development.

59. The sale of real property by a conditional installment contract of sale gives the buyers

    a. right of possession.
    b. an estate of inheritance.
    c. a freehold estate.
    d. All of the above

60. In single-family house construction the term *footing* refers to

    a. a beam under the floorboards.
    b. a girder running along the foundation, to which the ends of the floorboards are fixed.
    c. the spreading part at the base of the foundation wall or pier.
    d. a reinforced concrete slab over which asphalt tile may be laid.

61. Which of the following statements is correct when two or more parties hold title to real property as tenants in common?

    a. Any one tenant in common can force a division of the property through a partition action.
    b. In the event there is no conveyance of title by any one of the co-owners during his or her life, the last surviving party will own the property in severalty.
    c. Each tenant in common has a separate title to an undivided interest and can dispose of it as he or she desires without the consent of the other cotenants.
    d. None of the above

62. If the city acquires land for public streets by dedication, the grantor may seek to have the land returned if

    a. he or she retakes it by adverse possession.
    b. the conveyed easement has been abandoned by the city.
    c. the city failed to award "just compensation."
    d. the city fails to maintain the streets.

63. When appraising improved real property, it is least important for the appraiser to establish a separate value for the site when

    a. using the income approach.
    b. applying a gross rent multiplier.
    c. establishing a value for depreciation purposes.
    d. applying the cost approach.

64. Brokers Rodriguez and Lee each have an open listing on a property. Broker Rodriguez shows the property to a buyer and carries on negotiations, but the buyer decides not to buy. Two weeks later broker Lee contacts the same buyer and arranges a sale of the property. Regarding commission, the seller is obligated to pay

    a. the full amount to both broker Rodriguez and Lee.
    b. the full amount to broker Lee only.
    c. 50 percent each to broker Rodriguez and Lee.
    d. the full amount to broker Rodriguez, who will have to settle with broker Lee.

65. A joint tenancy holding can be created by a deed from

    a. joint tenants to themselves and others as joint tenants.
    b. tenants in common to themselves as joint tenants.
    c. a husband to himself and his wife as joint tenants.
    d. All of the above

66. The Mt. Diablo meridian line runs

    a. east and west.
    b. the same as township lines.
    c. north and south.
    d. north.

67. Each of the following could be a negotiable instrument, *EXCEPT* a(n)

    a. installment note.
    b. draft.
    c. personal check.
    d. trust deed.

68. Which of the following is the *LEAST* important factor when appraising a site for commercial purposes?

    a. Convenience of facility to shipping facilities and labor sources
    b. The community's purchasing power
    c. Zoning regulations
    d. Amenities

69. Which of the following would be classified as an encumbrance?

    a. Homestead
    b. Freehold estate
    c. Lease
    d. None of the above

70. The process of expressing anticipated future benefits of ownership in dollars and discounting them to a present worth at a rate that is attracting purchase capital to similar investments is called

    a. projection.
    b. yield evaluation.
    c. equity manipulation.
    d. capitalization.

71. Mae Smith owns a home that has a current market value of $100,000 and an existing first trust deed and note of $40,000 payable $350 per month including interest at 8½ percent. This existing loan contains no alienation clause. It is her desire to sell the home to her favorite nephew and wife for $100,000 and make the financing as low as possible. She enters into a sales agreement that calls for a $10,000 cash payment and for the nephew and wife to execute a new trust deed and note for $90,000 in her favor, payable $750 per month including interest at 9 percent. She plans to keep the existing $40,000 loan in effect and will continue to make the $350 monthly payments herself out of the monthly payments received from the nephew. This new $90,000 trust deed and note would be known as a

    a. blanket encumbrance.
    b. wraparound mortgage.
    c. real property sales contract.
    d. participation loan.

72. When a title company issues an ALTA policy, it customarily extends the risks normally insured against under the standard policy to include all but which one of the following?

    a. Rights of parties in possession
    b. Unrecorded physical easements
    c. Effects of zoning
    d. Unrecorded mechanics' liens

73. When a home has been kept in better than average condition, the effective age compared to the actual age would be

    a. less.
    b. the same.
    c. more.
    d. None of the above

74. If someone wishes to build a single-family residence, the three steps involved are

    a. land acquisition, mapping and planning approval, and construction.
    b. zoning approval, mapping and planning approval, and construction.
    c. mapping and planning approval, zoning approval, and construction.
    d. land acquisition, subdivision approval, and construction.

75. The most practical method of imposing restrictions on a new large subdivision is to

    a. publish the restrictions in a newspaper of general circulation.
    b. include the restrictions as covenants in all the deeds.
    c. record the restrictions in the manner provided by law and make reference to them in each deed.
    d. post the restrictions on the property.

76. A real estate licensee who misrepresents a property to a buyer while acting as agent for a seller may subject himself to

    a. disciplinary action by the licensing authority.
    b. civil action.
    c. criminal action.
    d. All of the above

77. A legal description of real property is considered to be defective if it does not describe a particular parcel of land with certainty. A property description that makes reference to monuments is usually considered to be less desirable because of

    a. failure to give clear evidence of range line designations.
    b. the possibility of the destruction of the monument.
    c. the fact that title practice does not permit monuments to be shown on the public record.
    d. the proximity of the monuments to appurtenances and other improvements.

78. Private deed restrictions may be imposed on real property by placing the restrictions in a

    a. deed.
    b. written agreement between two or more landowners.
    c. recorded declaration describing a general plan of restrictions for a tract and making reference to them in each deed.
    d. All of the above

79. A prospective client calls you and asks you to take a listing on his property. In reviewing his papers you discover that he is purchasing the property on a contract of sale, that it has no acceleration clause, and that there is no provision in the contract prohibiting a resale or an assignment. Which of the following is the most nearly correct statement? Your client could

    a. sell his interest in the property but only if he pays off the contract first.
    b. sell or assign his rights but not his duties under the original contract unless the contract seller's approval is obtained.
    c. properly give a warranty deed to the property to a purchaser, provided the deed recited "subject to the existing contract of sale."
    d. properly give a grant deed to the property to a purchaser, provided he took back a recorded purchase-money second trust deed to cover the payments due on the original contract of sale.

80. The purpose of the federal housing law is to

    a. provide fair housing throughout the United States.
    b. provide equal housing opportunities to minorities.
    c. provide fair housing in California.
    d. eliminate unfair rent.

81. Under the usual competitive circumstances, the vacancy rate attributable to a particular apartment property is fundamentally the result of

    a. the schedule of rents and the number of the units in the apartment building.
    b. the cost of money and the costs of construction.
    c. housing supply and demand in that particular area.
    d. employment fluctuation in the community.

82. Once a prospective real estate licensee has qualified for a new license by successfully passing the state examination, an application together with the proper fee must be filed with the Department of Real Estate within one year after

    a. passing the qualifying examination.
    b. the filing date of the examination application.
    c. entering into a written contract with the employing broker.
    d. the issuance of a temporary license.

83. On which of the following would the appraiser least likely use the cost approach?

    a. An old home in a commercial neighborhood
    b. A city library
    c. A new house on a suitable site
    d. A check against value estimates arrived at by other appraisal methods

84. An employee of a corporation licensed as a real estate broker who is working as a member of the corporation's sales staff

    a. does not require a real estate salesperson's license.
    b. must be a licensed real estate broker.
    c. must be a licensed real estate salesperson or broker.
    d. does not require a real estate license, provided that person is an officer of the corporation.

85. Mrs. Browne paid her regular monthly payment on her home loan of $550. Of that amount, $48.53 was applied to principal. The average balance owing on the note for that month was $56,500. The interest rate on the note was

    a. 8.5 percent.   c. 9.75 percent.
    b. 10.6 percent.   d. 12.5 percent.

86. Which of the following statements about real estate brokerage is correct?

    a. The amount of the broker's commission for the sale of a home is limited by law.
    b. An exclusive-agency listing permits the owner to sell without being liable for a commission.
    c. All agreements among brokers regarding the division of commissions must be in writing as required by the statute of frauds.
    d. Under no circumstances may a broker recover a commission if the sale was consummated after the listing expired.

87. Mark holds a three-year written lease that also contains an option to purchase the property at a stated price. If Mark were to assign the lease to Mike,

    a. Mike would now hold the option.
    b. Mark would retain the option.
    c. the option is automatically canceled.
    d. the assignment would be invalid because a lease with an option to purchase cannot be assigned.

88. An attachment is a(n)

    a. judgment.   c. assessment.
    b. lien.   d. fixture.

89. In California, a real estate appraiser must

    a. be licensed with the Department of Real Estate.
    b. be a California resident for at least one year.
    c. charge a fee based on a percentage of the appraisal value.
    d. None of the above

90. A contract between the seller of a home and a real estate broker, whereby the seller agrees to pay the broker a commission for procuring a buyer "ready, willing, and able" to buy and agreeing to use due diligence is called a

    a. unilateral executory contract.
    b. bilateral executory contract.
    c. unilateral executed contract.
    d. bilateral executed contract.

91. To transfer an interest in trade fixtures on the expiration of a lease, the lessee would use a

    a. chattel real.
    b. bill of sale.
    c. financing statement.
    d. None of the above

92. The broker who most likely has earned a commission is the one who has

   a. communicated acceptance to offeror.
   b. communicated offer to seller.
   c. secured acceptance to an offer.
   d. secured a substantial deposit with an offer.

93. An appraiser is hired to appraise a commercial office building whose value is believed to be approximately $575,000. What type of license does the appraiser need?

   a. Regular appraisal license
   b. Certified residential license
   c. Certified general license
   d. Any of the above

94. A balloon loan is a(n)

   a. standing loan.
   b. amortized loan.
   c. partially amortized loan.
   d. self-liquidating loan.

95. Although title insurance may be purchased to protect the insured against most every type of loss, title insurance may not be purchased to cover against a loss resulting from

   a. discovery of a forged document in the recorded chain of title.
   b. failure of one spouse to sign the deed in the transfer of community real property.
   c. unpaid city taxes not listed as an exception in the policy.
   d. a change in a city zoning ordinance, regulation, or plot plan.

96. In the appraisal of residential property, the cost approach is most appropriate in the case of _____ property.

   a. new   c. older
   b. middle-aged   d. multifamily

97. An attorney-in-fact is

   a. a lawyer acting as the executor or administrator of an estate.
   b. a principal who may act under implied powers.
   c. any legally competent person who has been given a power of attorney by another.
   d. a person acting in a dual-agency capacity.

98. An instrument that transfers possession of real property but not title is known as a(n)

   a. trust deed.   c. assignment.
   b. lease.   d. mortgage.

99. Mr. and Mrs. Bennett are purchasing a home and have applied for an FHA loan. When making an evaluation as to whether the lender will grant or deny the loan, the primary concern of the lender will be the

   a. marital status of the applicants.
   b. age and square footage of the home being purchased.
   c. credit characteristics of the applicants.
   d. anticipated term of the loan.

100. The term *highest and best* use of land is best defined as that use which

   a. best benefits the community.
   b. produces the highest gross annual income.
   c. meets deed and zone restrictions.
   d. results in the highest net income attributable to the land.

101. In the event the parties to a bulk sale do not comply with the provisions of the Bulk Sales Law as outlined in the Uniform Commercial Code, the party that would probably be injured the most would be the

    a. seller.
    b. buyer.
    c. creditor.
    d. lender.

102. When Adams transfers an interest in trade fixtures to a purchaser, she will use which of the following instruments to convey title?

    a. Chattel real
    b. Warranty deed
    c. Bill of sale
    d. None of the above

103. An owner of a liquor store received an original off-sale general license from the state two years ago and now wants to sell the business. The maximum he can charge for the license is

    a. $2,000.
    b. $4,000.
    c. $6,000.
    d. not limited by law.

104. When a business venture involving the use of a liquor license is transferred, the Department of Alcoholic Beverage Control can

    a. transfer an on-sale general license into any county that has a population of 35,000 or less.
    b. issue a license to any legally organized club after the club is formed and immediately applies for an on-sale general license.
    c. issue an on-sale general license to a business located in the area and doing business on a seasonal basis.
    d. issue an off-sale general license for the same location for which an on-sale beer and wine license previously was issued.

105. Under the Bulk Sales provisions of Division 6 of the Uniform Commercial Code, the publishing and recording requirements are intended to alert which of the following to the intended transfer?

    a. Broker
    b. Creditor
    c. Vendor
    d. Vendee

106. Under the Uniform Commercial Code, the document that is most often filed with the Secretary of State on the sale of a business is the

    a. security agreement.
    b. bill of sale.
    c. notice of intention to sell.
    d. financing statement.

107. An instrument that usually transfers the possession of real property without transferring its ownership is a(n)

    a. mortgage.
    b. sublease agreement.
    c. security device.
    d. easement.

108. In the sale of real property, a copy of the structural pest control report must be given, on request, to the

    a. buyer.   c. escrow holder.
    b. broker.   d. lender.

109. An acceleration clause is included in a negotiable note. This clause

    a. removes the negotiability of the note.
    b. is required for the note to be negotiable.
    c. does not affect the negotiability of the note.
    d. has no effect on negotiability and is of no benefit.

110. Successor's liability is set by the

    a. Franchise Tax Board.
    b. State Board of Equalization.
    c. Department of Corporation.
    d. Real Estate Commissioner.

111. If an owner of a business wants to know if a sales tax is to be imposed on the sale of property of the business, which of the following should the owner consult?

    a. Franchise Tax Board
    b. State Board of Equalization
    c. Department of Corporation
    d. Real Estate Commissioner

112. All of the following items are commonly found on a balance sheet *EXCEPT*

    a. goodwill.
    b. equipment used for deliveries.
    c. sales.
    d. prepaid expenses.

113. If there is no provision for a termination date in the escrow instructions, the parties have

    a. 30 days.
    b. 60 days.
    c. a reasonable time period.
    d. as long as either party wishes.

114. A valid bill of sale need not contain

    a. a date.
    b. an acknowledgment.
    c. a description of the property.
    d. mention of the consideration.

115. Which of the following is an example of a violation of fair housing laws as they relate to periodic tenancy?

    a. A landlord requires that each tenant have a good credit rating and a steady source of income.
    b. A landlord wants references from the previous landlord.
    c. A landlord requires a cosigner for a tenant who is single.
    d. A landlord demands the payment of the first, second, and last months' rents in advance.

116. A security agreement is usually given in connection with

    a. real property.
    b. agricultural property.
    c. rentals.
    d. personal property.

117. The north-south lines that are 24 miles apart are called

    a. base lines.
    b. meridians.
    c. Both *a* and *b*
    d. lot and tract.

118. A range is numbered to the

    a. east or west of a principal meridian.
    b. north or south of a base line.
    c. Both *a* and *b*
    d. None of the above

119. A township contains

    a. 24 sections.
    b. 36 sections.
    c. 18 sections.
    d. 6 sections.

120. A tier is numbered to the

    a. east or west of a principal meridian.
    b. north or south of a base line.
    c. Both *a* and *b*
    d. None of the above

121. The NW¼ of the NE¼ of the SW¼ of Section 12 contains how many acres?

    a. 10
    b. 40
    c. 20
    d. 160

122. The horizontal distance between range lines is

    a. 6 miles.
    b. 24 miles.
    c. 4 miles.
    d. 1 mile.

123. Which of the following contains the smallest parcel of land?

    a. 640 acres
    b. 9 square miles
    c. ½ of a township
    d. 36 square miles

124. Which of the following contains the largest parcel of land?

    a. 2 miles square
    b. 2 sections
    c. 10 percent of a township
    d. 43,560 feet by 43,560 feet

Refer to Figures 1–4 on pages 179 and 180 to answer questions 125 to 131.

125. Section 11 in a township is

    a. north of section 14 and south of section 2.
    b. north of section 17 and south of section 5.
    c. due west of section 10.
    d. due south of section 14.

126. Section 2 in a township is directly south of what section of the township directly to its north?

    a. 32
    b. 35
    c. 15
    d. 10

127. Each side of a square acre contains approximately

    a. 208 feet.
    b. 215 feet.
    c. 320 feet.
    d. 230 feet.

128. How many acres are in the N½ of SE¼ of the SE¼ of a section of land?

    a. 20
    b. 32
    c. 8
    d. 6

129. How many townships are there in a piece of land 24 miles square?

    a. 16
    b. 8
    c. 24
    d. 32

130. The NE¼ of SW¼ of Section 8 contains

    a. 40 acres.   c. 80 acres.

    b. 160 acres.   d. 20 acres.

131. What is the shortest distance between the closest borders of Section 2 and Section 35 of the same township?

    a. 6 miles   c. 1 mile

    b. 4 miles   d. 24 miles

FIGURE 1

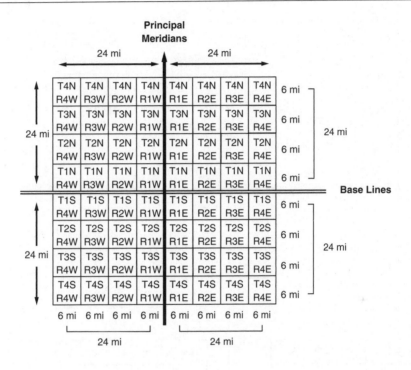

FIGURE 2

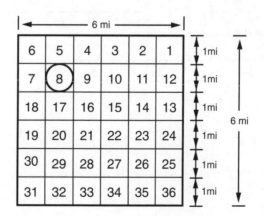

FIGURE 3

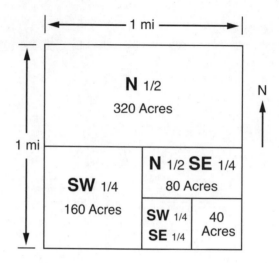

FIGURE 4

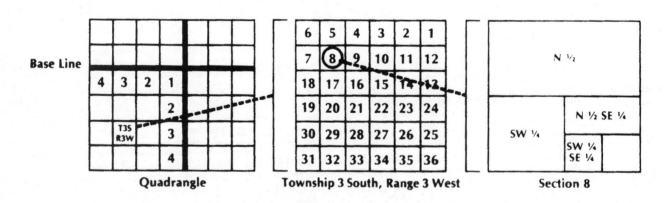

132. Which of the following is larger than a standard section?

    a. 16 parcels, 40 acres each
    b. 5,000 feet by 6,000 feet
    c. 1/36 of a township
    d. 5,280 feet by 5,280 feet

133. From a historical standpoint, the major function, objective, and aim of the FHA program have been provided by which of the following sections of the law?

    a. Title I
    b. Title II
    c. Title III
    d. Title II, 245 GPM

134. A partnership may take title to real property in the

    a. name of the partnership.
    b. individual names of one or more partners.
    c. name of a third party as trustee for the partnership.
    d. All of the above

135. All of the following are characteristics of an easement *EXCEPT* that it is

    a. an interest that can be protected against interference by third persons.
    b. capable of being created by a conveyance.
    c. considered as a nonpossessory interest.
    d. an interest that can be terminated at will by the possessor of the land.

136. The Real Estate Commissioner's Final Subdivision Public Report expires

    a. one year from date of report.
    b. never, unless a material change occurs.
    c. five years from date of issuance of report.
    d. when four or fewer lots remain to be sold.

137. Which of the following lenders would grant a lower loan-to-value ratio than other lenders?

    a. Savings and loans
    b. Insurance companies
    c. Mortgage companies
    d. Credit unions

138. The income approach would be used to appraise all of the following *EXCEPT*

    a. commercial retail properties.
    b. residences in a new subdivision.
    c. an industrial building on long-term lease.
    d. a neighborhood shopping center.

139. Urban industrial land is usually valued by

    a. front foot.
    b. square foot-acre.
    c. front foot-acre.
    d. None of the above

140. Which of the following parties would use a bench mark?

    a. An appraiser
    b. A surveyor
    c. An assessor
    d. A judge

141. Which of the following is a requirement for a deed to be valid and convey title?

    a. An acknowledgment
    b. Execution on a day of the week other than Sunday
    c. A property description
    d. Use of the phrase "to have and to hold"

142. Mr. David purchased a single-family residence and after moving into the dwelling, discovered that the roof eaves of his home come within two feet of his neighbor's property line. If the city zoning and building restriction required at least a five foot setback,

    a. the neighbor must adjust the property line.
    b. he would not be insured for any loss under a standard form policy of title insurance.
    c. he could not make an appeal for a variance to the local government body.
    d. the restriction cannot be enforced.

143. If prices decrease,

    a. the value of money increases.
    b. the value of money decreases.
    c. there is no effect on the value of money, as prices are not based on supply and demand.
    d. the monetary value of commodities increases.

144. Which of the following is correct with regard to townships and ranges?

    a. Ranges are numbered north and south from the base line.
    b. Township lines run east and west.
    c. Townships are numbered east and west from the principal meridian.
    d. Range lines run east and west.

145. A valid recorded homestead will not protect the homeowner against a foreclosure of a

    a. mortgage.
    b. trust deed.
    c. mechanic's lien.
    d. All of the above

146. Assuming that Able is a licensed real estate broker and Baker is a licensed real property securities dealer, which of the following is a correct statement?

    a. Baker may not sell out-of-state subdivision land as an agent for the owner of the land.
    b. Able may neither sell trust deeds to the public nor negotiate loans secured by real property.
    c. Able can perform any real estate acts that Baker can.
    d. Baker can perform any real estate acts that Able can.

147. A deed to real property located in Los Angeles County that is recorded in any other county of the state gives

    a. constructive notice in Los Angeles County.
    b. actual notice.
    c. constructive notice throughout the State of California.
    d. neither constructive notice nor actual notice.

148. A person who acquires real property through intestate succession does so as a result of

    a. a formal or witnessed will.
    b. a holographic will.
    c. a nuncupative will.
    d. direction of a probate court.

149. Of the following agreements, select the one that is not required to be in writing under the provisions of the statute of frauds.

    a. An agreement authorizing an agent to purchase or sell real estate for compensation

    b. An agreement that by its terms is not to be formed within a year of the making thereof

    c. A general partnership agreement to deal in real property

    d. An agreement for the leasing for a period of time longer than one year, or for the sale of real property or of an interest therein

150. In a business opportunity transaction the document that is used in the same manner as a trust deed in a real estate transaction is the

    a. financing statement.

    b. bill of sale.

    c. trust deed.

    d. security agreement.

■ ANSWER KEY

1. b. Once a lease expires but the landlord continues to accept the payment of rent, the relationship converts to what is called a *periodic tenancy*. In California, once the lease has expired yet rent continues to be paid, the relationship is clearly established as periodic tenancy.

2. d. Whenever a loan document allows for future additional advances without having to rewrite the loan instrument, the loan is referred to as an *open-end loan* or an *open-end trust deed*.

3. b. In the assumption of an existing loan, the party assuming becomes liable for the loan.

4. d. The question is asking for the exception. A promissory note is not an item that is recorded; the trust deed is recorded.

5. d. The cost approach formula states "land plus depreciated improvements is equal to the estimate of value." The procedure in the cost approach requires that the land valuation is arrived at by the market data approach. The value of the improvements is arrived at by determining the cost to replace and then allowing for accrued depreciation. Hence, separate approaches are used in the cost approach to estimating value.

6. b. The term *hypothecation* refers to using real property as security for a loan, yet retaining possession and rights thereto.

7. c. A junior lienholder may be successful in bringing about a foreclosure sale.

8. b. The question is asking for the exception. Choices *a, c,* and *d* are all examples of how the Federal Reserve System controls the flow of money in this country. It does not set the interest rate on govern-ment-guaranteed or insured loans. Other specific governmental agencies influence that decision, for example, FHA and VA.

9. d. The law of agency describes a fiduciary (a position of trust and confidentiality) relationship that exists between the real estate agent (broker) and the principal (owner).

10. b. Each title insurance company has the right to determine its own fee for services rendered.

11. b. An unlawful detainer action is the legal action a landlord seeks to remedy a default in rental payment.

12. b. If buyer and seller agree to release one another from the transaction and the seller instructs the broker to return any deposit received, then it is the broker's responsibility to follow the seller's instructions and return the deposit. Should the broker choose to sue the seller for the commission, the broker is entitled to do so, as the broker did the job that the seller hired the broker to do.

13. c. For a deed to become effective and transfer title, the deed must have a proper description of the property. True, there are other requirements, but choices *a, b,* and *d* are not any of those requirements. For the deed to be effective, it must be the intention of the grantor that the deed be delivered to the grantee. It is presumed delivered if either the deed is recorded or the grantee has possession of the document.

14. d. Look to the expression of buyer Sims paying commission to salesperson Pat. A salesperson cannot legally accept payment of commission from anyone other than

the salesperson's employing broker. Hence, the answer has to be "nothing."

15. b. Choices *a*, *c*, and *d* are all characteristics of fee simple absolute. The question is asking for the exception. The expression "a determinable fee" describes what is known as *fee simple defeasible*, which indicates some conditions are part of the transfer.

16. d. The question is asking for the exception. Choice *d* is correct as the receipt of any discounts on the purchase of supplies would be passed on directly to the owner of the building and not the property manager.

17. d. The question is asking for the correct statement. Without the ability to buy a commodity, value could not be easily determined.

18. d. Only the owner of the property can allow permission for a prospective purchaser of the property to move onto the property before escrow closes. That decision is not to be made by the broker in the transaction; it should be in the form of written consent.

19. d. The term *alienate* with reference to title means to transfer title. Customarily, that is done by the issuance of a grant deed.

20. b. There is a statutory requirement that there be an employment agreement between broker and salespersons; however, the Real Estate Commissioner is not required to approve of the format that is used for that agreement.

21. c. The question describes an exclusive authorization and right-to-sell listing. Such listing ensures that the broker will earn a commission whenever the property sells during the listing period, no matter

how the property sells. Even though the owner sold the property during the listing period without the broker's involvement, this kind of listing would pay a commission to the broker.

22. b. A writ of execution is a court order forcing the sale of property of a judgment debtor to satisfy a judgment. This is a postjudgment activity.

23. b. With reference to the documentary transfer tax in California, the rate of taxation is $.55 for each $500 of consideration, or for ease of calculation, $1.10 per $1,000 of the selling price. If there is an existing loan to be assumed by the buyer, then subtract the existing loan amount and tax the balance.

$150,000   selling price
− 25,000   existing loan
$125,000   subject to taxation

Take $125,000 times $1.10 per $1,000 equals $137.50. The answer is most nearly $138. Remember to subtract the existing loan from the sales price if it is to be taken over by the buyer. This tax is to apply only to new money created in the transaction.

24. b. The question asks for the exception. For example, underground sewer lines carry an easement by implication for use and are not visible on the inspection of the surface of the land. Hence, the use for an easement does not necessarily have to be visible.

25. a. Depreciation is defined as a loss in value due to any cause. This loss in value is subtracted from one's taxable income, thereby reducing the amount of taxable income, and is a form of tax shelter.

26. a. Under the statute of frauds, commission splits between brokers may be by oral agreement. Of course, in field practice it

would be preferred to put such an agreement into writing.

27. b.   An option agreement is merely a contract to keep an offer open.

28. a.   When a joint tenant does not sign for the debts of another joint tenant, then that surviving joint tenant is free of liability for the debts of the one who incurred such obligations solely. Because of the right of survivorship, the sister now takes the property free and clear of the debt incurred by the brother.

29. c.   Unlimited. Broker-made or arranged loans are not under usury laws.

30. c.   On a unit cost basis, a small house would cost more to build than a large house. The justification is that the small house would have the same initial construction costs of a larger house but simply utilize less space. Hence, a large house would cost on a unit cost basis, allowing for more space but with the same basic construction expenses.

31. b.   When a trust deed contains a subordination clause, it allows that trust deed to remain in a junior position. This would allow a construction loan to be granted, and construction loans are granted only if they can be recorded in the primary position. Hence, the future loan (probably the construction loan) on the property would have priority.

32. d.   Choices *a*, *b*, and *c* describe situations that would render a unit uninhabitable, thereby demonstrating what is known as *constructive eviction*. Such demonstration would justify a tenant's abandoning a property.

33. b.   Lowering the minimum reserve requirement of member banks increases the supply of money that member banks would have to make loans to members of the public.

34. d.   Choices *a*, *b*, and *c* are all examples of the exercise of police power.

35. b.   The question defines what is called a *sale-leaseback arrangement*. While there are several advantages to a sale-leaseback, the question asks for the most important of the advantages, which is to increase and free up any working capital that the business owner might have had tied up in the ownership of the real property.

36. b.   An injunction is a court order indicating that a violator is to stop the activity that is causing a problem to others and is to do so immediately.

37. c.   Currently an alienation clause, commonly known as a *due-on-sale clause*, is not allowed in an FHA-insured loan. This is currently a controversial subject, and that policy by FHA may change in the future.

38. b.   There is a total tax basis of $8,000 on the four lots the developer purchased ($2,000 apiece). The four lots are later sold for $10,000 each, totaling $40,000. Subtracting the tax basis of $8,000 total leaves a capital gain of $32,000 for tax purposes.

39. a.   As the depth of a lot increases beyond the typical lot depth, the value per front foot increases.

40. a.   Prior to issuing a title insurance policy, the title company investigates any and all documents and records available to it. Depending on the result of its search, it may or may not decide to issue a policy on a given piece of property.

41. c. Private mortgage insurance required by some lenders and to be paid for by borrowers is an example of what is called *loan default insurance*. With this type of protection, lenders are more inclined to make the higher loan-to-value ratios on single-family residential property.

42. a. While the lender beneficiary collects the payment of the mortgage insurance premium from the trustor (borrower), it is sent to the FHA. The receipt of the payment of this premium being paid by FHA borrowers across the country represents the bulk of the funds that cover the cost of the FHA program.

43. a. Lani has a legal right to enter the land and can proceed to drill on the land because of an implied right of entry that goes with a reservation of rights.

44. b. In California the minimum crawlspace requirement is 18 inches. Do not confuse with the requirement of 16 inches, which is the dimension for placement of vertical studs on center. The question here is discussing minimum required crawlspace.

45. c. Fannie Mae (the Federal National Mortgage Association) was created to buy up certain existing loans from lending institutions as a way to stabilize the mortgage marketplace. This activity allowed lenders to make more loans to consumers, thereby increasing the amount of housing credit available to the economy. Fannie Mae is not a lender and does not supervise public lending agencies, but rather is an investor.

46. a. There are 36 sections to a township. The numbering system for sections begins with Section 1 in the northeast corner of the township and proceeds from right to left, then left to right, in a back-and-forth fashion, ending up with Section 36 in the southeast corner. If you were to visualize two townships adjacent to each other using the numbering method just described, you would find that Section 13 would be due west of Section 18 *in the neighboring township*.

47. b. The expansion and contraction of the demand for residential housing is largely dependent on the cost and availability of the money supply in this country.

48. d. The question is asking for the exception. Choices *a*, *b*, and *c* will all have an effect on the final estimate of value in the appraisal process of an old family residential property.

49. d. Again, the question is asking for the exception. Because of the one unity of possession that exists in tenancy in common a tenant in common could occupy the land and not be legally obligated to make rental payments for the use of that land. Do not confuse this theoretical concept with the most practical occurrence in the field, which would probably cause rent to be paid to the other cotenant if only one tenant were to occupy the land.

50. d. Choices *a*, *b*, and *c* are all correct with reference to the payment of sales tax due on the sale of fixtures in a business opportunity.

51. a. Riparian rights extend to an owner of land that borders on a watercourse. Do not confuse with the rights of an owner of land that borders on a lake or ocean, which are not examples of a watercourse. If one has the right to access the water of a lake or an ocean, such rights are known as *littoral rights*. Do not confuse littoral rights with riparian rights, which refer to land bordering a watercourse, such as a river or stream.

52. b. The question asks, "In which of these instances is there a violation of law?" Choice *b* is a violation, because a real estate broker cannot do the escrow work of fellow brokers without being separately incorporated to do such work. Yet, a real estate broker can hold an escrow for a buyer or seller whom he or she has represented in a transaction.

53. b. The largest source of junior loans available today in the country is private investors. While savings and loan associations, commercial banks, and mortgage bankers will sometimes make junior loans, the bulk of their lending activity is found in the primary loan position. The primary loan position is a safer position for lenders, because if there is a foreclosure sale of the property, after deducting the costs and fees for this sale itself, the primary lender is paid ahead of any junior lienholders.

54. d. A survey of the property is not provided under a Standard Policy of Title Insurance.

55. d. Alliance Escrow Company should be used for escrow purposes because the seller accepted the buyer's offer, which stated Alliance Escrow Company would be used. Once the seller agreed to this condition, this agreement supersedes the information found in the listing agreement.

56. c. Life insurance companies like to buy up existing loans that are the more commonly found fully amortized loans. This type of an investment would ensure them many payments over a long period of time.

57. c. Multiply 1,980 feet by 1,980 feet which equals 3,920,400 square feet. Divide by 2 to give 1,960,200 square feet. Dividing by 43,560 (square feet in an acre) equals 45 acres in each parcel.

58. b. The Subdivision Map Act in California is enforced by local government and is concerned with the physical aspects of the subdivision.

59. a. The transaction is a land sales contract. In such a transaction the buyer is given the right of possession of the property but is not given a fee simple interest.

60. c. The term *footing* refers to the base or bottom of a foundation wall, pier, or column.

61. c. In tenancy in common, each tenant has separate title to an undivided interest and can dispose of such interest as he or she wishes without the consent of the other cotenants.

62. b. Of the choices given, if the city abandons the easement that had been conveyed, then the grantor may seek to have the land returned to him.

63. b. In the gross rent multiplier rule, the appraiser does not attempt to establish a separate value for the land. The appraiser attempts to seek fair market value of recently sold companies' income-producing property and will divide that figure by the economic annual gross rent for such property to arrive at a gross rent multiplier. The process of establishing a separate value for the land occurs when using the cost approach.

64. b. The seller is obligated to pay a commission on an open listing to only the broker who is the procuring cause. In this example, broker Lee is the one who brought in the buyer whose offer was accepted. There is no commission payment due to broker Rodriguez under an open listing.

65. d. A joint tenancy form of title taking can be created by a deed from those parties, as stated in choices *a*, *b*, and *c*.

66. c. Meridian lines run north and south. Township lines run east and west. Hence the Mt. Diablo meridian line runs north and south.

67. d. The question is asking for the exception. A trust deed or mortgage contract would not be a salable item because it is a security device. When a note is sold, for example, the trust deed or mortgage contract is assigned to the buyer of the note.

68. d. The least important factor in the appraisal of a site for commercial purposes would be the amenities of the property. Amenity-type properties would be more appropriately considered residential properties.

69. c. A lease is considered an encumbrance on real property. It is a possessory interest of the property. A homestead is a way to protect a certain amount of equity against unsecured creditors. A freehold estate describes the greatest interest one can have in the land. Neither the homestead nor the freehold estate would be considered an encumbrance.

70. d. The term *capitalization rates* is defined as the return on (such as interest) and the return of (depreciation recaptured) the investment. Capitalization refers to the process of expressing anticipated future benefits of ownership of income property in terms of dollars and discounting them to a present worth at a given rate. An appraiser attempts to determine a capitalization rate by taking the net operating income of recently sold similar income-producing properties and dividing that figure by the sales price to arrive at a given rate for that investment.

71. b. A "wraparound mortgage" is more formally known as an *all-inclusive trust deed* or *mortgage*. Out of the payments made to the seller of this property, the seller continues to make payments against an underlying existing loan on the property. A blanket encumbrance is used most often in subdivision activities. A real property sales contract is used in a sale of the property where a seller retains the legal title until the buyer completes the contract at a later date. A participation loan is one that is commonly made by an insurance company where the insurance company also acquires part ownership in the property as well as interest on the loan funds committed.

72. c. When a title company issues an ALTA policy, it covers risks that may occur as a result of the rights of parties in possession, such as tenants who may claim a lease with an option to purchase, and any off-record easements or unrecorded liens. The question asks for the exception. No title insurance policy will insure against the effects of zoning or zone changes.

73. a. The expression *effective age* indicates the apparent age of the property based on its observed condition. Hence, if the property is in better than average condition, the effective age would be less than the actual age of the property. Appraisers appraise property based on the effective age of property.

74. a. Statement of fact.

75. c. The simplest way to impose restrictions on a new subdivision would be to record the restrictions as legally required and then make reference to them in each subsequent deed as a unit in a subdivision

is sold. Commonly, these restrictions are recorded on a form called a *declaration of restrictions*, subsequently referred to in each transaction thereafter.

76. d. Choices *a, b,* and *c* could all occur against the real estate licensee who misrepresents a property to a buyer while acting as an agent for the seller.

77. b. Using monuments as a method to describe the land is the least desirable method because of the possibility of the destruction or the movement of a monument over the years. The use of monuments in land description is under the metes-and-bounds system.

78. d. Private deed restrictions may be imposed on real property by placing those restrictions (1) in a deed, (2) in a written agreement between two or more parties to the transaction, or (3) in the recorded declaration of restrictions.

79. b. The question is describing a land sales contract transaction. A buyer under a land sales contract may sell or assign his or her rights to another but remains primarily liable for the payment of a contract unless the contract seller's approval is obtained.

80. a. The purpose of the federal fair housing law is to provide fair housing opportunities for all throughout the United States, not specifically to just minorities, or to provide fair housing in California, or to eliminate unfair rent.

81. c. The vacancy rate attributable to a certain apartment building is usually a result of the supply of and demand for that kind of rental in that particular area.

82. a. An application, together with a proper fee, must be filed with the Department of Real Estate within one year after passing the qualifying examination.

83. a. The question is asking for the least likely example. Very likely the estimate of value for an old home in a commercial neighborhood would rest on the commercial zoning for the land as its primary focus of value.

84. c. If an employee of a corporation is working as a part of the corporation's sales staff, then such employee must also be licensed as either a real estate salesperson or broker. Whenever one is employed to do acts within real estate for compensation, either a salesperson's or broker's license is a requirement.

85. b. Take the monthly payment of $550 and subtract the amount applied to principal of $48.53, leaving a balance of $501.47. Multiply the $501.47 by 12 months of the year to total $6,017.04 annual interest. Divide the annual interest of $6,017.04 by $56,500 to equal 10.6 percent interest.

86. b. An exclusive-agency listing allows the owner to sell the property himself or herself without being liable for a commission. The amount of broker's commission is not set by law but by agreement between the parties. Agreements between brokers regarding the division of commission may be by oral agreement, as stated in the statute of frauds. There may be a situation where a broker recovers a commission even after the sale was consummated if a safety clause has been used.

87. a. If Mark were to assign the lease with an option to purchase to Mike, then Mike would now hold the option. The option would not be automatically canceled, and an assignment is a valid transaction.

88. b. An attachment is the legal seizure of the title to property by the court; it is an example of a lien and is a prejudgment activity.

89. d. Most appraisers are required to be licensed under the California Office of Real Estate Appraisers, not the Department of Real Estate; there is no residency requirement. According to the code of ethics subscribed to by most appraisers, the fee for the appraisal process cannot be based on a percentage of the appraised value.

90. b. A contract between the seller of a home and a real estate broker agreeing to list the property for sale wherein broker will use diligence in procuring such purchaser is known as a *bilateral* (two-sided) *executory contract*. The term *executory* means "to be done in the future," and the expression "a bilateral executory contract" is a way to define an exclusive right-to-sell listing agreement. The term *executed* means the work has already been done, which is not the case in a listing contract.

91. b. A bill of sale is used to transfer an interest in trade fixtures.

92. a. The broker who most likely has earned a commission is the one who has communicated the acceptance to the offeror (buyer). Do not confuse this with securing an acceptance to the offer. In real estate matters, there is no transaction until an acceptance has been communicated to the buyer (offeror).

93. c. A certified general license is required to appraise commercial property that has a value exceeding $290,000.

94. c. A balloon payment loan is one that has been only partially amortized (liquidated). This indicates that there will be a balance still due and owing on the loan.

95. d. Title insurance will not cover any losses due to a change in zoning ordinances, regulations, or plot plan.

96. a. The cost approach is used to appraise one-of-a-kind types of property, public service buildings, or new property.

97. c. An attorney-in-fact is one who has been given the power of attorney by another to sign on his or her behalf. An attorney-in-fact does not necessarily have to be an attorney at law.

98. b. A lease is a possessory interest in the land of another for a definite period of time but does not transfer title.

99. c. The question is asking for the primary concern of the lender—the credit characteristics of the applicants.

100. d. The expression *highest and best use* of the land is defined as that use resulting in the highest net income attributable to the land.

101. b. If the requirements of the Bulk Sales Law are not met, the creditor could move to unravel the sale between the seller and the buyer. The buyer would stand to lose any deposit monies presented into the escrow.

102. c. A bill of sale is used to transfer title to personal property items.

103. c. The maximum charge for a general liquor license that is up to and including five years of age is $6,000.

104. c. The Department of Alcoholic Control can issue an on-sale general license to a business located in the same area and doing business on a seasonal basis. The license is referred to as a *seasonal license*.

105. b. The creditor is protected by the publishing requirement of the Uniform Commercial Code's Bulk Sale provisions.

106. d. In a personal property loan transaction involving the sale of a business, a financing statement (do not confuse with financial statement) is filed with the Secretary of State in Sacramento. This document is used to give notice of who is the true extender of credit on that loan transaction. It is used to perfect the security agreement between the lender and the borrower.

107. b. A sublease transfers possession of the property from the original tenant to another tenant. It does not transfer ownership rights of the property.

108. a. Law requires that a copy of the structural pest report be given to the buyer if he or she requests it.

109. c. An acceleration clause in a note does not affect its negotiability (salability). In fact, it may enhance the desirability of the note.

110. b. Through the State Board of Equalization, successor's liability determines the collection of sales and use tax collected by a seller of a business and not turned in prior to the buyer's taking over the business. It is wise for the buyer of the business to obtain a "clearance receipt" from the State Board of Equalization indicating there are no taxes due from the seller before depositing all purchase funds into the seller's account.

111. b. The State Board of Equalization handles sales and use tax.

112. c. Sales do not show up on a balance sheet. Sales appear on the profit and loss statement under revenues. Both the balance sheet and the profit and loss statement make up a financial statement.

113. c. If no time period is specified for termination in the escrow instructions, a reasonable time period is allowed.

114. b. An acknowledgment (notarizing) is not a requirement for a bill of sale. The other three choices are customarily found on a bill of sale along with the seller's signature.

115. c. It is illegal to discriminate based on marital status. Requiring a cosigner because a prospective tenant is single is a violation of fair housing laws.

116. d. A security agreement is the security device used in a credit extension for personal property.

117. b. Meridians are the lines 24 miles apart running in a north-south direction that form the east-west sides of a quadrangle (since range lines are six miles apart, every fourth range line forms the side of a quadrangle).

118. a. Ranges are the land strips running in a north-south direction that lie to the east or west of the meridian. They are numbered starting at the meridian, with the numbers getting larger as they move to the east or west of that meridian.

119. b. There are 16 townships in a quadrangle and 36 sections in a township.

120. b. Tiers are the strips of land running in an east-west direction that lie to the north or south of a base line. They are numbered starting at the base line, with the numbers getting larger as they move to the north or south.

121. a. A section contains 640 acres. 640 acres × ¼ = 160 acres; 160 acres × ¼ = 40 acres; 40 acres × ¼ = 10 acres.

122. a. Each township is six horizontal miles across, or 24 miles across a quadrangle.

123. a. 640 acres = 1 square mile (1 section), and ½ of a township = 18 square miles.

124. a. Two miles square is equal to four square miles, or four sections.

125. a. See Figure 2.

126. b. See Figure 4.

127. a. 208^2 = 43,264. An acre equals 43,560 square feet.

128. a. See Figure 3.

129. a. See Figure 1.

130. a. See Figure 3.

131. b. See Figure 2.

132. b. All the other three choices equal one section.

133. b. The major function of FHA was to create loans for home purchasers. This has been actively provided for under Title II of the law.

134. d. California law allows a partnership to take title in any of the ways listed in choices *a*, *b*, and *c*.

135. d. The possessor of the land is the owner of the land but not the owner of the easement. The easement could be running across the land and cannot merely be terminated at the owner's will.

136. c. The final public report is good for five years. (Remember: final and five begin with the same letter.)

137. b. Insurance companies fund large commercial loans. They require a substantial down payment to minimize their risk.

138. b. Residential properties are commonly appraised by the sales comparison approach.

139. b. The square-foot or square-acre method is commonly used to appraise the value of industrial land of all types.

140. b. A bench mark is a permanent mark used by a surveyor to indicate property lines.

141. c. The deed must have an adequate property description. Acknowledgment is done for recording but is not a requirement for the validity of the deed.

142. b. Mr. David has problems but they will not be solved with the title insurance policy since the standard form only covers those matters of record. The standard form of a title policy does not cover unrecorded items, such as misplaced improvements or encroachments.

143. a. If prices decrease, then the dollar has a stronger purchasing power (i.e., you get more for your money).

144. b. Township lines run east and west: range lines run north and south. Ranges are numbered to the east and west of the meridian: townships are numbered north and south of the base line.

145. d. A homestead will protect against unsecured creditors but will not protect against loans or mechanics' liens against the property (because they are secured debts).

146. d. Both hold real estate licenses (which a real property securities dealer must have) and therefore can do the same real estate acts. Baker can also sell real property securities.

147. d. Recording a deed to real property in a county other than the county in which it is located does not give either constructive notice or actual notice.

148. d. Because the party died intestate (without a will), the distribution of the property is under the direction of the probate court according to the laws of the intestate succession.

149. c. General partnership agreements do not require a legal writing under the statute of frauds but it is strongly recommended.

150. d. A security agreement is used to secure a personal property loan.

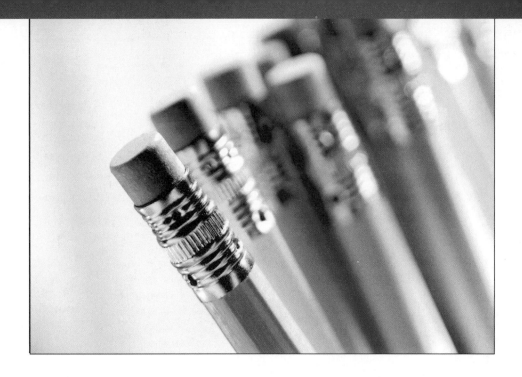

PRACTICE EXAMINATION VI

1. Broker Carter employs two salespersons to help in selling the property of Mr. Able. Salesperson One obtains an offer and a deposit on the property of Mr. Able. Salesperson Two also obtains an offer and a deposit on the same day as Salesperson One. Broker Carter does not tell Mr. Able of the second offer. He is waiting for the first offer to be rejected before telling of the second offer. This is

   a. permissible if the seller receives the better of the offers.
   b. permissible because broker Carter has fiduciary obligations to the buyer.
   c. not permissible because the broker must submit all offers.
   d. None of the above

2. Riparian rights of an owner refer to

   a. rivers and streams.
   b. subterranean caves.
   c. bays and arms of the sea.
   d. None of the above

3. Standard title insurance policies protect the insured from

   a. defects known to the insured that are not disclosed to the title insurance company.
   b. forgery in the chain of recorded title.
   c. zoning changes.
   d. All of the above

4. Who of the following may enter into a contract?

   a. Minors
   b. Aliens
   c. Convicts
   d. Children under the ward of the court

5. Successor's liability is set by the

   a. Franchise Tax Board.
   b. State Board of Equalization.
   c. Department of Corporations.
   d. Real Estate Commissioner.

6. If a licensee discriminates against a minority party, what action may the aggrieved party take?

   a. Collect punitive damages of no less than $250
   b. Collect actual and punitive damages
   c. Revoke and suspend the salesperson's license
   d. All of the above

7. Which of the following is a lien?

   a. Easement
   b. Trust deed
   c. Restriction
   d. None of the above

8. If an owner of a business opportunity wants to know if a sales tax is to be imposed on the sale of property of his business, which of the following should he consult?

   a. Franchise Tax Board
   b. State Board of Equalization
   c. Department of Corporations
   d. Real Estate Commissioner

9. Who may not terminate an agreement if a contract is not completed?

   a. Seller of residential property
   b. Buyer of an apartment building
   c. Attorney-in-fact representing a principal in a real estate transaction
   d. Broker representing the buyer

10. The primary cause for loss of value of property is

    a. tenant occupancy.
    b. obsolescence.
    c. incompetent management.
    d. deferred maintenance.

11. A lease for a definite period of years is

    a. real property.
    b. personal property.
    c. a freehold estate.
    d. None of the above

12. All of the following items are commonly found on a balance sheet EXCEPT

    a. goodwill.
    b. equipment used for deliveries.
    c. sales.
    d. prepaid expenses.

13. The tearing away or sudden loss of land by the action of water is known as

    a. accretion.   c. avulsion.
    b. accession.   d. alluvium.

14. Who would most likely use an unlawful detainer action?

    a. Trustor   c. Lessee
    b. Mortgagor   d. Lessor

15. In arriving at an estimate of value, which of the following would an appraiser be most interested in?

    a. The date the purchase agreement was signed
    b. The date of recordation of the grant deed
    c. The precise date of close of escrow
    d. The exact date and time the escrow was closed

16. In the event that no termination date of an escrow period is stated on the deposit receipt, how much time do the parties to the transaction have in which to complete the transaction?

    a. 30 days
    b. As long as they wish
    c. 60 days
    d. A reasonable time

17. Private restrictions for the use of land are created by

    a. private land use controls.
    b. written agreement.
    c. general plan restriction in subdivisions.
    d. All of the above

18. Mrs. Baker paid four points to the lender for a home loan. The lender then sold the mortgage to an insurance company for a 3.5 percent discount. The amount paid by the insurance company was $69,580. What was the original amount of the mortgage?

    a. $71,985.30   c. $71,103.63
    b. $73,363.20   d. $74,987.78

19. To perform the proper task of determining the worth of a certain parcel of real property as of a definite date, the appraiser makes a(n)

    a. determination of highest and best use.
    b. valuation.
    c. evaluation.
    d. None of the above

20. Of the following loans, which does not require a down payment unless demanded by a lender?

    a. FHA
    b. VA
    c. Cal-Vet
    d. All of the above

21. A lot contains 840 square yards and has a width of 45 feet. What is the depth of the lot?

    a. 18 feet   c. 168 feet
    b. 56 feet   d. 88 feet

22. There are no two parcels that are identical in size and features and consequently are nonsubstitutable; therefore, the courts use this basis to render their decision in

    a. a quiet title action.
    b. a lis pendens.
    c. an action for specific performance.
    d. decrees of partition.

23. A road with a total area of three acres runs along the southern boundary of a section. Of the following, which is most nearly the width of the road?

    a. 25 feet   c. 45 feet
    b. 35 feet   d. 55 feet

24. The builder's plan that indicates the piers, footing, and columns within a structure is known as the

    a. floor plan.
    b. plot plan.
    c. foundation plan.
    d. elevation plan.

25. The expression TTIP refers to

    a. divided interest.
    b. possession.
    c. right of survivorship.
    d. All of the above

26. If the cost of construction increases by 20 percent, what will be the percentage of loss in the value of the dollar?

    a. 20 percent   c. 16⅔ percent
    b. 25 percent   d. 83⅓ percent

27. Easements cannot be terminated by

    a. prescription by the owner of the servient tenement.
    b. release by the owner of the dominant tenement.
    c. revocation by the owner of the servient tenement.
    d. merger of the dominant and servient tenements.

28. When a buyer receives a commitment from a lender to provide loan funds to the buyer if needed, this type of loan is called a(n)

    a. standby loan.
    b. on demand loan.
    c. obligatory advance.
    d. conditional commitment.

29. In which of the following groups of terms is there an incorrectly spelled word?

    a. Tenement, forfeiture, obsolescence, encumbance
    b. Acknowledgment, jurisdiction, judgment, hypothecate
    c. Accommodate, appurtenance, amenities, alluvium
    d. Prescription, riparian, subordinate, subrogation

30. Mr. Johnson purchases a $200,000 property with 25 percent down and executes a first trust deed and note on the balance. During the next 10 years, the property doubles in value. Disregarding payments on the loan and all other variables, Mr. Johnson's initial investment is now worth

    a. $300,000.   c. $250,000.
    b. $200,000.   d. $100,000.

31. An appraiser is preparing a report on a house that has an actual age of 10 years. Because the house had been very well maintained, she assigns an age of only five years. This is known as _____ age.

    a. economic   c. effective
    b. physical   d. chronological

32. The term *warehousing* as used in real estate financing refers to

    a. subdivisions.
    b. trust deed foreclosures.
    c. mortgage portfolios.
    d. impound accounts.

33. An appraiser is asked to report on the economic feasibility of an addition of a swimming pool to a condominium project. In his valuation process, which principle would he refer to with respect to the pool?

    a. Supply and demand
    b. Contribution
    c. Progression
    d. Change

34. The parties to an existing contract agreed to its replacement by an entirely new contract substituting a different party for one of the principals. This is an example of

    a. subrogation.   c. novation.
    b. assignment.   d. rescission.

35. The type of roof that has four slopes rising to the ridge board is called a

    a. mansard.   c. gable.
    b. hip.   d. gambrel.

36. A strong indicator that the exchange value of the dollar has declined would be

    a. fewer capital investments.
    b. less credit has been made available and fewer dollars are in circulation.
    c. the cost of living index has risen significantly.
    d. prices have fallen overall.

37. If you were to visit a title plant, what would you find?

    a. Title insurance policies
    b. Grant deeds
    c. A collection of real estate records
    d. None of the above

38. In a "subject to" takeover, who remains responsible for the loan?

    a. Lender
    b. Buyer
    c. Seller
    d. None of the above

39. A valid grant deed vests title in the grantee at the time the deed is

    a. acknowledged.   c. recorded.
    b. signed.   d. delivered.

40. Of the following, which would most likely provide the investor with the best hedge against inflation?

    a. Savings account
    b. Government bonds
    c. Real property
    d. A note secured by a trust deed

41. When a seller of real property and a real estate licensee enter into a contract wherein the seller promises to pay a commission if the licensee procures a "ready, willing, and able" buyer and the licensee promises to use "diligence" in procuring a purchaser, what type of contract do they have?

    a. Bilateral executed contract
    b. Bilateral executory contract
    c. Unilateral executed contract
    d. Unilateral executory contract

42. Of the following, which is the superior lien or that which has first priority?

    a. 1911 Assessment Bond
    b. Homestead
    c. First trust deed
    d. Whichever was the first to be recorded

43. If a Cal-Vet loan is paid off within the first five years, what is the prepayment penalty, if any?

    a. 6 percent
    b. 2 percent
    c. Six months' interest if more than 20 percent of the loan is paid in each year of the first five years
    d. There is no prepayment penalty.

44. The Subdivision Map Act

    a. requires that a subdivider dedicate 10 percent of the area for recreational purposes.
    b. requires that a subdivider file a subdivision map with the California Department of Real Estate.
    c. is regulated by city and county planning commissions, and they standardize the regulations that govern subdivisions.
    d. is regulated by the Real Estate Commissioner.

45. Of the following, which entity enforces the state housing law?

    a. Real Estate Commissioner
    b. Corporations Commissioner
    c. State Contractor's License Board
    d. Local building inspector

46. The following description, "an estate in real property, which consists of an undivided interest in common in a portion of a parcel in real property, together with a separate interest in the space in a residential, industrial, or commercial building," is a partial definition of a

    a. stock cooperative.
    b. community apartment.
    c. condominium.
    d. planned development.

47. Functional obsolescence would not occur due to

    a. outside nuisances.
    b. massive cornices.
    c. a poorly designed floor plan.
    d. old-fashioned plumbing fixtures.

48. In a closing statement, there are debits and credits. In a seller's closing statement, which of the following would be considered a debit?

    a. Sale of personal property
    b. Prepaid rent by a tenant of seller
    c. Prepaid taxes by seller
    d. Prepaid insurance premiums

49. A loss in value due to the over-improvement of a house in as lesser neighborhood is an example of the principle of

    a. progression.
    b. regression.
    c. nonconformity.
    d. supply and demand.

50. The expression MPR is established by FHA and applies to loans FHA insures. MPR stands for

    a. maximum property requirements.
    b. minimum property requirements.
    c. mortgage property ratios.
    d. mortgage price ratios.

51. You are given the following information: straight-line income premise; 40 years remaining economic life; 11 percent interest rate. With this information, what will be the capitalization rate that is used to find the indicated building value?

    a. 2½ percent   c. 11 percent
    b. 8 percent   d. 13½ percent

52. From the following, select the legal meaning of the term *waiver* as it is most closely related to a real estate transaction.

    a. A unilateral act by one with its legal consequences
    b. One's act based on reliance on someone else's promise
    c. One's act based on reliance on some facts
    d. Estoppel

53. To arrive at value, on which type of property are amenities most often used?

    a. Public service buildings
    b. Income property
    c. Residential property
    d. All of the above

54. A fictitious business name statement, when filed in the office of the county clerk, is good

    a. for five years from December 31 of the year in which it was filed.
    b. for 10 years from July 1.
    c. annually.
    d. only when abandoned.

55. With reference to the cost approach, the value of improvements such as sidewalks, special landscaping, and concrete driveway are considered by the appraiser

    a. singly.
    b. jointly.
    c. as part of land value.
    d. as part of building value.

56. Of the following entities, which deals with "passthrough" securities?

    a. Ginnie Mae
    b. Fannie Mae
    c. Private investors and mortgage bankers
    d. All of the above

57. What rate of capital turnover would best describe a real estate transaction?

    a. Rapid by comparison with stocks
    b. Average by comparison with commodities
    c. Slightly below average by comparison with other commodities
    d. Slow by comparison with most other investments

58. Of the following, which is most active in buying and selling government securities?

    a. The Securities and Exchange Commission
    b. The Federal Trade Commission
    c. The Federal Open Market Committee
    d. None of the above

59. Select the best description of a "blind pool."

    a. A real estate trustee not yet knowing how many properties are to be purchased
    b. A form of syndication
    c. Limited partnerships
    d. Corporations

60. There are some instances in which the building code requirements of local government and the State of California differ from each other. Should this occur, which of the agency's requirements will take precedence?

    a. Local government
    b. The State of California
    c. The one that provides the highest degree of safety
    d. None of the above

61. When a flood hazard is found to exist, the flood hazard report will indicate the degree of frequency of such hazard. What are the three degrees of flood hazard?

    a. Water table, surface water, ponding
    b. Frequent, infrequent, rare
    c. Inundation, sheeting, and ponding
    d. None of the above

62. A real estate broker is responsible for the activities of the sales staff. Of the following, who has the authority to review and sign contracts on behalf of the broker?

    a. An individual who has accrued two years' full-time experience as a salesperson in the past five years
    b. An individual who has accrued two years' experience as a salesperson in the past five years with the same broker
    c. Anyone in the office as long as he or she is a licensed real estate salesperson
    d. None of the above

63. The California sales tax is a(n)

    a. ad valorem tax.
    b. tax charged on the sale of real and personal property.
    c. tax charged on the sale of tangible personal property.
    d. tax charged on the sale of stocks and debentures.

64. With reference to an unlocated easement, it is

    a. valid.
    b. void.
    c. invalid because it is not located.
    d. None of the above

65. According to the federal Truth-in-Lending Act (Regulation Z), all of the following would be wrong in advertising *EXCEPT*

    a. "assume a 7¾ percent mortgage loan."
    b. "take over a 7¾ percent annual interest rate loan."
    c. "assume a 7¾ percent annual percentage rate mortgage."
    d. All of the above

66. The use of "boot" is usually associated with the exchange of real property. The term boot may include

    a. notes and trust deeds.
    b. cars and jewelry.
    c. personal property.
    d. All of the above

67. The clearly stated policy of the California Real Estate Commissioner is to create a "color-blind" industry in which society can contribute to an environment of voluntary equal opportunity in fair housing. From the following, select the best interpretation of color-blind.

    a. Maintain an attitude that is actually free from bias and color-blind to appearance
    b. Race, creed, or color is not a material fact in real estate transactions
    c. Do unto others as you would have them do unto you
    d. All of the above

68. A lien is a money encumbrance. Which of the following liens does not need to be recorded?

    a. A money judgment
    b. A tax deed
    c. Real estate taxes
    d. A voluntary lien

69. Smith owns a grocery store that has existed for some time in an undeveloped area. Later, the area is zoned for single-family residential usage. If the grocery store is permitted to continue to operate, such permission would be an example of

    a. split-space zoning.
    b. down-space zoning.
    c. nonconforming space use.
    d. exclusive zoning.

70. With reference to bankruptcy claims, such claims are effective

    a. from the date of publication of the notice of bankruptcy in the newspaper.
    b. from the date of filing for the bankruptcy.
    c. for seven years.
    d. None of the above

71. With reference to an all-inclusive note and deed of trust, which of the following is most correct?

    a. The trustor is required to discharge all prior loans.
    b. The face amount of the loan does not include amounts of any senior loans.
    c. The beneficiary, by instructions in the note, must continue to make payments as they become due on any senior loans.
    d. This type of financing is recommended when the buyer wants to avoid the acceleration of the underlying loan due to an alienation clause.

72. Mr. Able dies intestate. His separate property is divided between his wife and two children as follows:

    a. ⅔ to his wife and ⅓ to his children.
    b. ½ to his wife and ½ to his children.
    c. ⅓ to his wife and ⅓ to each child.
    d. Property goes to his wife as community property.

73. If no notice of completion has been recorded, how many days are allowed in which to file for a mechanic's lien?

    a. 60 days   c. 90 days
    b. 30 days   d. 10 days

74. Examples of private restrictions would be conditions, covenants, and restrictions. How would one stop a violation of private restrictions?

    a. A desist and refrain order
    b. An injunction
    c. Junction
    d. Decrees of partition

75. If there is an alleged violation of the law under the federal fair housing law, a complaint must be filed within

    a. 60 days from occurrence.
    b. 90 days from occurrence.
    c. 180 days from occurrence.
    d. one year from occurrence.

76. Mortgage bankers, sometimes referred to as *loan correspondents*, often make direct loans to customers. These loans are

    a. kept in their own portfolio.
    b. sold to FHA/VA.
    c. sold to the secondary market.
    d. sold at a premium.

77. When called to appraise property, which of the following becomes the appraiser's primary concern in the analysis of residential property?

    a. Marketability and acceptability
    b. Square-foot area
    c. Functional utility
    d. Fixed and operating expenses

78. Frame construction, the parallel wooden members that support floors and ceilings are called

    a. joists.   c. footings.
    b. studs.   d. header.

79. Sometimes during the escrow period a dispute might arise between the seller and buyer, which, if remaining unresolved, could stop the closing of escrow. What action may the escrow holder take?

    a. Cancel the escrow and return all monies to the party
    b. Act as an arbitrator
    c. File an interpleader action in court
    d. All of the above

80. Owner Brown employs broker Jones to try to locate and arrange for a $200,000, 25-year loan on Brown's four-unit apartment building to refinance an existing high interest rate loan secured by a first trust deed and loan. Brown did not live in the building. Of the following, which is applicable under the Truth-in-Lending Act (Regulation Z)?

    a. If the loan is up to $200,000, apartment buildings containing four or more units are exempt from the provision of the Truth-in-Lending Act.
    b. A disclosure statement is required only from the lender and not the broker.
    c. The loan is not made for consumer credit and is exempt from the provisions of the Truth-in-Lending Act. A disclosure statement need not be given unless the owner lives in the building.
    d. The broker must provide Brown with a truth-in-lending statement.

81. An estate of inheritance is a(n)

    a. estate in fee.
    b. fee simple defeasible.
    c. life estate.
    d. estate for years.

82. A bearing wall

    a. can be at any angle to the doorway.
    b. is usually built stronger than any other interior walls.
    c. is usually left undisturbed when remodeling.
    d. All of the above

83. A father has a property put into the names of his three sons, Albert, Carl, and Bill, as joint tenants. Bill sells his interest to Wes. Then later, Albert dies. Albert's sole heir was his son Steve. How is title held?

    a. Steve owns ⅓ interest as a tenant in common.
    b. Carl owns ⅔ interest with Wes as a tenant in common.
    c. Ownership must be established by probate.
    d. None of the above

84. An escrow closed on May 1, 2000. Property taxes for the fiscal year 2000-2001 are

    a. the seller's personal responsibility.
    b. the buyer's personal responsibility.
    c. a lien on the property.
    d. None of the above

85. With reference to a real property sales contract, who holds equitable title?

    a. Vendee   c. Trustee
    b. Vendor   d. Beneficiary

86. With reference to a closing statement, the balance on both the buyer's and seller's statement

    a. must be different.
    b. can be different.
    c. must be the same.
    d. None of the above

87. When a buyer mortgages a home, she is the

    a. mortgagor.   c. trustee.
    b. mortgagee.   d. vendee.

88. There is a legal requirement that any person acquiring an interest in real property or a mobile home subject to local property taxation file a change of ownership statement with the county recorder or assessor. The change in ownership statement must be filed within

    a. 15 days.   c. 45 days.
    b. 30 days.   d. 90 days.

89. The appreciation accruing to a mortgaged home is to the benefit of the

    a. trustee.
    b. beneficiary.
    c. trustor.
    d. None of the above

90. Mr. Martin has an easement over Mr. Ross's property. However, Mr. Martin owns no land. What type of easement is this?

    a. Restricted easement
    b. Appurtenant easement
    c. Easement in gross
    d. A nonpossessory interest

91. Ms. Smith paid $14,000 down to Ms. Jones for her property. Ms. Smith then executes a purchase money trust deed in favor of Ms. Jones for the remaining balance. From whom did she get the money?

    a. A friend
    b. Ms. Jones
    c. An institutional lender
    d. All of the above

92. What is the value of a four-unit residential apartment building that rents for $206.25 per month per unit? The vacancy factor and uncollectible rents amount to 5 percent of the annual gross income. The annual expenses on the property total $4,140. The net operating income is capitalized at 8 percent. What is the value?

    a. $65,812.50   c. $71,384.25
    b. $68,400   d. $72,000

93. Mr. Able is leasing property from Mr. Baker for a period of 15 years. Charles, who is the owner of the house next door, wants an easement from Mr. Able.

    a. Able could give the easement.
    b. Able cannot give the easement, as only the owner has this right.
    c. Able can grant the easement, but only for the term of his lease.
    d. The easement can be granted only when the lease expires.

94. Under the Truth-in-Lending Act (Regulation Z), there is a right of rescission until midnight of the third business day following

    a. consummation of the transaction.
    b. delivery of all material disclosures.
    c. delivery of the notice of the right to rescind.
    d. the last of the above events to occur.

95. A brother and sister may take title in

    a. joint tenancy.
    b. tenancy in common.
    c. fee simple.
    d. All of the above

96. Mr. Green sold his house for $33,700, which was 7 percent less than he bought it for. If he could have sold the house without suffering the 7 percent loss, what would have been his selling price?

    a. $36,237   c. $31,272
    b. $36,090   d. $31,751

97. How many square miles are there in a section?

    a. 1
    b. 36
    c. 6
    d. None of the above

98. Who may investigate the records of the county recorder's office?

    a. Bank clerks
    b. Employees of the county assessor's office
    c. Private individuals
    d. All of the above

99. An investor purchased a $5,000 1911 Street Improvement Bond that paid 6 percent interest. If the investor is in a 28 percent tax bracket and a 5 percent state income tax bracket, the yield would be most nearly equal to which of the following investments?

    a. $9,000 savings account paying 5 percent interest
    b. $7,000 savings account paying 6 percent interest
    c. Income property paying $300 per month
    d. Preferred stock paying $300 per year

100. For purposes of advertising, which of the following are considered the four elements of successful advertising?

    a. Attract attention, arouse interest, create desire, promote the manufacturer
    b. Attract attention, promote the product, arouse interest, stimulate action
    c. Promote the manufacturer, arouse interest, create desire, stimulate action
    d. Attract attention, arouse interest, create desire, stimulate action

101. All of the following are correct assumptions about the formation of financial statements, *EXCEPT*

    a. assets minus liabilities equals net worth.
    b. assets minus expense equals net profit.
    c. assets equal liabilities plus net worth.
    d. expenses plus net profit equals gross income.

102. A contract for the sale of community real property signed by the husband only is

    a. valid.   c. illegal.
    b. voidable.   d. void.

103. A person who hires real property from the owner and is given the exclusive right to use it is known as a

    a. tenant.
    b. licensee.
    c. lodger.
    d. None of the above

104. The five requisites for a valid land contract are

    a. legality, capacity of the parties, mutuality, offer/acceptance, and writing.
    b. consideration, offer/acceptance, mutuality, capacity of the parties, and writing.
    c. mutuality, consideration, offer/acceptance, legality, and legal object.
    d. consideration, offer/acceptance, legality, capacity of the parties, and writing.

105. An appraiser was engaged to make an appraisal of a single-family residence. She decided to subtract a certain amount of value because of functional obsolescence. To which of the following was she referring?

    a. Dry rot
    b. Poor neighborhood
    c. Zoning
    d. Single-car garage

106. Which of the following circumstances might cause a loss in value that would be considered economic obsolescence?

    a. Poorly landscaped and cared for yard
    b. Excessively high property taxes
    c. Termites
    d. Massive cornices

107. As applied to real estate practice, an estate

    a. can be transferred only by grant.
    b. will always be passed on to heirs or to the estate by escheat on death of owner.
    c. always includes right of possession by owner.
    d. can exist with another estate in the same property at the same time.

108. Harris used a one-lane road to get to his mountain cabin. One day he found the road blocked by a chain across the road with a lock. This action by his neighbor probably had to do with which of the following?

    a. Easements by prescription
    b. Restrictions
    c. Insurance
    d. Eminent domain

109. A sublessor is one who

    a. assigns one's rights and duties for the unexpired term of the lease.
    b. transfers one's rights but not duties with right of return if the terms are breached.
    c. assigns one's duties with right of return if the terms are breached.
    d. assigns and records a short-form lease containing terms and conditions of the new lease.

110. A court order directing the sheriff to seize the property of a defendant as security for a legal action is known as a

    a. writ of attachment.
    b. writ of execution.
    c. foreclosure proceeding.
    d. probate.

111. The one similarity between a joint tenancy and tenancy in common is

    a. equal right of possession.
    b. right of survivorship.
    c. equal interest of all owners.
    d. tenant in possession can be charged rent for the use of the land.

112. A new well and pump are installed on a vacant parcel of land. For assessment purposes, the tax assessor considers these as

    a. improvements.
    b. additions.
    c. part of the land value.
    d. personal property.

113. A homestead recorded under California law may be invalidated by

    a. moving to another state.
    b. leasing the property.
    c. destruction of the home by fire.
    d. a prior homestead on another property.

114. Which of the following instruments require a listing or an inventory of the main buildings on real property being conveyed, sold, or insured?

    a. A grant deed
    b. A land contract of sale
    c. A CLTA policy of title insurance
    d. None of the above

115. As a general rule, which of the following sources would be least satisfactory in providing a legal description for a parcel of real property?

    a. Deeds
    b. Preliminary title reports
    c. Policies of title insurance
    d. Bills for real property taxes

116. In Title VIII of the Civil Rights Act of 1968, Congress declared a national policy providing fair housing throughout the United States. This policy applies to which of the following?

    a. Single-family dwelling, owned by private individuals who also own more than three such dwellings
    b. Multifamily dwelling of six units where the owner occupies one such unit as his or her residence
    c. Individually owned single-family residence offered for sale through a real estate broker
    d. All of the above

117. When estimating the loss in value due to depreciation, the real estate appraiser would primarily be concerned with

    a. economic life.
    b. actual age.
    c. chronological age.
    d. remaining life.

118. Effective gross income is the

    a. spendable income after taxes.
    b. gross income minus allowable expenses and payments of principal and interest.
    c. gross income minus a vacancy factor.
    d. gross income minus allowable expenses and depreciation.

119. A real estate appraisal is an estimate of value

    a. based upon replacement costs.
    b. based upon analysis of facts as of a specific date.
    c. derived from income data covering at least the preceding three months.
    d. None of the above

120. An increase in the appraised value of property that is considered an unearned increment would most probably result from

    a. an increase in population.
    b. capital improvements.
    c. the owner's decision to remodel.
    d. an increase in amenities.

121. A $200,000 house having been built among $75,000 to $100,000 homes would eventually seek the level of value of the surrounding homes. The principle of appraisal that best describes the influence on the value of the $200,000 house is

    a. balance.
    b. contribution.
    c. regression.
    d. anticipation.

122. An appraiser is preparing the income approach for an appraisal of income property. In his selection of a capitalization rate used, the higher the implied _____, the higher the capitalization rate.

    a. income   c. risk
    b. appreciation   d. value

123. An easement

    a. is a possessory interest in the dominant tenement.
    b. can be terminated with a merger of the dominant and servient tenement.
    c. can be created only by a deed.
    d. can be distinguished from a license because a license is a nonpossessory interest.

124. Which of the following appraisal methods would not be used by an appraiser in arriving at the cost of a new building?

    a. Observed condition
    b. Unit cost in place
    c. Quantity survey
    d. Comparison

125. When subdivisions are developed, subdividers place certain restrictions on each of the lots. Of these, experience has shown which of the following is least likely to be enforced?

    a. Minimum size for each lot
    b. Minimum limits on the amount of dollars allowed for improvements on each lot
    c. Minimum limits on the square footage of each home
    d. Limitations on the number of stories or total height of structures

126. Which of the following approaches to value tends to set the upper limit of value?

    a. Sales comparison
    b. Replacement cost
    c. Income approach
    d. Comparable sales method

127. The U.S. Attorney General would act to enforce the federal open housing law whenever

    a. state statutes are not enforced by the state officials.
    b. a conspiracy exists to practice resistance to the federal open housing law.
    c. a complaint is filed with the Secretary of HUD.
    d. the subject matter of a complaint filed by an aggrieved party indicates a violation by an owner of more than four units.

128. Which of the following would least likely cause title to real property to be unmarketable?

    a. Private restrictions contained in a deed
    b. Public restrictions contained in zoning ordinances and building codes
    c. A lis pendens
    d. A mechanic's lien

129. The lending institution that is permitted by law to offer the longest pay-off period on a conventional loan is the

    a. mutual savings bank.
    b. insurance company.
    c. savings and loan association.
    d. commercial bank.

130. In a lease, the leasehold interest lies in the

    a. lessor.   c. reversioner.
    b. lessee.   d. beneficiary.

131. For appraisal purposes a home is measured from

    a. outside measurements of house and garage.
    b. inside measurements of house as a whole.
    c. inside measurements of each room.
    d. outside measurements of house as a whole.

132. A homeowner can deduct a portion of which of the following as an expense for income tax purposes?

    a. Remodeling
    b. Painting a bedroom
    c. Depreciation
    d. Interest on the home loan

133. An intelligent investor would be concerned about his or her income taxes

    a. after purchasing property.
    b. at the time the first income is received.
    c. after the sale.
    d. before considering purchase.

134. The original cost basis can be adjusted by which of the following costs?

    a. Applicable closing costs
    b. Sales costs
    c. Capital improvements
    d. All of the above

135. In obtaining an FHA loan, each of the following is true EXCEPT

    a. FHA guarantees the loan.
    b. the customer must qualify.
    c. the loan is obtained through a lending institution.
    d. property must meet certain standards.

136. Closing costs are divided into two major areas, recurring and nonrecurring costs. Which of the following is a nonrecurring closing cost?

    a. Real property tax proration
    b. Hazard insurance premium
    c. Interest on new real estate loan
    d. Title insurance fee

137. Which of these types of title insurance is usually required by a lender?

    a. A CLTA policy
    b. An ALTA owner's policy
    c. A standard title policy
    d. An ALTA lender's policy

138. A purchaser may withdraw an offer to purchase

    a. only with the seller's permission.
    b. at any time prior to acceptance by the seller and communication of acceptance to the buyer.
    c. only if the broker agrees.
    d. if he or she signs an agreement to forfeit any deposit.

139. An agency relationship may be terminated by

    a. expiration of the term.
    b. death of the agent.
    c. agreement.
    d. All of the above

140. An agency relationship may be created by

    a. agreement.
    b. ratification.
    c. estoppel.
    d. All of the above

141. Nondisclosure of a dual agency by a broker can result in

    a. contract rescission.
    b. loss of commission.
    c. disciplinary action.
    d. Any of the above

142. A material fact that must be disclosed to a purchaser would include all the following *EXCEPT*

    a. a leaky roof.
    b. a septic tank.
    c. the racial composition of the neighborhood.
    d. plans for a nearby freeway.

143. The individual for whom a licensee acts is known as a(n)

    a. broker.   c. principal.
    b. employee.   d. agent.

144. A license may be suspended for which of the following reasons?

    a. Acting for more than one party without the consent of each
    b. Making any secret profit
    c. Dereliction of duty
    d. All of the above

145. A real estate broker who employs salespersons must execute a written agreement with each one. The agreement must show the

    a. amount and type of supervision to be exercised by the broker.
    b. compensation to be paid.
    c. duties of the parties.
    d. All of the above

146. A real estate agent is under a duty to use which of the following in the performance of his duties?

    a. Care
    b. Skill
    c. Diligence
    d. All of the above

147. A REALTOR® is defined as

    a. anyone licensed as a real estate agent.
    b. a member of a real estate board affiliated with NAR.
    c. any licensed real estate partnership.
    d. any person licensed under federal law.

148. A real estate broker should regard himself as a

    a. fiduciary.
    b. substitute for an attorney.
    c. legal adviser.
    d. None of the above

149. The AIDA approach to real estate advertising includes which one of the following?

    a. Interest
    b. Attention
    c. Desire and action
    d. All of the above

150. A method of selling investment property that allows the taxpayer to spread any gain realized over a period of years is called a(n)

    a. installment sale.
    b. sale-leaseback.
    c. tax-deferred exchange.
    d. None of the above

■ ANSWER KEY

1. c. The law of agency requires that all offers be submitted to the owner. The broker cannot withhold offers. The fiduciary relationship exists between the broker and the seller, yet the broker must be "honest and fair" to the buyer.

2. a. Riparian rights refer to the access rights of property owners adjacent to a moving body of water (i.e., a watercourse). Do not confuse with littoral rights, which are those affecting property adjacent to an ocean, lake, or pond.

3. b. Forgery is one of several items covered by the CLTA standard title policy. There is no title company that would protect against zoning or known defects.

4. b. There is virtually no restriction against aliens in the purchasing of property in California. The other choices are examples of those who are incompetent with reference to the ability to contract.

5. b. Through the State Board of Equalization, successor's liability is imposed with reference to the collection of sales and use tax collected by a seller of a business and not turned over to the state before the business's buyer takes over. It is wise for the buyer of the business to obtain a "clearance receipt" from the State Board of Equalization indicating there are no taxes due from the seller before depositing all purchase funds into the seller's account.

6. b. Actual and punitive damages are possible through the proper court action by the injured party. Only the Real Estate Commissioner can revoke or suspend one's license, not the court or an individual.

7. b. A trust deed is an example of a voluntary lien. While an easement and a restriction are also examples of forms of encumbrances, they are not liens. Liens are money encumbrances.

8. b. The State Board of Equalization handles matters of sales and use tax.

9. d. A broker cannot move to terminate a contract in which the broker is representing others. Only the principals to the contract can move to take such action.

10. b. Obsolescence is the primary cause for loss in value due to reduced desirability and usefulness of a structure as its design and construction become obsolete. It may be due to functional or economic obsolescence.

11. b. A lease is an example of a "chattel real"—an interest in real property but still only a form of personal property, meaning the contract itself is a movable item.

12. c. Sales do not show up on a balance sheet. Sales appear on the profit and loss statement under revenues. Both the balance sheet and the profit and loss statement make up a financial statement.

13. c. Avulsion refers to a sudden loss of property due to violent action of the water, such as flooding conditions.

14. d. An unlawful detainer action is the court action a landlord (lessor) might choose to take to legally remove a tenant who has defaulted in rental payment.

15. a. The date the purchase agreement was signed reflects the value the buyer and seller agreed on, which was probably influenced by market conditions of that date.

16. d. When a specific time period is not indicated for an escrow period, a "reasonable time" is allowed. Of course, it is preferred to state a specific time to minimize the possibility of misunderstanding between the parties.

17. d. Private restrictions can be created by all choices presented.

18. c. When calculating the face amount of a note, first take 100 percent and subtract the discount amount paid. Then divide the purchase price of the note by the remainder. 100% – 3.5% = 96.5%. Divide $69,580 by .965 = $72,103.63. Disregard the fact that four points were paid for the loan. Points represent a one-time charge by a lender for the loan and do not affect the amount of the loan or the face amount of the note.

19. b. An appraisal is a "valuation" process, not an evaluation. A determination of highest and best use is merely one of the many steps in the appraisal process.

20. b. The VA loan guarantee program does not require a down payment unless the lender requires it of the borrower. Both FHA and Cal-Vet require down payments.

21. c. 840 square yards times 9 square feet to a yard equals 7,560 square feet, divided by 45 feet wide equals 168 feet depth. Formula: Area divided by width equals depth.

22. c. Action for specific performance may be used here when the injured party does not want dollar damages but wants the specific property stated in the contract. The injured party in this action hopes the defendant will be ordered to perform specifically as promised, for example to proceed with the sale of the property.

23. a. Three acres times 43,560 (square feet to an acre) = 130,680 square feet, divided by 5,280 (linear feet in a mile, the distance on any edge of a section) = 24.75. The nearest choice would be 25 feet. Formula: Area divided by depth equals width, and area divided by width equals depth.

24. c. Foundation plans indicate piers, footings, and columns.

25. c. The four unities of *time, title, interest,* and *possession* (TTIP) make up joint tenancy, whose distinguishing characteristic is the right of survivorship.

26. c. 100% divided by 120% equals 83.3%. From 100%, subtract 83.3% to arrive at 16⅔%.

27. c. The servient owner cannot revoke the easement. There are several ways to terminate an easement, and choices *a, b,* and *d* are all possible methods.

28. a. The key here is reading the expression "if needed" in the question. Based on only a possible need, the "standby loan" is requested.

29. a. The term *encumbance* is misspelled. The correct spelling is "encumbrance."

30. c. Do not select choice *d,* which simply doubles the down payment of $50,000 (25 percent of $200,000). If Mr. Johnson were to place $50,000 down on a purchase of $200,000 that doubled in value in the next ten years to $400,000, his initial investment of $50,000 would be worth $250,000.

31. c. Effective age refers to the appearance and the condition of the property and is used for the appraisal process if it differs from actual age in the opinion of the appraiser. Effective age could be younger than, or older than, or the same as the

actual age, simply depending on the care of the property.

32. c. *Warehousing* is a term used to indicate the activities of a mortgage company that borrows for a short term from a commercial bank, sets up various direct consumer loans, and sells off the portfolio to investors. It is usually hired back by the investor to service the loans.

33. b. The principle of contribution is applied to determine how much value the pool will add to the overall value of the total property. A pool will not usually add value equal to its cost because not all buyers will find a pool a plus factor.

34. c. *Novation* refers to the substitution of a new obligation or contract for an old one by the mutual agreement of the parties.

35. b. A hip roof has four sides. A gable roof has two sides. A mansard is flat with downslopes, and a gambrel roof looks like a barn-style roof.

36. c. If the cost of living index rises significantly, it is telling us that it takes more dollars to buy the same commodity; therefore, the exchange value of the dollar has declined.

37. c. Title plants provide classified and summarized histories of real estate transactions and of other activities that might affect ownership of the land.

38. c. The seller remains responsible for the loan in a "subject to" takeover. Some older FHA and VA loans are still "subject to" takeovers.

39. d. The deed must be delivered to have an effective transfer of title. There is no legal requirement in California for the recording of a grant deed. Of course, it is in the best interest of the buyer (grantee) to do so.

40. c. Real property values tend to fluctuate with the trends of inflation; hence, real estate investment may provide an opportunity for greater return. Savings accounts, bonds, and notes remain constant during inflationary periods and may not be considered as good an investment.

41. b. A promise for a promise makes up a bilateral contract. The term *executory* refers to something to be done at a future time, such as the selling of the property in this case.

42. a. Property taxes and special assessments, of which a 1911 Street Improvement Bond is an example, are on a parity (equal basis) with each other and have priority over all other liens.

43. c. Six months' interest if more than 20 percent of the loan is paid off each year of the first five years is how Cal-Vet currently sets the prepayment penalty. There is no prepayment penalty after five years.

44. c. Local authorities have control over physical aspects of the subdivision under the Subdivision Map Act.

45. d. Local building inspectors enforce the state housing laws.

46. c. The quotation in the question defines a condominium.

47. a. Outside nuisances would be an example of economic or social obsolescence, whereas functional obsolescence defines that which is occurring inside the property lines, such as the examples in choices *b*, *c*, and *d*.

48. b. Prepaid rent would be a debit or charge to the seller, as in the case of security monies. This represents advance payment, which would be transferred to the buyer of the property.

49. b. The principle of regression refers to the property, not the neighborhood, and an overbuilt house would be an example of this principle. This misplaced improvement would regress in value due to its incorrect placement.

50. b. MPR stands for minimum property requirements, not maximum requirements.

51. d. An overall capitalization rate is made up of the return on (interest) and the return of (depreciation recaptured) the investment. The term *economic life* refers to the building's useful life and is usually shorter than its actual life. To find the cap rate for this building, take the premise of 100 percent potential economic life and divide by 40 years remaining to arrive at a 2½ percent annual recapture rate. This indicates that over 40 years, this building will return the value of the investment to the owner at the rate of 2½ percent a year. The 11 percent interest rate is a given in the question. Combine the 2½ percent recapture rate (return of) and the 11 percent interest rate (return on) to equal 13½ percent capitalization rate for this building.

52. a. To waive a right means to relinquish it or to forgo a right. The expression *unilateral* indicates one-sided action. Therefore, a one-sided act of an individual who may choose to waive his or her rights means accepting whatever consequences may follow.

53. c. Residential properties are considered amenity-type properties, indicating that additional value is attributed to the residential property for any amenities such as central air-conditioning or forced-air heating. Income property and public service buildings would not be considered amenity-type properties.

54. a. A fictitious business name statement is good for five years from December 31 of the year in which it was filed.

55. a. In the cost approach, the appraiser would attempt to estimate the value of improvements such as sidewalks, special landscaping, and a concrete driveway separately and apart from the land and building value.

56. d. Mortgage-backed securities involve a plan whereby a lender sells a group or pool of mortgages in exchange for a like amount of security. The security holders then receive a "passthrough" of the principal and interest payment on the pool of mortgages, less any amounts to cover servicing costs and certain fees. While it was Ginnie Mae's idea originally to use mortgage-backed securities as a means of purchasing blocks of other loans, today Fannie Mae, private investors, and mortgage bankers also participate in this program.

57. d. The turnover of real estate transactions is considered to be slow by comparison with other types of investments, such as stocks or commodities. A real estate transaction customarily involves finding a purchaser, then entering into an escrow period that may involve several months, etc.

58. c. The Federal Open Market Committee is made up of the seven-member board of governors of the Federal Reserve System and five of the district bank presidents, also under the Fed. This committee meets periodically and actively participates in buying or selling government securities, depending on whether it wants to tighten up or loosen up the flow of money in this country.

59. b. A blind pool is made up of often several hundred to several thousand limited partner investors. At the time of forming the blind pool, the property to be purchased has not yet been identified. The best description of this activity would be that of syndication, because a blind pool is a form of syndication.

60. c. In California one governmental agency cannot take precedence over another agency with reference to matters such as building codes. If there is a conflict between the agencies concerning building code requirements, the agency's requirement that provides the highest degree of safety is the one that will prevail.

61. c. The three degrees of flood hazards are inundation, sheeting, and ponding.

62. a. The broker or broker-appointed office manager must review, initial, and date all contracts created in that office. A broker can appoint one who has accrued two years' full-time experience as a salesperson in the past five years to handle this matter in the broker's absence.

63. c. Sales tax is the tax charged on the sale of tangible personal property. Do not confuse with taxation on real property as well.

64. a. An unlocated easement is valid. As an example, there may be an old public utility company easement whose precise location is unknown.

65. c. The Truth-in-Lending Act requires that the expression *annual percentage rate* be fully spelled out in the advertisement.

66. d. When the equity of the properties involved in an exchange of real property is unequal, the deficient party must give something to equalize the equity. The something extra given is referred to as *boot*. Boot may be defined as those items stated in choices *a*, *b*, and *c*.

67. d. Choices *a*, *b*, and *c* would all be a good interpretation of the expression *color-blind*.

68. d. Choices *a*, *b*, and *c* all represent items that must be recorded. While it is wise to record a voluntary lien, it is not necessarily a legal requirement. An example of a voluntary lien is a trust deed or mortgage. A lender chooses to record that trust deed or mortgage to protect its interest, even though it is not a legal requirement.

69. c. The question cites an example of what is called *nonconforming use*. An example of downzoning would be changing a lot zoned for commercial usage to one zoned for residential use. The terms *split zoning* and *exclusive zoning* are not applicable here.

70. b. Bankruptcy claims become effective immediately on the date of filing for the bankruptcy action and not from the date that the publication of the notice is shown in the newspaper.

71. c. An all-inclusive note and deed of trust is most often used when there is an underlying loan against the property that the seller does not wish to pay off at this time. The beneficiary is the seller of this property and is obligated by instructions in the note to continue to make payments on the underlying loans so as not to jeopardize this new loan created in the all-inclusive trust deed transaction. The face amount of the note in this transaction would include any other debts against the property, and the trustor (borrower) simply makes one payment to the beneficiary (seller), who becomes obligated to make the payment on the underlying debt.

72. c. When one dies intestate, it means that no will was left. In this case, Mr. Able's separate property is divided, with one-third going to his wife and two-thirds going to two or more children. In this question there are only two children; therefore, each child receives one-third.

73. c. If no notice of completion has been recorded, any unpaid persons on a job have 90 days in which to file a mechanic's lien.

74. b. If one is violating private restrictions, then it is the legal action of an injunction that is sought to stop those violations.

75. c. Under the Civil Rights Act of 1968, known as the federal Fair Housing Act, complaints must be filed within 180 days of the occurrence of the alleged violation.

76. c. Mortgage bankers' loans are sold to the secondary market, as bankers wish to generate cash from the sale of these loans to pay off the lines of credit against which they made these loans initially. The mortgage banker is then hired back by the investor to service the loans and ends up making the bulk of its income from service fees.

77. c. The appraiser's main concern in the analysis of residential property is the functional utility of the property, meaning its flow of traffic pattern, the room layout, and ease of livability.

78. a. Joists are the parallel wooden members that support floors and ceilings. Do not confuse with studs, which are vertical supports.

79. c. An escrow holder may turn over to the court any monies held and request that the court resolve the disputed matter. Such action is called an *interpleader*. The escrow entity does not have the authority to cancel the escrow or act as an arbitrator.

80. c. This is a refinanced loan that is not on an owner-occupied building. Nonowner-occupied buildings are exempt from the truth-in-lending requirements.

81. a. An *estate in fee* is another way to say *fee simple* or an *estate of inheritance* or *perpetual estate*. It describes the greatest interest one can have in the land.

82. d. Choices *a*, *b*, and *c* are all descriptions for a bearing wall.

83. b. Carl now owns ⅔ interest with Wes as tenants in common due to the right of survivorship in a joint tenancy transaction. Heirs of a joint tenant would not have a rightful claim. The use of joint tenancy avoids the probate procedure.

84. c. Real property taxes are neither the seller's nor the buyer's personal responsibility. Property taxes become a lien on the property, and must be paid accordingly, no matter who pays them.

85. a. It is the vendee on a real property sales contract who holds equitable title only. The vendee is the purchaser. The vendor (seller) retains legal title until a later date.

86. b. It would be very unusual to have the balances on a buyer's and seller's closing statement be exactly the same. Customarily, those balances are different on each party's statement, depending on the costs accruing to each party.

87. a. The borrower under a mortgage is called the *mortgagor*.

88. c. The change in ownership statement must be filed with the county recorder within 45 days of the transfer.

89. c. The trustor (borrower) or buyer of the property benefits from the appreciation accruing to the property. This refers to the growing value of the property.

90. c. An easement in gross goes with a person and not a property.

91. b. Ms. Jones extended the credit and in essence is the lender on this transaction. Do not read more into the question than exists.

92. a. The formula for appraising income property is scheduled annual gross income, less vacancy factor and rental loss, less all allowable expenses (taxes, utilities, maintenance, management, insurance, and reserves for replacement, if any) equals the net operating income—divided by the capitalization rate equals value.

    4 units at $206.25 each per month = $825 × 12 months = $9,900.00
    $9,900 – $495 (vacancy factor and
    rental loss) = $ 9,405
    Less annual expenses   – 4,140
    Net operating income $ 5,265
    $5,265 (Net operating income)
    ÷ .08 (Capitalization rate) = $65,812.50
                                        (VALUE)

93. c. The lessee, Mr. Able, has a possessory interest in the land and can grant an easement to the neighbor, Charles, but only for the period of the lease that Able holds—15 years.

94. d. The right of rescission under the Truth-in-Lending Act (Regulation Z) is until midnight of the third business day following the last of choices *a*, *b*, and *c* to occur.

95. d. A brother and sister may take title in any manner they wish other than in community property (only for husband and wife). Fee simple describes the interest that they have in the land, fee simple being the greatest ownership interest anyone can have. Do not confuse ownership with matters of title.

96. a. Use the Selling Price Rule: subtract from 100 percent and then divide: 100% – 7% = 93%; $33,700 ÷ .93 = $36,237.

97. a. There are 36 sections to a township, with each section being a one-mile square and containing one square mile.

98. d. The county recorder's records are public records; therefore, anyone who wishes may investigate such records during normal business hours.

99. a. Combine the tax brackets: 28% + 5% = 33%. Savings account of $9,000 pays 5% interest = $450. Bond: $5,000 pays 6% interest = $300. Bond interest is free from federal income tax; hence, take 100% – 33% (tax bracket) = 67% net after taxes. Bond interest: $300 ÷ 67% = $447.76. Thus, receiving $300 in bond interest (after tax savings) is equivalent to having received $447.76, which is closest to the interest yield of $450.

100. d. Memorize the word *AIDA* for *a*ttention, *i*nterest, *d*esire, *a*ction.

101. b. Assets, liabilities, and net worth are found in the balance sheet. Gross profit, expenses, and net income are found in the profit and loss statement. Assets are not found in the same statements. The balance sheet and the profit and loss statement together make up a "financial statement."

102. b. Both signatures are required if either the husband or the wife signs a contract for the sale of community real property. The other spouse has one year in which to void the sale. This makes the sale agreement voidable during that year.

103. a. A person who grants, leases, or hires real property is a tenant. The term *hire* would indicate a lease or rental.

104. d. A valid land contract must be in writing, just like any other real estate contract, in addition to having the other four elements of any simple contract, which are consideration, consent, capacity, and lawful object.

105. d. Few homes are built today with a single-car garage. Today, this would be considered functionally obsolete.

106. b. Economic obsolescence is a loss caused by outside (extraneous) factors. If the city has an excessively high tax rate, it might affect all properties within that area.

107. d. The fact that a lease will exist on a property creates two interests: the legal owner holds a fee simple estate and the lessee holds a less-than-freehold or leasehold estate.

108. a. Blocking access might stop a claim of easement by prescription by Harris.

109. b. A sublessor is the original lessee who has given up part of his or her interest in the property. As a sublessor he or she is still primarily liable for the rent.

110. a. Statement of fact.

111. a. Under any type of co-ownership, each owner has equal right of possession. This means that any owner can go anywhere on the property regardless of the percentage of his or her overall interest.

112. a. Even though the well and pump are put in the ground, the tax assessor classifies these as improvements.

113. d. A homeowner can have only one homestead at a time in California. If there is a valid homestead recorded on one home and the owner decides to place it on a second home, the first one has to be removed officially before the second takes effect.

114. d. None of these requires a list of all the buildings. They do require a description of the property.

115. d. The county tax assessor uses individual parcel numbers on each tax bill, not a legal description of real property.

116. d. The Civil Rights Act of 1968 applies to all of the types of housing listed in the question.

117. a. The appraiser is concerned with the loss due to depreciation up to this point. He or she looks to the productive life (economic life) of the property and considers how much of this has been used up.

118. c. *Effective gross income* is the term used to indicate the amount remaining after deducting vacancies from the gross income.

119. b. The appraiser bases an appraisal on facts obtained from a survey, and the result is an estimate as of a specific date.

120. a. An unearned increment means there has been an increase in value due to no efforts on the part of the owner. This could result from an increase in population or perhaps inflation.

121. c. This placement of a $200,000 home in a lower valued neighborhood would affect its value. The value will decrease based on the principal of regression. The worth of the better house is adversely affected by its presence among the lesser houses.

122. c. The capitalization rate (a risk rate) indicates the return that the owner expects on the purchase price. The higher the risk involved in the investment, the higher the capitalization rate.

123. b. When the dominant and servient tenement merge (come under one owner), the easement terminates.

124. a. Observed condition is a technique used to establish depreciation, and because this is a new building, it would not be used in this process.

125. b. The amount each owner spends on improvements cannot be restricted by the subdivider.

126. b. Most buyers will not pay more for property than what they would pay for an acceptable substitute or for new construction.

127. b. The U.S. Attorney General will not get involved in disputes of an ordinary nature. Most of these are turned over to the state officials if there has been a violation under the open housing law. If a conspiracy exists, however, the Attorney General would be called in to enforce the provisions of the law.

128. b. Most property sold today is subject to some type of public restriction. Most buyers are aware of this.

129. b. Insurance companies are not regulated as the others are with respect to their real estate loans.

130. b. In a lease there is a lessor (landlord), who is owner of the property; the lessee is the party that takes possession of the property and is given the leasehold interest.

131. a. When calculating the square footage of a home, you must consider the house and garage, and you measure from the outside areas.

132. d. A homeowner can deduct only the property taxes, interest payments, and a prepayment penalty.

133. d. Tax consciousness should begin prior to the purchase.

134. d. Statement of fact.

135. a. FHA "insures" the loan; it does not "guarantee" it.

136. d. The title insurance policy premium is a once-only fee. The policy protects the owner and heirs for certain items until the property is sold. The other choices are examples of costs that recur.

137. d. The lender requires that the borrower pay for an ALTA lender's policy. This type of policy protects only the lender (not the borrower) for the loan balance. It is one of the conditions for obtaining the loan.

138. b. The buyer can revoke the offer at any time up to the point where the seller's acceptance has been communicated to the buyer.

139. d. Statement of fact.

140. d. While it is common to create an agency relationship by written agreement (the listing), it can be created by ratification (consenting to acts of the agent) and estoppel (principal stopped from denying an inconsistent position in the representation).

141. d. Failure to disclose a dual agency can result in rescission of the contracts as well as loss of commission and disciplinary action against the licensee.

142. c. Racial composition is not a material fact in the buying and selling of real property. Discussing racial makeup of a neighborhood could be construed as violating law.

143. c. The term *principal* is used to define the party whom the broker is representing.

144. d. Statement of fact.

145. d. Statement of fact.

146. d. Statement of fact.

147. b. Only members of NAR can use the term *REALTOR*®. It is a trade name owned by the National Association of REALTORS®.

148. a. A broker acts as a fiduciary, which includes faithful service to the principal being represented by the broker.

149. d. Advertisements should be written to get someone's attention and stimulate their interest so that they will have the desire to buy and will take action.

150. a. An installment sale is a seller carry-back of the loan. The seller is taxed only on the profit as received over several years instead of being taxed on the entire profit in the year of sale.

PRACTICE EXAMINATION VII

1. Legally and technically, property is defined as

   a. freehold estates.
   b. things that buyers and sellers own.
   c. rights or interests that a person has in the thing owned.
   d. only personal property.

2. When comparing condominiums and rented apartments, which of the following would be true?

   a. The person who occupies each unit would have an estate in real property.
   b. The occupier has a fee estate.
   c. The local tax assessor must assess each unit of the subdivision separately.
   d. None of the above

3. Another name for an estate of inheritance is

   a. fee simple defeasible.
   b. estate at sufferance.
   c. estate in fee.
   d. probate estate.

4. David gave a grant deed to John transferring title to a property. This title is subject to a condition stating that title will be forfeited if alcoholic beverages are ever sold on the property. John would have which of the following types of estates?

   a. Fee simple absolute
   b. Fee simple defeasible
   c. Estate in forfeiture
   d. Less than freehold estate

5. A person who held a life estate leased the property for five years and then died before the end of the five-year term. The new owners ordered the lessee to move out. The lease was

   a. valid for the five years.
   b. valid until the man died.
   c. invalid from the beginning.
   d. invalid unless the deceased's executor confirmed it.

6. Which of the following would be defined as a fixture in the law?

   a. Something that is made part of a chattel real
   b. Something referred to by actions but not referred to in the sales contract
   c. Something incorporated into the land
   d. Something used in an extraordinary way with the land

7. As used in real property law, which of the following is most nearly correct as a meaning for the word *tenancy?*

   a. The landlord-tenant relationship
   b. The obstinacy of a holdover tenant
   c. The mode or method of holding title to real property by a lessee or owner
   d. None of the above

8. What is the meaning of a quiet title action?

   a. Purchasing property through a dummy transaction
   b. An action to quiet a noisy tenant
   c. Foreclosure action
   d. Court action to remove a cloud on the title

9. Which of the following would be the best and most complete definition of the term *encumbrance?*

   a. The degree, quantity, nature, and extent of interest that a person has in real property
   b. The use of property by a debtor to offer a creditor security for a debt
   c. Any action taken relative to property, other than acquiring or transferring title
   d. Anything that affects or limits the fee simple title to property

10. Which of the following statements, if any, is correct concerning the relationship between an effective interest rate and a nominal interest rate?

    a. The effective rate is the rate the buyer will pay; the nominal rate is the rate named in the loan application.
    b. The effective interest rate is always lower because the nominal interest rate includes charges other than interest.
    c. The effective interest rate is the rate actually paid by the borrower for the use of the money; the nominal interest rate is the rate specified in the note.
    d. None of the above

11. When loaning money to two or more coborrowers on a single promissory note, the lender would be best advised to increase the security on the note by inserting which of the following phrases after the names of the coborrowers?

    a. Personally and corporately
    b. Together as individuals
    c. Individually and severally
    d. Jointly and severally

12. Which of the following is true concerning promissory notes?

    a. They are used as security for trust deeds.
    b. They are recorded at the county recorder's office.
    c. They are always used when real estate is sold.
    d. They are the evidence of the debt.

13. When comparing a straight note with an installment note, the straight note will have

   a. equal annual principal reduction payments.
   b. no principal payments during the term of the loan except on the last payment.
   c. a total effective interest rate greater than if the loan were an installment loan.
   d. None of the above

14. When making a loan, amortization tables are used to determine the

   a. interest rate.
   b. monthly payment.
   c. term of the loan.
   d. annual percentage rate.

15. Mr. James sold Blackacre to Ms. Woods. Before he sold it, Blackacre had an appurtenant easement across Whiteacre, which was owned by Mr. Sommers. When Ms. Woods tried to use the easement, Mr. Sommers protested. Which of the following is correct?

   a. Mr. Sommers owns the servient tenement, and his consent must be obtained for Ms. Woods to use the easement.
   b. An appurtenant easement always passes when the property is sold.
   c. Mr. James owns the dominant tenement and the easement upon it.
   d. Mr. James owns the easement and can grant it to anyone.

16. Which of the following would be an illustration of the government's police power?

   a. The creation of restrictive conditions by the original subdivider
   b. Eminent domain proceedings against property in the path of a proposed freeway
   c. Adjudication of conflicting claims between present and former owners of a parcel of real property
   d. The enactment of zoning laws limiting the use that may be made of a parcel of real property

17. Which of the following is the legal method that a city uses to implement its general plan?

   a. Variances
   b. General land use
   c. Zoning
   d. Conditional use permits

18. According to a certain contract, the buyer will be taking the property subject to the existing loan. "Subject to" most nearly means that

   a. both buyer and seller will be liable for the loan.
   b. the seller has no liability for the loan.
   c. only the buyer will be liable for the loan.
   d. the buyer will not be personally liable for the loan.

19. A trust deed note taken by a state savings and loan association on a single-family owner-occupied residence could be prepaid without penalty

    a. if the loan is more than seven years old.
    b. if the lender exercises the due-on-sale provision in the note and signs a waiver of right to prepay.
    c. if the loan is assumed by a buyer of the house.
    d. at any time, whether or not there is a written prepayment penalty clause.

20. Which of the following would impair the security of a trust deed recorded on real property?

    a. The trust deed is recorded after a declaration of homestead.
    b. The trust deed is recorded after a work of improvement was commenced and a mechanic's lien is recorded on the work.
    c. A judgment lien is placed on the property.
    d. None of the above

21. Which of the following would be true about a lis pendens?

    a. It can be removed only by a court order.
    b. It can be recorded no matter what the type of lawsuit is.
    c. It may affect the title to real property based on the results of the lawsuit.
    d. None of the above

22. A title company could make a title search by searching the records of the

    a. county clerk's office.
    b. county recorder's office.
    c. federal land office.
    d. All of the above

23. Bascomb purchased a parcel of real property and received a standard policy of title insurance. Bascomb would be protected against all of the following items *EXCEPT*

    a. the forgery of the signature of the grantor.
    b. easements and liens on the property not revealed by public records.
    c. the delivery of a previous deed in the chain of title without the intent of the grantor.
    d. the insanity of the grantor.

24. An ALTA policy of title insurance goes beyond the protection afforded by a CLTA policy in guarding against

    a. existing liens and encumbrances as disclosed by the public records.
    b. a deed or reconveyance issued by a minor.
    c. the location of property lines according to formal survey.
    d. an error in the sequence of recording trust deed loans.

25. Jones, who does not have a real estate license, is the owner and president of an investment firm. He advertises and sells properties for his clients. Because these transactions involve real estate, who will prosecute him for violating the real estate law?

    a. The district attorney
    b. The state attorney general
    c. The Real Estate Commissioner
    d. The local police

26. Who of the following is authorized to manage property for the general public?

    a. A licensed real estate broker
    b. One holding a Certified Property Manager designation
    c. Any affiliate member of the California Association of REALTORS®
    d. All of the above

27. According to the regulations of the Real Estate Commissioner, the broker must have a signed employment agreement with each of his or her salespersons. According to those regulations, a copy of this agreement must be kept by both parties for

a. one year from date of termination.
b. two years from date of termination.
c. three years from date of termination.
d. three years from date of employment.

28. Broker Jones, who is not a member of any trade organization, has been using a new advertising slogan: "a new breed of realtor." Concerning this practice

a. it is grounds for revocation or suspension of his real estate license.
b. it is permissible, providing the word *realtor* is not capitalized.
c. it is acceptable as long as he is not licensed in more than one state.
d. it is a violation of fair housing laws.

29. When budgeting for a real estate office, the phrase *company dollar* means the

a. money required to establish an office and run it for a given period of time.
b. income of an office after all expenses are subtracted.
c. income of an office after all commissions are subtracted.
d. None of the above

30. A broker advertises the sale of "Mega Bucks Trust Deed" in a newspaper. In the advertisement she offers a specific yield that she arrives at by looking at her yield for the past year. Which of the following is true concerning this advertisement?

a. This is illegal according to the Truth-in-Advertising law.
b. It is legal if the Department of Real Estate has confirmed the yield that is stated.
c. It is legal if she gives the actual interest rate specified in the note and the discount rate from the outstanding loan balance.
d. There is no law covering this subject.

31. When a licensee negotiates a loan secured by real property, the licensee must deliver a mortgage loan disclosure statement to the borrower

a. within three days of the time the borrower signs it.
b. when it is signed by the borrower.
c. within 24 hours of the time the borrower signs it.
d. when escrow closes.

32. Under the Truth-in-Lending Act all of the following are correct EXCEPT

a. "FHA financing available."
b. "VA financing available."
c. "$5,000 down, 8% interest."
d. "easy financing, call us today."

33. Which of the following state agencies would receive complaints concerning fair housing laws?

a. Department of Real Estate
b. Department of Fair Employment and Housing
c. Department of Community Development
d. None of the above

34. In which of the following years did the U.S. Supreme Court prohibit all racial discrimination when real property is sold, leased, or rented?

    a. 1962
    b. 1968
    c. 1974
    d. 1982

35. A real estate licensee has a practice of avoiding showing property found in integrated areas to minority buyers. This is an example of

    a. redlining.
    b. blockbusting.
    c. steering.
    d. proper conduct.

36. Generally, as both the employment rate and the GDP (gross domestic product) rise,

    a. the level of personal income rises.
    b. new residential developments will increase in number.
    c. sales of existing homes will remain level or increase.
    d. All of the above

37. Changes in which of the following would have an impact on real estate in the future?

    a. The real estate industry
    b. Land-use controls
    c. Consumer concerns
    d. All of the above

38. A real estate investor who wishes to operate by using the principle of leverage would

    a. use his personal funds insofar as possible.
    b. use borrowed funds and personal funds on an equal basis.
    c. use borrowed money to the maximum extent possible.
    d. invest in real properties with values that are declining.

39. Carter bought 10 acres of vacant land for $20,000 per acre, making a cash down payment of $20,000, and executing a straight note and a blanket deed of trust for the balance. As a part of the note, the lender agreed that when Carter made an additional payment of $20,000 on the principal, the trustee would issue a partial reconveyance for one acre. Carter has paid a total of $40,000 on the note and now owns two acres free and clear. The percentage of his equity in the encumbered property

    a. has been eliminated.
    b. remains the same.
    c. has increased.
    d. has decreased.

40. When the term *warehousing* is used in connection with real property financing, the term would normally describe

    a. a jumbo loan on a self-storage facility.
    b. the underwriting of stock issues with loans against industrial property.
    c. loans regulated by Article 7 of the California Real Estate Law.
    d. a mortgage banker collecting loans prior to sale.

41. Both buyer and seller have signed a real property conditional sales contract, the effect of which would be

    a. all rights and interest of the seller now pass to the buyer.
    b. an equitable title passes to the buyer.
    c. the legal title passes to the buyer.
    d. no title to the real estate passes.

42. A buyer defaulted on a real property installment sales contract that had been recorded by the seller. If a quitclaim deed were to be used to extinguish the cloud on the title, it must be executed by

    a. both buyer and seller.
    b. seller only.
    c. buyer only.
    d. None of the above

43. If an advertisement is placed in a newspaper advertising a house for sale and only the annual percentage rate is stated,

    a. total finance charges must be included.
    b. the number of payments must be included.
    c. the amount of the down payment must be included.
    d. additional disclosures are not required.

44. The federal right-to-cancel notice must be given to a borrower by the agent if

    a. a commercial building is being used for the security for the loan.
    b. the loan is not secured by the borrower's dwelling and more than $25,000 is being borrowed.
    c. the borrower's residence is the security for the loan.
    d. the money will be used for business expansion.

45. According to the Truth-in-Lending Act, consumers must be informed of credit terms by the

    a. trustee.
    b. broker.
    c. lender.
    d. escrow company.

46. A mortgage loan may be insured by

    a. VA.
    b. FHA or a private mortgage insurer.
    c. Fannie Mae.
    d. the beneficiary.

47. According to generally accepted practices, an escrow agent is authorized to

    a. give the buyers advice about the best financing that is available.
    b. change the escrow instructions when asked to by the listing broker.
    c. call for funding of the buyer's loan.
    d. authorize a pest control company to make corrective repairs.

48. When a trust deed is sold, the parties often use an escrow in order to

    a. obey the civil code.
    b. be a witness for the transaction.
    c. make sure that the conditions and terms are met prior to the closing of the transaction.
    d. provide a legal recourse against the escrow company for the two parties involved.

49. Under current law, the seller of real property does not have to disclose that a prior occupant of the property died of AIDS. However, it must be disclosed only if

    a. the lender asks.
    b. the loan is an FHA loan.
    c. an inquiry is made about this subject.
    d. None of the above

50. Which of the following would be considered the primary purpose of RESPA?

    a. To regulate all real estate loans
    b. To choose lenders that can process applications for loans
    c. To regulate home improvement loans
    d. To require that disclosures be made by lenders that make loans on one-unit to four-unit dwellings

51. If a contract for the purchase of real estate is to be enforceable, the consideration must be sufficient relative to value in order to enforce a suit for

    a. rescission.
    b. specific performance.
    c. lawful detainer.
    d. damages.

52. When a licensee is acting as the buyer's agent, the licensee will disclose this fact to others

    a. as soon as is practicable.
    b. after the offer has been presented and accepted.
    c. when the loan is funded.
    d. after the licensee receives a commission.

53. What is the best way to create an agency relationship?

    a. By actions
    b. By being considerate
    c. By written agreement
    d. By cooperating with other brokers

54. In which of the following ways could an agency relationship *not* be created?

    a. Implied contract
    b. Oral contract
    c. Written contract
    d. Voluntary offer by the agent

55. A dual agency is legal if

    a. all parties are told before the close of escrow.
    b. the buyer and seller consent to it.
    c. the broker and the escrow company agree to it.
    d. all parties are told after they sign the contracts.

56. The buyer's earnest money deposit may be

    a. a promissory note.
    b. a postdated check.
    c. anything that the seller considers valuable.
    d. All of the above

57. When a broker has two offers on the same property, both from salespeople within his or her office, and both with a deposit, the broker is placed in a dilemma. The broker decides not to present the second offer until the first offer has been accepted or rejected by the seller. The seller is not informed of the second offer. The broker's action is

    a. permissible if the second offer is substantially the same as the first.
    b. permissible only if the commission is divided equally between the salespersons.
    c. not permissible because the broker owed the fiduciary obligation to both buyers.
    d. not permissible.

58. Which of the following would be a fiduciary duty of the agent to the buyer according to the law of agency in the civil code?

    a. Acting with the utmost care, integrity, loyalty, and honesty when dealing with the buyer
    b. Giving the buyer advice about how to hold title
    c. Telling the buyer which escrow company to use
    d. Being a subagent

59. A broker's ad in a local newspaper says that if a buyer or seller will bring this ad to his office and either list or buy property through him, he will give the person $50. Which of the following is true?

    a. The broker cannot give $50 to the buyer or seller.
    b. The broker cannot give $50 to the buyer.
    c. This would violate real estate law because he would be compensating unlicensed persons for performing real estate acts.
    d. The broker can give $50 to the buyer or seller.

60. In July, Hall bought Welch's home through the listing broker, Cruz. In November, when the first rain came, the tile roof leaked badly in many places. Hall sued Welch and Cruz for the cost of the necessary new roof. Testimony in court showed that Welch had mentioned the need of a roof to Cruz, but Cruz had not mentioned it to Hall because "he had not asked about it." The most likely result was that

    a. Hall was successful in the suit against Welch, who was entitled to recover damages, in turn, from Cruz.
    b. Hall recovered from Welch, but Cruz was not liable to Welch.
    c. Cruz was liable to Hall, but Welch was not.
    d. on the basis of "caveat emptor," Hall is not entitled to recover from either Welch or Cruz.

61. An exclusive right-to-sell listing agreement is a(n)

    a. promise for a promise.
    b. bilateral contract.
    c. employment contract.
    d. All of the above

62. To be entitled to a commission, a broker must show that he or she was the procuring cause of the sale under all of the following types of listings *EXCEPT*

    a. exclusive agency.
    b. exclusive authorization and right to sell.
    c. open listing.
    d. nonexclusive listing.

63. When the deposit receipt on the sale of a house states that the property is being sold "as is," it

    a. also requires a real estate transfer disclosure statement.
    b. provides that the buyer should beware.
    c. means that nothing is warranted.
    d. does not require a real estate transfer disclosure statement.

64. Which of the following would not terminate an offer to purchase real property?

    a. The offeror communicates notice of revocation after the offeree has properly posted acceptance
    b. A counteroffer from the offeree
    c. Death or insanity of the offeror
    d. The offeree fails to accept within the prescribed period given by the offeror

65. None of the following would automatically terminate an offer to buy real property *EXCEPT*

    a. revocation of the offer by the offeree.
    b. rejection of the offer by the offeror.
    c. an inquiry by the offeree as to whether the offeror will accept different terms.
    d. rejection of the offer by the offeree.

66. In a real estate purchase contract, the liquidated damages clause is initialed and the buyer defaults. The deposit will be

    a. no more than 3 percent of the selling price or the amount of the deposit, whichever is less.
    b. used to pay any escrow expenses and the balance returned to the buyer.
    c. divided equally between the seller and the listing agent.
    d. given to the seller when escrow is opened.

67. The Internal Revenue Service would define the marginal tax rate as the

    a. tax rate that is used for the next dollar of taxable income earned.
    b. 15 percent tax rate.
    c. tax rate used for your state income tax.
    d. None of the above

68. If a person owns two personal residences, sells one, and then buys another one under conditions that comply with the gain deferral rules, which of the following is true?

    a. The person must sell both residences to qualify for deferral.
    b. Only the residence that has the greater value can use the deferral rules.
    c. Current tax laws allow for a certain amount of gain exemption on the sale of the principal residence.
    d. Deferral of the gain can be use for either residence.

69. Which of the following is real property?

    a. Growing trees
    b. A leasehold interest
    c. An easement in gross
    d. None of the above

70. Ms. Smith, who owns an apartment, sustained a $3,000 operational loss for the tax year. For income tax purposes, she may

    a. deduct only $1,000 of the loss on her income tax return.
    b. offset the loss against any capital gains.
    c. deduct the full amount from her ordinary income.
    d. deduct only one-half of the loss from her ordinary income.

71. According to income tax laws, which of the following is true about depreciation of land?

    a. Land has a residual value but improvements do not.
    b. The ACRS method of depreciation can be used when depreciating land.
    c. Land is considered to be 25 percent of the total value and is depreciated.
    d. Land is not depreciated.

72. John sold a property to Sam on an installment sale for income tax purposes. The buyer assumed an existing loan that exceeded John's basis in the property. John thus had loan relief (excess mortgage over basis). The excess amount must be

    a. deducted from the basis.
    b. made a part of the sales price.
    c. added to the basis.
    d. made a part of the down payment whether cash was received or not.

73. Sampson owned a triplex valued at $160,000, with an adjusted basis of $70,000. King owned a duplex valued at $155,000. Both properties were owned free and clear. They exchanged their properties, with King giving Sampson $5,000 in cash. For federal income tax purposes

    a. both will be taxed on the difference between the value and the basis.
    b. King has a taxable gain.
    c. Sampson has a recognized gain.
    d. neither has a taxable gain.

74. In which of the following situations would an IRC Section 1031 exchange not be allowed?

    a. The properties are not of a like kind.
    b. The exchanged properties are both vacant land.
    c. One of the properties is a leasehold over 30 years.
    d. One property is in California and the other is in Arizona.

75. Which of the following would not be subject to property tax?

    a. Mobile homes properly installed on a permanent foundation
    b. Vacant land located in an unincorporated area of the county
    c. Intangible personal property
    d. Possessory interests of lessees in tax-exempt public property, such as leases on oil and gas properties

76. If the owner of a property thinks that the property has been overassessed by the county assessor, the owner would contact the

    a. Department of Real Estate.
    b. Board of Supervisors.
    c. Assessment Appeals Board.
    d. county tax collector.

77. Which of the following must be given by the seller of a condominium to the buyer?

    a. The CC&Rs
    b. The bylaws
    c. A copy of the most recent financial statement
    d. All of the above

78. In a condominium complex a sidewalk would be

    a. part of the common area.
    b. at least four feet wide.
    c. made of asphalt.
    d. owned as a fee simple estate.

79. What would be the value of a fourplex rental property if each unit rented for $206.25 per month; vacancies were 5 percent of gross rents; operating expenses were $4,140 per year; and the net earnings represented an 8 percent return on the investment?

    a. $65,812.50   c. $71,484
    b. $68,400   d. $72,000

80. Jones bought a house for $125,000. He obtained a loan for 88 percent of the purchase price payable $1,549 per month at 12 percent interest. Before he made his first payment, he sold the house for $139,750. His equity at the time of sale was

    a. $15,000.
    b. $29,750.
    c. $139,750.
    d. None of the above

81. Ms. Smith bought a property for $72,000 with a $20,000 cash down payment and a $52,000 loan. The loan did not require interest and did not require any payments for one year. One year later, she sold the property for double its purchase price. Each dollar of her original cash investment is now equal to

    a. $2.00.   c. $7.30.
    b. $4.60.   d. $9.20.

82. A highrise office building has a quarterly income of $265,000. The expenses amount to 32 percent of the income. What is the annual net income?

    a. $106,000   c. $349,800
    b. $189,200   d. $720,800

83. If a 32-unit apartment building shows an annual net income of $117,800, and the appropriate capitalization rate is 8 percent, what is the approximate value of the property?

    a. $867,008   c. $1,017,792
    b. $942,400   d. $1,472,500

84. An agent supplies the following information concerning an apartment building: Gross income, $80,000; Operating expenses $25,000; Depreciation, $10,000; Vacancies, 10 percent; Value, $450,000. What would be the capitalization rate?

    a. 8.2 percent   c. 10.4 percent
    b. 9.3 percent   d. 11.5 percent

85. An income property rents for $1,000 per month. The operating expenses are $3,000 a year. During the past five years it has been vacant for three months. If an appraiser uses a 10 percent capitalization rate, the value of the property would be

    a. $74,951.   c. $84,000.
    b. $79,000.   d. $91,000.

86. A man borrowed 80 percent of the value of his home. The loan had a 9 percent interest rate. The first year's interest on the loan was $4,050. What was the value of the property?

    a. $36,000   c. $48,000
    b. $45,000   d. $56,250

87. Johnson negotiated a $20,000 loan to purchase his home. He was charged four points to get the loan. The loan required 2 percent of the original amount as a prepayment penalty. Monthly payments were $163, including interest at 8 percent per annum. Five years later, Johnson sold his home and paid the loan in full. If during the time he had it, the loan had an average outstanding balance of $18,500, what were the lender's gross earnings?

    a. $6,750   c. $7,140
    b. $6,840   d. $8,600

88. When creating a fully amortized loan for $5,000 at an 11 percent interest rate for 20 years, the lender will require equal monthly payments of $51.61, including principle and interest. How much of the first monthly payment will be used to reduce the principal balance?

    a. $45.83   c. $11.56
    b. $25.80   d. $5.78

89. If the Smiths sold their house for $73,700, and this was 17 percent more than what they paid for it, the purchase price was most nearly

    a. $58,380.   c. $62,992.
    b. $61,920.   d. $65,420.

90. Johnson bought a parcel of land for $63,360. Disregarding interest charges on any financing involved, property taxes, and all other variables, if it costs 12 percent of the future selling price to market this lot, how much must the property increase in value before it can be resold without a loss?

    a. 24 percent   c. $4,320
    b. 112 percent   d. $8,640

91. The owner of a single-family home gave a listing to salesperson Grove, provided Grove's broker, Ms. King, would appraise the property to verify the listing price. Which of the following best describes the activity performed by broker King?

    a. Broker King can appraise the property only if she is a licensed appraiser.
    b. Broker King cannot legally appraise the property unless she charges an additional fee.
    c. Broker King must provide a narrative appraisal report.
    d. Broker King is acting within the law because no claim of being an expert appraiser was made by King.

92. An appraiser is appraising a single-family residence and notices an abandoned gasoline station next door. The appraiser would recommend which of the following?

    a. A structural pest control report
    b. A toxic waste report from the EPA
    c. Rezoning the property
    d. A soils report by a civil engineer

93. Which of the following defines a fee appraiser?

    a. A person who is employed by a lending institution to do its appraisal
    b. A person who appraises property for the State of California
    c. A person who appraises property for the federal government
    d. A person who is self-employed and charges a fee

94. When an appraiser is appraising a property, he or she usually considers all of the following *EXCEPT*

    a. a definition of value.
    b. the property identification.
    c. the property rights to be appraised.
    d. the assessed value.

95. In estimating the value of a parcel of real property, an appraiser considers the value of which of the following?

    a. The bundle of rights
    b. Utility
    c. Physical land and the improvements thereon
    d. All of the above

96. When real property increases in value because of an increase in population, this is classified as

    a. economic value.
    b. economic obsolescence.
    c. an unearned increment.
    d. None of the above

97. Of the following approaches to value used by appraisers, which is the one most readily adaptable for use by real estate licensees?

    a. The market approach
    b. The capitalization approach
    c. The square-foot approach
    d. The cost approach

98. When a licensee is appraising an improved parcel of property using the market data method, that person must make adjustments to the estimates of value because

    a. the property will eventually have a greater value because of inflation.
    b. the property will depreciate.
    c. any two properties are rarely alike concerning all features.
    d. All of the above

99. When using the market data method of appraising a single-family residence, the unit of comparison is the

    a. gross multiplier.
    b. cubic feet.
    c. entire property.
    d. capitalization rate.

100. An appraiser, in appraising a special-purpose property, would probably use the

    a. market data approach.
    b. cost approach.
    c. income approach.
    d. land residual approach.

101. The value of a parcel of real property is best measured by which of the following groups of characteristics?

    a. Utility, scarcity, depreciation, demand
    b. Cost, demand, utility, transferability
    c. Scarcity, utility, feasibility, cost
    d. Demand, scarcity, transferability, utility

102. Normally, a structure used primarily as a warehouse would be valued by the

    a. square foot.   c. front foot.
    b. square yard.   d. cubic foot.

103. When an appraiser compares the phrase *reproduction cost* with the phrase *replacement cost*, replacement would be more closely associated with which of the following concepts?

    a. The cost to replace a building with another building that would use the land to its highest and best use
    b. The original cost to replace a building
    c. The present cost to replace the building with the exact replica
    d. The present cost to replace the building with another building having the same utility

104. An appraiser in appraising a restaurant building would probably use the

    a. market data approach.
    b. cost approach.
    c. income approach.
    d. All of the above

105. When gross income is changed into value in one operation, which of the following describes this occurrence?

    a. Fixed factor
    b. Rent multiplier
    c. Comparison
    d. Cost

106. An investor wants to buy a vacant parcel of land, build a building on it, and lease it as a hardware store for $5,000 a month. He estimates that the building will cost $300,000 and the expenses will be $12,000 per year. If he wants to use a 12 percent capitalization rate, what is the most he can pay for the land?

    a. $10,000
    b. $100,000
    c. $200,000
    d. None of the above

107. When an appraiser is considering the economic life and the physical life of a building, the economic life is usually

    a. longer.
    b. shorter.
    c. the same.
    d. None of the above

108. An appraiser defines depreciation as

    a. recapture that has been realized.
    b. loss in value from any cause.
    c. wear and tear of the improvements.
    d. a loss in the value of the land.

109. A substantial difference in value between two properties that were built concurrently on adjoining lots of equally valuable land with construction and maintenance costs the same would most likely be caused by

    a. physical depreciation of one of the properties.
    b. economic obsolescence in the neighborhood.
    c. nonconforming uses opposite the properties.
    d. functional obsolescence within one of the properties.

110. The primary purpose for which an appraiser would use a site analysis is to determine the

    a. correct zoning laws.
    b. type of soil.
    c. highest and best use.
    d. ocean views.

111. A kiosk is the term used to identify a(n)

    a. information booth in a mall.
    b. construction crane.
    c. addition to a shopping center.
    d. special compartment to hold a security key for use by the fire department.

112. An architect often draws a plot plan for the purpose of

    a. showing the details of the foundation construction.
    b. guiding building construction.
    c. showing exterior sides of the houses.
    d. guiding placement of construction and related land improvements.

113. During the wintertime, an appraiser finds that the inside of an exterior wall of a building is about the same temperature as the other interior walls. The appraiser would come to the conclusion that

    a. the furnace is doing a good job.
    b. the wall insulation is adequate.
    c. heat is leaking into outside walls.
    d. the heating duct system is faulty.

114. Which of the following conditions would not cause a building to be declared substandard?

    a. There is dampness in the habitable rooms.
    b. The electrical wiring does not comply with present code, but it did when it was installed and it is now safe and is working properly.
    c. There is no heating.
    d. There is defective weather protection on the outside of the building.

115. As a general rule, when residences are being sold, the buyer or lender requires a termite inspection. A good strategy for the seller is to have the termite report issued at which of the following times?

    a. Before putting the property on the market
    b. After determining the sales price
    c. Before opening escrow
    d. Only if the lender has already completed the appraisal

116. An escrow closing statement that refers to "recurring costs" would be describing

    a. deed transfer taxes.
    b. title insurance.
    c. impound items.
    d. escrow charges.

117. An executrix of an estate is

    a. appointed by the probate court.
    b. named in the decedent's will.
    c. selected by the devisee.
    d. appointed by the decedent's attorney.

118. The fundamental purpose for setting up a depreciation reserve as shown on a balance sheet is for

    a. income tax benefits.
    b. allowable property tax deductions for wear and tear.
    c. interest that can be earned on invested reserve funds.
    d. preservation of invested capital.

119. All of the following are items commonly found on a balance sheet *EXCEPT*

    a. goodwill.
    b. equipment used for the business.
    c. sales.
    d. prepaid expenses.

120. Which of the following would least apply in the definition of "goodwill"?

    a. The habit of patronage
    b. The value added to the business due to advertising over a period of time
    c. Courteous treatment accorded to customers in the past
    d. Ample stock in modern fixtures

121. Which document authorizes a broker to receive a deposit from a prospective buyer?

    a. The listing agreement
    b. The deposit receipt
    c. The owner-buyer statement
    d. The settlement statement

122. Which of the following statements most accurately describes mortgage companies that act as mortgage loan correspondents?

    a. Companies that prefer negotiating loans that are sold on the secondary market
    b. Companies that were organized under federal laws and are subject to strict supervision
    c. Companies that do not service the loans that they originate
    d. Companies that are not active in the field of government-insured loans

123. As a general rule, purchasing a home for reasons of financial enhancement or its speculative possibilities is a(n)

    a. primary motive.
    b. secondary motive.
    c. exclusive notice.
    d. None of the above

124. An offer to sell a franchise in California must be registered with the Department of Corporations unless it is exempted because the franchisor

    a. has a net worth of not less than $5 million.
    b. has a net worth of not less than $1 million.
    c. is a subsidiary of a corporation having a net worth of not less than $1 million.
    d. is incorporated in another state.

125. A real estate broker is liable to a buyer if he or she

    a. executes a contract in the name of the seller.
    b. acts in excess of the authority given him or her by the seller.
    c. turns the buyer's deposit over to the seller and thereafter the contract fails due to no fault of the broker.
    d. innocently makes a misrepresentation based upon information received from the seller.

126. Two of the most important items for a borrower to be advised of regarding the Truth-in-Lending Act are

    a. disclosure and discount rates.
    b. finance charge and annual percentage rate.
    c. advertising and interest rates.
    d. installment payments and cancellation rights.

127. A note on which only interest is paid during its term and that can be used for leverage is a(n)

    a. straight note.
    b. amortized note.
    c. installment note.
    d. level payment note.

128. Under which of the following listings must an owner pay a commission even though the owner sells entirely through his or her own efforts?

    a. Exclusive agency
    b. Exclusive authorization to sell
    c. Open listing
    d. Net listing

129. Personal property can be

    a. hypothecated.
    b. alienated.
    c. assessed.
    d. All of the above

130. In a percentage lease, the rental is usually based on a percentage of the
    a. value of the building.
    b. monthly gross sales with a minimum rent.
    c. annual net sales with a minimum rent.
    d. assessed value.

131. The interest of a lessee in real property is known as a
    a. reversion.
    b. remainder.
    c. freehold.
    d. chattel real.

132. One of the distinguishing economic characteristics of real property is that it is
    a. immovable.
    b. a long-term investment.
    c. very expensive.
    d. likely to increase in value.

133. Which of the following activities would normally require great involvement in accounting duties and procedures?
    a. Appraising
    b. Exchanging
    c. Property management
    d. Negotiation of real property sales

134. A permit must be secured from the Corporations Commissioner before anyone can offer which of the following to residents of California?
    a. Real property partnership syndications
    b. An out-of-state subdivision
    c. A guaranteed trust deed or real property sales contract
    d. All of the above

135. Which of the following would be exempt from the "Discrimination and Unlawful Act" chapter in the Health and Safety Code?
    a. Owner-occupied residence financed by the VA
    b. A fourplex financed by the FHA
    c. An owner-occupied single-family residence that is unencumbered
    d. None of the above

136. Which of the following types of loans may have a variable interest rate?
    a. Cal-Vet
    b. FHA
    c. VA
    d. Any of the above

137. The members of the National Association of Real Estate Brokers are called
    a. Realtists.
    b. REALTORS®.
    c. broker-realtists.
    d. united brokers.

138. The primary justification for zoning ordinances is that they
    a. promote conformity in the outward appearance of structures.
    b. limit the supply of specific businesses within a zoned area.
    c. promote the general health, safety, and welfare of the community.
    d. increase the tax base of the local governing body.

139. Which of the following is required for a valid escrow in the conveyance of title to real property?

    a. The services of a licensed real estate broker
    b. A binding contract between the buyer and the seller
    c. A complete chain of title
    d. No conditions in the escrow instructions

140. The type of legal action that would most likely be taken in the event of a default on a land contract would be a

    a. lis pendens.
    b. writ of execution.
    c. foreclosure by trustee's sale.
    d. quiet title action.

141. The party that is benefited the most by a subordination clause in a trust deed and note is the

    a. trustor.
    b. beneficiary.
    c. holder of the note.
    d. trustee.

142. No subdivision lots can be legally sold or leased prior to

    a. furnishing a copy of the commissioner's final public report to the buyer.
    b. giving the buyer a chance to read it.
    c. obtaining the signature of the buyer for a copy of the report.
    d. All of the above

143. The maximum commission rate allowed on a five-year loan secured by a junior trust deed of $6,000, which comes under the provisions of the Real Property Loan Brokerage Law, is

    a. 5 percent.
    b. 10 percent.
    c. 15 percent.
    d. None of the above

144. A person sold her home and took back a note secured by a purchase-money deed of trust. She selected a real estate broker from the telephone book and asked him to service this loan. If the broker takes on this duty, state law requires him to

    a. convey a broker's loan statement.
    b. be a real property securities dealer.
    c. have a written authorization from the holder of the note.
    d. be a loan correspondent or a mortgage broker.

145. A real estate salesperson notifies his broker that he is terminating his employment. He asks the broker to give him his license. The broker should

    a. give the salesperson his license and notify the commissioner in writing within five days of he termination.
    b. return the license to the commissioner for cancellation.
    c. mark the license canceled, and give it to the salesperson.
    d. destroy the license and notify the commissioner of the termination of employment immediately.

146. Withdrawals from the real estate broker's trust account cannot be made without the signature of the broker or the signature of at least one of which of the following persons when authorized by the broker?

    a. A salesperson in the broker's employ
    b. Any corporate officer of a corporation licensed as a broker
    c. Any unlicensed employee, provided such employee is covered by a sufficient fiduciary bond indemnifying the broker against losses due to the acts of the specific employee
    d. All of the above

147. Within one month after the closing of a transaction, a real estate broker handling the transaction shall cause information to be given to both seller and the purchaser in writing regarding the

    a. name, address, and license number of the escrow holder.
    b. true selling price of the property.
    c. exact amount of the licensee's compensation on the transaction.
    d. All of the above

148. For mechanic's lien purposes, all of the following are considered equivalent to completion of improvements *EXCEPT*

    a. a cessation of labor for a continuous period of 60 days.
    b. the elapse of an 18-month period of construction on a single-family home improvement.
    c. acceptance of the work of improvement by the owner.
    d. occupation by the owner accompanied by cessation of labor of the improvement.

149. A township is

    a. six square miles.
    b. 36 sections.
    c. larger than a range.
    d. one square mile.

150. A policy of title insurance requires a careful search of the public records. The public records covered are located at the

    a. county recorder's office.
    b. federal land office.
    c. county clerk's office.
    d. All of the above

■ ANSWER KEY

1. c. The definition of property is "the rights or interest that a person has in the thing owned."

2. a. The question compares condominium interests and rental interests. An owner has a fee simple interest in the airspace in the condominium unit. A tenant has a leasehold interest in the unit. Both are types of estates in real property.

3. c. An estate in fee, or *fee simple* as it is commonly known, is an interest that can be inherited; hence, another name is *estate of inheritance*.

4. b. When there are deed restrictions on property, it is known as *fee simple defeasible*. This means that title can be "defeated" or lost if the conditions are violated.

5. b. All interests on a life estate terminate when the person on whose life the estate depends dies. Even though the lease was for five years, it is only valid until the one who holds the life estate dies.

6. c. Something incorporated (attached or affixed) into the land is defined as a fixture.

7. c. *Tenancy* refers to a mode or method of holding title to real property. It does not refer to leasehold matters as used in this context.

8. d. A quiet title action is a court action that "quiets" or settles a dispute concerning title. It is often used to clear a cloud on the title.

9. d. An encumbrance is a burden of some type on the title (i.e., a loan, property taxes, or mechanic's lien). It is anything that affects or limits the fee simple title to property. Most real property is subject to some type of encumbrance.

10. c. The effective interest rate is another way of saying annual percentage rate. It is the rate the borrower is actually paying for the use of someone else's money. It includes finance charges as well as the interest rate. The nominal rate is the interest rate only and is stated or named in the note.

11. d. Jointly and severally mean together or alone (as severed). This means that the borrowers are fully responsible for the repayment of the loan together or individually.

12. d. The note is the evidence of the debt. It contains the promise to pay and is a contract complete unto itself. The deed of trust is a security device used to secure the note.

13. b. A straight note calls for the payment of interest only with the entire principal due and payable at the end of the term of the note.

14. b. Amortization tables are commonly used to determine the monthly payment of a debt.

15. b. The term *appurtenant* means "runs with"; therefore, an easement appurtenant runs with the land. The appurtenant easement across Whitecare held by Blackacre can be used by the new owner of Blackacre.

16. d. The enactment of zoning laws is a common example of government's use of police power.

17. c. The creation of a general plan for a city's growth and development includes allocating a certain number of parcels for residential, commercial, and industrial usage. Zoning is a way to implement usage. Zoning is a way to implement the plan to best serve the needs of the general public within a city.

18. d. The term *subject to* comes from "subject to the original terms and conditions of this loan." This indicates that the original borrower, who is now a seller of the property, is still liable for the loan. Therefore, the buyer will not be personally liable for the loan. There are not many "subject to" takeover loans anymore because of the enforcement of the due-on-sale clause. Often, an older VA loan can be taken over on a "subject to" basis.

19. a. There is no prepayment penalty allowed on most loans for single-family owner-occupied residential purposes after seven years under the Business and Professional code 10242.6. (Under Civil Code 2954.9 there is no prepayment penalty allowed after five years on certain loans.)

20. b. A trust deed recorded after work has officially begun on the property puts it in a subordinate position to a mechanic's lien. The date that a mechanic's lien takes is the date the work of improvement commences on the job. In this case if the property is sold, the mechanic's lien would be paid before the trust deed and note.

21. c. A lis pendens is a lawsuit that is pending concerning the title to property. It clouds the title until the matter of the lawsuit is resolved.

22. d. Title companies customarily search many public records before issuing a title policy ensuring that a good title is passing to the buyer. This includes a search of the records at the local, state, and federal levels.

23. b. Unrecorded liens and easements are not protected by a standard policy of title insurance. Many title companies will insure for these unrecorded items on an owner's extended title policy.

24. c. An ALTA owner's (extended coverage) policy usually protects the matter of property lines and possible encroachments.

25. a. The question indicates that Jones is not licensed. It is the district attorney who has the right to prosecute for violations of real estate law by unlicensed persons. The Real Estate Commissioner has authority over only those who are licensed in real estate.

26. a. A real estate broker's license of record is required for the firm or person who manages other people's property for compensation or in anticipation of compensation.

27. c. Both the broker and the salesperson are required to keep a copy of the employment agreement for three years from the date of termination of the employment.

28. a. The term REALTOR® is a trade name owned by the National Association of REALTORS®. Only its members are legally entitled to use the term. The illegal use of this term could lead to suspension or revocation of the real estate license.

29. c. The definition of *company dollar* is the income that remains after all commissions (including cooperative broker commission splits) are paid. The income that remains is used to run the company.

30. c. What makes the ad legal is the inclusion of the actual interest specified in the note shown separately from the discount rate.

31. b. The mortgage loan disclosure statement must be given to the borrower at the time of signing.

32. c. Under the Truth-in-Lending Act, when advertising consumer credit, either advertise in general terms, such as those found in choices *a*, *b*, and *d*, or if one

detail in the ad is given about credit terms, all details must be given. The question asks for the exception. Choice *c* gives two details of credit. It is incorrect. Remember, if one detail is given, all of the details pertinent to this loan must be given. Or just the annual percentage rate could be advertised as long as it is fully spelled out, not abbreviated.

33. b. The California Department of Fair Employment and Housing is the agency that will receive complaints of alleged violations of fair housing laws.

34. b. In 1968, the U.S. Supreme Court ruled in *Jones v. Mayer* that there shall be no racial discrimination in the United States concerning property matters.

35. c. Avoiding showing properties found in integrated areas to minority buyers is an example of the illegal practice of steering.

36. d. As employment increases and production rises, there is more personal income, which typically creates a greater demand for housing.

37. d. Any change in the real estate industry, including changes in the use of land and the concerns of consumers, will affect the real estate market either in a positive or negative way.

38. c. Leverage is a concept in which one uses little or none of one's own money for a purchase of property. Therefore, the purchase is made almost exclusively with borrowed funds.

39. c. When Carter first bought the parcels, he owned 10 lots and owed $180,000, or $18,000 per lot. Now he owes $140,000 ($20,000 down payment plus $40,000 paid on the note equals $60,000 paid for the property; $200,000 minus $60,000 equals $140,000). $140,000 divided by eight encumbered lots equals $17,500 owed per lot. His equity has increased.

40. d. Warehousing in the loan industry refers mainly to a mortgage banker who makes loans to the general public, then packages the loans (warehouses them) for sale to the secondary mortgage market. It is a holding or collecting of the loans until they are sold.

41. b. A real property conditional sales contract is another way to say *land contract*. In a land contract, only equitable and not legal title passes to the buyer at the time of the sale. Legal title passes to the buyer when the terms of the loan contract are met (until then the legal title to the property remains with the seller). This type of sale is sometimes used for a buyer who has little money down coupled with a seller who is willing to carry the loan for this high-risk buyer.

42. c. It is the buyer who must sign the quit-claim deed to remove the claim to the title to the property, and in doing so the buyer removes the cloud on title.

43. d. It is permissible to advertise just the annual percentage rate (fully spelled out) with no additional disclosures required under the Truth-in-Lending Act that regulates consumer credit offerings.

44. c. A right-to-cancel notice applies to all consumer credit transactions in which the obligation is secured by a lien on the consumer's principal dwelling. However, be aware that there are some exemptions to the right-to-cancel notice (right of rescission), such as a loan for the purchase of one's personal residence.

45. c. It is the lender who is responsible for informing the consumer of credit terms.

46. b. Both FHA and PMI (private mortgage insurance) insure loans.

47. c.   As an escrow is preparing to close, the escrow holder sends a completed "loan package" with completed loan documents in it to the lender and awaits confirmation that the lender is ready to fund the loan when requested by the escrow holder. An escrow holder cannot give legal advice. Also, he or she cannot change or authorize anything without the written consent of the parties to the escrow, who are the buyer and the seller, not the broker.

48. c.   Putting the sale of a trust deed into the hands of a neutral third party (escrow) is a wise practice to minimize the chances of terms and conditions not being met or being overlooked.

49. c.   AIDS is not a required disclosure unless asked.

50. d.   RESPA is a federal law that requires that certain disclosures be made to borrowers on one-family to four-family dwelling transactions. An example of an important disclosure is the good-faith estimate of loan costs that a lender must give on receipt of loan application or within three business days thereof.

51. b.   A specific performance lawsuit is a way to enforce a valid real estate contract. One of the requirements for a valid contract is sufficient consideration.

52. a.   The form of representation must be disclosed as soon as is practicable.

53. c.   The most common and preferred way to create an agency relationship is by written agreement. In practice it is done by a written exclusive right-to-sell listing agreement in which the principal (owner) employs the broker to act as the owner's agent in the sale of the property.

54. d.   Voluntary offer by one party does not create an agency relationship. The other choices are possible ways.

55. b.   In California, a dual agency relationship is legal with the "informed consent" of all parties to the contract.

56. d.   An earnest money deposit may be money or its equivalent. The other three choices are all examples of equivalents.

57. d.   Not permissible. The seller must be informed of all offers and be given the opportunity to consider them.

58. a.   Choice *a* is a good definition of the fiduciary duty of an agent to a buyer.

59. d.   It is legal for a real estate sales brokerage to advertise a gift, provided the conditions for earning the gift are in the ad.

60. a.   Since Cruz was Welch's agent, Welch had responsibility for the representations made by Cruz. This was why Hall was able to sue Welch, who then had the right to sue Cruz for not disclosing the information to Hall.

61. d.   All three choices are ways to describe a listing agreement.

62. b.   The question asks for the exception. In all but choice *b*, the broker would have to prove procuring cause (the cause of the purchase) to earn a commission.

63. a.   Even when residential property one-family to four-family units are sold "as is," a real property transfer disclosure statement is required to be given by the seller to the buyer. However, a disclosure is not a warranty of condition.

64. a.   The question asks for the choice that would not terminate an offer. Once an offeree (seller) has communicated the acceptance of an offer to the offeror (buyer), a contract between them is formed. An attempt by an offeror to revoke the offer at that point would not terminate it.

65. d. The question asks for the exception. Rejection of the offer by the offeree (seller) automatically terminates the offer. (Watch for the play on words. The correct expressions would be "revocation by offeror" or "rejection by offeree.")

66. c. The question states "the deposit will be . . ." The liquidated damages clause, if initialed and activated, states that the most the buyer can lose is 3 percent of the purchase price of the deposit, whichever is less. This question asks about the disposition of the deposit. The broker is entitled to one-half of what the seller collects of the deposit, after deducting costs of collection, if any. In any event, the broker's share shall not exceed the amount the broker would have earned as commission.

67. a. Choice *a* is a good definition of the marginal tax.

68. c. Statement of fact.

69. a. Statement of fact.

70. c. It is deductible for income tax purposes.

71. d. Because land is not a wasting asset, it is not depreciated for income tax purposes.

72. d. Statement of fact for tax purposes.

73. c. Sampson had a recognized gain, which means taxable gain because she acquired a less expensive property instead of exchanging for one that was equal or greater in value than what she sold.

74. a. Internal Revenue Code 1031 requires the exchange of like-kind properties. Choices *b, c,* and *d* fit the category of "like kind."

75. c. The question asks which one would not be subject to property tax. Intangible personal property would not be; however, the other choices would be.

76. c. Statement of fact.

77. d. Choices *a, b,* and *c* include some of the disclosures required on the sale of a condominium.

78. a. A sidewalk is part of the common area and not the unit itself.

79. a. $206.25 × 4 units × 12 months = $9,900. $9,900 × .95 (100% − 5% for vacancy) = $9,405 (effective gross income). $9,405 − $4,140 (operating expenses) = $5,265 (net operating expenses) = $5,265 divided by .08 (rate of return) = $65,812.50.

80. b. $125,000 × .88 (percent borrowed) = $110,000 (loan amount). $139,750 (selling price) − $110,000 (loan amount) = $29,750 equity. Remember that at the time he bought the house, his down payment became instant equity in the house.

81. b. $72,000 doubled in value to $144,000. $144,000 sales price − $52,000 loan = $92,000 current equity. $92,000 divided by $20,000 original down payment = 460% return on equity or $4.60 for each original dollar of equity. Again, remember that the original down payment is treated as instant equity in the property.

82. d. The question gives quarterly income. Take $265,000 × 4 to arrive at annual income of $1,060,000 × .68 (100% − 32%) that equals $720,800 net income.

83. d. $117,800 divided by the capitalization rate of .08 = $1,472,500.

84. c. $80,000 × .90 (100% − 10% vacancy) = $72,000 (effective gross income). $72,000 − $25,000 operating expenses = $47,000 (net operating expenses). $47,000 divided by value $450,000 = 10.4% capitalization rate.

85. c. $1000 monthly × 12 months = $12,000 annual income. Three months of vacancies divided by 60 months in 5 years equals 5 percent vacancy factor. $12,000 × .95 (100% − 5% vacancy) equals $11,400 (effective gross income). $11,400 − $3,000 expenses equals $8,400 net operating income divided by a .10 cap rate equals $84,000 value.

86. d. $4,050 annual interest divided by .09 equals $45,000 (loan amount) divided by .80 (percentage of loan-to-value ratio) equals $56,250.

87. d. $20,000 loan × .02 = $400 (prepayment penalty). $20,000 × .04 = $800 (points charged). $18,500 (average loan balance) × .08 (interest rate) = $1,480 (annual interest) × 5 years = $7,400 (total interest) + $400 (prepayment penalty) + $800 (points) = $8,600.

88. d. 11% (interest rate) × $5,000 (loan amount) = $550 (annual interest) divided by 12 = $45.83 (monthly interest). $51.61 (total payment) − $45.83 (interest) = $5.78 (principal).

89. c. $73,700 (selling price) divided by 1.17 (100% representing the unknown cost plus 17% profit) = $62,991.45.

90. d. $63,360 (purchase price) divided by .88 (100% representing the unknown selling price − 12% to cover selling costs) = $72,000 (selling price) − $63,360 = $8,640 increase in value needed to cover the selling costs.

91. d. Statement of fact.

92. b. The concern by the appraiser is that there could be some leakage of the underground gasoline tanks that might exist on the abandoned gasoline station property, in addition to other environmental concerns.

93. d. A fee appraiser is one who is self-employed and charges a fee for each appraisal report.

94. d. The assessed value to the property by the tax assessor does not influence the appraiser's estimate of value. Choices *a*, *b*, and *c* are all considerations in the appraisal process.

95. d. Choices *a*, *b*, and *c* are all considered in the appraisal process.

96. c. *Unearned increment* refers to an increase in value of property due to no effort on the part of the owner. The increase could be the result of an increase in population that creates a higher demand for property, or the increase could be due to inflation.

97. a. The market data approach is the simplest approach to value and is familiar to most real estate licensees, as real estate agents are used to comparing property values.

98. c. Statement of fact.

99. c. Statement of fact.

100. b. The cost approach is used for one-of-a-kind properties, including special-purpose properties (e.g., libraries, courthouses, hospitals).

101. d. The four elements or characteristics that create value can be remembered by the memory jogger called *DUST*: *d*emand, *u*tility, *s*carcity, and *t*ransferability.

102. d. Industrial property, such as a warehouse, has value based on its volume; therefore, the cubic contents are appraised.

103. d. *Replacement cost* refers to the cost to replace a building that is similar to the existing building and has the same utility factor. (*Reproduction cost* refers to an exact replica of the existing building).

104. c. A restaurant is an income-producing property; therefore, the income approach is used.

105. b. The gross rent multiplier is a number that shows the relationship between value and gross rent in one step. The formula is: Sales Price divided by Gross Rent = the Gross Rent Multiplier.

106. b. $5,000 × 12 months = $60,000 annual income – $12,000 (expenses) = $48,000 (net operating income) divided by .12 cap rate = $400,000 (total value) – $300,000 (cost of building) = $100,000 (amount that can be spent on the land).

107. b. *Economic life* refers to the productive life of property and is usually shorter than the number of years that the building actually stands (physical lines).

108. b. *Depreciation* refers to a loss in value from any cause.

109. d. *Functional obsolescence* refers to features that are outdated (e.g., old-fashioned kitchen appliances, out-of-date plumbing fixtures). Those could cause one property to be less valuable than the other.

110. c. The first step in site analysis is to determine its highest and best use.

111. a. A kiosk is a small freestanding building used for information purposes, such as the type found in a shopping mall, or at an entrance to a subdivision development, or a university.

112. d. A plot plan guides the placement of construction and related land improvements.

113. b. If the interior side of an exterior wall feels the same as other interior walls, then the insulation is doing its job. Heat and air are not being lost.

114. b. Statement of fact.

115. a. Having the termite report (properly called a *structural pest control report*) ready at the time the property is put on the market for sale is good practice. It becomes one less item to be concerned with regarding the condition of the property.

116. c. The term *recurring costs* refers to those expenses that will have to be paid again within the next year or two. Impound items are monthly payments held by the lender to pay for taxes and insurance.

117. b. An executrix is a female person who is named in the will to administer the estate of the deceased person.

118. d. Depreciation provides for a recapture of the invested capital in improvements. A certain amount of income is set aside each year to allow for the wearing out or depreciation of the improvements.

119. c. The total amount of sales would be found in the profit and loss section of a financial statement, not in the balance sheet section. The question asks for the exception.

120. d. The question asks for the choice that least applies which is choice *d*. Choices *a*, *b*, and *c* can all be applied to what makes up goodwill.

121. a. The listing agreement, when signed by the seller, authorizes the broker to act in the seller's behalf. The listing agreement is an employment contract between the owner and the broker, even if the salesperson for the broker takes the listing.

122. a. Mortgage loan correspondents are mortgage companies that, after making loans sell them into the secondary mortgage market.

123. b. Most homebuyers buy for the primary need of shelter. Speculation for most buyers is a secondary motive.

124. a. A franchisor (seller) who has a net worth of at least $5 million is exempt from certain parts of the Franchise Investment Law when selling franchises to the general public.

125. b. If the broker exceeds the authority given by the seller, then the broker becomes liable to the buyer for the excessive acts.

126. b. Of the many disclosures required of a lender, the two most important ones are the finance charge and the annual percentage rate.

127. a. A straight note calls for the payment of interest only with the principal still due and payable at the end of the term. This type of note is often used by investors who want leverage. In other words, this is a way to buy property where investors use little or none of their own money for the purchase, with the intent to resell at a profit at a later date, having used someone else's money for the transaction.

128. b. Under an exclusive authorization and right-to-sell listing, an owner promises to pay the broker a commission, regardless of how the property sells during the listing period. This promise is made in exchange for the broker's promise to use diligence in procuring a purchaser for the property.

129. d. Personal property can be used as security for a loan (hypothecated), transferred (alienated), and assessed (for personal property tax purposes).

130. b. Most percentage leases are based on a percentage of the monthly gross sales of a business along with a minimum rent.

131. d. A lessee (tenant) has a leasehold interest in property. The term *chattel* is an old English expression that means personal property. The lease or document is a personal property item; therefore, the term *chattel real* applies to a leasehold interest.

132. a. Real property is all that is immovable, which is its most distinguishing characteristic.

133. c. The job of a property manager is multifaceted; however, the accounting requirements are extraordinary.

134. a. Real property syndications are under the jurisdiction of the Commission of Corporations (not the Real Estate Commissioner). Choices *b* and *c* are under the jurisdiction of the Real Estate Commissioner.

135. d. Choices *a*, *b*, and *c* are not exempt.

136. a. Cal-Vet has a variable interest rate loan.

137. a. Realtists is a tradename owned by the National Association of Real Estate Brokers. REALTORS® is a trade name owned by the National Association of REALTORS®. Only members of these organizations are legally entitled to use the appropriate trade name.

138. c. The intent of a zoning ordinance is to promote the general health, safety, and welfare of the community.

139. b. The two legal requirements for a valid escrow are a binding contract between the buyer and the seller and the conditional delivery of the transfer instrument (deed) to a third party (escrow holder).

140. d. A quiet title action is a court action used to clear a cloud on title. This action can be used to clear a cloud on a land contract default.

141. a. A trustor is a borrower. This clause allows the borrower to obtain a construction loan that a lender requires to be recorded as a first trust deed to protect its position.

142. d. All must be completed before sale.

143. c. 15 percent commission is allowed for junior trust deeds under $20,000 to be paid in three years or more.

144. c. Written authorization from the noteholder is required before the broker can service the loan for the noteholder.

145. a. Currently, the broker is to notify the Real Estate Commissioner within five days of a salesperson's leaving or joining the firm.

146. d. The parties listed in choices *a, b,* and *c* are authorized to make withdrawals.

147. b. When the broker performs escrow services for in-house transactions, the broker must notify the seller and buyer of the true selling price within one month after close of escrow. However, in the more usual real estate transaction, an escrow holder (other than the broker) is the one who sends a settlement statement to all parties at the close of escrow.

148. b. The question asks for the exception. Choices *a, c,* and *d* are considered equivalent to completion.

149. b. A township is a six-mile square that contains 36 square miles called *sections*. Notice that the term *mile square* refers to shape, while the term *square mile* refers to area.

150. d. A title company routinely checks the records at the local, state, and federal levels and usually protects against those matters of record at those offices.

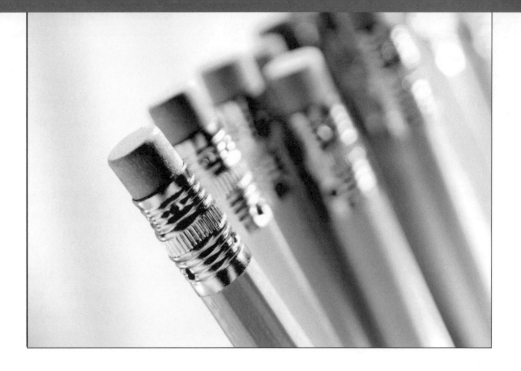

PRACTICE EXAMINATION VIII

1. Current California laws regarding residential rental and lease agreements provide that landlords have how many days to return the unused portion of a security deposit?
   a. 30 days
   c. 10 days
   b. 21 days
   d. Immediately

2. The provisions of the California State Housing Act are enforced by the
   a. Real Estate Commissioner.
   b. local officials who regulate the issuance of building permits.
   c. FHA and VA.
   d. local health officers.

3. To gain a hedge on inflation, one would most likely put money into
   a. a savings account.
   b. government backed trust deeds or mortgages.
   c. long-term government bonds.
   d. equity assets.

4. The opposite of "alienation" is
   a. subrogation.
   c. subordination.
   b. acquisition.
   d. hypothecation.

5. The city is interested in constructing an airport on Ace Corporation's property. The city presents to the board of directors of the corporation an offer to purchase the property. If the corporation refuses to sell the property to the city, what is the city's other method of acquiring this property?
   a. Execution sale
   b. Adverse possession
   c. Eminent domain
   d. Police power

6. Laws that are enacted to protect the "health, safety, and welfare" of the general public are enforced through
   a. eminent domain.
   b. police power.
   c. the majority vote of the people.
   d. the Internal Revenue Service.

7. When creating a new subdivision, which of the following would be least economical?

   a. Long blocks
   b. Left-angled intersections into a major street
   c. Cul-de-sac designs
   d. Short blocks

8. Able refuses to take an oath but is required to make a public statement. This can be done by a(n)

   a. notarization.
   b. affirmation.
   c. affidavit.
   d. acknowledgement.

9. The sale of a business opportunity is conveyed by a

   a. chattel mortgage.
   b. bill of sale signed by the vendee.
   c. bill of sale signed by the vendor.
   d. grant deed.

10. On the roof of a residence, the wooden shingles are nailed to the

    a. joists.   c. sheathing.
    b. rafters.   d. ridge board.

11. The supports that are parallel to the floor and ceiling are called

    a. joists.   c. rafters.
    b. studs.   d. beams.

12. In the sale of a business opportunity, which of the following would require the payment of sales tax?

    a. Fixtures and/or furniture
    b. The value of goodwill
    c. Accounts receivable
    d. All of the above

13. When selling a business opportunity, the Bulk Sales Law under the Uniform Commercial Code requires a person to

    a. notify individual creditors.
    b. post a notice of the intention to sell.
    c. publish the notification of sale.
    d. All of the above

14. Buyer Able and seller Baker enter into a contract whereby the parties made a conditional delivery of all the required items to the escrow company. During the escrow period, Baker asked that the deed be released so he could show it to his attorney. Able refused to consent to the release of the deed, although the escrow company was willing to comply with all requests of the parties. The escrow company

    a. could release the deed to Baker.
    b. could not release the deed to Baker.
    c. could file an interpleader action concerning the deed.
    d. had to give the deed to Baker as it was acting as an agent for both parties.

15. Title VIII of the Civil Rights Act of 1968 is also known as the federal Fair Housing Act. The act prohibits discrimination in the sale, rental, or leasing of a dwelling. If a person believes he or she has been discriminated against in buying property in California, all of the following action could be taken *EXCEPT*

    a. a lawsuit for monetary damages.
    b. a lawsuit filed in either a state or federal court.
    c. having the broker's licenser suspended or revoked.
    d. suing for any actual expenses incurred.

16. Johnson genuinely believes she was discriminated against. What action could she take?

    a. File private action in a state or federal court
    b. File civil action in a State Superior Court
    c. File criminal action in a state court
    d. File criminal action in a federal court

17. The "statutory dedication process" is completed when the

    a. dedicated area is completed.
    b. final subdivision map is recorded.
    c. appointed representative of the city or county signs off, accepting the dedicated parcels.
    d. local authorities deliver a signed acceptance to the subdivider.

18. The term *boot* usually has an impact on

    a. income tax.
    b. grant deeds.
    c. promissory notes.
    d. financing concessions.

19. The maximum space permitted between wall studs under most building codes is

    a. 6 inches.
    b. 16 inches on center.
    c. 12 inches on center.
    d. 24 inches on center.

20. When does a subdivision preliminary public report expire?

    a. After one year
    b. On issuance of the final public report
    c. When a material change occurs
    d. All of the above

21. If the Real Estate Commissioner believes that fraudulent statements are being made in the sale of subdivision property under his or her jurisdiction, the commissioner can prevent the continuation of sales by

    a. immediately revoking the final public report.
    b. issuing a desist and refrain order.
    c. issuing a notice of pendency of action.
    d. issuing a writ of possession.

22. Which of the following would be the least effective document to search for a legal description?

    a. A preliminary title report
    b. The tax assessor's bill
    c. A title insurance policy
    d. A deed to real property

23. In the regulation of the sale of subdivisions under the control of the Real Estate Commissioner, which of the following would be of most concern?

    a. Streets
    b. Sewers
    c. Financing of the facilities in the common area
    d. All of the above

24. For federal income tax purposes, a taxpayer could adjust the basis of her personal residence for

    a. depreciation.
    b. interest on loans.
    c. premiums on insurance.
    d. cost of a new swimming pool and new patio.

25. The "band of investment" theory is used to calculate a

    a. discount rate.
    b. interest rate.
    c. capitalization rate.
    d. annual percentage rate.

26. For income tax purposes, which of the following qualifies for depreciation?

    a. Unimproved land
    b. Owner-occupied residences
    c. Owner-occupied farmhouses
    d. Commercial peach orchards

27. From the following, select the best definition of a *commercial acre*.

    a. Any area within a commercially zoned neighborhood
    b. Any acre that contains retail stores and offices
    c. Any acre between residential and industrial areas
    d. An acre in a subdivision after deducting for streets, sidewalks, and other public areas

28. Evans builds a new personal residence. The transportation agency wants to move it back to widen the street. This is an example of

    a. functional obsolescence.
    b. economic obsolescence.
    c. physical deterioration.
    d. accrued depreciation.

29. The best method to use in appraising land is

    a. the averaging of the results of the three appraisal approaches.
    b. the capitalization of net income approach.
    c. the market data approach.
    d. to determine the cost of the improvements appropriate for this type of land and add back the land cost.

30. The main cause of depreciation is

    a. loss of physical life.
    b. deferred maintenance.
    c. obsolescence.
    d. deterioration.

31. Willett owns income property and is considering adding a swimming pool to the property. Which principle of value should he be concerned with?

    a. Balance   c. Substitution
    b. Anticipation   d. Contribution

32. When appraising income property by means of the cost approach, the appraiser would also use the market data approach to

    a. estimate the capitalization rate.
    b. determine the value of the land.
    c. determine the depreciation schedule.
    d. estimate the duration of the income stream.

33. The instrument used to remove a lien of a trust deed from the records is called a

    a. deed of reconveyance.
    b. release.
    c. satisfaction.
    d. certificate of redemption.

34. Joan Roberts recorded the title to her existing property as "a single woman." Later, she married John Smith and changed her name on her deed to read, "Joan Smith, a married woman." This name change

    a. would probably not affect any future reconveyance of title.
    b. would have little effect as the legal description on the deed is sufficient for any future transfer.
    c. could create a cloud on the title.
    d. would indicate that the property is held as community property.

35. *Value* is most closely related to

    a. cost.
    b. price.
    c. utility.
    d. worth.

36. Which instrument transfers title from a sovereign to a member of the general public?

    a. A government patent
    b. A deed
    c. A quitclaim deed
    d. A warranty deed

37. In the conveyance of title to real property, which of the following is a requirement?

    a. Delivery of the grant deed
    b. Recordation of the grant deed
    c. Issuance of a title insurance policy
    d. A buyer in possession of the property

38. Regarding the sale of probate property, who sets the broker's commission?

    a. The executrix of the estate
    b. The administrator of the estate
    c. The court
    d. The real estate broker

39. All of the following are essential to acquiring an easement by prescription *EXCEPT*

    a. open and notorious use of the land of another.
    b. use that is hostile to the owner.
    c. payment of real property taxes for five years.
    d. some claim of right or color of title.

40. All of the following are capable of being assigned *EXCEPT*

    a. trust deed.
    b. grant deed.
    c. deposit agreements.
    d. lease agreements.

41. Susan Johnson decides to look for property while her husband Bill is out of town. Susan locates what she believes is the perfect property for them. Because she wants to act quickly before anyone else buys this property, she instructs a broker to write an offer in their behalf. She gives the broker a check for the deposit and signs the purchase agreement. The contract should be signed as

    a. the Johnsons, by Susan Johnson.
    b. Bill Johnson and Susan Johnson, Husband and Wife.
    c. Bill Johnson and Susan Johnson, by Susan Johnson.
    d. Susan Johnson.

42. The term *et ux* means

    a. "and others."
    b. "and children."
    c. "and wife."
    d. None of the above

43. The position of the parties to a real property sales contract would be similar to

    a. trustor to trustee.
    b. mortgagor to mortgagee.
    c. landlord to tenant.
    d. trustee to beneficiary.

44. Regarding the Real Estate Settlement Procedures Act, known as RESPA,

    a. the borrower must be provided with a good-faith estimate of settlement costs on application for the loan or within three business days thereof.
    b. the borrower is entitled to inspect the actual settlement statement one business day prior to the close of escrow, unless this right is waived by the borrower.
    c. if the lender or the escrow holder requires the use of specific title company services or pays or receives kickbacks, it could be subject to a fine and possible imprisonment.
    d. All of the above

45. An institutional lender would be interested in all of the following *EXCEPT* the

    a. value of the property.
    b. borrower's income and credit history.
    c. amount of the down payment.
    d. borrower's desire for the property.

46. The majority of money used for home loans comes from

    a. individual savings accounts.
    b. federal reserves.
    c. government bonds.
    d. insurance reserves.

47. All of the following are noninstitutional lenders *EXCEPT*

    a. university endowments.
    b. pension funds.
    c. insurance funds.
    d. mortgage companies.

48. Which of the following lenders is least likely to make a home loan?

    a. Banks
    b. Savings and loans
    c. Mortgage companies
    d. Insurance companies

49. Which of the following signs a reconveyance deed?

    a. The trustor   c. The beneficiary
    b. The trustee   d. The grantor

50. The prepayment penalty clause in a deed of trust is a benefit to the

    a. trustor.   c. beneficiary.
    b. trustee.   d. All the above

51. The mortgagor is the one who

    a. holds the trust deed.
    b. sells the property.
    c. signs the note.
    d. sells the mortgage.

52. Regarding the deed of trust, it

    a. is the evidence of the debt.
    b. is held by the trustor.
    c. outlaws in four years.
    d. is the security for the note.

53. An alienation clause in a note

   a. causes the note to be nonnegotiable.
   b. does not affect its negotiability and may enhance its desirability.
   c. is of no benefit to a note.
   d. allows the note to be assumed more easily.

54. Mrs. Dawson sells a $10,000 note secured by a deed of trust to investor Lee for $7,500. This transaction can be described as

   a. leveraging.   c. illegal.
   b. usurious.   d. discounting.

55. The secondary mortgage market could be described as

   a. where loans are made directly to borrowers.
   b. mortgages passed between mortgagees.
   c. mortgages passed between mortgagors.
   d. seller carryback transaction.

56. Loan-to-value ratios refer to loan amounts compared with

   a. the original amount due on the note.
   b. percentage of assessed value.
   c. percentage of sales price.
   d. percentage of appraised value.

57. Which of the following is the most commonly used title insurance policy?

   a. American Land Title Association
   b. Standard and extended coverage policies are used equally
   c. California Land Title Association standard coverage
   d. California Land Title Association extended coverage

58. From the following, select the terms that are synonymous.

   a. Interim loan, construction loan
   b. Short-term loan, takeout loan
   c. Takeout loan, construction loan
   d. Short-term loan, standby loan

59. The reason a lender charges loan points is to

   a. be competitive in interest rates.
   b. equalize interest rates.
   c. make adjustments between fixed rate loans and ARMs in its loan portfolio.
   d. increase the lender's yield.

60. Which of the following is usually in writing and is a revocable and assignable instrument?

   a. An easement
   b. A license
   c. An appurtenance
   d. A trust deed

61. For federal income tax purposes, which of the following may a homeowner deduct?

   a. The expenses for fixing up the property
   b. The mortgage interest
   c. Depreciation from wear and tear
   d. The cost to landscape the slope behind the property

62. The current depreciation rate for commercial property is

   a. 15 percent.   c. 27½ percent.
   b. 28 years.   d. 39 years.

63. For what period of time is an appraisal good on a single-family residence?

    a. For six months from the date of the appraisal
    b. As of the date of property inspection and report
    c. On the date the appraisal is given to the client
    d. Indefinitely

64. What is the ultimate test of functional utility?

    a. Marketability
    b. Layout
    c. Adequacy
    d. Deferred maintenance

65. Which type of depreciation is the most difficult to overcome in a property?

    a. Physical deterioration
    b. Functional obsolescence
    c. External obsolescence
    d. Future depreciation

66. The key factor in a developer's decision in choosing the best site for a shopping center is the

    a. traffic count.
    b. purchasing power.
    c. marketing study.
    d. population.

67. The expression "numerous buyers and sellers, with equal knowledge about products and prices" defines a(n)

    a. imperfect market.
    b. perfect market.
    c. real estate market.
    d. changing market.

68. Equity in real property is defined as the

    a. cash-on-cash return.
    b. total of all mortgage payments made to date.
    c. difference between mortgage indebtedness and market value.
    d. appraised value.

69. Under the Truth-in-Lending Act, who must inform consumers of credit terms?

    a. The lender
    b. The broker
    c. The escrow company
    d. The trustee

70. A dual agency relationship is legal in California if

    a. all parties are informed before the close of escrow.
    b. the buyer and the seller consent to it.
    c. the broker and the escrow company agree to it.
    d. all parties are advised after they sign the purchase contract.

71. Broker Willet is not a member of any trade organization. Yet, he has been using "a new breed of Realtor" in his advertisements. This practice

    a. could lead to revocation and suspension of his real estate license.
    b. is permissible if he does not capitalize the term *realtor*.
    c. is a clear violation of fair housing laws.
    d. is permissible, as it is common practice.

72. Which of the following comprises the largest area?

    a. 5,280 feet × 10,560 feet
    b. 1 mile × 1 mile
    c. 10 percent of a township
    d. 4 sections

73. An acre of land is divided into four equal lots that are parallel to each other. The depth of the lots is 240 feet. What is the width of each lot that faces the sunny side of Evergreen Lane?

    a. ¼ acre
    b. 181.5 feet·
    c. 45.4 feet
    d. 4 rods

74. The Uniform Commercial code document (UCC-1) to be filed with the Secretary of State on financing the purchase of a business opportunity is the

    a. bill of sale.
    b. security agreement.
    c. financing statement.
    d. financial statement.

75. The U.S. Supreme Court case that prohibits racial discrimination in the sale, lease, or rental of property was in

    a. 1988.
    b. 1974.
    c. 1968.
    d. 1962.

76. Which of the following acts provides for the handicapped?

    a. Americans with Disabilities Act
    b. California Fair Employment and Housing Act
    c. Title VIII of the Civil Rights Act of 1968
    d. None of the above

77. Greene put a six-foot-wide cement sidewalk on the outside of a corner lot that measures 100 feet by 100 feet. At $1.20 per square foot, approximately how much would Greene pay for the sidewalk?

    a. $1,350
    b. $1,390
    c. $1,440
    d. $1,485

78. Developer Steve owns 80 acres with a ¼-mile frontage on the street. In order to take some soil tests, he hired a tractor operator to bulldoze four paths, each 50 feet wide. One path is to be lengthwise in the center of the lot and three paths are to be widthwise, one in the center and one at each end. At $60 an acre to clear the land, approximately how much will he pay for this work?

    a. $460
    b. $455
    c. $465
    d. $444

79. Perez purchased a lot for $63,360. Setting aside interest charges on the financing, property taxes, and all other variables, how much must the property increase in value in order for Perez to pay for closing costs and appraisal fees, which will be 12 percent?

    a. 25 percent
    b. 112 percent
    c. $4,075
    d. $8,640

80. The combination of lots A, B, and C sold for $39,000. Lot B was priced at $6,400 more than Lot A. Lot C was priced at $7,100 more than Lot B. What was the price of Lot A?

    a. $5,000
    b. $5,666.33
    c. $6,366.67
    d. $6,400

81. Louise has an $1,800 assessment lien on her property, payable in equal payments over 10 years beginning January 1 at 6 percent interest. She has made her payments for the past two years. On January 1 of the third year, she sells her home and states that all liens will be paid by the close of escrow, which will be April 1. Approximately how much will she pay at the closing?

    a. $1,440
    b. $1,462
    c. $1,526
    d. $1,708

82. Which of the following is the best illustration of a straight note?

    a. $16,000 × 8.5% for 4 years; $446 per month
    b. $19,000 × 9% for 5 years; $459 per month
    c. $11,000 × 9.5% for 3 years; $393 per month
    d. $28,000 × 12.5% for 4 years; $292 per month

83. Chung purchased a home for $72,000 with $20,000 down. The new deed of trust for $52,000 was a straight note. The value of the home doubled in value and sold for double the purchase price. What was his investment worth per dollar?

    a. $3.60
    b. $4.60
    c. $6.10
    d. $9.20

84. Ms. Crowell bought the contents of a store for $27,900. She sold the goods for 33⅓ percent more than they cost but lost 15 percent of the selling price in bad debts. Her profit on the venture was

    a. 18⅓ percent.
    b. $3,720.
    c. $5,580.
    d. $9,300.

85. Mr. Roberts appraised a 20-unit apartment building at $240,000 based on a 10 percent capitalization rate. Later, the monthly rental was increased by $10 per apartment. If the capitalization rate were raised to 12 percent, what would be the present value of the apartment building?

    a. $200,000
    b. $220,000
    c. $264,000
    d. None of the above

86. Which of the following is the best legal definition of a fixture?

    a. Something that is made part of a chattel real
    b. Something used in a usual way with the land
    c. Something incorporated into the land
    d. Something referred to in the sale contract

87. In comparing condominiums with apartment rentals, all of the following are incorrect EXCEPT the

    a. person who occupies each unit has an estate in real property.
    b. occupier has a fee estate.
    c. local tax assessor must assess each unit separately.
    d. None of the above

88. A real estate broker arranges a lease for 25 years on a building whose annual rent will always be $30,000. He arranges as his commission 7 percent of the rent for the first year, 5 percent for the next 4 years, 3 percent for the next 15 years, and 1 percent for the balance of the lease term. What would be his total commission for the years after the first 19?

 a. $1,200
 b. $1,500
 c. $2,400
 d. None of the above

89. How does a *lis pendens* affect title?

 a. Because it affects marketability of the property, only the court can clear up the matter.
 b. It clouds the title and affects the marketability of the property.
 c. It does not affect subsequent owners.
 d. It does not affect marketability.

90. What is a *quiet title* action?

 a. An action to settle noise disturbances
 b. An execution sale
 c. Purchasing property by a secret sale
 d. Court action to remove a cloud on title

91. Which of the following defines government's right of police power?

 a. Eminent domain proceedings against property to be taken for a freeway
 b. Adjudication of conflicting claims between past and present owners of a given parcel
 c. The placement of restrictive conditions on property by a prior grantor
 d. The enactment of zoning laws limiting the use that may be allowed for a piece of property

92. Jason has an income of less than $100,000 and is actively involved in the management of his commercial office building. He experienced a $10,000 operational loss for the tax year. For income tax purposes, he may

 a. deduct only half of the loss.
 b. offset the loss against any capital gains.
 c. deduct the full amount from his ordinary income.
 d. deduct only $2,500 of the loss from ordinary income.

93. Combining small adjoining lots into one large single-family ownership is done in anticipation of

 a. assemblage.
 b. progression.
 c. contribution.
 d. plottage increment.

94. Of the three appraisal approaches, which one is most adaptable for use by real estate licensees?

 a. Square-foot approach
 b. Market data approach
 c. Cost approach
 d. Income approach

95. When a licensee is appraising an improved parcel of property using the market data approach, there are adjustments to be made to the estimates of value. Why are these adjustments made?

 a. The property will likely depreciate.
 b. It is likely that the property will increase in value.
 c. Rarely are two properties similar concerning all features and benefits.
 d. None of the above

96. The position of trust assumed by salesperson Jackson, who is employed by broker Able, whose company will represent seller Baker is a(n)

    a. gratuitous relationship.
    b. trustor relationship.
    c. fiduciary relationship.
    d. employment relationship.

97. When an appraiser uses the term *reproduction cost* and the term *replacement cost*, replacement is most closely related to which of the following concepts?

    a. The original cost to replace the building
    b. The current cost to replace the building with an exact replica
    c. The cost to replace a building with another described as being of highest and best use
    d. The present cost to replace the building with another building with the same utility factor

98. The portion of prints that illustrate the footings and piers of a building is

    a. a plot plan.
    b. the schematics.
    c. the foundation plan.
    d. an elevation sheet.

99. If the interior surface of an exterior wall is the same temperature as the room temperature,

    a. the insulation is sufficient.
    b. the insulation is insufficient.
    c. heat is escaping.
    d. None of the above

100. A valid bill of sale must contain

    a. a date.
    b. an acknowledgment.
    c. the seller's signature.
    d. a verification.

101. Sometimes a borrower prefers a straight note to an amortized note. The straight note will have

    a. equal annual principal reduction payments.
    b. a total effective interest rate greater than if the loan were amortized.
    c. no principal payments during the term of the loan except on the last payment.
    d. None of the above

102. A buyer defaulted on a recorded real property sales contract. Whose signature would be required on a quitclaim deed to extinguish the cloud on title?

    a. Both the buyer and the seller
    b. The seller only
    c. The buyer only
    d. The trustee only

103. Which of the following best describes the relationship between an effective interest rate and a nominal interest rate? The effective interest rate is

    a. the rate the buyer will pay; the nominal rate is the same as the annual percentage rate.
    b. lower due to the nominal rate including charges other than the interest rate on the note.
    c. the rate the borrower is actually paying for the use of money; the nominal rate is the rate named in the note.
    d. None of the above

104. The primary purpose of RESPA is to

    a. regulate all types of loans.
    b. regulate only commercial loans.
    c. regulate industrial loans.
    d. require that lenders make certain disclosures on loans on one-unit to four-unit dwellings.

105. When a deed of trust is sold to an investor, the sale is usually processed by an escrow holder to

    a. meet the requirements of law.
    b. act as a witness to the sale.
    c. make certain that the terms and conditions of the sales contract are met prior to the close of escrow.
    d. take legal action against one of the parties if there is a default.

106. The good-faith estimate of loan costs required to be given to the borrower on certain loans includes the

    a. sum of the total direct and indirect costs of obtaining credit.
    b. sum of the total direct and indirect costs, excluding appraiser's fees.
    c. cost of credit expressed as a percentage.
    d. total direct and indirect loan costs, including title, appraisal, and loan escrow fees.

107. Usually when homes are to be sold, the buyer or lender will require a pest control report. Concerning the seller, it is wise for the seller to have the pest control inspection and report prepared

    a. before listing the property for sale.
    b. after the opening of escrow.
    c. before the opening of escrow.
    d. only if the lender request that it be done.

108. An exclusive right-to-sell listing agreement is a(n)

    a. promise for a promise.
    b. employment contract between the principal and the broker.
    c. bilateral agreement.
    d. All of the above

109. None of the following would terminate an offer to buy real property *EXCEPT* a(n)

    a. revocation of the offer by the offeree.
    b. rejection of the offer by the offeror.
    c. inquiry by the offeree as to whether the offeror will consider a longer escrow period.
    d. rejection of the offer by the offeree.

110. Seller Jansen has found a buyer for her condominium. She must give the buyer a copy of the

    a. CC&Rs.
    b. most recent financial statement of the homeowners' association.
    c. bylaws.
    d. All of the above

111. The most common way to create an agency relationship in the real estate industry is by

    a. cooperating with all brokers.
    b. actions of the parties.
    c. written agreement.
    d. estoppel.

112. Mrs. Landon purchased a residential income property for $375,000. If the land is valued at $100,000 and she obtained a loan for $300,000, what would be the first year's depreciation?

    a. $8,725   c. $12,000
    b. $10,000   d. $13,600

113. Where would a person file a complaint under the California Fair Employment and Housing Act?

    a. Department of Housing and Community Development
    b. Department of Fair Employment and Housing
    c. Department of Housing and Urban Development
    d. Federal Housing Administration

114. A real estate licensee avoids showing properties found in certain neighborhoods to minority buyers. This is an example of

    a. blockbusting.
    b. panic selling.
    c. steering.
    d. appropriate conduct.

115. Mr. Diaz wants to manage property for the general public. In order to do this, he must

    a. hold a real estate broker's license.
    b. have the Certified Property Manager designation.
    c. be a member of the California Association of REALTORS®.
    d. None of the above

116. The city decides to take a piece of property for public use. A condemnation action follows, and the owner is paid money for the taking. This is known as an

    a. insurance loss.
    b. involuntary conversion.
    c. inverse condemnation.
    d. involuntary lien.

117. Mr. and Mrs. McNalley have a combined income of $22,600. Both are 64 years of age and want to apply for a postponement of the payment of their real property taxes on their home. Where would they go for claim forms?

    a. The State Controller's Office
    b. The County Tax Assessor
    c. The County Tax Collector
    d. The Assessment Appeals Board

118. The Truth-in-Lending Act covers a(n)

    a. business loan.
    b. improvement loan for a duplex rental property.
    c. personal loan secured by a borrower's home.
    d. agricultural loan.

119. All of the following could create an agency agreement *EXCEPT* a(n)

    a. appointment by the principal.
    b. implied agreement between two parties.
    c. oral agreement.
    d. voluntary offer by the salesperson.

120. Seller Smith lists a property for sale with broker Brown. The property is purposely listed at a very high price with the intent to keep minorities out of the neighborhood. Several prospective buyers who are minorities see the property and make offers to purchase. Their offers are refused. Smith later sells to a nonminority buyer at a lower price than any other offer received. All are in violation of the law *EXCEPT* the

    a. seller.
    b. broker.
    c. nonminority buyer.
    d. None of the above

121. Who requires that there be a written employment agreement between the real estate broker and the salesperson?

    a. The Real Estate Commissioner
    b. The local Board of REALTORS®
    c. The Code of Ethics
    d. The National Association of REALTORS®

122. Under no circumstances may a broker

    a. receive a commission from both buyer and seller.
    b. appoint a salesperson to act for the broker as a manager.
    c. misrepresent material facts.
    d. sell the principal's property to a relative.

123. Jones held an easement over Smith's property. Jones no longer needed the easement. To terminate the easement, Jones could sign a

    a. partial release.
    b. quitclaim deed.
    c. grant deed.
    d. reconveyance deed.

124. Mr. Gilbert bought a new home with a loan secured by a first deed of trust. Mr. Anderson refinanced his home loan with the use of a first deed of trust and was able to take out some equity. Regarding the loan,

    a. neither Gilbert nor Anderson has the right to rescind their loans.
    b. both have the right to rescind.
    c. Gilbert has the right to rescind; Anderson does not.
    d. Anderson has the right to rescind; Gilbert does not.

125. Of the following loans, which would not require a down payment for a qualified borrower?

    a. Cal-Vet   c. FHA
    b. VA   d. Conventional

126. Ms. Frederick feels she has been discriminated against. What action could she take?

    a. File a civil action
    b. File a federal action
    c. File a complaint with the Department of Housing and Urban Development
    d. All of the above

127. The relationship of the escrow holder to all parties in a real estate sale is that of an

    a. employee.
    b. agent.
    c. advocate.
    d. independent contractor.

128. All of the following are required for a valid contract *EXCEPT*

    a. competent parties.
    b. lawful object.
    c. sufficient consideration.
    d. money.

129. Broker Davis says to buyer Smith, "You've got to buy this property, and I guarantee that it will double in value in two to three years." Smith buys the property and after three years realizes that similar properties are selling for a great deal less than they were three years ago. What action could Smith take?

    a. Nothing, as the broker did not do anything wrong
    b. File a lawsuit against the broker
    c. Revoke the broker's license
    d. Ask the court to restrict the broker's license

130. Often a neighborhood analysis of property is required in urban areas as

    a. area employment affects demand.
    b. real estate is immobile.
    c. transactions affect value.
    d. All of the above

131. A real estate broker who uses the expression *tax shelter* is referring to

    a. income tax.
    b. interest payments.
    c. depreciation.
    d. deferred maintenance.

132. Able sold a house to Baker subject to a VA loan. If Baker defaults on the loan, who is liable to the lender?

    a. Able
    b. Baker
    c. Both Able and Baker
    d. The VA retains liability

133. Under a deed of trust, if the trustor defaults and a notice of default is recorded, the trustor has up to five business days before sale to reinstate the loan. Who is in possession of the property during the reinstatement period?

    a. The trustor
    b. The trustee
    c. The beneficiary
    d. An officer of the court

134. Newer air-conditioning units carry a designation called EER (energy efficiency ratio). The higher the number, the

    a. more efficient the unit.
    b. less efficient the unit.
    c. more electricity the unit requires.
    d. higher the BTU output.

135. Regarding a percentage lease, which type of business opportunity would pay the highest percentage?

    a. Parking lot
    b. Retail store
    c. Chain department store
    d. Supermarket

136. A less-than-freehold estate is a(n)

    a. life estate.
    b. estate in remainder.
    c. estate for years.
    d. All of the above

137. A contract based on illegal consideration is

    a. valid.   c. legal.
    b. void.   d. enforceable.

138. Of the three appraisal approaches, which is the most complete appraisal?

    a. Letter form
    b. Short form
    c. Narrative
    d. Competitive market analysis

139. If the time period for the closing of an escrow is not specified in the purchase contract, then the time to use is

    a. 30 days.
    b. 45 days.
    c. 60 days.
    d. a reasonable time.

140. An unlocated easement is

    a. valid.
    b. void, as exact locations are required.
    c. unenforceable, due to lack of location.
    d. valid, as only public utilities must indicate the location of the easement.

141. A default in a mortgage could be the result of not

    a. making mortgage payments.
    b. keeping up the property.
    c. paying property taxes.
    d. All of the above

142. Manufacturer Jim is building a factory. Developer Baker finds that this will be an opportunity for women to find work. Baker builds housing accommodations suitable for women and instructs his broker to do the following: (1) advertise for "single working women" and (2) limit applicants to equal numbers of Asians, Chicano, and other minorities by indicating that the apartments are already taken.

    a. Only statement 1 is illegal.
    b. Only statement 2 is illegal.
    c. Neither statement 1 nor 2 is illegal.
    d. Both statements 1 and 2 are illegal.

143. On which of the following dates would property taxes become a lien for the 2003/2004 fiscal year?

    a. January 1, 2003
    b. March 1, 2003
    c. March 1, 2004
    d. February 1, 2004

144. Regarding real estate financing, the smaller the down payment, the longer the loan, the

    a. less interest is paid on the loan.
    b. more interest is paid on the loan.
    c. greater the amount of the total principal paid over the life of the loan.
    d. interest would be the same.

145. Sheet metal used in construction to avoid seepage of water is called

    a. sheathing.   c. flashing.
    b. shingles.   d. header.

146. All of the following are negotiable EXCEPT

    a. bills of exchange.
    b. mortgages.
    c. notes.
    d. personal checks.

147. Which financial institutions make large loans but are not subject to state controls?

    a. Commercial banks
    b. Savings and loans
    c. National banks
    d. Insurance companies

148. All of the following are liens EXCEPT

    a. judgments.
    b. mortgages.
    c. property taxes.
    d. restrictions.

149. The term *short rate* refers to

    a. appraisals.
    b. insurance premiums.
    c. prepayment penalties.
    d. interest on loan payments.

150. The soil pipe is used for

    a. irrigation water.
    b. gas pipes.
    c. sewer lines.
    d. hot water pipes.

■ ANSWER KEY

1. b. As of January 1, 1994, there are now 21 days to return unused security deposits on residential units, with an itemized statement for any money withheld.

2. b. The State Housing Act is enforced by local government in charge of issuing building permits and planning.

3. d. Equity assets have the opportunity to grow in value right along with inflation. The other choices typically have fixed or limited rates of return.

4. b. *Acquisition* means to acquire or receive something. It is the opposite of *alienation*, which means to transfer title.

5. c. Under eminent domain, there is a provision for a condemnation action that could force the taking through court action. Typically, eminent domain requires payment of just compensation to the owner based on fair market value.

6. b. Laws that are enacted to protect the "health, welfare, and safety" of the people are enforced and upheld under police power.

7. d. Least economical would be short blocks, as they would cause many additional expenses, such as having to create more streets and increase all the lighting and utilities.

8. b. An affirmation is a way to make a public statement without having to take an oath or swear. Some persons who for personal reasons will not take an oath may choose to and/or be allowed to use the affirmation.

9. c. A bill of sale signed by the vendor (seller) is the instrument used to transfer the title of a business opportunity.

10. c. Wooden shingles are nailed to the sheathing.

11. a. Joists are supports that are parallel (horizontal) to the floor and ceiling. Supports that are vertical to the floor and ceiling would be called *studs*.

12. a. In a sale of a business opportunity, sales tax would be charged on furniture and fixtures, but not on the other choices.

13. c. The Bulk Sales Law requires that a notification of the sale of the bulk of the inventory of a business be published. This is designed to alert any creditors to the sale.

14. b. The escrow holder cannot release any documents without the approval of all parties to the escrow, namely the buyer and the seller.

15. c. The question asks for the exception. The only party that can suspend or revoke the broker's license is the Real Estate Commissioner, not the court or a private party. The court can recommend to the commissioner that the license be removed, but the decision is up to the commissioner.

16. a. Private action in a state or federal court is available, as discrimination laws are found in both federal and state law.

17. b. Statement of fact.

18. a. Boot is money or its equivalent that is used to equalize equities in an IRC 1031 tax-deferred exchange of real property. Boot or any mortgage relief received is taxable in the year received.

19. b. 16 inches on center is a requirement.

20. d. Statement of fact.

21. b. A desist and refrain order is an order to immediately stop subject activity.

22. b. The tax assessor's bill does not include the "legal description" of property. It shows only the "assessor's parcel number."

23. c. The commissioner would be most interested in the financing of community facilities and language as to financing found in the sales contract. The intent of the commissioner is to focus on minimizing the chance of fraud or misrepresentation in the sale of subdivisions to the general public. Streets and sewers would be matters under the control of local government under the Subdivision Map Act.

24. d. Improvements of a permanent nature, such as a new patio, can be added to the owner's cost basis of the property.

25. c. The "band of investment theory" is one method used to calculate a capitalization rate.

26. d. Commercial orchards (e.g., commercial peach orchards) can be depreciated for income tax purposes.

27. d. Statement of fact.

28. b. Economic obsolescence is a form of depreciation that occurs outside the property, over which the owner has little or no control.

29. c. The market data approach is the most common way to appraise land.

30. c. Statement of fact.

31. d. The question asks about an income property, not a personal residence. The owner would have to consider how much the pool would contribute to the increase in rent, which would contribute to the potential increase in value of the income property. Regarding income property, value is a functioning of income.

32. b. The market data approach is the preferred way to appraise the value of the land.

33. a. A reconveyance deed is issued by a trustee to a trustor. When it is recorded, it removes the lien of the trust deed from the public records.

34. c. Without making reference to the prior used name as well as the new name on the new deed, a cloud on the title is created.

35. d. Value is most closely related to the worth of the property.

36. a. A government patent transfers title from a sovereign to a member of the general public. The term *sovereign* can be used for a government entity.

37. a. The delivery of a grant deed is required to transfer title to property from a grantor to a grantee. Delivery is evidenced by recordation of the deed or possession of the deed by the grantee.

38. c. The court determines the commission rate in a probate sale. The amount the court allows can be different from the commission rate the broker includes in the contract.

39. c. The question asks for the exception. Payment of real property taxes is not a requirement for easement by prescription. It is a requirement for adverse possession.

40. b. A grant deed is not assignable. A new grant deed is made up for each new buyer of property.

41. d. A person can sign only his or her name, not also another person's name, to the contract. If Susan had a power of attorney from her husband to sign in his behalf, then she could do so.

42. c. Statement of fact.

43. c. In a land contract, no legal title passes at the time of the sale. Legal title passes when the terms of the sales contract are met (which is at some time in the future). Therefore, the seller is known as a *vendor* and the buyer is called a *vendee*. Of the choices offered, this would be closest to landlord/tenant.

44. d. Statement of fact.

45. d. The question asks for the exception. The lender is not primarily interested in the borrower's desire for the property but quite interested in the other three choices. The other three choices will influence the lender's decision to make the loan.

46. a. Money in individual savings accounts is mainly used for home loans, especially at savings and loan associations that make the bulk of home loans.

47. c. The question asks for the exception. Insurance companies are under the category of "institutional lenders."

48. d. Insurance companies make large commercial loans and are not in the business of making home loans.

49. b. It is the trustee who issues and signs the reconveyance deed per the instructions of the beneficiary.

50. c. The prepayment penalty benefits the beneficiary (lender). It is a lump sum payment of interest to the lender by the borrower for the privilege of being released from the contract, which calls for long-term payments.

51. c. The mortgagor is the borrower who signs the note.

52. d. The trust deed is the favored security device in California for real estate loans. It secures the promissory note.

53. b. An alienation clause in a note is the due-on-sale clause. It calls for payment in full if the property is sold and this clause is enforceable. However, its inclusion in a note has no effect on the negotiability (salability) of the note.

54. d. Discounting a note means it is sold for less than its face amount.

55. b. In the secondary mortgage market, loans are bought and sold between lenders (mortgagees). An easy way to remember that the word *mortgagee* means lender is to think of two e's in both lender and mortgagee.

56. d. Statement of fact.

57. c. The CLTA or California Land Title Association standard coverage of title insurance is the most commonly purchased type of policy for most home sales.

58. a. *Construction loan* and *interim loan* refer to the same thing. It is the short-term, higher cost loan obtained for the period of construction. It is ultimately replaced with long-term financing, usually at a better rate of interest, called a *takeout loan*.

59. d. Statement of fact.

60. b. A license is a form of revocable permission, such as parking lot signs, driver's licenses, and real estate licenses. Another example: Able says to Baker, "You can cross my property until I say you can't." The portion that says, "until I say you can't" makes it a license.

61. b. Statement of fact.

62. d. Currently, the number of years to depreciate commercial property for income taxation purposes is 39 years.

63. b. Statement of fact.

64. a. Marketability (salability) of property is the ultimate test of functional utility (functional usefulness or appeal).

65. c. External obsolescence is sometimes called *economic obsolescence*. It is the most difficult to overcome for property owner, as it occurs outside the property lines where the owner has little or no control. Examples include bad sewer lines in the entire neighborhood, freeway construction, and downzoning of property.

66. b. The purchasing power of the population in the area designated for a shopping center is a key factor in the decision to build. Also, it will determine what stores to bring in and services that would be most marketable in that area.

67. b. Statement of fact.

68. c. Equity is the difference between what is owed against the property and what it could sell for. In other words, it is the owner's interest in the property.

69. a. It is the lender's responsibility to disclose credit terms to the consumer (borrower).

70. b. A dual agency is legal in California if there is informed consent of all of the parties to the agency.

71. a. The term REALTOR® is owned by the National Association of REALTORS®, and only members may use it. Misuse of a tradename is grounds for loss of license.

72. d. Four sections (four square miles) is larger than the other choices. Choice *a* refers to one mile by two miles. Choice *b* is one mile by one mile. Choice *c* refers to 3.6 miles. (A township contains 36 square miles and 10 percent of it equals 3.6.)

73. c. One acre equals 43,560 square feet. 43,560 divided by 240 feet equals 181.5 feet. 181.5 divided by four lots equals 43.375 feet. The nearest choice is 45.4 feet.

74. c. Under the Uniform Commercial Code, the financing statement (not financial statement) is to be recorded with the Secretary of State. On its recording, a lien is created against the personal property used as security for the credit extension for the purchase of a business opportunity.

75. c. In 1968, *Jones v. Mayer* was decided. It states there shall be no racial discrimination in the sale or rental of property in the United States.

76. a. Statement of fact.

77. d. Be sure to measure around the outside of the lot. 100 × 6 = 600 square feet on one side and 600 square feet on the other side equals 1,200 square feet. Be certain to add 36 square feet for the corner piece (6 feet × 6 feet) for a total of 1,236 square feet. At $1.20 per square foot × 1,236, the total is $1,483.20. The nearest choice is *d*.

78. d. 80 acres ÷ 1,320 feet (¼ mile) = 2,640 feet. The property is 1,320 × 2,640. One path is 2,640 × 50 feet = 132,000 square feet. Three paths are widthwise. 1,320 × 50 × 3 = 198,000 square feet. Combine 132,000 and 198,000 equal to 330,000 total square footage of paths. Be certain to deduct for the overlap of the paths 3 times, 3 × 50 × 50, which equals 7,500 square feet. 330,000 − 7,500 = 322,500 square feet ÷ 43,560 = 7.4 acres. 7.4 acres × $60 per acre equals $444 (remember there are 4 paths in this question, and the answer is $444).

79. d. 100 percent represents the unknown selling price. 100% − 12% for costs and fees = 88%. $63,360 ÷ .88 = $72,000 that the property must sell for to cover costs and fees. $72,000 − $63,360 = $8,640.

80. c. Lot A + Lot B + Lot C = $39,000. Lot A = X (unknown to us at this point). Lot B = X (the value of Lot A) + $6,400. Lot C = X (the value of Lot A) + $6,400 + $7,100. Add the known lot values: $6,400 + $6,400 + $7,100 = $19,900. Take the total sales price of $39,000 and subtract the $19,900 to equal $19,100, which represents the unknown total value attributed to Lot A. Divide by 3 because Lot A's value is found in itself, Lot B, and Lot C. $19,100 ÷ 3 lots = $6,366.67 as the answer. In other words, add up the known numbers and subtract from the total sales price to identify the unknown number. Divide by the number of lots, which in this question is three, to find the answer. For those who know algebra, it is easily used to solve this problem.

81. b. $1,800 ÷ 10 years = $180 per year × 2 years = $360. $1,800 − $360 = $1,440, which is the current balance. $1,440 × 6% = $86.40 annual interest. $86.40 divided by 12 months = $7.20 × 3 months = $21.60. $1,440 + $21.60 (interest) = $1,461.60. $1,462 is the closest choice.

82. d. A straight note calls for the payment of interest only. $28,000 × .1250 = $3,500 ÷ 12 months = $291.67. Therefore, monthly payments of approximately $292 would be for interest only, with the entire principal amount due at the end of the loan term. The other choices all include more than interest in the payments.

83. b. $72,000 × 2 = $144,000 because the house doubled in value. The equity is found by subtracting the mortgage debt of $52,000 from the value of $144,000. Remember that the down payment on property is instant equity. Therefore, the initial down payment of $20,000 is treated as equity. $144,000 − $52,000 = $92,000 equity. $92,000 divided by the down pay-

ment (investment in property) of $20,000 equals a 460% or $4.60 per dollar return.

84. b. $27,900 × 33⅓% = $9,300 + 27,900 = $37,200 sales price. $37,200 × .15 = $5,580 loss for bad debts. $37,200 − $5,580 = $31,620 after loss is deducted. $31,620 − $27,900 purchase price leaves $3,720 profit.

85. b. Value $240,000 × .10 capitalization rate = $24,000 net operating income. There is an increase of rent by $10 per month per unit. 20 units × $10 × 12 months = $2,400 annual increase in rental income. Original net operating income of $24,000 is increased by $2,400 and now is $26,400. Use the formula Net Operating Income divided by Capitalization Rate equals Value. $26,400 divided by the new capitalization rate of .12 equals $220,000. Remember, a higher capitalization rate usually means a higher risk investment. The higher the risk, the lower the value.

86. c. Statement of fact.

87. a. The question asks for the exception to the comparisons. Choices *b, c,* and *d* are incorrect. A condominium owner does have an estate in real property. A tenant does not have an estate in real property, only a leasehold interest.

88. c. $30,000 × 7% × 1st year = $2,100. $30,000 × 5% × 4 years = $6,000. $30,000 × 3% × 15 years = $13,500. $30,000 × 1% × 5 years = $1,500. The question asks about the commission after 19 years, which means to figure years 20, 21, 22, 23, 24, and 25. Year 20 is $30,000 × 3% = $900. Years 21, 22, 23, 24, and 25 are at 1 percent each year. $30,000 × 1% × 5 years = $1,500 plus $900 from year 20 = $2,400.

89. b. A lis pendens is a pending lawsuit on the title to property. It does affect the mar-

ketability of property because a cloud is created on the title. The new owner could be affected by this legal action. Typically, a lis pendens can be terminated by an action for removal, dismissal, or final judgment being rendered.

90. d. A *quiet title* action is a court action that "quiets the title" or settles a dispute and thereby removes a cloud on title.

91. d. Zoning laws are upheld under police power. Also under police power are building code and rent control provisions.

92. c. Statement of fact.

93. d. Plottage increment (bonus or higher value) is the purpose for combining smaller adjoining parcels into one large parcel.

94. b. The market data approach is most familiar to and easily adaptable for most real estate licensees. The comparative market analysis routinely done by an agent follows a similar concept to that found in the market data approach.

95. c. Statement of fact.

96. c. A fiduciary relationship will be created between the broker and the principal, which refers to honesty, loyalty, integrity, and utmost care.

97. d. Statement of fact.

98. c. Statement of fact.

99. a. If the inside surface of an outside wall is the same temperature as the room temperature, then the insulation is doing its job and is sufficient.

100. c. The bill of sale must include the seller's signature.

101. c. A straight note requires only payment of interest. On the last payment, the entire principal is due and payable.

102. c. A quitclaim deed can be used to clear the cloud on the title. In this case, it requires the signature of only the buyer.

103. c. Statement of fact.

104. d. RESPA requires that lenders of loans on one-unit to four-unit dwellings make certain disclosure to borrowers, such as the good-faith estimate of settlement costs and a special information booklet.

105. c. Statement of fact.

106. d. Statement of fact.

107. a. It is wise for a seller to have the pest control report done just before putting the property up for sale. If there is any work to be done, it can be arranged for and taken care of, which could eliminate needless delays during an escrow period. It is customary for a buyer to request such a report. Many lenders will also want to see the report.

108. d. Statement of fact.

109. d. The question asks for the exception. Rejection of the offer by the offeree (seller) would terminate an offer.

110. d. Statement of fact.

111. c. Creation of an agency relationship can occur in several ways. However, the preferred method would be by express written agreement.

112. b. Land is not depreciable. The deed of trust has no bearing on depreciation, so disregard it. Depreciation is based on the purchase price of the income property minus land value. $375,000 − $100,000 (land) = $275,000 for depreciation. $275,000 divided by 27½ years (for residential income property equals $10,000 for depreciation each year for 27½ years.

113. b. Complaints concerning California fair housing laws can be filed with the California Department of Fair Employment and Housing.

114. c. Steering is the illegal practice of avoiding showing property in certain neighborhoods to minority buyers.

115. a. A real estate broker's license is required to manage other people's property for compensation or in anticipation of it.

116. b. Statement of fact.

117. a. The State Controller's Office has claim forms for the postponement of the payment of property taxes for qualified senior citizens. An easy way to remember which office has the forms is SC for State Controller and SC for senior citizen. Currently, the requirements are (1) at least 62 years of age; (2) own at least 20 percent equity in the home; (3) occupy the residence; and (4) have limited annual household income.

118. c. Statement of fact.

119. d. A voluntary offer by one side does not create an agency relationship. It would require the participation of both parties.

120. c. The question asks for the exception. The nonminority buyer is not in violation of the law. However, the seller and the broker are in violation.

121. a. Statement of fact.

122. c. Statement of fact.

123. b. The signing of a quitclaim deed by the easement holder is a way to terminate the easement.

124. d. Refinancing of an existing loan has a right of rescission. A new loan for the purchaser of a personal residence does not have a right of rescission.

125. b. There is no down payment required of a qualified veteran on a loan under the Department of Veterans Affairs program.

126. d. Statement of fact.

127. b. The escrow holder becomes a limited agent of the buyer and seller. The limitation extends to the proper preparation and processing of documents and the proper handling and processing of funds.

128. d. The question asks for the exception. Money is not an element that is required for a valid contract. It is merely an example of the element of "sufficient consideration." The other choices are requirements.

129. b. Statement of fact.

130. d. Statement of fact.

131. a. The term *tax shelter* is commonly used to mean an investment that will provide tax benefits such as depreciation, which is a way to reduce one's taxable income.

132. d. The VA guarantees the lender against loss.

133. a. During the reinstatement period, the trustor (borrower) remains in possession of the property.

134. a. Statement of fact.

135. a. A smaller dollar operation such as a garage or other type of parking facility tends to have to pay a higher percentage lease than a higher dollar business. The lower the income, the higher the percentage. The higher the income, the lower the percentage.

136. c. An estate for years is a lease agreement and is a less-than-freehold estate.

137. b. Statement of fact.

138. c. The narrative report is a complete documentation of all pertinent facts about the

property. It is the most extensive and complete type of report but the least often used.

139. d. A reasonable time is allowed. Reasonable can be defined as a "statement of fact, based on circumstances."

140. a. An unlocated easement is valid. Sometimes it is difficult to know exactly where the points of entrance and exit are found on the property.

141. d. Statement of fact.

142. d. Statement of fact.

143. a. Property tax becomes a lien against property on January 1 preceding the fiscal (business) year for property taxation. The tax year begins on July 1 and ends on June 30 of each year.

144. b. This indicates that interest will be paid for a longer period of time, which means more interest will be paid over the life of the loan than would have been paid on a shorter-term loan.

145. c. Flashing is used to protect a building from seepage of water.

146. b. Mortgages are not negotiable (salable), but the other choices are.

147. c. National banks are not subject to state controls.

148. d. Restrictions are private deed limitations placed on the property by an earlier grantor. They are commonly known as *CC&Rs* and are not liens (liens are money encumbrances).

149. b. The insurance term *short rate* refers to the insurance company penalizing the insured for canceling a policy by retaining a portion of the unused premium.

150. c. The soil pipe carries waste from the house to the main sewer line.

PRACTICE EXAMINATION IX

1. When prices decrease, the value of a dollar

    a. increases.
    b. decreases.
    c. is not affected.
    d. is only slightly affected.

2. Which of the following is the formula for the gross rent multiplier rule?

    a. Sales price divided by gross rent
    b. Gross rent divided by sale price
    c. Gross rent divided by market value
    d. Gross rent divided by assessed value

3. Which one of the following can apply for rezoning?

    a. The buyer
    b. The developer
    c. The subdivider
    d. All of the above

4. When zoning changes from C-1 to R-1, this is usually

    a. downzoning.
    b. upzoning.
    c. split zoning.
    d. nonconforming use.

5. Owner Able sells her property for $100,000. Buyer White agrees to assume the seller's existing deed of trust of $60,000. Based on $.55 for each $500 of the selling price, what will be the amount of the documentary transfer tax?

    a. $44   c. $88
    b. $66   d. $110

6. In the event of a default by a buyer in a purchase that involves a deed of trust, the power of sale clause is granted from

    a. trustor to beneficiary.
    b. trustor to trustee.
    c. buyer to lender.
    d. seller to lender.

7. If a buyer agrees to take over a seller's existing loan where the seller wants no further liability for the loan, how should he or she take it over?

   a. Assumption
   b. Subject to
   c. A release clause should be added to the mortgage.
   d. A subordination clause should be included in the mortgage.

8. Due to court action, a lien is placed on all of a person's property in a given county. This is a

   a. general lien.
   b. specific lien.
   c. lis pendens.
   d. notice of default.

9. When can a real estate salesperson lawfully refuse to show a minority buyer a house that he or she has requested to see?

   a. When the sellers have requested that no one be shown the house when the seller is absent
   b. It is never lawful not to show a minority buyer a house if he or she requests to see it.
   c. When the selling price seems inappropriate
   d. After usual business hours

10. A property is valued at $800,000 with a return of $72,000 a year based on a 9 percent capitalization rate required by investors. If the rate increases to 12 percent, what would the value be?

    a. $400,000   c. $846,000
    b. $600,000   d. $920,000

11. A broker prepared an offer to purchase for a buyer and placed the deposit given by the buyer into the broker's trust account. The offer was accepted by the seller. Later, the parties to the contract became involved in a dispute and legal action followed. To clear her trust account, the broker gave the clerk of the court the earnest deposit. This action is called a(n)

    a. assignment.
    b. condition precedent.
    c. interpleader action.
    d. None of the above

12. All are part of the market data approach *EXCEPT*

    a. open market sales.
    b. material cost.
    c. adjustment to comparable sales.
    d. reconciliation.

13. All of the following are not required to create a valid deed *EXCEPT*

    a. the date.
    b. recording the deed.
    c. name of the beneficiary.
    d. granting clause.

14. The following are debits on a buyer's closing statement *EXCEPT*

    a. insurance premiums.
    b. property tax prorations.
    c. VA loan discount points paid by the seller.
    d. selling price.

15. Gross, triple net, flat, and percentage are terms most often used with

    a. linkage.
    b. leases.
    c. subdivisions.
    d. land markets.

16. A minor under 18 years of age enters into a purchase agreement with a seller. The seller accepts the terms of the offer. Shortly after escrow closes, the grant deed is recorded as is customary. Later it is discovered that the buyer is under the legal age for entering into a contract. The grant deed is

    a. void.
    b. illegal.
    c. valid if approved by a trustee.
    d. valid because it is recorded.

17. Contractor Glenn installs a six-foot-wide sidewalk around a condominium unit. The sidewalk is

    a. public property.
    b. in the common area, which is under the control of the homeowners' association.
    c. real property of the specific unit owner.
    d. None of the above

18. Mr. Smith is leasing a parcel of land from Ms. Jones for a 10-year period. If Mr. Diaz, the owner of the next-door property, requests an easement from Mr. Smith,

    a. Smith could give him the easement.
    b. Smith cannot give an easement, as only the one who has the freehold interest can convey this right.
    c. Smith could give him the easement but only for the 10-year period.
    d. an easement cannot be granted until the lease has terminated.

19. A person can file a complaint under the federal fair housing law. According to the statute of limitations, it must be done within _____ days of the alleged violation of law.

    a. 60   c. 180
    b. 90   d. 360

20. An insurance company agrees to lower the interest rate on a loan that it is carrying on a piece of property if the borrower gives it a 10 percent share in the property. This is known as a(n)

    a. interim loan.
    b. participation loan.
    c. package loan.
    d. equity loan.

21. Regarding the handwritten part of a real estate contract versus the printed portion,

    a. the printed portion takes precedence over the handwritten portion.
    b. the handwritten portion takes precedence over the printed portion.
    c. both the handwritten portion and the printed portion are treated with equal importance.
    d. oral agreements reached after signing the contract will prevail.

22. The terms *blank*, *restricted*, and *qualified* refer to

    a. trust deeds.
    b. endorsements.
    c. reconveyance deeds.
    d. lease agreements.

23. Broker Tim was showing a piece of property on which he held an option. Tim should advise the prospective buyer that he is a(n)

    a. seller.   c. optionor.
    b. principal.   d. agent.

24. A property has been foreclosed by judicial sale. For what time period does the mortgagor retain possession of the property?

    a. 30 days
    b. 120 days
    c. 180 days
    d. A one-year redemption period applies.

25. Frieda James was denied a loan due to a poor credit report. The credit bureau refused to provide Ms. James with a copy of the report. What recourse can Ms. James follow?

    a. There is no recourse.
    b. Sue for damages and court costs.
    c. Pay a certain fee to have the poor credit ratings removed from the report.
    d. File a complaint with the local business bureau.

26. Which of the following could be construed as fraudulent misrepresentation by a broker?

    a. Misrepresentation of a material and major fact
    b. Misrepresentation of a material and major fact with the full knowledge and intent of the broker
    c. Misrepresentation of a material and major fact that influenced the buyer to purchase the property with the buyer subsequently suffering a loss
    d. All of the above

27. An appraiser views market value as meaning nearly the same as

    a. utility.   c. assessed value.
    b. probable price. d. inherent value.

28. In risk management, the lender considers

    a. diversification of assets.
    b. liquidity of assets.
    c. reserve accounts.
    d. All of the above

29. The truth-in-lending disclosure statement is not required on a loan

    a. for agricultural property.
    b. on a revolving credit line.
    c. where a security agreement is used.
    d. for an owner-occupied residence secured by a deed of trust.

30. When a business firm awards a person the right to market its services, name, or products, this is known as a

    a. business sale.
    b. franchise.
    c. syndication.
    d. limited partnership.

31. In a real estate transaction, all of the following may sue for specific performance or dollar damages *EXCEPT* a(n)

    a. seller of land.
    b. buyer of a house.
    c. broker on behalf of a principal who has a written exclusive right-to-sell listing with the broker.
    d. attorney-in-fact on behalf of his or her principal.

32. Which of the following is a real property item?

    a. Chattels real
    b. Leasehold interests
    c. A promissory note
    d. Vegetation

33. Smith had a life estate interest on property that he leased for 10 years to Baker. Six years later Smith died. The new owners of the property demanded that Baker move out. Regarding the lease, it is

    a. valid for the 10-year period.
    b. valid until Smith died.
    c. invalid unless court action confirms it.
    d. invalid, as a hold of a life estate cannot lease it.

34. BTUs are a way to rate the capacity of which of the following systems?

    a. Heating   c. Electrical
    b. Sewage   d. Water

35. A lis pendens is effective when

    a. it is filed.
    b. a judgment has been rendered.
    c. an action is pending on property.
    d. an execution sale is ordered.

36. Which of the following is used by a city to implement its general plan?

    a. Conditional use permits
    b. General land-use controls
    c. Zoning
    d. Variances

37. Which of the following is not correct concerning a lis pendens placed on property?

    a. The new owner is not affected by the lis pendens.
    b. It is filed at the county recorder's office.
    c. The marketability of title may be affected by the lis pendens.
    d. A lis pendens can be removed by a court order or by posting a bond.

38. All of the following are subject to property tax EXCEPT

    a. vacant land located in an unincorporated area.
    b. mobile homes installed on a permanent foundation.
    c. intangible personal property.
    d. properties to which there are oil and gas leases.

39. According to income tax laws, which of the following is true regarding land?

    a. It is considered to be about 25 percent of total property value.
    b. Improvements have no residual value, but land does.
    c. It is subject to accelerated depreciation.
    d. It is not depreciable.

40. All of the following terms are closely associated EXCEPT

    a. heir.   c. sale.
    b. executrix.   d. will.

41. Jack buys a property that he might use as a personal residence and is hoping to create an exchange for tax purposes. The IRC 1031 exchange would not be allowed if

    a. the properties to be exchanged are not like-kind.
    b. the exchanged properties are both vacant land.
    c. one of the properties has a leasehold interest of over 30 years.
    d. one property is in California and the other is in Oregon.

42. Appraiser Greene does not follow FHA guidelines when appraising property for an FHA loan. She

    a. has committed a felony.
    b. has committed a misdemeanor.
    c. will be disciplined by the Real Estate Commissioner.
    d. would not be given a beneficial review.

43. If an appraiser were hired to appraise a restaurant or shopping center, which of the following approaches to value would be appropriate?

    a. Market data approach
    b. Cost approach
    c. Income approach
    d. Short-form

44. Jack grants to Joan an option to purchase Jack's farm. The option is a(n)

    a. voluntary lien on Jack's farm.
    b. contract to keep an offer open.
    c. fiduciary agreement.
    d. offer to keep a contract open.

45. In the cost approach, an appraiser uses market data comparisons to determine

    a. selling price.
    b. highest and best use.
    c. land value.
    d. fixed depreciation.

46. When using the market data method of appraising a single-family residence, the unit of comparison is the

    a. capitalization rate.
    b. unit-in-place method.
    c. property as a whole.
    d. gross rent multiplier.

47. A thin string of stores along a business street is called a

    a. neighborhood shopping center.
    b. commercial strip center.
    c. cluster project.
    d. None of the above

48. Presenting competing offers to purchase property to an owner in a way that influence the owner to accept an offer that is favorable to the agent is

    a. unethical.
    b. illegal.
    c. acceptable practice.
    d. Both a and b

49. An appraiser would most likely use which of the following methods to appraise a warehouse?

    a. Square foot   c. Square yard
    b. Front foot   d. Cubic foot

50. The primary purpose of site analysis is to determine its

    a. type of soil.
    b. zoning laws.
    c. highest and best use.
    d. possible views.

51. Changes in which of the following will have an impact on real estate in the future?

    a. The real estate industry itself
    b. Land-use controls
    c. Consumer concerns
    d. All of the above

52. Another term for *nondisclosure* is

    a. false promise.   c. Neither a nor b
    b. negative fraud.   d. Both a and b

53. When arranging a loan, amortization tables are used to determine the

    a. interest rate.
    b. monthly payment.
    c. term of the loan.
    d. annual percentage rate.

54. When a buyer and seller execute a real property sales contract, which type of title transfers?

    a. All rights and interest of the seller pass to the buyer.
    b. An equitable title passes to the buyer.
    c. A legal title passes to the buyer.
    d. No type of title passes to the buyer.

55. The security of the deed of trust recorded on property would be jeopardized if

a. a judgment lien were recorded on the property.
b. the deed of trust were recorded after the recording of a declaration of homestead.
c. the deed of trust were recorded after construction work commenced on the property and a mechanic's lien were later recorded.
d. None of the above

56. A mortgage loan may be insured by

a. the beneficiary.
b. FHA or PMI.
c. Fannie Mae.
d. the VA.

57. An ALTA policy of title insurance offers protection that is beyond the protection of a CLTA title insurance policy because it guards against

a. an error in the sequence of recording deeds of trust liens.
b. a deed of reconveyance issued by a minor.
c. the location of property lines according to a formal survey.
d. existing recorded liens and encumbrances.

58. To be entitled to a commission, a broker must prove that he or she was the procuring cause of the sale on all of the following listings EXCEPT a(n)

a. exclusive agency.
b. exclusive authorization to sell.
c. open listing.
d. nonexclusive listing.

59. All of the following terminate an offer to purchase real property EXCEPT

a. the offeror's communication of notice of revocation after the offeree has properly posted acceptance
b. death or insanity of the offeror.
c. a counteroffer by the offeree.
d. the offeree's failure to accept the offer within the prescribed period given by the offeror.

60. What is the definition of a company dollar?

a. The amount that remains after subtracting overhead and expenses
b. The amount that remains after all commissions, including cooperating broker splits, have been paid
c. The amount that remains after subtracting commission and management expenses from gross sales
d. The amount of capital available to open an office

61. The UCC document that must be filed with the Secretary of State that is part of the financing for a purchase of a business is a

a. bill of sale.
b. financial statement.
c. financing statement.
d. security agreement.

62. Smith has a property worth $660,000 with a basis of $440,000. He trades for Diaz's property, which is worth $770,000. Diaz receives boot to equalize the equities. What is Smith's basis on the new property?

a. $440,000   c. $660,000
b. $550,000   d. $770,000

63. A real estate broker supplies the following information regarding a residential income property: gross income is $80,000; vacancy is 10 percent; operating expenses are $25,000; depreciation is $31,000; value is $450,000. Based on this information, what is the capitalization rate?

    a. 8.3 percent
    b. 9.3 percent
    c. 10.4 percent
    d. 11.5 percent

64. Steve bought a second deed of trust with a face value of $1,400 at a 15 percent discount. He received payments of $122 per month including 9 percent interest for one year. What was Steve's percentage return on his investment?

    a. 23 percent
    b. 31 percent
    c. 34 percent
    d. 40 percent

65. Jane bought a house for $125,000 and obtained a loan for 88 percent of the purchase price payable at $1,549 per month at 12 percent interest. Before she made her first payment, she sold the house for $139,750. Her equity at the time of sale was

    a. $15,000.
    b. $29,750.
    c. $139,750.
    d. None of the above

66. Mary's estate was distributed as follows: 37 percent to her husband, 18 percent to each of her two sons, 18 percent to her daughter, and the balance to a college that received $37,000. How much did her daughter receive?

    a. $74,000
    b. $102,000
    c. $148,000
    d. $152,000

67. Investor Clark purchased a parcel of land that was ¾ of an acre and 110 feet deep. He later purchased the adjoining parcel for $1,400 that was the same depth but was ⅔ the size of the first parcel. He then subdivided the combined parcels into lots with a frontage of 82½ feet each. If he sold the lots for $750 each and made a profit of 50 percent over what he paid for both parcels, what was the cost of the first parcel?

    a. $1,600
    b. $2,000
    c. $2,400
    d. $2,600

68. Mr. and Mrs. Jenson sold their home for $73,700, which was 17 percent more than they paid for it. What was the approximate original purchase price?

    a. $61,170
    b. $62,992
    c. $86,229
    d. $88,695

69. Mr. Dawson purchased a ¼-acre parcel that was 90 feet deep. He paid $1 per square foot as the purchase price. He wants to sell and make a 25 percent profit on the sales price after paying $100 in costs and 6 percent commission. How much would the property have to sell for per front foot?

    a. $115
    b. $120.56
    c. $128.54
    d. $131.63

70. Greg sold his house for $84,000. If buyer Sue assumes an existing first deed of trust of $21,000 at the rate of $.55 cents per each $500 of the sales price, how much will the documentary tax be?

    a. $23.10
    b. $69.30
    c. $92.40
    d. $115.50

71. A tract of ground is bisected by a canal, leaving two triangular lots. One lot has a street frontage of 500 feet and a depth of 760 feet. Approximately how many acres are there in this lot?

   a. 4 acres
   b. 5 acres
   c. 8.5 acres
   d. 9 acres

72. A lot that faces the shady side of West Avenue measures 50 feet wide by 150 feet deep. Baker wants to build his home on this lot. The county building department requires a 20-foot setback on the front of the lot, a 4-foot setback at the back and a 4-foot sideyard setback. How many buildable feet remain?

   a. 5,292 square feet
   b. 5,460 square feet
   c. 6,300 square feet
   d. 7,500 square feet

73. There is a three-acre easement that runs along the south edge of a section. About how wide is the easement?

   a. 25 feet
   b. 28 feet
   c. 30 feet
   d. 33 feet

74. If a square parcel contains 160 acres, how long is each side?

   a. ¼ mile
   b. 2,640 feet
   c. 180 chains
   d. 145 rods

75. How many feet to a rod?

   a. 3 feet
   b. 16½ feet
   c. 33 feet
   d. 5,280 feet

76. Ms. Brown negotiated a $20,000 loan on her home and paid four points to obtain the loan. There was a required prepayment penalty of 2 percent of the original loan amount. The monthly payments were $163 including interest at 8 percent annually. Five years later, Ms. Brown sold her home and paid the loan in full. If while Ms. Brown had the loan the average outstanding balance was $18,500, what were the lender's gross earnings?

   a. $6,750
   b. $6,840
   c. $7,140
   d. $8,600

77. Where would one file a complaint under the California fair housing laws?

   a. California Department of Real Estate
   b. California Department of Fair Employment and Housing
   c. California Department of Community Development
   d. Federal Trade Commission

78. In arriving at an effective gross income figure for an apartment building, appraiser David makes a deduction for

   a. real property taxes.
   b. repairs.
   c. vacancy factor.
   d. depreciation.

79. According to the law of agency, the agent of the buyer has a fiduciary duty. This duty requires the agent to

   a. act with loyalty, integrity, honesty, and the utmost care.
   b. give the buyer advice as to how to take title.
   c. tell the buyer which escrow and title service to use.
   d. be a subagent.

80. The main purpose of the Real Estate Settlement Procedures Act is to

    a. regulate all real estate loans.
    b. choose lenders that can process the paperwork efficiently.
    c. regulate property improvement loans.
    d. require that disclosures be made by lenders who loan on one-family to four-family dwellings.

81. Fannie Mae's primary objective is

    a. buying FHA/VA loans in the primary mortgage market.
    b. selling FHA/VA loans in the primary mortgage market.
    c. buying and selling FHA/VA loans in the secondary mortgage market.
    d. buying and selling conventional loans in the secondary mortgage market.

82. The lack of government intervention in private economic affairs is described by the term

    a. mixed economy.
    b. laissez-faire.
    c. competition.
    d. command economy.

83. When one is appraising an improved parcel of property using the market data method, one must make adjustments to the estimates of value, as

    a. the property will depreciate.
    b. the property will eventually increase in value due to inflation.
    c. any two properties are rarely similar in all ways.
    d. All of the above

84. Which of the following would be an example of economic obsolescence?

    a. A leaking roof
    b. No parking at the site
    c. An oversupply of like properties
    d. Poor architectural design

85. Appraiser Able would consider all of the following *EXCEPT*

    a a definition of value.
    b. the identification of the property.
    c. the assessed value.
    d. the property rights to be valued.

86. A permit must be secured from the Real Estate Commissioner before an owner or his or her agent sells or offers to sell

    a. stock in a corporate real estate syndicate.
    b. a lot in a Washington subdivision being offered for sale in California.
    c. property that was acquired by a government patent.
    d. lots being sold in a California land project.

87. If two or more real estate brokers or salespersons enter into an agreement to purchase a commercial building, they must have

    a. a real estate license.
    b. a partnership license.
    c. the approval of the Real Estate Commissioner.
    d. None of the above

88. Owner Hall added a patio to her personal residence. For federal income tax purposes, this will be

    a. added to her cost basis of the property.
    b. taken as a deductible expense in the year of installation.
    c. of no tax consequence because it is her personal residence.
    d. depreciated over the life of the improvement.

89. Regarding rental property, "gross income minus vacancy factor and collection losses" equals

    a. effective gross income.
    b. net income.
    c. before-tax cash flow.
    d. net spendable income.

90. The expression "present worth of future benefits" refers to the

    a. market data approach.
    b. comparative market analysis.
    c. capitalization of net income.
    d. reproduction cost analysis.

91. An easement for light and air may be created by

    a. prescription.   c. implied grant.
    b. express grant.   d. All of the above

92. If there are wide cracks in the corner of a basement that appear to be spreading up the walls, this condition is likely due to

    a. the property settling.
    b. deterioration.
    c. weak joints in the walls.
    d. None of the above

93. Which of the following are the two implied warranties carried by a grant deed?

    a. The property is free of encumbrances; title has not been previously conveyed.
    b. The grantor is the only owner; no other encumbrances exist other than those disclosed.
    c. Title has not been conveyed to another; the grantor is the only owner.
    d. The grantor has not already conveyed title to another; the estate conveyed is free from encumbrances other than those disclosed.

94. All of the following could cause a residential income property to become economically obsolete EXCEPT

    a. a heating system that has become outmoded.
    b. stores that move out of the area.
    c. flight patterns of air traffic that have changed.
    d. a neighborhood that is in its decline stage.

95. A grant deed

    a. transfers title from one party to another.
    b. shows the persons involved in the title transfer.
    c. creates a written document suitable for recording.
    d. is signed by a grantee.

96. A deed that has been recorded

    a. transfers title.
    b. conveys a valid title.
    c. guarantees ownership to the grantee.
    d. presumes delivery.

97. The statute of frauds requires that certain contracts be in writing to

    a. employ a real estate broker to arrange a lease for one year.
    b. employ a real estate broker to sell personal property.
    c. employ a person to give advice on a real estate matter.
    d. create an agreement not to be performed within one year of the making.

98. Comparing the CLTA standard coverage title insurance policy with the extended title coverage, the extended would protect against

    a. forgery.
    b. lack of capacity of the parties.
    c. matters of public record at various government levels.
    d. physical aspects of the property.

99. Owner Grey sells property using a real property sales contract. Buyer Johnson records the contract but subsequently defaults and vacates. Later, Grey finds another buyer and wishes to transfer the title using a grant deed. To do this, Grey must obtain a

    a. quitclaim deed from the vendee.
    b. notice of nonresponsibility.
    c. reconveyance deed.
    d. notice of default.

100. Under the Cal-Vet program, the title to the veteran's home is in the name of the

    a. Veterans Administration.
    b. veteran.
    c. Department of Veterans Affairs.
    d. institutional lender.

101. What is the maximum amount of commission that a broker could charge for arranging a second deed of trust for $9,000 for a three-year period?

    a. $450
    b. $900
    c. $1,350
    d. None of the above

102. There are certain instances when a lender looks to a borrower's personal assets. In which of the following could that occur?

    a. A corporation
    b. A general partnership
    c. A limited partnership
    d. None of the above

103. Aside from unusual fluctuations in the mortgage market, junior loans most often are secured through

    a. private investors.
    b. savings and loan associations.
    c. commercial banks.
    d. insurance companies.

104. Ray sold his home and carried back a $175,000 first deed of trust. Later, he sold the note to Jones, endorsing it "without recourse." The borrower on the note subsequently defaulted in his payments to Jones.

    a. Jones would have to foreclose to collect the balance due.
    b. If Jones suffers a loss, he could collect from Ray.
    c. Jones does not have the right to foreclose.
    d. Ray would have to foreclose.

105. Which of the following must provide federal insurance to protect the accounts of their depositors?

    a. State-chartered savings and loans
    b. Federally chartered savings and loans
    c. Both *a* and *b*
    d. Neither *a* nor *b*

106. The procedure to evict a nonpaying tenant is

    a. physical ejection by the lessor.
    b. court action for specific performance.
    c. an unlawful detainer action.
    d. None of the above

107. Under inflationary conditions, who would most benefit from the purchase of a house?

    a. The beneficiary
    b. The trustee
    c. The trustor
    d. Either *a* or *b*

108. Which of the following would offer a greater amount of protection to the holder of a junior trust deed?

    a. Recording the note
    b. Recording the trust deed
    c. Recording the trust deed and the note
    d. Recording the trust deed and a request for notice of default

109. The term *seasoned note* refers to a(n)

    a. loan made during a certain season of the year.
    b. loan with a previous history of prompt payments.
    c. extended due date on the loan.
    d. open-end loan.

110. To be binding, every real estate contract must be

    a. in writing.
    b. supported by adequate consideration.
    c. acknowledged.
    d. All of the above

111. The title given to the person who has been given authority to sign for another person under a "power of attorney" is

    a. attorney at law.
    b. attorney-in-fact.
    c. trustor.
    d. guarantor.

112. A grant deed to a person under an assumed name is

    a. void.
    b. voidable.
    c. permissible.
    d. prohibited.

113. The cost of homeownership includes the

    a. amenities.   c. equity.
    b. interest.   d. principal.

114. When remodeling property, which of the following would be least likely removed?

    a. Floor joist   c. Partition wall
    b. Bearing wall   d. Header

115. Under the Sales and Use Tax Law, a seller's permit is required of every

    a. retailer.
    b. wholesaler.
    c. Neither *a* nor *b*
    d. Both *a* and *b*

116. The duties of a property manager include

    a. collection of rent.
    b. caring for the needs of the occupants.
    c. maintenance and upkeep of the property.
    d. All of the above

117. The sale of a business opportunity is the concern of the

    a. secretary of state.
    b. Department of Alcoholic Beverage Control.
    c. local and federal governments.
    d. State Board of Equalization.

118. An injured party under Title VIII of the Civil Rights Act of 1968 could file a lawsuit with the

    a. civil court.
    b. criminal court.
    c. court commissioner.
    d. Real Estate Commissioner.

119. Under the Bulk Sales Law, the party who would assume responsibility and liability for the inventory being sold if no notice of the sale is given is/are the

    a. seller.
    b. buyer.
    c. broker and creditors.
    d. creditors only.

120. To obtain a judgment lien, an abstract of judgment must be recorded in the county where the

    a. debtor resides.
    b. creditor resides.
    c. property is located.
    d. judgment was obtained.

121. A subdivider would be most interested in a(n)

    a. subordination clause.
    b. release clause.
    c. alienation clause.
    d. or-more clause.

122. A minority buyer tells a local real estate broker that she is interested in a property in a particular neighborhood. The broker could assume that the buyer

    a. is testing the broker.
    b. is interested in property in a certain area.
    c. is interested in buying only in a minority area.
    d. cannot qualify to purchase in a more expensive area.

123. Covenants, conditions, and restrictions may be created by

    a. deed.
    b. agreement.
    c. recorded declaration of restrictions.
    d. All of the above

124. The Housing Financial Discrimination Act of 1977 covers

    a. private offerings.
    b. physical handicaps.
    c. equal rental opportunity.
    d. the practice of redlining.

125. If you own an undivided interest in the common areas and a separate interest in a certain unit of an industrial, commercial, or residential building, you own a

    a. community apartment project.
    b. condominium.
    c. land project.
    d. stock cooperative.

126. A grant deed has been issued to "John Darrel, et ux." The Latin term *et ux* means

    a. and others.
    b. without warranties.
    c. and wife.
    d. amount over and above.

127. A 10-year lease is agreed on, requiring the lessee to pay the first and the last month's rent in advance. For income tax purposes,

    a. all will be taxable at the time of sale of the property.
    b. the first month's rent is taxable in the first year and the last month's rent is taxable in the tenth year.
    c. all will be taxable in the year received.
    d. this is treated as a proration over the life of the lease.

128. A person could check for liens on a seller's fixtures or stock in trade when a business opportunity is being sold. The office to contact is the

    a. State Board of Equalization.
    b. Office of the Secretary of State.
    c. County Recorder's Office.
    d. County Clerk's Office.

129. Appraiser Clark is hired to appraise a commercial office building. All of the following are relevant to the appraisal *EXCEPT*

    a. principal and interest payments.
    b. net operating income.
    c. property taxes.
    d. maintenance costs.

130. The terms *quantity survey*, *cubic foot*, *square foot*, and *unit in place* refer to

    a. escrow terminology.
    b. appraising, using the cost approach.
    c. appraising, using the income approach.
    d. construction application.

131. An office building was rented from September 1 to November 5 by an election committee. This is known as a(n)

    a. periodic tenancy.
    b. estate for years.
    c. tenancy at sufferance.
    d. tenancy at will.

132. The tax that a city may apply against a real estate brokerage firm based on its gross receipts is a

    a. sales tax.
    b. use tax.
    c. documentary transfer tax.
    d. business license tax.

133. The land that accumulates on property due to the splash-up action of water is called

    a. avulsion.   c. erosion.
    b. reliction.   d. alluvium.

134. Select from the following statements the one that is often true regarding real estate loans arranged through a commercial bank.

    a. The interest must be paid in advance.
    b. These loans increase the bank's cash position.
    c. Discount points are always charged.
    d. Any discount points charged will be in direct proportion to the amortization period.

135. All of the following are correct regarding the court disposition of probate property *EXCEPT*

    a. commissions are set by law based on the listed price of property.
    b. the executrix of the estate may enter into an exclusive listing agreement with a real estate broker.
    c. the court will not accept an initial offer less than 90 percent of the court's appraised value.
    d. the executrix may purchase the property subject to court approval.

136. Riparian rights typically are

    a. a matter of public record.
    b. stated in a title insurance policy.
    c. stated in a grant deed.
    d. None of the above

137. Ms. Baker owns a fee simple estate. If she leases it to Mr. Able for 10 years, Ms. Baker has a

    a. fee simple estate with a reversionary interest.
    b. less than freehold estate.
    c. net lease.
    d. life estate.

138. Which of the following is true when the Federal Reserve System increases its discount rate by ½ percent?

    a. Banks will decrease their interest rates.
    b. Sellers will be less inclined to pay off existing loans.
    c. It is favorable news from a borrower's position.
    d. It is an inflationary measure.

139. A seller who has owned her property for two years sells the property to a buyer who is paying all cash. In which of the following loans is she likely to pay a prepayment penalty when paying the lender the entire balance due in the first two years of her loan?

    a. VA
    b. FHA
    c. A hard-money junior loan
    d. A conventional loan

140. The major cause of depreciation of real property is

    a. deterioration.
    b. deferred maintenance.
    c. obsolescence.
    d. the passing of time.

141. Sam and Harry have recently purchased homes. Sam made a much smaller down payment than Harry made. Conventional loans were obtained for both parties. As far as most lenders are concerned, Harry

    a. probably obtained financing at a lower rate than Sam.
    b. will likely build a better record for loan payments.
    c. is likely to maintain his property in a better condition.
    d. All of the above

142. If a deed is to be used as prima facie evidence in a court of law, it must be

    a. recorded.   c. acknowledged.
    b. certified.   d. verified.

143. The liquidity of a business is measured by

    a. capital minus liabilities.
    b. total assets minus total liabilities.
    c. current assets minus current liabilities.
    d. assets divided by liabilities.

144. To determine accrued depreciation under the straight-line method, each year of economic age is assigned a(n)

    a. rate that varies according to the life of the improvements.
    b. decreasing rate set by the Internal Revenue Service.
    c. progressive rate.
    d. equal weight.

145. There are many different ways to form a business opportunity. It can be formed as a sole ownership, a form of partnership, or a corporation. An advantage of a partnership over sole ownership could be that

    a. the personal liability of each general partner is limited to the amount of his or her investment.
    b. partners can make decisions independently of each other.
    c. each partner is considered a co-owner of the partnership assets.
    d. None of the above

146. Mr. Stewart, the owner of Greenacre, sold it to Ms. Turner but retained a life estate interest and remained in possession. Later, Mr. Stewart sold his life estate interest to Mr. Reed and gave up possession. Ms. Turner demanded immediate possession of the property because she had the fee simple interest. What is the current status?

    a. Ms. Turner is entitled to possession.
    b. Mr. Reed should sue for the return of his original purchase price.
    c. Mr. Stewart is liable for damages to Ms. Turner.
    d. Mr. Reed can retain possession as long as Mr. Stewart is living.

147. A parcel of land is 660 feet wide and 1,320 feet deep. How many acres are contained in this parcel?

    a. 10 acres   c. 30 acres
    b. 20 acres   d. 40 acres

148. An acre is being divided into four equal lots. If the lots are designed to be parallel to each other, 200 feet deep, and in a rectangular layout, what would be the approximate width of each lot?

    a. 15 feet
    b. 55 feet
    c. 200 feet
    d. There is not enough information to calculate the width.

149. A valid enforceable contract requires a

    a. genuine offer and a genuine acceptance.
    b. meeting of the minds.
    c. Either *a* or *b*
    d. Neither *a* or *b*

150. The statement, "The REALTOR® shall not publicly disparage the business practices of a competitor" would be found in the

    a. Business and Professions Code.
    b. Commissioner's Code of Ethics
    c. NAR Code of Ethics.
    d. Real Estate Law.

■ ANSWER KEY

1. a. When prices decrease, a person can buy more for a dollar. Therefore, the value of a dollar increases.

2. a. The formula for the "gross rent multiplier rule" is "sales price divided by gross rent equals the gross rent multiplier" (*SP* divided by *GR*).

3. d. Rezoning can be initiated by buyers, developers, subdividers, and even local government, following a change in the general plan for a given community.

4. a. Zone changes from a commercial use to a residential use in most communities is an example of downzoning.

5. a. When a loan is being assumed by a buyer, it is subtracted from the selling price and only the balance is taxed. $100,000 – $60,000 = $40,000 to be taxed at the rate of 55 cents per each $500. The easier way to figure the tax is $40,000 × $1.10 per each $1,000 (40 × $1.10) = $44. The $60,000 was taxed in its original transaction. This tax applies only to new money created in the sale.

6. b. When the trustor (borrower) signs the note and deed of trust, he or she gives the power of sale to the trustee. Remember, the trustee (not the beneficiary) is the one who will handle a foreclosure sale and, if necessary, will also issue a reconveyance deed when the loan is paid in full.

7. a. In an assumption, the seller has no further liability, as the buyer becomes responsible for the loan.

8. a. A general lien affects all property of a owner.

9. a. A real estate licensee can lawfully refuse to show property to anyone when instructed by the owner not to do so while the owner is away.

10. b. $72,000 return (net operating income) ÷ 12 percent = $600,000.

11. c. An interpleader action allows holders of a deposit to distance themselves from a dispute by placing the deposit into the hands of a clerk of the court.

12. b. Material cost is not part of the market data approach. It is part of the cost approach.

13. d. The question asks for the choice that *is* a requirement. A granting clause is required in a deed; that is, "I hereby grant and convey."

14. c. The question asks for the exception. VA discount points paid by the seller would be a debit on the seller's closing statement, not on the buyer's closing statement.

15. b. These terms are commonly found in lease agreements.

16. a. The contract is void (or invalid), as the element of capacity is missing from the contract.

17. b. Sidewalks are part of the common area, not the unit.

18. c. Lessee Smith could grant an easement to Diaz, but only for the term of the lease. Remember, the lessee has possession and control over the property for only the term of the lease agreement.

19. c. The question asks about federal law. Under federal law, the time period for the filing of a complaint is 180 days (under California law, it would be 60 days).

20. b. A participation loan gives the lender an ownership share in the property and/or its profits upon sale.

21. b. The handwritten parts of a contract prevail over the printed parts.

22. b. These terms refer to types of endorsements.

23. b. Because the broker has an interest in the property, he must disclose that he is a principal as well as an agent.

24. d. The maximum time period allowed for the mortgagor to retain possession after a judicial (court) sale is one year if the sale proceeds do not satisfy the debt. If sale proceeds do satisfy the debt, court costs, and interest, then the redemption and possession period is only three months. The question is a general one; therefore, the answer is one year.

25. b. Ms. James can sue for court costs, and damages.

26. d. Statement of fact.

27. b. Market value is also known as *probable price*, *objective value*, and *value in exchange*.

28. d. Before granting a loan, a lender looks at liquidity, diversification of assets, and reserve amounts.

29. a. A Truth-in-Lending statement is not required on loans for agricultural purposes, but is for the other choices.

30. b. The question presents a good description of a franchise.

31. c. The question asks for the exception. A broker cannot sue on behalf of the principal. The principal him or herself may file a lawsuit directly if it becomes necessary.

32. d. As long as the roots of the plant, bush, vine, or tree are still part of the earth, vegetation is considered to be real property.

33. b. The lease was valid only as long as Smith was alive, as the life estate was based on Smith's life. When Smith died, the lease terminated.

34. a. Statement of fact. BTU = British thermal unit of heat.

35. a. A lis pendens is a pending lawsuit on the title to property that becomes effective when it is filed (recorded).

36. c. Zoning has been the most important legal tool in carrying out local general plans.

37. a. This is the choice that is not correct. A new owner is affected by the lis pendens action until it is either removed, dismissed, or final judgment is rendered.

38. c. The question asks for the exception. Intangible personal property (such as the value of goodwill in a business opportunity) is not subject to property tax.

39. d. Land is not depreciable, as it is not a wasting asset.

40. c. The question asks for the exception. The terms *heir*, *executrix*, and *will* have to do with estates and inheritances. The term *sale* is broad and may be used in other types of transactions.

41. a. An IRC 1031 tax-deferred exchange requires like-kind property (does not include a personal residence).

42. d. The appraiser would not be given a beneficial review if she did not use the proper FHA guidelines for an appraisal for an FHA loan.

43. c. The income approach is appropriate for a restaurant, as it is an income-producing property.

44. b. An option is clearly a type of contract that keeps an offer open. The optionee (prospective buyer) is not forced to buy at

the option date but may or may not exercise the right to buy.

45. c. In the cost approach, land is appraised using the market data approach.

46. c. In the market data approach, comparable properties are compared as a whole unit with the subject property as a whole unit.

47. b. A commercial strip center is defined as a "thin string of stores along a main street."

48. d. Both *a* and *b* (unethical and illegal).

49. d. The cubic-foot method of appraising a warehouse is often used because of the building's storage capacity. The cubic-foot method is more commonly used on the east coast than on the west coast.

50. c. A most important task for the appraiser of a site (land) is to determine its highest and best use.

51. d. Statement of fact.

52. b. Nondisclosure is also known as *negative fraud*. Negative fraud carries with it the intent to commit fraud.

53. b. The monthly payment of property loans can be found by using amortization tables.

54. b. A real property conditional sales contract (land contract) transfers "equitable title" to the buyer. Legal title passes when the terms of the loan contract are met.

55. c. The mechanic's lien would then take priority over the deed of trust.

56. b. Both FHA and PMI (private mortgage insurance) insure loans.

57. c. The question of property lines is covered in the ALTA owners' extended coverage of title insurance.

58. b. In an exclusive authorization and right-to-sell listing, the owner promises to pay a commission regardless of how the property sells during the listing period. The broker does not have to be the agent who finds the buyer to earn the commission.

59. a. The question asks for the exception. The buyer's attempt to revoke an offer after the seller has posted an acceptance is too late for the revocation. Once the seller's acceptance is conveyed back to the buyer, what was an offer becomes a contract between them.

60. b. Statement of fact.

61. c. The financing statement (not financial statement) is filed (recorded) with the Secretary of State.

62. b. Old basis of $440,000 plus $110,000 (difference between $770,000 and $660,000) equals $550,000. A way to remember how to calculate the basis on the new property in an exchange, for testing purposes, is to "carry over old basis like baggage when you move" to the new property. Add any boot paid to effect the exchange (difference in sales prices) and that equals the new basis on the target property. While this is a simplistic way to calculate your answer, it will work for testing purposes.

63. c. $80,000 – $8,000 for the 10 percent vacancy factor = $72,000 effective gross income. $72,000 – $25,000 operating expenses = $47,000 net operating income. Disregard the depreciation, as it is a distractor in the question. $47,000 ÷ the value of $450,000 = 10.4 percent capitalization rate.

64. a. $1,400 × 15% = $210. $1,400 – $210 = $1,190. $122 × 12 months of payments = $1,464. $1,464 – $1,190 = $274. $274 ÷ $1,190 = 23%.

65. b. $125,000 × 88% = $110,000. $139,750 – $110,000 = $29,750.

66. a. Husband received 37%, two sons 18% each, and 18% to the daughter (37% + 18% + 18% + 18%) = 91%. 100% of the estate − 91% that went to the family leaves 9% that went to the college. If 9% that the college received is worth $37,000, then simply double it for the 18% that the daughter received. $37,000 × 2 = $74,000.

67. a. First parcel is 43,560 × .75 (¾ of an acre) = 32,670 square feet ÷ 110 feet = 297 feet. Second parcel is 32,670 × .667 (⅔ the size of the first parcel) = 21,790.89 square feet ÷ 110 feet = 198.1 feet. 297 + 198 = 495 feet. 495 feet ÷ 82.5 feet = 6 lots. $750 × 6 lots = $4,500. The profit for both parcels is $4,500 ÷ 150% = $3,000 for both parcels. $3,000 − $1,400 paid for the second parcel leaves $1,600 for the first parcel. (Simply remember the answer to this question "as the $1,400 two-parcel lot question" is $1,600. That is, 14 + 2 = 16.) It never hurts to keep a sense of humor.

68. b. You can use 100 percent in place of the unknown cost. Add the profit of 17 percent to it. Take the sales price of $73,700 and divide by 1.17 to equal cost of $62,991.45. Nearest choice is b.

69. d. 43,560 (square feet to an acre) ÷ 4 = 10,890 ÷ 90 = 121 feet to the front footage. 10,890 × $1 = $10,890 plus the costs of $100 = $10,990. 25 percent profit plus 6 percent commission = 31 percent. 100% − 31% = 69%. $10,990 ÷ .69 = $15,927.54. $15,927.54 ÷ 121 feet = $131.63 cost per front foot.

70. b. The easiest way to calculate the documentary transfer tax (a county tax, not a city tax) is to use $1.10 per $1,000. Be certain to deduct the existing loan that is being taken over from the sales price and tax the balance. This tax applies only to new money created in the sale. The assumed loan was taxed in its original transaction. $84,000 − $21,000 =$63,000. $63,000 ÷ $1,000 = 63 × $1.10 = $69.30.

71. a. The question asks for the number of acres in one of the triangular lots. To find the area of a triangle, take ½ of width times depth of a rectangle. ½ of 500 × 760 = 190,000 (500 × 760 ÷ 2). Take 190,000 square feet and divide by 43,560 square feet to an acre to equal 4.36 acres. The nearest choice is four acres.

72. a. You cannot place a building on the setback area of a piece of property. Setback requirements differ from city to city. You own the whole parcel and can landscape the setback area if you wish, but you cannot build on it. The question asks for the amount of land you can build on, so you must deduct the setbacks from the dimensions of the lot or parcel. For sideyard setbacks, remember to deduct from both sides. 50 feet wide − 8 feet (4 + 4) = 42 feet wide. 150 feet length − 24 feet (20 feet off the front and 4 feet off the rear) = 126 feet long. The formula to use is Area = Wide × Length. Multiply 42 × 126 = 5,292 buildable square feet to the lot.

73. a. Any side of a section of land is 1 mile or 5,280 feet. The number of square feet to an acre is 43,560. Multiply 3 acres × 43,560 = 130,680 square feet. 130,680 ÷ 5,280 = 24.75 feet. Nearest choice is 25 feet.

74. b. The distance on the side of a 160-square-acre parcel is ½ mile or 2,640 feet.

75. b. One rod equals 16½ feet. Rods are sometimes used by engineers and surveyors. There are 320 rods to 1 mile.

76. d. $20,000 × 4% = $800 (a point is 1 percent of the loan amount). $18,500 × 8% ×

5 years = $7,400 interest. $20,000 × 2% = $400 prepayment penalty. $800 + $7,400 + $400 = $8,600 gross earnings to lender.

77. b.   Remember the state agency that receives complaints about fair housing laws is the California Department of Fair Employment and Housing.

78. c.   The vacancy factor is subtracted from the building's schedule gross income to find its effective gross income.

79. a.   The question asks about the fiduciary duty of the agent of the buyer. The fiduciary relationship requires that the agent act with loyalty, integrity, honesty, and utmost care.

80. d.   The federal law called RESPA requires that certain disclosures be made on loans for one-unit to four unit dwellings. Typical disclosures include a special information booklet and a good-faith estimate of settlement costs.

81. c.   While Fannie Mae can buy and sell many types of loans, including conventional, it focuses heavily on buying and selling FHA and VA loans in the secondary mortgage market.

82. b.   Laissez-faire refers to a policy of non-intervention or "hands off" by the government.

83. c.   Rarely are any two properties alike in all features and benefits.

84. c.   Economic obsolescence has to do with what occurs outside the property lines, such as an oversupply of property.

85. c.   The assessed value of property is the tax assessor's value for property tax purposes. It is not considered by the appraiser in the usual appraisal process.

86. b.   Out-of-state property being offered for sale in California requires a permit from the Real Estate Commissioner.

87. d.   Because they are acting as principals, no license is required.

88. a.   The cost of the patio, which is an improvement of a permanent nature, is added to the cost basis of the property.

89. a.   Effective gross income remains after the deduction of either just the vacancy factor or the vacancy factor plus collection loss (bad rent checks that were not made good), if any.

90. c.   The expression "present worth of future benefits" refers to the capitalization approach. The "present worth" refers to the value of the property. The "future benefits" refers to the anticipated income from the property.

91. d.   Statement of fact.

92. a.   "Hairline" splits that spread upward found on walls are usually from the settling of the property.

93. d.   Statement of fact.

94. a.   The question asks for the exception concerning economic obsolescence. A heating system that is outmoded is an example of functional obsolescence, not economic obsolescence.

95. a.   A grant deed transfers title from the seller to the buyer. (A trust deed is a security device in which the borrower gives up legal title to the trustee as security for the debt, and a reconveyance deed returns the legal title to the borrower when the loan is paid in full.)

96. d.   One of the ways to evidence that a deed has been delivered to the receiver of the title is to have the deed recorded. The

other method is for the receiver of title to have possession of the deed.

97. d. An agreement not to be performed within one year of its making must be in writing under the statute of frauds.

98. d. Certain physical aspects of the property are customarily covered under an owner's extended title insurance policy (e.g., encroachments and survey lines, which would not be covered under a CLTA standard title insurance policy).

99. a. A real property sales contract is another way of saying "land contract." If the buyer defaults and vacates after recording the purchase, a way to clear the cloud on title is to have the vendee (buyer) sign a quitclaim deed. (Sometimes court action is required.)

100. c. The Department of Veterans Affairs is the name of the department in the Cal-Vet program that processes property purchases for the qualified veteran. Title to the property is held by this agency until the terms of the loan contract are fulfilled.

101. c. $9,000 × 15% = $1,350. Remember that on Article 7 loans, junior trust deeds of less than $20,000 with a term of three years or more allow a 15 percent commission for loan brokerage services (plus a limited amount for costs). The question asks about maximum commission.

102. b. In a general partnership, each general partner is fully responsible for all debts of the partnership. This responsibility extends to the personal assets of each partner.

103. a. Historically, private investors are the largest source of union mortgage money. This is usually through a junior loan being carried back by the seller of property or money made available for junior loans through other private parties.

104. a. The endorsement "without recourse" indicates that the seller of the note is not responsible for payment to the buyer of the note if the borrower on the note defaults.

105. b. Federally chartered savings and loan associations must provide federal insurance protection to their depositors (state chartered savings and loans may provide federal insurance protection—many do).

106. c. The unlawful detainer action is the legal action for the eviction of a nonpaying tenant.

107. c. A trustor is a borrower and is the buyer and present owner of the property. In a period of inflation, prices rise. The higher price of the house would benefit the present owner due to the potential profit if he or she sells.

108. d. Recording the deed of trust and a request for notice of default benefits a junior lienholder. The recording gives constructive (public) notice of the claim of the junior lienholder. The "notice" would alert the junior lienholder if the first trust deed went into default.

109. b. A "seasoned note" is one with a previous payment history of more than 36 months (36 months and one day or longer). It is said that within this time period one is able to see what type of payment habit the borrower has established on the note.

110. b. Adequate (or sufficient) consideration is one of the required elements for the contract to be binding. The writing requirement under the statute of frauds for a real estate contract is for the contract's enforceability.

111. b. An *attorney-in-fact* is the title given to a person who has been given the authority to sign for another person under a power of attorney.

112. c. It is permissible to issue a grant deed to an assumed name (e.g., a business name).

113. b. The interest portion of the monthly payment is a cost of homeownership.

114. b. A bearing wall supports the roof. It is usually left alone when remodeling and is built heavier than other interior walls.

115. d. A seller's permit is required of all retailers and wholesalers.

116. d. Statement of fact.

117. d. The State Board of Equalization administers the Sales and Use Tax law, which is part of the sale of a business.

118. a. Action can be filed in a civil court.

119. b. The buyer becomes responsible. This is why the burden to put the bulk sales notice in a newspaper is put on the buyer. The purpose of the notice is to alert any creditors of the stock-in-trade that it is being sold. There is a greater chance that the ad will be placed as required if the burden to do so is placed on the buyer, who has the ultimate responsibility for the stock-in-trade.

120. c. Statement of fact.

121. b. A release clause in a deed of trust benefits a subdivider. It allows the subdivider to sell each of the houses in the subdivision without paying off the entire blanket lien of a trust deed on the subdivision. Each house can be released from the blanket lien when a buyer arranges for funds for the purchase of a house.

122. b. The proper conduct of a real estate agent is to assume that the minority purchaser is interested in purchasing property in the neighborhood of her choice.

123. d. Statement of fact.

124. d. The Housing Financial Discrimination Act of 1977 prohibits redlining by lenders on residential properties of one-dwelling to four-dwelling units.

125. b. The question includes a definition of a condominium.

126. c. *Et ux* means "and wife."

127. c. Rental income is taxed as ordinary income in the year received.

128. b. A UCC-1 form (a financing statement) is filed with the secretary of state, often as part of the sale of a business opportunity where a credit extension was granted. On filing (recording) the form, a lien is placed on the items listed on the UCC-1 form, as security for the credit granted. Sometimes the filing is done with the County Recorder's office.

129. a. The question asks for the exception. Principal and interest payments are not considered when estimating the value of income property. They would be a consideration in calculating the cash flow of property for taxation purposes; however, the question addresses the appraisal process.

130. b. These terms are part of the cost approach in the appraisal of property. They are used to describe the four methods of estimating cost new.

131. b. An estate for years is a lease agreement that includes the use of property for a period that is fixed in advance.

132. d. Most cities charge a business tax that is based on the gross receipts of a business.

133. d. The alluvium (or alluvion) is the name given to the land or soil that has splashed up onto a person's property as a result of the gradual depositing (accretion) of the soil by water, wind, or glacial ice.

134. d. Often banks will charge discount points especially on long-term amortization periods to help equalize or increase their yield.

135. a. The question asks for the exception. Commissions are not based on the listed price of probate property. Typically, they are based on the purchase price. The court sets the rate of commission on court probate sales, regardless of what the purchase contract states.

136. d. Riparian rights are appurtenant to the land. They do not have to be recorded or shown in a policy of title insurance.

137. a. Baker has a fee simple interest and has given Able a leasehold interest on the property for 10 years. Baker also has a reversionary interest, which means that the possession of the property reverts to Baker when the lease agreement terminates.

138. b. The Federal Reserve System includes banks that are bankers' banks. It is not where the general public banks. When the Fed increases its discount rate, member banks will have to pay a higher rate when they borrow from the Fed. This will increase the interest rate charged to the general public. Sellers will be less inclined to pay off existing loans as they are very likely to be at a lower rate of interest.

139. d. Conventional residential loans on one-dwelling to four-dwelling units for owner occupancy would have a prepayment penalty in the first five to seven years depending on who makes the loan.

140. c. Obsolescence or "obsolete" features contribute strongly to the depreciation of property.

141. d. Harry is the stronger purchaser. The lower cost of the financing will leave him with a greater financial ability to maintain his property. His financial strength will probably allow him to build a better payment record than a purchaser who is financially weak.

142. c. Acknowledgment (recordation) is a requirement of the grant deed before the court will accept it as prima facie (on its face) evidence in a court case.

143. b. Statement of fact.

144. d. The straight-line method of depreciation means the same amount is depreciated each year for the depreciation period.

145. c. In a general partnership, each partner is a co-owner of the partnership assets of the other partner. A benefit is that the partners share in the responsibilities and the assets.

146. d. The life estate interest is based on the life of Mr. Stewart. As long as Mr. Stewart is living, Mr. Reed can retain possession of the property. When Mr. Stewart expires, the possession by Mr. Reed terminates and Ms. Turner can then claim possession under her fee simple interest.

147. b. 660 feet × 1,320 feet = 871,200 square feet ÷ 43,560 square feet to an acre = 20 acres.

148. b. Area divided by depth or length = width. 43,560 ÷ 200 = 217 ÷ 4 lots = 54.25 (55 is the nearest choice).

149. c. Some of the requirements of a valid contract include a genuine offer coupled with a genuine acceptance that is a meeting of the minds.

150. c. The quotation is taken from the Code of Ethics of the National Association of REALTORS®.

PRACTICE EXAMINATION X

1. An appraiser wishes to use the gross rent multiplier formula on a home that rents for $640 monthly. A comparable sale of a neighbor's home can be used. It rented for $600 monthly and sold for $90,000. Based on this information, what would be the approximate value of the property being appraised?

   a. $90,240
   b. $96,000
   c. $126,900
   d. There is not enough information to estimate value.

2. A buyer purchased a home for $300,000 with a down payment of $75,000. During the first year, the value of the home increased by $30,000 on her $75,000 equity investment. This is an example of

   a. escalation.
   b. leverage.
   c. profitability.
   d. liquidity.

3. Mr. Smith is selling his land. He also owns stock in a mutual water company that "runs with the land." If Mr. Kim is purchasing the land and wants the stock,

   a. Mr. Kim must buy the stock in a separate transaction.
   b. Mr. Kim need not buy the stock separately because it "runs with the land."
   c. it is like an appurtenant easement.
   d. Mr. Smith can charge up to $10,000 for the stock.

4. A person buys a condominium and uses it for her own residential purposes. She does not rent it out for income. For income taxation purposes, she may deduct which of the following from her gross income?

   a. Assessments on recreational amenities
   b. Mortgage interest on the common areas she owns
   c. Costs of repair and maintenance of the condominium
   d. Mortgage interest on the unit

5. Henry purchased a home for $380,000 with a 10 percent down payment. The market price was listed at $390,000. The county shows the assessed value as $370,000. For income taxation purposes, what is the cost basis of the property?

   a. $360,000   c. $380,000
   b. $370,000   d. $390,000

6. The highest support in the construction of a home is the

   a. collar beam.   c. cripple.
   b. ridgeboard.   d. header.

7. Johnson bought a home with a roof style that has four sides. In describing this roof to a friend, Johnson could call it a

   a. hip.   c. gable.
   b. gambrel. d. mansard.

8. Trust deeds have priority when they are _____ first.

   a. executed
   b. executed and delivered
   c. acknowledged
   d. recorded

9. Which title insurance policy is most often used?

   a. Standard   c. ALTA
   b. Extended   d. CLTA

10. When a real estate transaction has been completed, which of these contributing members is responsible for "noticing" the Internal Revenue Service?

    a. Lender   c. Agent
    b. Escrow holder d. Appraiser

11. A property has a net operating income of $30,000. If the investor uses a 6 percent capitalization rate instead of a 5 percent rate, what will be the difference in value?

    a. $30,000
    b. $90,000
    c. A decrease by $100,000
    d. An increase by $200,000

12. Property falls under the regulations of the Subdivision Map Act if it is divided into as few as _____ or more lots.

    a. two   c. four
    b. three d. five

13. If Clare sold her property to Baker and carried back a note and deed of trust as a junior lien, it would indicate a

    a. tight money market.
    b. VA loan.
    c. conventional loan.
    d. None of the above

14. What is the quickest way for a lender to take a property back when a borrower has defaulted on a loan?

    a. Sheriff's sale
    b. Judgment
    c. Foreclosure sale
    d. Power of sale clause

15. Baker sold his property under a land sales contract. He accepted $25 from the buyer, who moved in and did make intermittent payments to Baker. Later, the buyer moved out in the middle of the night. What effect did this action have?

    a. It created a cloud on Baker's title.
    b. It had no effect, as the buyer moved out.
    c. Baker could get a deficiency judgment.
    d. A new buyer would have problems.

16. Muriel sold her property and took back a note and second deed of trust for $30,000. Later, she sold the note for less than its face amount. This is known as

a. discounting the note.
b. terminating the note.
c. splitting the note.
d. collateraling the note.

17. The Seller Transfer Disclosure Statement Act allows the selling broker to

a. make a visual inspection of the property and report pertinent facts.
b. inspect even the inaccessible area and report material details.
c. pay for a pest control inspection.
d. inspect common areas in a subdivision.

18. For federal income taxation purposes, seller Smith's payment of $9,000 commission to broker Jones is treated as a(n) _____ to Smith.

a. capital gain
b. standard deduction
c. expense of the sale
d. item to add to cost basis

19. A good example of functional obsolescence is

a. adverse zoning.
b. a leaking roof.
c. a one-bath house.
d. freeway construction.

20. There are four important elements that create value. Of the four, which one is the least important?

a. Demand
b. Utility
c. Scarcity
d. Transferability

21. Which one of the following runs with the land?

a. Covenant
b. Easement granted for life
c. Appurtenant easement
d. All of the above

22. Recently, a neighborhood experienced bad sewer lines in the entire area and a downzoning of property usage. These are examples of

a. deterioration.
b. economic obsolescence.
c. functional obsolescence.
d. All of the above

23. Which of the following is not essential to a valid grant deed?

a. Acknowledgment of the grantor's signature
b. In writing
c. Signature of the grantor
d. A competent grantor

24. A deed can be construed as void if the

a. grantor does not sign his or her actual name.
b. grantee is a fictitious person.
c. grantor signs correctly, but his or her name is misspelled.
d. grantee is described sufficiently.

25. A quitclaim deed

a. warrants no encumbrances.
b. warrants nothing.
c. conveys after acquired title.
d. None of the above

26. Mr. David purchased a one-half acre of land and agreed to a condition stated in the deed. Subsequently, David violated this condition of ownership. This would likely

    a. allow the other owners the right to sue for damages through court action.
    b. allow the other owners the right to file an injunction.
    c. cause the possible forfeiture of ownership.
    d. All of the above

27. Mrs. Jenner died intestate and left no heirs. She left a sizable estate in California. It is likely that

    a. the property will be sold for taxes that accrue if no one claims the property within five years.
    b. the property will escheat to the State of California if no claim is made by any possible heirs within a five-year period.
    c. the will determines the disposition of the estate.
    d. a will might be located.

28. When a judgment is made by the court ordering the sale of property, the document issued is called a(n)

    a. writ of execution.
    b. attachment.
    c. abstract of judgment.
    d. sheriff's deed.

29. All of the following are required legal essentials for a valid and binding basic contract *EXCEPT*

    a. a proper writing.   c. mutual consent.
    b. capacity.   d. lawful object.

30. Broker Riley sold property to a buyer who was under 18 years of age and an unemancipated minor. The contract is

    a. illegal.   c. void.
    b. valid.   d. voidable.

31. A deposit receipt and offer to purchase becomes enforceable

    a. immediately.
    b. immediately on the seller's signature accepting the offer.
    c. on the buyer being notified of the seller's accepting the offer.
    d. when the escrow closes.

32. Of the following title insurance policies, which one provides coverage against all possible defects in the condition of title?

    a. California Land Title Association Standard Coverage
    b. American Land Title Association Extended Coverage
    c. California Land Title Association Extended Coverage
    d. None of the above

33. According to the Real Estate Commissioner's regulations, the broker and salesperson must enter into a written employment agreement. A copy of this agreement must be kept by

    a. the broker for five years from termination of employment.
    b. the salesperson for three years from date of employment.
    c. both the broker and the salesperson for three years from termination of employment.
    d. both the broker and the salesperson for three years from date of employment.

34. Under the Truth-in-Lending Act, the right to rescind the loan is allowed on the refinancing of home loans. The rescission period is not allowed on loans for the purchase of a personal residence. The rescission period, if it applies, is for three days after the

    a. signing of the note.
    b. loan application is received.
    c. loan application is approved.
    d. None of the above

35. A commercial office building shows a quarterly income of $265,000. The operating expenses on the property are 32 percent of the income. Based on this information, what is the building's annual net operating income?

    a. $84,800
    b. $180,200
    c. $339,200
    d. $720,800

36. Real estate salesperson Smith deliberately avoids showing properties found in integrated areas to minority buyers. This is an example of

    a. appropriate conduct.
    b. blockbusting.
    c. steering.
    d. redlining.

37. A piece of property that faces the shady side of a stream measures ½ mile by ½ mile. Approximately how many acres does this property contain?

    a. 40
    b. 80
    c. 160
    d. 320

38. How many square one-acre lots can be sold along one side of a ¼ section that faces a road?

    a. 13 lots
    b. 12 lots
    c. 6 lots
    d. 3 lots

39. Within three business days, a real estate broker deposits or places trust funds received into

    a. a neutral escrow depository.
    b. the hands of the principals.
    c. the broker's trust fund account.
    d. All of the above

40. Currently, residential income property is depreciable over

    a. 31 years.
    b. 39 years.
    c. 27½ years.
    d. 29½ years.

41. Expansion and contraction of available space for rent or sale is influenced mainly by the

    a. elasticity of demand.
    b. supply and demand concept.
    c. regression and progression principles.
    d. imperfect market and perfect market concept.

42. Jones lists his lot for sale at $6,500, which represents a 30 percent increase in a one-year period. He decides to reduce the listed price by 25 percent, hoping it will sell, and also agrees to pay the broker a 6 percent commission. How much will Jones probably lose in this transaction?

    a. Less than $450, more than $400
    b. More than $450, less than $525
    c. Less than $550, more than $525
    d. More than $575, less than $600

43. Money that is paid for property that is condemned describes a(n)

    a. involuntary conversion.
    b. voluntary conversion.
    c. downzoning.
    d. rezoning.

44. Which of the following is the longest distance?

    a. 66 feet   c. 1 rod
    b. 100 chains   d. 1 mile

45. One section of land can be described as

    a. 320 rods by 320 rods.
    b. 5,280 feet by 5,280 feet.
    c. a one-mile square.
    d. All of the above

46. A land locator is

    a. a real estate broker who helps sell government land to the public, earns a commission, and, therefore, must be licensed in real estate.
    b. one who does not require a real estate license.
    c. a government employee.
    d. None of the above

47. An apartment building of 16 units or more requires

    a. a nonresident manager.
    b. a resident manager.
    c. an owner to be on the property during normal business hours.
    d. management by a professional firm.

48. A real estate license is required for

    a. mortgage bankers and brokers.
    b. property managers for compensation.
    c. real estate salespeople for compensation.
    d. All of the above

49. An abstract of judgment creates which of the following liens on property?

    a. Attachment lien   c. Involuntary lien
    b. Judgment lien   d. Voluntary lien

50. If there is a conflict between a promissory note and a deed of trust, the prevailing instrument would likely be the

    a. deed of trust.
    b. lender's loan disclosure statement.
    c. promissory note.
    d. The note and the deed of trust are in parity, so the conflict would have to go to arbitration.

51. Tobey gives a grant deed to Webster, transferring title to a piece of property. The title is subject to a condition that title will be forfeited if alcoholic beverages are ever sold on the property. The estate that Webster has is a(n)

    a. fee simple absolute.
    b. fee simple defeasible.
    c. estate in forfeiture.
    d. less-than-freehold estate.

52. Who can make a secret profit on the sale of property?

    a. The broker
    b. The salesperson
    c. The owner
    d. All of the above

53. Able uses statements like "Sell now before your property goes down in value, as minorities are moving in" to induce owners to list their property for sale. This illegal practice is called

    a. panic selling.   c. Both a and b
    b. panic peddling.   d. steering.

54. In estimating the value of a parcel of real estate, appraiser Leslie considers the value of the

    a. physical land and the improvements thereon.
    b. bundle of rights under fee simple ownership.
    c. utility factor of the property.
    d. All of the above

55. The primary purpose for combining lots is to create

    a. plottage in anticipation of taxation.
    b. assemblage in anticipation of plottage increment.
    c. plottage in anticipation of assemblage increment.
    d. plottage in anticipation of highest and best use of land.

56. To estimate the value of improved property as a single unit, an appraiser would use the

    a. land residual technique.
    b. property residual technique.
    c. building residual technique.
    d. capitalization method.

57. If the employment rate and the gross domestic product both rise, usually the

    a. level of one's personal income rises.
    b. new home development increases.
    c. sales of existing homes will begin to increase.
    d. All of the above

58. A real property transfer disclosure statement must be given by a seller/transferor of one-dwelling to four-dwelling units under a

    a. sale or exchange of property.
    b. land sales contract.
    c. lease option.
    d. All of the above

59. A transfer of title to property under a real property sales contract would be signed by the

    a. transferee.   c. vendor.
    b. trustee.   d. vendee.

60. A real estate investor is interested in applying the technique of leverage. She could accomplish this by

    a. using most of her personal funds.
    b. using equal amounts of personal funds and borrowed funds.
    c. using borrowed funds to the highest amount possible.
    d. investing in property in the decline phase of its life cycle.

61. A divorced person under the age of 18 wants to list her property for sale with the local broker. Regarding the listing, the broker

    a. cannot take the listing.
    b. must first obtain court permission to take the listing.
    c. can take the listing.
    d. can take the listing, but it is not enforceable if a legal problem arises.

62. In an advertisement offering a house for sale, if only the annual percentage rate is given,

    a. total finance charges and payments must be listed.
    b. only the total number of payments must be listed.
    c. the required down payment must be shown.
    d. additional disclosures are not required.

63. A title insurance company would most likely search the records of the

    a. county recorder's office.
    b. county clerk's office.
    c. federal land offices.
    d. All of the above

64. The term *negative declaration* in regards to an environmental impact report indicates

    a. a negative influence on the environment due to the development.
    b. no negative influence on the environment must be listed.
    c. the developer's subdivisions are not of the highest standards.
    d. the developer's financial ability to satisfy creditors.

65. For a contract for the purchase of real property to be enforceable, the consideration must be sufficient in relation to value to enforce which of the following actions?

    a. A rescission of the contract
    b. A lawsuit for specific performance
    c. An unlawful detainer action
    d. An action for dollar damages

66. Which of the following types of easements could be more easily removed than the others because of nonuse by the easement holder?

    a. An easement created by deed or reservation
    b. An easement by express reservation
    c. An easement by implication
    d. An easement by prescription

67. There is a difference between special assessments and property taxes. Special assessments

    a. provide for local improvements.
    b. are placed on the property only by improvement districts.
    c. are always subordinate to property taxes.
    d. if delinquent in payment, require a court sale of property.

68. A site analysis is mainly concerned with factors relating to

    a. developments outside and around the site.
    b. the site itself.
    c. existing improvements on the site.
    d. All of the above

69. In an appraisal of income property, the appraiser's estimate should

    a. allow a lender to provide the highest possible loan amount.
    b. indicate the highest and best use compared to its present use.
    c. approximate value in an unidentifiable market.
    d. approximate value in an identifiable market.

70. A purchase-money transaction is identified as a

    a. loan from a private individual.
    b. seller carryback.
    c. loan from an institutional lender.
    d. All of the above

71. An owner of a single family residence lists it for sale with broker Jones under an exclusive right-to-sell listing agreement. During the listing period, the owner decides to unilaterally cancel the listing due to personal reasons. Under these circumstances, the owner

    a. can cancel without any further liability to the broker.
    b. might be sued for damages by the broker.
    c. cannot cancel, as the listing is a binding contract.
    d. cannot cancel, as it is a valid contract until the expiration date of the listing.

72. In a listing agreement, the expression, "I will use diligence in procuring a purchaser" appears. This statement creates which type of contract?

    a. A unilateral contract
    b. A bilateral contract
    c. A voidable contract
    d. An open listing

73. A broker arranges for a seven-year lease agreement between a tenant and the property owner. The usual method of compensation is by a

    a. flat fee.
    b. percentage of the first year's rent.
    c. percentage of the total lease paid up front.
    d. percentage of the total lease to be paid monthly or annually.

74. On a settlement statement for an FHA loan, the points paid by the buyer would be stated as a

    a. debit to the buyer.
    b. credit to the buyer.
    c. debit to the seller.
    d. None of the above

75. There are five essential elements for an enforceable listing agreement for the sale of real property. They are

    a. mutual consent, lawful object, legal objectives, consideration, and money.
    b. mutual consent, offer and acceptance, legal objective, consideration, and competent parties.
    c. mutual consent, legal objective, competent parties, consideration, and a proper writing.
    d. mutual consent, mutuality, legal objective, competent parties, and in writing.

76. A real estate broker offers and accepts a plan to be paid his commission in the form of part cash and part ownership in a business opportunity he is negotiating for a client. This is

    a. unethical.
    b. illegal.
    c. legal.
    d. a proprietary arrangement.

77. Broker Johnson accepts a deposit from a prospective purchaser who wishes to buy a specific property when the owner did not authorize the broker to act as the seller's agent. The buyer gave written instructions to the broker to hold the check, uncashed, until the offer was accepted or rejected. The broker

    a. must immediately place the deposit into escrow.
    b. must immediately place the check into the broker's trust account, as that is safer than merely holding the check.
    c. becomes the buyer's agent with respect to the deposit and must act according to the buyer's instructions.
    d. and the seller would both be responsible to the buyer for the deposit if it were misplaced.

78. A broker who owned a real estate company died leaving a large sales staff and many listings with the company. The broker's daughter, who also held a real estate broker's license, took over the company. Regarding the existing listings,

    a. the daughter would have to relist the properties in her name for the listings to continue.
    b. the daughter cannot refuse to relist the properties, as she is now the broker of record for the company.
    c. the listings would automatically transfer to the daughter.
    d. a simple telephone call of explanation to the owners would be sufficient.

79. A grant deed is to a real property transfer what a(n) _____ is to a business opportunity transfer.

    a. bill of sale
    b. security agreement
    c. financial statement
    d. inventory list

80. Disregarding a down payment, when buying a home, which of the following loans would have the fewest closing costs?

    a. Cal-Vet
    b. Veterans Administration
    c. Federal Housing Administration
    d. Conventional loans

81. When a principal employs an agent to do certain acts, this creates

    a. an agency relationship.
    b. a fiduciary relationship.
    c. Both *a* and *b*
    d. Neither *a* nor *b*

82. Owner Smith tells broker Gray that he wishes to sell his house immediately and would like $175,000 for it. Gray tells buyer Jones that Smith has financial troubles and will accept a much lower price, perhaps $150,000. Smith ultimately accepts the $150,000 offer made by Jones. Gray is guilty of

    a. nothing, as he did his job and found a buyer.
    b. violating the fiduciary duty to Smith.
    c. unethical behavior and a violation of the fiduciary duty, but it is not serious because Smith accepted the offer.
    d. unethical behavior and a violation of the fiduciary responsibility.

83. An attachment lien outlaws (terminates) in

    a. two years.
    b. three years.
    c. four years.
    d. no amount of time until a judge dismisses the matter.

84. A grant deed is invalid if

    a. no date appears on its face.
    b. there is no statement of how title is to be held by the buyers.
    c. it is not recorded.
    d. None of the above

85. It is customary that mineral rights on land

    a. remain with the original grantor.
    b. not be leased.
    c. not be separated from the land.
    d. transfer with the land.

86. What is the fee that a lender can charge for the preparation of the Uniform Settlement Statement?

    a. Nothing
    b. A minimum of $10
    c. A percentage of the loan amount
    d. No more than $50

87. Which of the following would automatically invalidate a homestead declaration?

    a. Moving out of the property
    b. Leasing the property
    c. Moving out of state
    d. Prior homestead that was recorded

88. When can an eviction actually occur?

    a. After the three-day notice to "pay or quit" has been sent
    b. Thirty days after the notice to vacate has been given
    c. On filing an unlawful detainer action
    d. On receiving a judgment that calls for an eviction

89. If the Federal Reserve System wants to take certain measurers to tighten up the money supply, it could

    a. sell bonds.
    b. buy bonds.
    c. raise the discount rate and buy bonds.
    d. raise the discount rate and sell bonds.

90. The inside measurements of a new suburban industrial building are 24 feet by 30 feet. The building has six-inch walls. How many square feet of land does the building occupy?

    a. 693   c. 735
    b. 720   d. 775

91. How many acres are there in the SE ¼ of the NE ¼ of the NW ¼ of section 36?

    a. 10 acres   c. 40 acres
    b. 20 acres   d. 80 acres

92. The expression *demise* refers to

    a. the passing on of a right.
    b. real property left by a will.
    c. title insurance coverage.
    d. a will.

93. The type of lease agreement that is based on the gross sales of a business is a _____ lease.

    a. gross   c. fixed
    b. percentage   d. net

94. A sublease

    a. assigns the rights to another, who accepts full responsibility for the lease.
    b. transfers the rights, but not the duties, attached to the lease with the right of return if the terms are breached.
    c. assigns and records an abstract of a lease.
    d. assigns the rights for an unexpired term.

95. Real property is

    a. crops after harvest.
    b. fruit on trees that has been sold.
    c. minerals and gas removed from the earth.
    d. stock in a mutual water company.

96. The term *property* includes

    a. personal property if it is a lease agreement.
    b. real property if it is not personal.
    c. real property if it is a fixture.
    d. All of the above

97. A beneficiary statement is issued by the

    a. borrower to the lender for credit approval purposes.
    b. lender to the borrower to identify the current status of the loan.
    c. borrower to the lender to verify past employment.
    d. lender to identify the party who benefits from the loan proceeds.

98. The primary function that the Department of Real Estate's Recovery Fund serves is

    a. to develop educational offerings for real estate agents.
    b. for brokers to receive earned, but unpaid, commissions.
    c. for members of the general public who hold uncollectible court judgments against licensees to collect limited damages.
    d. None of the above

99. A two-year lease agreement was drawn up and was subsequently signed by the lessor. The lessee did not sign the lease but moved in. After paying the first few months of rent, the lessee moved out. Which of the following statements is true?

    a. The lease is valid, as only the signature of the lessor is required on the lease agreement.
    b. The lease is void, as only the lessor signed it, and there is no recourse against the lessee.
    c. The lease is void because it was not acknowledged.
    d. The lease is void because it was not recorded.

100. Riparian rights can be described as those of a landowner by

    a. rivers and streams.
    b. oceans and bays.
    c. subterranean caves.
    d. All of the above

101. When personal property becomes permanently attached so that it becomes part of the real property itself, it is known as a(n)

    a. attachment.   c. fixture.
    b. appurtenance.   d. trade fixture.

102. Community property is property that was

    a. purchased before marriage.
    b. purchased with the income of both husband and wife.
    c. purchased with separate income.
    d. acquired by gift or inheritance.

103. If a property owner pays an appraiser to appraise her property, who can the appraiser discuss the appraisal with?

    a. Anyone who inquires
    b. Only the owner
    c. The lender
    d. The local real estate brokers

104. Able says to Baker, "You can use my property until I say you can't." This is a statement of

    a. license.
    b. easement.
    c. easement by prescription.
    d. use that is not hostile to the owner.

105. Broker Joe and sister Sarah acquire title to a property as joint tenants. Later, Sarah deeds half of her interest in the property to her husband, Bill. This would

    a. leave only the brother as a joint tenant.
    b. create a joint tenancy between all of them.
    c. require that they go to court to seek permission to do so.
    d. create a tenancy in common for three parties.

106. If an owner refuses to pay a swimming pool contractor his fees for installation of the pool, the recourse of the contractor is to file a(n)

    a. attachment lien.
    b. specific lien.
    c. general lien.
    d. notice of default.

107. A piece of choice property was purchased subject to an easement. The easement is

    a. appurtenant to the property.
    b. an encumbrance.
    c. a specific lien.
    d. an encroachment.

108. Penalties under the Unruh Civil Rights Act include

    a. actual damages.
    b. punitive damages.
    c. Both *a* and *b*
    d. up to $1,000 in damages.

109. The formula for the gross rent multiplier rule is

    a. sales price divided by gross rents.
    b. gross rents divided by sales price.
    c. gross rents divided by market value.
    d. None of the above

110. The legal method used by a city to implement its general plan is

    a. variances.
    b. general land use.
    c. zoning.
    d. conditional use permits.

111. William did not pay his property taxes and they are now delinquent. Regarding the redemption of the property, which of the following is true?

    a. Delinquent taxes and penalties may be paid in installments.
    b. The owner remains in possession during the redemption period.
    c. The owner has one year from the foreclosure sale to redeem the property.
    d. There is no redemption period.

112. An investor enjoys a certain capitalization rate of return on her investment and a potential recapture of her investment over the next 25 years. The overall capitalization rate is the

    a. return on the investment.
    b. return of the investment.
    c. return on and of the investment.
    d. rate used to determine depreciation.

113. Who controls the Subdivision Map Act?

    a. The Real Estate Commissioner
    b. Local government
    c. The State Housing Law
    d. The local building inspector

114. The expression "numerous buyers and sellers with equal knowledge about products and prices" refers to a(n)

    a. imperfect market.
    b. perfect market.
    c. real estate market.
    d. capital market.

115. Deregulation is a process

    a. of removing all government restraints.
    b. whereby some government restraints are gradually loosened.
    c. whereby depositors can withdraw their funds from lending institutions.
    d. to revoke an offer.

116. A subdivider would order a percolation test

    a. to determine soil compaction.
    b. to determine geologic hazards.
    c. for sewage disposal.
    d. to test for toxic waste.

117. Mrs. Jenner believes she has been discriminated against in the rental of an apartment unit. What action can she take?

    a. File a civil suit
    b. File a suit in federal court
    c. File a complaint with HUD
    d. All of the above

118. The person who is entitled to a copy of a pest control report upon payment of the appropriate fee to the Structural Pest Control Board in Sacramento is

    a. the seller.
    b. the seller and the buyer.
    c. anyone who requests it.
    d. the escrow agent, who can then distribute copies to all parties in the transaction.

119. What is the usual time period for an exclusive-agency listing agreement?

    a. Whatever time period the parties agree on
    b. Three months
    c. Six months
    d. The time period is open.

120. An owner and a real estate broker enter into an exclusive-agency listing agreement. During the listing period, the owner sells the property to a neighbor. Regarding the commission,

    a. a full commission is due the broker.
    b. the broker is entitled to only one-half of the commission because the owner found the buyer.
    c. the broker is not entitled to a commission.
    d. the broker will have to file court action to collect the commission.

121. A rectangular parcel contains 1,263.6 square yards. If one side of the parcel is 105.3 feet, what is the length of the other side?

    a. 12 feet
    b. 108 feet
    c. 13 yards
    d. 108 yards

122. An owner/transferor of a home gives a lease option to a tenant. Under the Real Property Transfer Disclosure Statement Act,

    a. no transfer disclosure statement is required because it is not a sale.
    b. the owner must give a completed transfer disclosure statement to the lessee/buyer before the lease-option contract is signed.
    c. lease options are not under this act.
    d. None of the above

123. Greene enters into a real estate purchase contract with Rich. Both parties initial the liquidated damages clause. If Rich defaults, Greene will be entitled to

    a. no more than 3 percent of the selling price or the amount of the deposit, whichever is less.
    b. collect dollar damages to cover any escrow charges.
    c. recover nothing.
    d. go to court to recover the deposit.

124. Any discrepancy or ambiguity in a legal description of property on a deed

   a. will place a cloud on the title.
   b. is curable by the seller.
   c. will require confirmation action.
   d. All of the above

125. In a tight money market, an investor who is concerned that interest rates will rise and does not want long-term investments should

   a. purchase short-term investments, which might bring a higher interest rate and offer more liquidity.
   b. invest in trust deeds and mortgages.
   c. place all of his or her money into a savings account.
   d. purchase equities in real estate as a hedge against inflation.

126. A veteran purchased a home through conventional financing. He now wants to borrow money and decides to use his VA entitlement for the refinancing of his home. The lender is willing to make the loan and charges discount points to the borrower. Regarding the position of the VA, it

   a. will guarantee the loan only if the seller and not the buyer pays the discount points.
   b. might guarantee the loan if the discount points are set by the VA and not the lender.
   c. will guarantee the loan.
   d. does not guarantee the loan for refinancing purposes.

127. Which of the following is not a form of obsolescence?

   a. A misplaced improvement
   b. Wear and tear from use
   c. An overbuilt improvement
   d. An outdated kitchen

128. When a government body, such as a city, county, or the state, obtains an easement over a piece of property by statutory dedication, it comes under

   a. eminent domain.
   b. the Subdivision Map Act.
   c. easement by prescription.
   d. escheat.

129. An architect has been hired to draw a plot plan. It is for the purpose of

   a. guiding the placement of construction and related land improvements.
   b. guiding the construction of the building.
   c. showing the exterior sides of the houses.
   d. showing the details of the foundation construction.

130. There are two properties that were built concurrently on adjoining lots of equal value. The construction and maintenance costs were almost the same. A major difference in value between them today would probably be due to

   a. economic obsolescence in the neighborhood.
   b. physical depreciation of one of the properties.
   c. nonconforming uses across the street from one of the properties.
   d. functional obsolescence within one of the properties.

131. To arrive at an estimate of value, the appraiser

   a. averages the three indicators of value.
   b. reconciles the three indicators of value.
   c. revises the three indicators of value.
   d. finalizes the three indicators of value.

132. When negotiating a sale of real property, the conditions of sale will have an effect on the

    a. price of the property.
    b. basis of the property.
    c. loan-to-value ratio of the property.
    d. utility of the subject property.

133. Which of the following describes the action of gross income being changed into value in one operation?

    a. The use of a fixed rate of return
    b. The use of a rent multiplier
    c. The comparison approach
    d. The cost approach

134. In periods of tight money, if the interest or yield increases, the capitalized value of the building

    a. decreases.
    b. increases.
    c. remains the same.
    d. is subject to strong fluctuations.

135. In an IRC 1031 tax-deferred exchange, value is based on

    a. book value.
    b. fair market value.
    c. purchase price minus depreciation plus capital improvements.
    d. equity value.

136. The term *encumbrance* is best defined as

    a. the use of property by a debtor to be offered as security for a debt.
    b. any action relative to creating a transfer.
    c. the degree, quantity, nature, and extent of interest that one has in real property.
    d. anything that affects or limits the fee simple interest in property.

137. What is the method used to attempt to stop a violation of private restriction?

    a. Decrees of partition
    b. An injunction
    c. A junction
    d. A desist and refrain order from the Real Estate Commissioner

138. Sometimes a "quiet title" action is sought. What does this refer to?

    a. A foreclosure action
    b. Purchasing property through a dummy buyer
    c. An action to quiet a noisy neighbor
    d. Court action to remove a cloud on title

139. A California real estate license is needed by a

    a. trustee selling foreclosure property.
    b. a secretary in a real estate company who sells tract homes on the weekends.
    c. a woman who manages her own apartment building.
    d. All of the above

140. The Real Estate Commissioner has the duty to

    a. screen and qualify applicants for licensing.
    b. investigate complaints filed by the general public against a licensee.
    c. review and approve or disapprove public reports for subdivisions.
    d. All of the above

141. Currently in California, the Commissioner of Corporations has control over

    a. real estate investment trusts.
    b. limited partnerships.
    c. blind pools.
    d. All of the above

142. The main purpose of fair housing laws is to prevent discrimination in housing based on race, color, religion, age, sex, marital status, national origin, ancestry, handicap, and familial status. A violation of these laws is

    a. against public policy.
    b. unlawful.
    c. Both *a* and *b*
    d. Neither *a* nor *b*

143. Of the many duties of the county tax assessor, a main duty is to

    a. assess the taxes.
    b. adjust the taxes if requested by property owners.
    c. estimate the amount of taxes a property owner must pay.
    d. set the market value of property for taxation purposes.

144. The principle that states "Most people will not pay more for property than the cost of an equally desirable substitute property" is taken from the principle of

    a. conformity.   c. regression.
    b. substitution.   d. progression.

145. Owner Hopkins has many types of real estate investments. For federal income taxation purposes, the type of property that she can depreciate is

    a. her personal residence.
    b. a condominium used as her second home.
    c. a duplex used as rental property.
    d. vacant land that she is holding for future development.

146. Regarding the Uniform Settlement Statement, which is issued at the close of a RESPA transaction, which of the following would appear on the statement?

    a. A finder's fee
    b. Any kickbacks
    c. Fees paid for the preparation of the statement
    d. Appraiser's fee

147. Broker Murray has a habit of exaggerating the features of a property. This is known as

    a. puffing.   c. panic selling.
    b. panic peddling.   d. blockbusting.

148. There are five ways to acquire title to real property in California. Which of the following is/are used?

    a. By succession
    b. By deed
    c. By occupancy
    d. All of the above

149. All of the following conditions are necessary to acquire title by adverse possession *EXCEPT*

    a. open and notorious use.
    b. a color of title or claim of right.
    c. residency on the property.
    d. a minimum of five years of occupancy on the property.

150. Should there be a forced sale of homesteaded property, which of the following would be paid before the homestead exemption?

    a. A deed of trust and a mechanic's lien
    b. Real property taxes
    c. Both *a* and *b*
    d. Neither *a* nor *b*

■ ANSWER KEY

1. b.   Use the neighbor's sale as comparable sales data and apply the formula for the gross rent multiplier rule, "sales price divided by gross rent equals the multiplier." Take the sales price of the $90,000 comparable and ÷ $600 a month = 150 as a monthly gross rent multiplier. Take 150 × $640 a month on subject property, and that equals $96,000 as the estimated value on the subject property.

2. b.   Leverage is the ability of the borrower to control a large investment with a relatively small amount of his or her own money.

3. b.   Because the stock in the mutual water company runs with the land, the buyer does not pay extra for it.

4. d.   The interest portion of the mortgage payment on only the unit is a deduction from taxable income. The other choices are not allowable deductions for owner occupants (but are for investors in condominium units). The question indicates that the unit is for the owner's personal use.

5. c.   For income taxation purposes, the cost basis of the home will be the purchase price, not market price or assessed value.

6. b.   The ridgeboard is the highest member of frame construction. Its job is to support the upper ends of the rafters.

7. a.   A hip roof is a four-sided roof. It is a pitched roof with sloping sides and ends.

8. d.   First to record is first in right.

9. d.   The CLTA (California Land Title Association) is the formal name for the commonly obtained standard type of title insurance coverage used.

10. b.   The escrow holder is responsible for any required notifications to the IRS. For example, under the Foreign Investment in Real Property Tax Act (FIRPTA), every buyer must, unless an exemption applies (and there are many), deduct and withhold 10 percent of the gross sales price from the seller's proceeds and send it to the IRS, if the seller is a "foreign person" under the statute. However, it is the escrow holder who would actually process the funds and notices of the transaction to the IRS, in the buyer's behalf.

11. c.   Remember the concept, "the higher the risk, the higher the capitalization rate, the lower the value." Therefore, expect that if the rate increases, value decreases. The net operating income of $30,000 ÷ a capitalization rate of 5% = $600,000. $30,000 ÷ 6% = $500,000. With the higher capitalization rate of 6 percent, the value decreases by $100,000. A simple way to remember this concept is to think of a seesaw with a capitalization rate at one end and value at the other end. When one end of the seesaw is up (capitalization rate), the other (value) is down and vice versa.

12. a.   The Subdivision Map Act, which is controlled by local government, begins its controls at, and applies to, a division of one lot into two or more lots. A subdivision of five or more lots would come under both the Subdivision Map Act and the Subdivided Lands Law (controlled by the Real Estate Commissioner).

13. a.   In a tight money market, there is more use of seller financing. Sellers often find that to make a sale, they might have to carry back some or all of the loan if funds are not readily available through lending institutions.

14. d.   The power of sale clause, which is usually found in a deed of trust, when signed by the borrower (trustor), allows the trustee in behalf of the lender to sell the secured property if there is a default. This clause allows the sale to occur by trustee's public sale and not a court sale, which is a quicker method of remedying the default. The term *foreclosure sale* could mean a court sale or a trustee's (public) sale.

15. a.   Baker's title will be clouded. It is possible to remove the cloud and one way to do that is to have the buyer sign a quitclaim deed. In the question, the buyer moved out. It would become a matter of trying to find the buyer in order to have the quitclaim deed signed. If this action is not workable, legal action might be needed to help the seller clear up the cloud.

16. a.   The question describes "discounting of a note." The reason sellers would consider selling a note they are holding for a lesser amount is to obtain the bulk of their funds now as opposed to waiting for a longer period of payment.

17. a.   Statement of fact.

18. c.   The seller's payment of commission along with most other expenses of sale can be deducted for income taxation purposes.

19. c.   A one-bath house in today's life style would be considered an example of functional obsolescence. Think of functional obsolescence as involving items that are either old-fashioned or out of date. If you encounter the term *physical deterioration* in other questions, it refers to items that are either worn out or are not working. *Economic obsolescence* refers to conditions that occur outside the owner's property lines that decrease value but that the owner has little or no control over (e.g., downzoning or freeway noises).

20. d.   The question asks for the least important characteristic of value, and that happens to be "transferability" (title matters), which can be more easily resolved than other issues. The "most" important would be "utility" (usefulness of the property).

21. c.   An appurtenant easement runs with the land. An easement for life (by its name) is based only on a person's lifetime; when that person's life terminates, so does the easement. Therefore, it does not run with the land. A covenant (a promise) might or might not run with the land.

22. b.   Economic obsolescence occurs outside the owner's property and is difficult for the owner to overcome.

23. a.   An acknowledgement (notarization) of the grantor's signature is not a requirement for a valid deed. It becomes a requirement for the recording of the deed. The question asks about validity of the deed.

24. b.   A deed to a fictitious "person" is void. It means no such person exists. Do not confuse this with the term *fictitious name*. A deed to a fictitious name or assumed name is valid, as it could be a business name.

25. b.   A quitclaim deed does not warrant anything. It removes the present claim of a grantor (one who is on title) to subject property.

26. c.   A violation of a condition of ownership could lead to the forfeiture (loss) of title.

27. b.   The property escheats (reverts) to the state, which waits for five years before it sells property. This gives any possible heirs an opportunity to come forth and place a claim on the estate.

28. a.   Statement of fact. A writ of execution is a forced sale of property to satisfy a judgment.

29. a.   A proper writing is not a requirement for a valid contract under contract law.

However, under the statute of frauds, certain contracts must be in writing for enforceability purposes, and this includes a real estate contract.

30. c.   The contract is void, as the element of capacity is missing.

31. c.   When the seller's acceptance has been communicated back to the buyer in the manner stated in the offer, a contract is formed between the parties.

32. d.   None of the policies listed in the choices protect against "all" possible losses. There are some policies that give more protection than others, but it is virtually impossible to protect against all possible losses.

33. c.   Both the broker and the salesperson must keep a copy of the employment agreement for three years from the date of termination of the employment.

34. a.   If the right of rescission applies, it runs for three business days after the signing of the note. A business day is any day other than Sunday and federal legal holidays. Yes, Saturday is counted as a business day.

35. d. $265,000 (quarterly) × 4 = $1,060,000 × 32% = $339,200. $1,060,000 − $339,200 = $720,800.

36. c.   Steering is the illegal practice of deliberately avoiding the showing of properties in certain areas to minority buyers and "steering" them elsewhere.

37. c.   One-half mile by one-half mile describes a one-quarter section of land that contains 160 acres.

38. b.   One square acre has 208.71 feet on each side. The distance on the side of a one-quarter section is ½ mile or 2,640 feet. 2,640 feet divided by 208.71 = 12.65 lots. You cannot get 13 lots out of 12.65, so realistically 12 lots could be developed.

39. d.   Most offers to purchase used today authorize a broker to hold the deposit until an offer is accepted or rejected. On acceptance or rejection, the broker has three business days to do choices *a*, *b*, or *c*.

40. c.   Currently, residential income property can be depreciated over 27½ years. Remember that only improvements are depreciable and not the land. In other questions, if the land value is given, be sure to subtract the land value and depreciate only the value of the improvements.

41. a.   The amount of available space is influenced by the amount of demand by the potential users of the space (i.e., buyers or tenants). The *elasticity of demand* refers to a strong demand or a weak demand, and it changes, depending on the different phases of a business cycle.

42. a. $6,500 ÷ 1.30 (100% + 30%) = $5,000 (original cost). $6,500 × 75% (100% − 25%) = $4,875. $4,875 × 94% (100% − 6%) = $4,582.50. $5,000 (original cost) − $4,582.50 = $417.50 loss.

43. a.   A *condemnation action* is the legal action for the taking of private property (under eminent domain) for the good of the public. This legal taking is considered an involuntary conversion from the owner's viewpoint.

44. b.   100 chains = 6,600 feet. One rod = 16.5 feet, and one mile = 5,280 feet.

45. d.   The three other choices are just different ways of identifying one mile. There are 320 rods to a mile. One mile equals 5,280 feet. A section is a one-mile square (one mile on each side).

46. a.   Statement of fact.

47. b.   A resident manager is required for apartment buildings of 16 or more units. As long as the resident manager handles

only the affairs of the subject property, no real estate license is required for the resident manager. Remember, a real estate broker's license of record is required for property managers who manage other people's property for compensation.

48. d. Statement of fact.

49. c. An abstract of judgment is the result of court action against a person. It is an involuntary lien.

50. c. The promissory note is the evidence of the debt, contains the promise to pay and signature of the borrower, and is a contract complete unto itself. The deed of trust is a security device and secures the promissory note. It contains many protective clauses for the lender. If there is a conflict between the note and the deed of trust, in usual circumstances the note prevails.

51. b. When title is passed with conditions of ownership, it is known as *fee simple defeasible*, which means title may be defeated or lost if the conditions are violated.

52. c. Owners can make secret profits as they do not have to reveal what the original cost of the property was. When real estate licensees act as principals, they must disclose this fact to the other parties to the transaction.

53. c. Choices *a* and *b*. The term *panic selling* is found in law. Panic peddling is another term for panic selling. Both terms are used to describe the same activity, which is illegal and unethical practice.

54. d. Statement of fact.

55. b. *Assemblage* refers to combining small adjacent lots into one large parcel for plottage increment (bonus).

56. b. The property residual technique is used to appraise the total value of income property without separating the land value from the value of the improvements.

57. d. Statement of probability.

58. d. The three choices listed all require a real property transfer disclosure statement.

59. c. A "real property sales agreement" is another way of saying "land contract." In a land contract, no legal title passes at the time of the sale, only equitable title passes. Because a grant deed is not issued until the terms of the contract are met, the seller cannot be called a grantor. Therefore, the land contract is signed by the "vendor" (seller).

60. c. Remember, leverage is the process of using as little of your own money and as much borrowed money as possible to control a large investment.

61. c. The broker can take the listing, as a person under 18 and divorced is within the category of emancipated minors who can contract.

62. d. If the annual percentage rate (fully spelled out) is stated in the ad, then other disclosures are not required.

63. d. Statement of fact.

64. b. A negative declaration is actually good news for the developer. It means that local government believes the proposed development will have no negative influence on the environment. This eliminates the time and cost of the preparation of an environmental impact report.

65. b. Statement of fact.

66. d. Statement of fact.

67. a. The purpose of special assessments is to provide funds for specific local improvements for the general public (e.g., streets, sewers, and sidewalks).

68. b. The main concern of a site (land) analysis is the site itself (i.e., what is its highest and best use?).

69. d. Statement of fact.

70. d. The three other choices are all examples of purchase-money loans.

71. b. A listing agreement is a formal contract between the owner and the broker. If either the owner or the broker breaches the contract, there is the potential for a lawsuit for damages.

72. b. A bilateral contract is a two-sided contract. It is a promise for a promise. The promise of "diligence" by the broker occurs when the broker signs the listing agreement. However, the owner is the first to sign, with a promise of payment of commission on sale of property. Hence, the owner's promise to pay coupled with the broker's promise of diligence in finding a buyer creates a bilateral agreement.

73. d. Statement of fact.

74. a. Points paid by the buyer are treated as debits (charges) to the buyer.

75. c. Statement of fact.

76. c. It is legal for a broker to accept cash, check, or part ownership in some type of business or property that the owner and broker agree on as compensation.

77. c. Without authorization from a seller to accept a deposit for the purchase of property, the broker acts as the buyer's agent with respect to the deposit. This means that the broker must follow the buyer's instructions regarding the deposit.

78. a. Listings are personal service contracts that employ brokers to act for sellers in the sale of property. When the broker of record expires, the listings also expire. In this question, the daughter would have to relist the properties in her name to be able to continue to represent the sellers.

79. a. A bill of sale transfers the title of a business opportunity. A grant deed transfers the title of real property.

80. a. Cal-Vet has fewer closing costs than other types of loans, as there are no points to be paid. There is no institutional lender in this loan. It is the veteran who deals with Cal-Vet's Department of Veterans Affairs for the loan.

81. c. Statement of fact.

82. d. The broker's action was a clear violation of the fiduciary duty and ethical standards of a real estate licensee. (If the seller had authorized the broker to reveal this information and willingness to accept a much lower offer, then the action would be permissible.)

83. b. An attachment lien is an involuntary specific lien against property that terminates in three years. If the property owner expires during the three-year period, the lien continues for its full term, unless there is an action for dismissal or removal or judgment is rendered.

84. d. A valid grant deed does not require a date, method of title taking, or recordation.

85. d. Mineral rights, unless exempted, transfer with the land.

86. a. No fee can be charged for the preparation of the Uniform Settlement Statement (RESPA).

87. d. Statement of fact.

88. d. Statement of fact.

89. d. If the Federal Reserve System raises the discount rate it charges its member banks, banks will have to charge a higher rate of interest to borrowers. Higher inter-

est rates discourage borrowing. If the Federal Reserve System decides to sell bonds to the public, money is taken from bank accounts by those who buy the bonds from the Federal Reserve System. This action reduces the amount of cash for lending purposes.

90. d. Be sure to add the six-inch walls to all four sides of the building. The width of 24 feet is increased by one foot (6″ + 6″) to equal 25 feet. The 30-foot length of the building is also increased by one foot (6″ for walls at the front and 6″ for the rear wall) = 31.25 × 31 = 775.

91. a. Calculate backward. For testing purposes, disregard the directions shown and concentrate on the numbers. One quarter of any section is 160 acres. Take ¼ of 160 and there are 40 acres left. Take ¼ of 40 acres and there are 10 acres left. An easy way to remember the right answer to this question is when you have three ¼'s listed in a row, the answer is 10 acres.

92. a. The term *demise* refers to the passing of a right to another. For example, in lease agreements, while the expression "I hereby let and demise these premises" is not required to be written in the lease, the landlord is actually passing the possession of the property to the tenant. Do not confuse the term *demise* with the term *devise*. Devise is a gift of real property by last will and testament.

93. b. A percentage lease is often based on a tenant's monthly gross income to the business. There is usually a minimum amount of rent due with the percentage of gross income on top of basic rent.

94. b. Statement of fact.

95. d. Because stock in a mutual water company runs with the land, it is treated as a real property item.

96. d. Statement of fact.

97. b. A beneficiary statement shows the current status of the loan (i.e., unpaid balance, interest due, due date, etc.).

98. d. Statement of fact.

99. a. Only the lessor's signature is required on a valid lease agreement, although it is customary to obtain the signatures of all parties. Signature of the lessor and possession of the premises by the lessee forms a valid lease agreement.

100. a. Riparian rights refer to those of a landowner by a river or stream (a watercourse).

101. c. A fixture is an item that was once personal property but has been affixed to real property in such a way that it becomes part of the real property itself.

102. b. Property acquired during marriage with the income of both husband and wife becomes community property.

103. b. The appraiser can discuss the appraisal with only the client who hired the appraiser. In this case, it is the owner.

104. a. A license is a form of permission that can be revoked. The part of the statement that says "until I say you can't" makes it a license.

105. d. They would all be tenants in common. Recall that there are four unities to a joint tenancy: time, title, interest, and possession. If one or more of the unities is missing, a tenancy in common is created. In this question, the sister broke the unity of "time" by deeding some of her interest away.

106. b. Because work was done on a specific piece of property and the contractor remains unpaid, a specific lien that affects just subject property can be filed.

107. b. An encumbrance is anything that burdens, limits, or affects the fee simple interest on property. This includes easements, trust deeds, property taxes, mechanics' liens, zoning, CC&Rs, etc.

108. c. Statement of fact.

109. a. The formula for the gross rent multiplier rule is Sale Price divided by Gross Rent = the Gross Rent Multiplier. This formula is sometimes used on income property as just a way to quickly estimate value. It is dependent on comparable sales data, as it is ineffective in an inactive market. The more formal and preferred method for appraisal of income property is the "capitalization of income approach."

110. c. Zoning is a tool commonly used by a city to implement its general plan.

111. b. During the redemption period, the owner remains in possession of the property.

112. c. An overall capitalization rate is made up of both the "return on" and the "recapture of" the investment. It is a rate that each investor seeks for his or her investment purposes.

113. b. Local government (the local planning commission) administers the Subdivision Map Act. This act is concerned with the physical aspects of the subdivision and how the subdivision will affect the community.

114. b. Statement of fact.

115. b. Deregulation is a process whereby government restraints are gradually relaxed.

116. c. Percolation tests are conducted to determine how well the soil will absorb fluids. These tests are often used in conjunction with septic tank installations for sewage disposal.

117. d. Statement of fact.

118. c. Statement of fact.

119. a. Statement of fact.

120. c. The broker is not entitled to a commission. In an exclusive-agency listing, the seller reserves the right to sell the property during the listing period and not pay a commission.

121. b. 1263.6 square yards × 9 square feet to a square yard = 11,372.40 square feet to the area of the rectangle. 11,372.40 ÷ 105.3 feet (width) = 108 feet. Read the choices carefully; the correct answer is 108 feet, not 108 yards.

122. b. Notice that the seller must give the statement to the lessee/buyer before the lease-option contract is signed.

123. a. Statement of fact.

124. b. An ambiguity in the legal description of property can be corrected by the seller/grantor. A correction deed or "deed of confirmation" can be completed by the seller.

125. a. Statement of fact.

126. c. The VA will guarantee the loan for refinancing as well as for the purchase of a home by a qualified veteran.

127. b. Wear and tear from use is an example of physical deterioration.

123. a. Statement of fact.

129. a. The purpose of the plot plan is to show lot dimensions and to guide the placement of construction and related improvements.

130. d. Functional obsolescence (outmoded appliances or old-fashioned features and fixtures) could cause value to differ between adjacent properties.

131. b. To estimate value, the appraiser reconciles (not averages) the three indicators of value, which are the three appraisal

approaches (market data, cost, and capitalization).

132. a. The conditions of sale will have a marked effect on the sales price of property. For example, if the seller will carry back the loan, the ease of financing will usually drive up the sales price. Or if the purchase is by all cash, the sale price is usually lowered.

133. b. Statement of fact. Recall the formula for the gross rent multiplier rule: Sales Price divided by Gross Rent equals the Gross Rent Multiplier. Take the appropriate multiplier and multiply it by rent and it equals value. For example, property sells for $75,000 and is rented for $500 per month. $75,000 divided by $500 = 150. The neighbor's house is renting for $550 per month. Based on the above comparable sales data, multiply 150 × $550, which equals $82,500 value for the neighbor's house.

134. a. An interest rate is part of a capitalization rate. It is the "return on" the investment. If an interest rate increases, so does the capitalization rate. If the capitalization rate increase, value decreases.

135. d. Tax-deferred exchanges are based on equity value, not market value. The first step in creating the exchange is to balance the equities of each owner.

136. d. Statement of fact.

137. b. An injunction is a court action to stop an activity or to bring about forced compliance.

138. d. A quiet title action is a court action brought to remove a cloud on title.

139. b. A real estate license is required for this activity.

140. d. Statement of fact.

141. d. The Commissioner of Corporations and not the Real Estate Commissioner has control over all types of corporations and syndications (including real estate syndications).

142. c. Violations of fair housing laws are against public policy and unlawful.

143. a. Of the many duties of the county tax assessor, the main responsibility is to assess the property taxes.

144. b. The principle of substitution states that most people will not pay more for property than they would have to pay for an acceptable substitute.

145. c. Rental property can be depreciated for income taxation purposes. However, property that is owner occupied (a personal residence) as well as vacant land cannot be depreciated.

146. d. A fee can legally be paid for the appraiser's services. However, finder's fees, kickbacks, and fees to prepare the RESPA documents are prohibited; therefore, you would never find these fees on a RESPA settlement statement.

147. a. Puffing is an exaggeration of a property's features and benefits; it is an opinion or a form of sales talk. Often the court tends to treat puffing as a representation of material fact, as unsophisticated parties tend to rely on these statements in their decision to buy property.

148. d. The Civil Code indicates there are five ways to transfer title to real property. The five ways are by will, succession, accession, occupancy, and transfer (includes deeds).

149. c. Statement of fact. The question asks for the exception.

150. c. Choices *a* and *b* are examples of secured liens. They take priority over a homestead exemption, which protects to some extent against the claims of unsecured creditors.

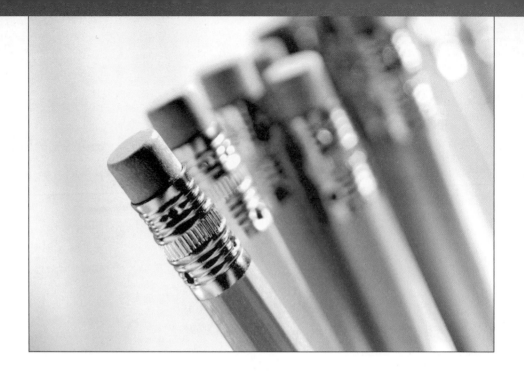

BROKER APPENDIX

■ INSTRUCTIONS TO THE READER

The practice examinations in this supplement are geared specifically to the reader who is preparing for the California Real Estate Broker license examination. These exams should be used in conjunction with the Hot Notes, test-taking tips and additional practice exams found in *California Real Estate Exam Guide*.

All practice exams should be taken until a 90 percent or better score is achieved. The Hot Notes should also be studied until they are totally familiar to you. Best wishes on your state examination!

BROKER APPENDIX
Hot Notes

Following are additional Hot Notes for the broker applicant. (It is important for the broker applicant to also study all of the *California Real Estate Exam Guide*, its Hot Notes, and its practice questions in addition to the Broker Supplement.)

1. "As is" refers to observable defects.
2. An officer of a corporation does not require a real estate license when selling corporate property, provided the officer receives no special compensation.
3. A Fictitious Business Statement is good for five years from December 31 in the year filed. It is filed with the county clerk. Requires approval by the Real Estate Commissioner.
4. Worker's compensation is required for all employees, including real estate licensees.
5. A prepaid rental listing service must provide at least three actual rentals within five days of receipt of a client's rental fee.
6. An advance fee agreement must be in not less than 10-point type and approved by the Real Estate Commissioner at least 10 business days prior to its use.
7. Failure to disclose a material fact, not in real estate, is an example of fraudulent misrepresentation.
8. Dual agency is likely to occur in a for-sale-by-owner transaction in which an agent brings an offer to an owner.

9. A single agent acts for a buyer *or* a seller but not both, is client-oriented, and must be fair and honest with all parties.

10. In an exclusive authorization to locate property, the broker becomes the single agent of only the buyer.

11. Under subagency which is no longer offered through the Multiple Listing Service, when a salesperson brings in a buyer for a salesperson's broker's listing (dual agency), a salesperson becomes a subagent of a seller.

12. A salesperson with two years' experience out of the last five with any real estate broker may be selected as a manager of the branch office.

13. Blind advertising indicates there is nothing stated in an ad that identifies an advertiser as a real estate licensee.

14. A Code of Ethics is a moral science.

15. A real estate broker's license is required for property management.

16. The broker of record must be named as trustee on any trust fund account.

17. Any excess of more than $200 of a broker's own funds must be removed from any trust fund account within 25 days of deposit to avoid a charge of commingling funds.

18. Any overage in a trust account must be accounted for and kept in the trust fund account.

19. It is legal to advertise gifts as an incentive to attract business, provided the conditions for earning the gifts are in the ad.

20. An owner can use "reasonable means" to protect against floodwater.

21. Stock in a mutual water company (real property) is appurtenant to the land; a utility company easement is not. Vegetation is real property.

22. If a life estate is based on the life of another, it is called a *life estate pur autre vie*.

23. A leasehold estate is not real property, it is a chattel real.

24. The definition of *voidable* is "valid on its face, but may be rescinded by an injured party."

25. An agreement in a deed is called a *covenant*.

26. A quiet title action is one way to terminate an adverse possession claim.

27. A quiet title action may be used to enforce a forfeited recorded land contract.

28. An auctioneer offers property in behalf of a seller.

29. Escheat is not a way for an individual to receive title. It is a way for the state to ultimately take ownership of unclaimed property after a five-year wait.

30. Just compensation to an owner based on fair market value due to a taking under eminent domain is based on the Fifth Amendment of the U.S. Constitution.

31. A corporation seal authorizes an officer to sign for a corporation.

32. A grantee who is judicially declared mentally incompetent and who inherits property can legally receive it.

33. Reliance on title insurance has limited the use of warranty deeds.

34. The main disadvantage to a lender in a deed in lieu of foreclosure is that it does not wipe out junior liens. The first trust deed holders would have to assume any junior liens (which they do not like to do).

35. A recorded deed is an example of constructive notice.

36. A subordination agreement in a trust deed benefits a trustor (borrower). It allows subsequent encumbrances to have priority.

37. A mechanic's lien recorded today has priority over an unrecorded deed delivered a week ago.

38. A trust deed recorded before the mechanic's lien has priority over it.

39. A writ of execution is one way to satisfy a judgment.

40. A judgment is good for 10 years in the county where recorded and is a general lien.

41. The Uniform Building Code regulates remodeling, demolition, and new construction.

42. If city, state, or county codes overlap, the one that provides the highest degree of safety applies.

43. The Subdivision Map Act is administered by the Local Planning Commission, which also develops zoning regulations. This act applies to two or more lots. The developer who does not want a performance bond to be of record will have to deposit funds into escrow to certify easements and public improvements.

44. The Real Estate Commissioner administers the Subdivided Lands Law. This law applies to in-state and out-of-state offerings made to Californians.

45. With a preliminary public report, an agent can take only reservations.

46. A final public report can be issued without a preliminary report.

47. Owner-occupants of a condominium project (the units and the common areas) cannot deduct the homeowners' association dues for income tax purposes. The bearing walls and sidewalks belong to the common areas.

48. Bearing walls can be built at any angle to the doorway, are usually left undisturbed when remodeled, and are built heavier than other interior walls.

49. If the interior side of an exterior wall feels the same as the outside temperature, it is likely that heat and air are being lost through wall outlets.

50. If the inside surface of an exterior wall feels the same as the temperature of the surface of the interior wall, the insulation system is sufficient.

51. *Puffing* is a high exaggeration of property features and is both unethical and illegal.

52. The fiduciary duty is established between the principal and the broker, even when the salesperson of the broker takes the listing.

53. Estoppel does not terminate agency. It is one way to create an agency relationship.

54. Consideration is not a requirement for an agency relationship. A gratuitous agent (no fee) must present all offers.

55. The use of a postdated check with an offer to purchase is not illegal if it is disclosed to the seller.

56. The listing contract authorizes the broker to accept a deposit.

57. The clause "time is of the essence" is found on a deposit receipt.

58. Under warranty of authority, the principal (seller) is liable for the acts of the agent within the scope of authority granted. If the agent exceeds the authority, the agent may be liable for resulting damage. This warranty is invalid if the broker does not disclose the principal's name.

59. Negative fraud is actual fraud.

60. The Agency Relationship Disclosure Act applies to one-family to four-family units and became law in 1988.

61. The safety clause is found in the listing agreement.

62. Competing brokers agreeing to set commissions at a specific percentage are in violation of antitrust laws.

63. Waiver is the voluntary giving up of a right and may have legal consequences.

64. An exclusive right-to-sell listing is a bilateral executory agreement. Executory means something remains to be done, for example, the sale of the property.

65. An option is a contract to keep an offer open and is a unilateral contract. In a lease-option, the provisions of the lease are sufficient for consideration.

66. Any counteroffer is a rejection of the original offer.

67. In a court sale of probate property, the first overbid formula is 10 percent of the first $10,000 and 5 percent of any excess. The court sets the broker's commission.

68. Escrow is a neutral stakeholder, which must follow the written instructions of principals, cannot give legal advice, and is not a legal requirement for the majority of residential sales.

69. If there is a dispute over deposits, the escrow-holder can file an interpleader action and turn the matter over to the court.

70. Escrow instructions must be executed (signed) by the buyer and seller.

71. There are 360 days to a banker's or escrow year.

72. The CLTA title policy covers matters of public record at the offices of the county clerk, the Secretary of State, and the federal land office. No on-site inspection of the property is required. It is the most common type of policy.

73. The ALTA owners' extended title policy covers encroachments and matters a buyer would be unaware of, for example, off-record liens and unrecorded easements.

74. An appraisal is an estimate of value of property as of a specific date. It is usually the date of property inspection or contract date.

75. An appraisal may be by oral or written means.

76. A fee appraiser is an independent contractor.
77. Market value is worth.
78. Shelter is the primary motive of most property buyers.
79. Functional utility is a main concern of an appraiser.
80. The ultimate test of functional utility is the property's marketability.
81. Property on a hill or near water tends to have a higher value.
82. Demography is the study of the population.
83. The principle of substitution is part of all three appraisal approaches.
84. The principle of change is always present.
85. The principle of progression refers to a fixer-upper. The worth of the lesser property is enhanced by its presence among the better properties.
86. The first step in highest and best use analysis is to estimate the value of the land.
87. Cost equals value when improvements are new and are of highest and best use.
88. If current highest and best use is to change, current use is called *interim use*.
89. The first step in the appraisal process is to define the problem.
90. The second to the last step is to reconcile the three appraisal approaches.
91. The last step in the appraisal process is to state the estimated value.
92. Some irregularity in the topography of land is desirable in residential subdivisions.
93. Nonconforming use means an inconsistent use is allowed.
94. Assemblage anticipates plottage increment.
95. The methods for site valuation are sales comparison, land development, and allocation.
96. Always adjust comparable sales to subject property. If a comparable sale is inferior, adjust it upward; if superior, adjust it downward.
97. Financing is the first adjustment the appraiser makes for comparable sales.
98. Calculate the value of a house built in 1910 by using historic cost indexed to current construction cost.
99. The appraiser would likely use the cost approach replacement method on a commercial building that is at the end of its economic life.
100. The cubic-foot method of appraisal is often used on warehouses.
101. Depreciation is a loss in value from any cause. The major cause of depreciation is obsolescence. Depreciation occurs from both inherent and extraneous causes.
102. Deferred maintenance is often overlooked by property owners.
103. One version of the gross rent multiplier rule is to divide the selling price by the monthly rent to arrive at the monthly multiplier. Divide by annual rent to arrive at the annual multiplier. If you are given an annual multiplier, for example, a one-digit or two-digit number and monthly rent, convert the monthly rent to annual rent, then multiply by the annual multiplier.

104. An overall capitalization rate is made up of both the return on the investment and the recapture of the capital investment.

105. Capitalization is the process of converting a single year's income stream into an estimate of value. Economic rent is used for the appraisal of income property.

106. The land residual technique is used to establish only land value.

107. The building residual technique is used to establish the building value. It is used on older properties with dissimilar buildings on similar lots.

108. The depth table rule is used on commercial lots.

109. Urban industrial lots are valued by the square-foot or square-acre method.

110. Backfill is used to fill in around trenches and the foundation of a building.

111. Drywall is also called *gypsum board*.

112. The elevation shows the front and side views of a structure.

113. Foundation plan shows the foundation, subfloors, footing, and pier placement.

114. To strengthen the loadbearing factor of a roof, place the rafters closer together.

115. The *R* in R-value refers to heat "resistance."

116. Schematics refers to preliminary drawings and sketches by an architect.

117. If you give a real estate transfer disclosure statement (TDS) after acceptance of an offer, the buyer has three days if it is given in person, or five days if by mail, to rescind the contract.

118. The seller (transferor) must present the buyer with a TDS in the sale of residential property of one to four units. The broker cannot fill in the seller's portion of the TDS, even if the seller has never seen the property.

119. Exempted from the TDS disclosure is a fiduciary administering an estate.

120. Information on pest control reports can be obtained from the Structural Pest Control Board in Sacramento by anyone who requests it and pays a fee. It keeps its records for two years.

121. The Truth-in-Lending Act applies to businesses who offer consumer credit, for example, brokers and financial institutions. It does not apply to homeowners who market their own properties.

122. The two most important disclosures under Truth-in-Lending are the finance charge, which includes any direct and indirect loan charges, and the annual percentage rate.

123. HUD enforces the Real Estate Settlement Procedures Act (RESPA). Its purpose is to allow borrowers to shop for loan services. It applies to first trust deeds, junior loans, and refinancing loans on one to four residential units. Under RESPA, the lender must provide a good-

faith estimate of loan costs not later than three business days after receipt of loan application.

124. An agent is prohibited from paying a finder's fee/referral fee under RESPA.

125. A referral fee from an escrow company to a broker is a violation of RESPA.

126. Under the Interstate Land Sales Full Disclosure Act, anyone who requests it is entitled to a copy of the property report. Any purchaser has a seven-day right of rescission after the purchase of these vacant lots.

127. The Federal Open Market Committee of the Fed actively buys and sells government securities.

128. When the Fed sells its securities to the public, it is attempting to tighten up the money supply.

129. The lender's mortgage yield is based on the total amount of dollars received, less the cost of the lender's funds.

 130. Rising interest rates indicate rising inflation.

131. The Internal Revenue Service can impute a legal rate of 10 percent interest on zero interest rate loans.

132. A beneficiary statement to a borrower shows the current status of the loan.

133. Federal Land Banks make large land loans.

134. A package mortgage is a real estate loan that includes personal property.

135. A construction loan (short-term loan) is synonymous with interim loan. Commercial banks prefer short-term loans.

136. Insurance companies prefer takeout loans (long-term loans). They make participation loans. You would least likely refinance a home loan with an insurance company.

137. Mortgage bankers warehouse (hold) loans for sale to the secondary mortgage market.

138. Mortgage brokers do not lend their own money.

139. Mortgage companies are subject to minimum supervision.

140. In the secondary mortgage markets, loans are bought and sold between mortgagees (lenders).

141. The best hedge against inflation is a real estate investment that holds its value.

142. The term *capital markets* refers to long-term accounts, for example, bonds, mortgages, and treasury certificates.

143. The nominal interest rate is the rate stated on the note; the effective interest rate (APR) is the rate the borrower actually pays (includes finance charges).

144. An appraiser would be reprimanded and would not receive a beneficial review if he or she did not use FHA guidelines when completing appraisals for FHA loans.

145. An appraiser could be fined and face legal action for intentionally misrepresenting value (a possible felony), thereby causing a loss for a lender.

146. Discount points are charged to increase a lender's yield.

147. Mutual mortgage insurance (a mortgage insurance premium fund) protects the lender against any deficiency.

148. The VA loan is based on the Certificate of Reasonable Value. The origination fee on a VA loan is paid to the lender.

149. Reasonable discount points may be charged to the veteran on a refinance or purchase using the VA loan program.

150. A veteran can buy a farm on the Cal-Vet program.

151. FHA will but VA will not provide for a duplex purchased for rental.

152. A real property sales contract is used in the Veterans Farm and Home Purchase Act (Cal-Vet).

153. No prepayment penalty is a similarity between FHA and VA loans.

154. On a reverse annuity mortgage, the mortgagee (lender) makes periodic payments to the mortgagor (borrower).

155. There is a maximum interest rate fluctuation of 5 percent over the life of a renegotiable rate mortgage.

156. An alienation clause is a due-on-sale clause, benefits the lender, and is enforceable.

157. Trust deeds and mortgages are not negotiable (they are assignable).

158. The one similarity between a trust deed and a mortgage contract is the *security*.

159. The major difference between a trust deed and a mortgage contract is the *title*.

160. The beneficiary is the lender under a trust deed. The trust deed can be foreclosed by a trustee's sale or a judicial (court) foreclosure.

161. A request for notice of default benefits any junior lienholder.

162. A trust deed loan can be reinstated up to five business days prior to the trustee's sale.

163. There is no right of redemption at a trustee's sale.

164. A sheriff's deed is issued after the one-year redemption period under a mortgage contract.

165. Prepaid taxes are a credit on a seller's closing statement.

166. Senior homeowners can contact the assessor's office for information on carrying over an old property tax base to a new home.

167. Senior citizen property owners can contact the State Controller's Office for information on property tax postponement.

168. Special assessments are foreclosed through a tax sale.

169. The clearance receipt from the State Board of Equalization protects the buyer of a business from successor's liability for sales taxes not turned in to the state by the prior business owner.

170. The marginal tax applies to the next dollar of income earned.

171. Discount points on the refinancing of a loan are to be amortized over the life of a loan, like interest.

172. A homeowner who owns two homes and spends six months in each one can declare only one of them every two years as a principal residence for the tax exclusion benefits.

173. IRC 1031 tax-deferred exchanges are based on equity value. Any boot paid to equalize the exchange can be by cash or mortgage relief.

174. Qualified owners who materially participate in the management of their property and who earn less than $100,000 per year may be able to deduct up to $25,000 against nonpassive income each year.

175. If a broker decides to open an office, it should be located near the broker's area of specialization. The broker should have at least six months of working capital in reserve.

176. The desk cost is found by dividing the number of salespersons into the total operating expenses of the company. It does not include a profit margin for the broker.

177. A bill of sale transfers title to personal property. It is required for the sale of personal property valued at over $500.

178. Bulk sale notices are designed to warn any creditor of the seller's inventory that the inventory is being sold. The transferee (buyer) must place an ad in the legal notice section of the newspaper 12 business days before the transfer. The ad need only appear one time. The notice will not show the names and addresses of the creditors.

179. The bulk sale notice is recorded in the county where the goods (bulk sales) are located.

180. Alcoholic Beverage Control regulates liquor licensing. A bona fide club must be in operation at least one year to be able to apply for the license.

181. S corporations: All losses and profits are passed through to each stockholder to calculate against ordinary income.

182. A real estate investment trust must distribute 95 percent or more of its ordinary income to its shareholders annually. Seventy-five percent of its income must be from real estate investments.

183. The Corporations Commissioner regulates real estate syndications.

184. When the broker sets up a financing package for the buyer, the broker becomes the agent for the buyer and accepts the fiduciary responsibilities as the buyer's agent.

185. *Book value* is described as the original cost of the land and buildings plus the cost of any additions, less any depreciation.

186. The County Board of Supervisors sets the real property tax rate.

187. Closely spaced internal columns is an example of incurable functional obsolescence.

188. Verbal agreements between brokers for commission splits are legal. An unpaid cooperating broker can file a civil suit against a broker who did not keep a promise to share a commission.

189. If John grants to Mary an interest that is less than John has, John has created an estate in reversion for himself.

190. On the signing of a real property sales contract (land contract), equitable title passes to the purchaser (vendee).

191. A balance sheet includes goodwill, prepaid taxes, and any sales tax deposit. It does not include gross sales. (Gross sales would appear on a profit and loss statement.)

192. A commercial peach orchard can be depreciated. Land is not depreciable. Residential income property is depreciated over 27½ years, and commercial over 39 years.

193. The California Unruh Act prohibits discrimination by businesses. It does apply to the real estate industry.

194. The California Fair Housing Act (Rumford Act) applies to all persons in the state. Complaints can be submitted to the Department of Fair Employment and Housing within 60 days of the violation. Penalties include proceeding with the sale or lease, making the next vacancy available, and paying up to $1,000 in damages.

195. The American with Disabilities Act provides for the handicapped.

196. A 1968 United State Supreme Court landmark decision (*Jones v. Mayer*) bars racial discrimination by anyone in the sale or rental of property.

197. A person can file a complaint regarding fair housing matters with HUD, a state court, or a federal court.

198. A man buys a property for 20 percent less than the asking price. He later sells it for the asking price, and makes 25 percent profit on his 80 percent investment.

199. There are 48 board feet in lumber that measures 12 inches by 2 inches by 24 feet (1 board foot measures 12 inches by 12 inches by 1 inch).

200. A property owner sells a house and takes back a note for $11,220 as a second deed of trust. If he sells the note for $7,293, the discount rate is 35 percent. ($11,220 − $7,293 = $3,927; $3,927 ÷ $11,220 = 35%.)

201. *Infill* is the redevelopment of existing urban developments. It brings in multistory residential buildings with retail usage on the ground floor.

202. *Attornment* is to consent to the transfer of a right. It is where a tenant agrees to become a tenant of a new landlord by staying on after the sale of the property.

203. A brownfield site is an abandoned contaminated real property that may be difficult to develop.

204. GPAM stands for graduated payment adjustable mortgage.

BROKER APPENDIX
Practice Examination I

1. Developing zoning regulations is primarily the responsibility of the

   a. county or city engineer.
   b. planning commission.
   c. county tax assessor.
   d. State Board of Equalization.

2. In years past, subdividers, developers, and builders have realized significant profits by taking large parcels of land and subdividing them into smaller tracts. What would be the incentive for this type of development?

   a. Industrialization
   b. Migration
   c. Urbanization
   d. All of the above

3. It is unlawful for any person to effect the sale of a franchise that is regulated by the Franchise Investment Law unless a proper application is made to the Commissioner of Corporations, and the person is licensed by the

   a. Real Estate Commissioner.
   b. Corporations Commissioner.
   c. franchise tax board.
   d. Both a and b

4. The phrase "as is" in the sale of a residence refers to

   a. title defects.
   b. observable defects.
   c. unobservable defects.
   d. habitability defects.

5. A lump-sum cost required because of overdue repairs is generally known as

   a. economic obsolescence.
   b. functional obsolescence.
   c. Both a and b
   d. deferred maintenance.

6. In the three appraisal approaches, the one that requires land and improvements to be valued separately is known as the

    a. income approach.
    b. cost approach.
    c. sales comparison approach.
    d. All of the above

7. An individual should consult a real estate appraiser when he or she intends to

    a. remodel or rehabilitate.
    b. rent or lease.
    c. sell or buy.
    d. All of the above

8. When using the cost approach to determine value, an appraiser would make use of the market data approach to determine the

    a. value of the improvements.
    b. accrued depreciation.
    c. value of the land.
    d. value of comparable sales.

9. Which of the following statements is *LEAST* related to the term *depreciation?*

    a. A decrease in value due to any cause
    b. Obsolescence due to neighborhood infiltration of unharmonious property usage
    c. The ability of the inventive mind to design, which could result in adequate or inadequate features due to style, size, or age
    d. A value resulting from special supply and demand forces for specific properties or inflation in general

10. The promise to list a property for sale in exchange for a promise to perform is called a(n)

    a. consideration.
    b. option.
    c. executed agreement.
    d. unilateral contract.

11. The Real Estate Settlement Procedures Act requires that the settlement statement be delivered by the lender to the borrower in the absence of a waiver by the borrower

    a. within 10 days of receipt of the loan application.
    b. on or before the settlement date.
    c. three days prior to the settlement date.
    d. one day prior to the settlement date.

12. Which of the following is known to have done the most to stabilize the mortgage market?

    a. The Federal Savings and Loan Corporation
    b. A homeowners' association
    c. Federal Housing Association
    d. Federal Housing Administration

13. When the Truth-in-Lending Act applies to the advertising of real estate for sale, which of the following would be mentioned?

    a. Specific terms for payments
    b. A specific amount for the down payment
    c. A specific time period for the payments
    d. All of the above

14. When comparing the advantages of corporate ownership over private ownership of real property, which of the following is a correct statement?

    a. Only the stockholders—not the corporation—are permitted to own real property.
    b. The corporation does not have to pay taxes.
    c. The corporation would be taxed at a lower rate than a private owner in the highest tax bracket.
    d. The corporation can transfer the title to its real property without having a tax liability.

15. A good example of an investment that is purchased as a hedge against inflation is a(n)

    a. investment that will have the characteristics of an annuity.
    b. income-producing investment that will maintain its value.
    c. investment that maintains a high degree of liquidity.
    d. risk-free investment.

16. Broker Carter wants to offer promotional notes for sale to the public using newspaper advertising. This advertising must first be submitted to the Real Estate Commissioner for approval how many days prior to its use?

    a. 3 days   c. 10 days
    b. 5 days   d. 30 days

17. Broker Baker is found guilty of misrepresentation in a real estate transaction. Baker could be

    a. subject to civil action.
    b. subject to criminal action.
    c. subject to disciplinary action by the Real Estate Commissioner.
    d. All of the above

18. Which of the following agreements cannot be assigned without the consent of the parties to the agreement?

    a. Trust deed
    b. Lease agreement
    c. Option to purchase
    d. Power of attorney

19. The Real Estate Commissioner has regulations requiring the impounding of deposits for purchases in subdivisions. One of the reasons for this impounding is to protect the

    a. subdivider's funds.
    b. buyer's legal title until a proper release is obtained from any existing blanket encumbrances against the subdivision.
    c. buyer from a mechanic's lien.
    d. lender.

20. All of the following are ways to terminate an easement, *EXCEPT*

    a. a quitclaim deed from the holder of the dominant tenement.
    b. nonuse of the easement.
    c. destruction of the servient tenement.
    d. a merger of the servient tenement and the dominant tenement.

21. Which of the following statements is correct concerning appurtenant easements as they belong to and affect certain parcels of land?

    a. The parcels of land may be abutting and involve two separate parcels
    b. The one parcel, called the *dominant tenement*, has an advantage, while the other parcel, the *servient tenement*, is burdened by the easement
    c. The parcels may be contiguous and have separate owners
    d. All of the above

22. Mr. Jones sells his property to Mrs. Dale. They agree that Jones will retain possession of the property for four months after the close of escrow. At the close, a grant deed received by Dale went unrecorded. Later, Jones sold the property to Green, who was unaware of the prior sale. Green obtained a new loan for the purchase, recorded the deed, and took possession of the property. Which of the following is correct?

    a. Dale can sue Green for fraud.
    b. Jones is the legal owner of the property.
    c. Green is the legal owner of the property.
    d. The loan held by the bank is void.

23. Which of the following is not real property?

    a. Trade fixtures
    b. A detached garage
    c. Growing crops
    d. All of the above

24. Abel leased his real property to Cain. Cain leased the property to Green with Abel's consent. If Cain dies, which of the following statements would be correct?

    a. Green's leasehold is still valid.
    b. Green must renegotiate the terms of the lease.
    c. Cain's lease would terminate.
    d. Green's lease is no longer valid.

25. An undivided interest in land coupled with the right of exclusive occupancy of an apartment unit describes a

    a. stock cooperative.
    b. planned unit development.
    c. community apartment.
    d. condominium.

26. In which of the following is the cost of owning real property excluded?

    a. Interest on the loan balance
    b. Amortization of the loan
    c. Depreciation of the improvements
    d. Loss of interest on the owner's equity in the property

27. The effect of the Truth-in-Lending Act on the broker extends to

    a. the hiring of salespersons.
    b. the manner in which the broker advertises properties for sale.
    c. the closing of the transaction.
    d. closing the escrow.

28. Which of the following are considered to be packaged mortgages?

    a. Loans that allow additional monies to be made available to the borrower as an open-end type of loan
    b. Loans that allow additional purchases to be added onto an existing loan without having to refinance
    c. Loans that cover the land, improvements, and built-in appliances
    d. Loans that apply to several properties at the same time

29. An apartment building was constructed prior to the enactment of a zoning ordinance that does not permit multiple-family units in subject neighborhood. The existing building is an example of a

    a. violation of zoning.
    b. violation of the applicable master plan.
    c. nonconforming use.
    d. variance.

30. Which of the following is an example of a valid acknowledgement?

    a. An acknowledgement by a notary who notarizes a deed in which he or she is the grantor
    b. An acknowledgement of a deed that has been drawn and acknowledged out of state by a notary who is commissioned in that state
    c. An acknowledgement taken out of state by a notary commissioned in California
    d. All of the above

31. To perfect a claim to title under adverse possession, all of the following are required, *EXCEPT*

    a. payment of taxes for a continuous five-year period.
    b. open and notorious use of the property.
    c. some color of title or claim of right.
    d. that the land is owned by a government agency and designated for public use.

32. A lease that has been executed

    a. would grant or convey an interest in the land.
    b. would be illegal if the property were community property and signed only by the wife.
    c. must contain the words "let and demise" to be valid.
    d. must be recorded if the property is owned by the federal government.

33. To which of the following would an equitable title to real property pass?

    a. The vendee under a land contract
    b. The beneficiary under a deed of trust
    c. The trustee under a deed of trust
    d. Both *a* and *b*

34. Regarding financing, who would be most interested in a line of credit?

    a. The borrower
    b. The lender
    c. The seller
    d. The secondary mortgage market

35. A buyer wanting protection against unrecorded encumbrances in the purchase of real property would

    a. obtain an ALTA policy.
    b. include a request in the deposit receipt that extended coverage be provided.
    c. obtain a warranty deed.
    d. obtain an extended coverage policy.

36. Mr. Sato purchased a lot from Ms. Diaz that would be suitable for an apartment building. Sato paid 10 percent down and financed the balance as a first trust deed. To obtain a construction loan, which clause should he insist be included as part of the first trust deed?

    a. An alienation clause
    b. An acceleration clause
    c. A subordination clause
    d. None of the above

37. The imposition of restrictions on a new, large subdivision is most practically achieved by

    a. including them as covenants in the deed to each individual parcel.
    b. duly recording them with adequate reference made thereto in the deed to each parcel.
    c. including them in the body of the Real Estate Commissioner's final public report.
    d. publishing them 10 days prior to sale in a newspaper of general circulation.

38. Mr. Greer dies intestate with no known heirs. Which event is most likely to occur?

    a. Title to his real property will vest in the state immediately and automatically.
    b. The property escheats to the state through legal proceedings.
    c. The property can be claimed by anyone who wishes to pay any property tax that is due.
    d. Title to the property will vest in the state if no heirs come forth with a valid claim within ten years of the death of Greer.

39. Mrs. Able has a fee simple estate. It will become a less-than-freehold estate when she does which of the following?

    a. Allows a right-of-way for her neighbor
    b. Assigns all oil and mineral rights to her creditors
    c. Assigns a 49-year lease for agricultural purposes
    d. None of the above

40. Buyer Able gave broker Baker a deposit with an offer to purchase. Which of the following is true regarding the deposit?

    a. It never belongs to the broker.
    b. It is always refundable to the buyer.
    c. The broker must release the deposit to the seller.
    d. If the sale is canceled, the broker decides what happens with the deposit.

41. If a broker obtains an option to purchase property, he or she is required by law to disclose to each potential buyer of the property that he or she is a(n)

    a. optionor.   c. principal.
    b. beneficiary.   d. trustor.

42. The holder of a life estate cannot file a homestead on the property. Only a fee simple estate can be homesteaded. What is known about these statements?

    a. The first statement is true and the second statement is false.
    b. The first statement is false and the second statement is true.
    c. Both statements are true.
    d. Both statements are false.

43. From the following, which is the form of co-ownership that makes it difficult for one person to sell without the other person's consent?

    a. Joint tenancy
    b. Tenancy in common
    c. Community property
    d. Tenancy in partnership

44. Abel gives a life estate to Cain for the life of Black. Later Black dies. The interest held by Abel is a(n)

    a. estate in remainder.
    b. reversionary interest.
    c. less-than-freehold estate.
    d. fee simple estate.

45. When appraising an apartment building, the projection for gross income is based on

    a. contract rent.
    b. net rent.
    c. economic rent.
    d. None of the above

46. Which is the most effective way for a developer to finance the cost of off-site improvements and pass the cost on to the buyers?

    a. Improvement bonds
    b. Bank loans
    c. Grant deeds
    d. None of the above

47. A broker takes a listing on a retail business. The best way to determine the actual gross sale of the business is to

    a. check last year's financial statement.
    b. check the balance sheet.
    c. confirm the cost of the goods sold.
    d. verify the sales tax receipts.

48. Mr. Chang leased a commercial building for a period of 10 years. The lease will produce an annual income of $10,000 for the owner. Six percent is considered to be a realistic rate for leaseholds in the same area. What is the value of the lessor's interest in this lease?

    a. Less than $94,000
    b. $100,000
    c. $110,000
    d. More than $110,000

49. The Street Improvement Act of 1911 provides which of the following payment methods for property owners when the unpaid balance has "gone to bond"?

    a. The bondholder must include only interest on his income tax report.
    b. The owner can deduct principal and interest amounts from his annual income tax return.
    c. The owner can deduct interest charges from his annual income tax return.
    d. None of the above

50. Based on the assumptions presented, appraiser Jennings is justified in selecting straight-line depreciation in the capitalization of which of the following statements?

    a. The income imputable to the improvements will decline at a fixed annual rate commensurate with the fixed annual decline in market value.
    b. The market value of the improvements will decline at a fixed annual rate based on their remaining useful life.
    c. The land value remains constant, and the income imputable to the land is level in perpetuity.
    d. All of the above

51. Regarding commercial properties, as the depth of a lot decreases from the depth of a typical lot in the area

    a. the front-foot value decreases and the square-foot value increases.
    b. the front-foot and the square-foot value decrease.
    c. only the square-foot value decreases.
    d. the total lot value increases.

52. The statute of frauds provides that certain contracts are unenforceable unless they, or some note or memorandum, are in writing. Which of the following contracts would not be enforceable in court?

    a. An oral agreement to pay a broker a commission for negotiating the exchange of two businesses
    b. An oral agreement between a broker and a salesperson to share a commission
    c. An exclusive listing taken orally by a broker to sell a single-family home
    d. An oral agreement to sell a business opportunity

53. RESPA provides for all of the following, *EXCEPT*

    a. a limitation of the buyer's cost for the lender's preparation of the uniform settlement disclosure statement.
    b. the imposition of a penalty of up to three times the cost of the title insurance, if the seller bases his or her acceptance on the buyer's purchase of a title insurance policy through a specific company.
    c. a prohibition on the payment of kickbacks.
    d. the establishment of a commission split between cooperating brokers.

54. There are certain advantages to a borrower when obtaining FHA financing as compared with conventional financing. All of the following are benefits, *EXCEPT*

    a. FHA's minimum building requirements.
    b. the monthly mortgage payments are budgeted to meet the borrower's income.
    c. mortgage insurance rates are lower.
    d. there is no need for short-term financing.

55. A mortgagee when analyzing an FHA loan application considers the

    a. mortgagor's credit rating.
    b. purchaser's motivation.
    c. purchaser's available funds for the transaction.
    d. All of the above

56. When using the cost approach to appraise real property, an appraiser would use

    a. a single method of appraising the value of the land and the improvements and then average both into an overall estimate of value.
    b. separate methods for estimating the value of the land and the improvements and then combine the estimates into one overall estimate of value.
    c. the same method for estimating the value of the land and the improvements and then arrive at a separate estimate for each.
    d. None of the above

57. Because the housing market involves many different types of desires and needs, it is said to be

    a. structured.   c. fractionalized.
    b. stratified.   d. fractured.

58. The elevation sheets of a construction plan usually provide which of the following?

    a. Thickness of slab floor, kind and size of steel wire reinforcements
    b. Exterior sides of the structures as they will appear after construction
    c. Construction details and arrangements of interior areas
    d. Contour of the plot elevations of the land in relation to streets and boundaries

59. An indirect method of estimating depreciation would include which of the following?

    a. Engineering
    b. Capitalized income
    c. Age-life depreciation
    d. Only straight-line depreciation

60. Most people will not pay more for real property than the price of an acceptable substitute that is available without undue delay. To which principle of value does this refer?

    a. Anticipation   c. Conformity
    b. Competition   d. Substitution

61. Effective gross income less operating expenses minus debt service on a parcel of income property is known as

    a. accounts payable.
    b. cash flow.
    c. net income.
    d. cash receipts.

62. Two lots were purchased for $18,000 each. Later they were divided into three lots and sold for $15,000 each. The gross profit percentage is

    a. 15 percent.   c. 25 percent.
    b. 20 percent.   d. 40 percent.

63. An avocado grove is bisected by a concrete irrigation canal and leaves two triangular lots. One lot has a frontage of 750 feet and a depth of 970 feet. The lot contains approximately

    a. 5.3 acres.
    b. 8.3 acres.
    c. 10.6 acres.
    d. None of the above

64. In measuring the relative liquidity of a business operation, which of the following ratios would be used?

   a. Fixed assets to fixed debts
   b. Fixed assets to capital
   c. Current assets to current liabilities
   d. Capital to total liabilities

65. Under the jurisdiction of the California Environmental Quality Control Act, a public agency determines that a nonexempt proposed project has no significant impact on the environment and that a full environmental impact report is not required. The public agency must issue a

   a. declaration of beneficial conditions.
   b. negative declaration.
   c. positive declaration.
   d. statement of project condition.

66. Owner Alexis exchanged a shopping center worth $227,000 that was free and clear with a cost basis of $207,000 for a farm worth $247,000, also free and clear. Alexis paid $20,000 in boot to effect the exchange and to equalize the equities. For income tax purposes on the farm, Alexis would have

   a. $207,000 cost basis and no recognized gain.
   b. $227,000 cost basis and $20,000 recognized gain.
   c. $227,000 cost basis and no recognized gain.
   d. It cannot be calculated from the information given.

67. John and Susan Andrews purchased a home for $100,000 and took title as community property. Shortly thereafter, John died. At the time of his death, the property had a fair market value of $140,000. Later, Susan sold the home for $140,000. For federal income tax purposes, the gain from the sale of the home would be

   a. $40,000.
   b. $140,000.
   c. $100,000.
   d. There is no gain.

68. Diaz enters into an option to purchase real property from seller Cano. When does this agreement become a mutually binding contract?

   a. When consideration for the option passes from Diaz to Cano
   b. When Diaz exercises the right to purchase
   c. When the option is granted to Diaz by Cano
   d. All of the above

69. An offeror dies several hours prior to a seller's acceptance of an offer to purchase the seller's property. Which of the following is most correct?

   a. A contract exists and cannot be rescinded by the executor of the offeror's estate.
   b. A contract exists, and either party may rescind within a reasonable period of time.
   c. The offer was revoked by operation of law on the offeror's death.
   d. A contract exists, and it can be rescinded by the executor of the offeror's estate.

70. An offer to fully perform a purchase contract is known as a

    a. covenant.   c. demand.
    b. condition.   d. tender.

71. There are no two parcels that are exactly alike in all features and benefits. This concept forms the basis for courts of law to enforce a

    a. decree of partition.
    b. lis pendens.
    c. specific performance.
    d. quiet title action.

72. Under the federal Truth-in-Lending Act, which of the following may not be included as part of the finance charge?

    a. Loan discount points
    b. Time price differential
    c. Finder's fees
    d. Appraisal fees

73. The most common form of real estate syndication is a

    a. general partnership.
    b. blind pool.
    c. corporation.
    d. limited partnership.

74. Broker Nance adopted the following policies in the management of an apartment building. These policies were authorized by the owner of the building: (1) Single males are required to post a higher security deposit than single females or married couples. (2) The existing tenants, who are primarily Caucasian, are asked to solicit prospective renters from among their friends. The federal Fair Housing Act prohibits

    a. only statement 1.
    b. only statement 2.
    c. both statements 1 and 2.
    d. neither statements 1 nor 2.

75. Concerning equal opportunity housing, which of the following is incorrect?

    a. Panic selling occurs when the buyer is also a seller of a home.
    b. White prospects do not have to be shown any homes in racially changing neighborhoods unless they ask to see such properties.
    c. The federal Fair Housing Law applies equally to purchases of recreational properties.
    d. All prospective purchasers are entitled to full information concerning the availability of home loans.

76. Champion Swimming Pool Corporation installed a swimming pool for Mr. and Mrs. Thomas on their residential property. After completion, Champion filed a lien to ensure payment of the contract price. Which type of encumbrance would be created?

    a. A general lien
    b. An execution lien
    c. A voluntary lien
    d. None of the above

77. Subdivider Greg wishes to impose restrictions on a new large subdivision. These restrictions would most likely be

    a. included as covenants in the deed to each individual parcel.
    b. recorded with adequate reference made in the deed to each parcel.
    c. included in the Real Estate Commissioner's final subdivision public report.
    d. published in a newspaper of general circulation.

78. It is possible that constructive notice to homebuyers could occur in all of the following ways, *EXCEPT*

    a. knowledge of a stranger in possession under an unrecorded deed.
    b. the existence of utility lines on subject property.
    c. a defective property description that was revealed in the search of the public records.
    d. a person's possession under a recorded deed.

79. In a court probate sale, the price offered for the property must be at least

    a. 75 percent of the court appraisal.
    b. 80 percent of the court appraisal.
    c. 90 percent of the court appraisal.
    d. 100 percent of the court appraisal.

80. Broker Abel represented the seller of a home but was unaware of the seller's age. After the deed was signed, the title insurance company advised Abel that the grantor was not 18 years of age. The grant deed is

    a. valid.   c. illegal.
    b. voidable.   d. void.

81. The term *reversion* as it refers to a real estate transaction, most nearly means the

    a. interest of a lessor in a leased property.
    b. title to land changed by the action of water or wind.
    c. rights of a mortgagee should there be a default.
    d. action of the state under the process of escheat.

82. Mrs. Goodman executes and delivers a quitclaim deed to Mr. Whitman, who does not record the deed. Regarding the failure to record, the deed is

    a. invalid between the parties and invalid as to the third parties with constructive notice.
    b. invalid between the parties and valid as to the third parties with constructive notice.
    c. valid between the parties and valid to subsequent recorded interests without notice.
    d. valid between the parties and invalid to subsequent recorded interests without notice.

83. A purchaser buys a parcel of real property "as is." The fact that most of the plumbing is missing is not revealed to the buyer by the seller or the broker. After purchasing the property, the buyer sues. Which of the following is true?

    a. The suit is valid because of the lack of disclosure.
    b. The suit is invalid because of "caveat emptor" (let the buyer beware).
    c. The suit would be valid only if filed against the broker.
    d. The suit would be valid only if filed against the seller.

84. An attachment lien terminates in

    a. two years.
    b. three years.
    c. four years.
    d. It is ongoing until dismissed.

85. There is a line of stores along a major transportation route. This would best be described as a

    a. cluster development.
    b. neighborhood shopping center.
    c. strip commercial development.
    d. None of the above

86. Mr. and Mrs. Baker purchased a home and wished to protect it against a forced sale by filing a declaration of homestead. Mr. Baker was transferred out of state. The homestead is

    a. valid.
    b. invalid because he moved out of state.
    c. valid if he moves back within a three-year period.
    d. None of the above

87. Ms. Grayson owns a home near a neighboring municipal airport. Because flight patterns were recently changed, planes now pass directly over her property. As this has proven to cause property values to decrease greatly in the area, Ms. Grayson asks the city to buy her property. This is an example of

    a. police power.
    b. inverse condemnation.
    c. eminent domain.
    d. a voluntary conversion.

88. An income property valued at $250,000 produces a net return of 6 percent to its owner. A prospective buyer wishes to receive an 8 percent return if the investment is made. What would be the value of the property based on 8 percent?

    a. $250,000
    b. $235,000
    c. $187,000
    d. None of the above

89. Mr. Butler wishes to receive an income of $250 per month. What total amount must be invested to ensure a 4 percent return?

    a. $3,000
    b. $75,000
    c. $7,500
    d. It cannot be determined from the information given.

90. From the following, select the correct statement.

    a. A broker must have office records audited quarterly.
    b. A broker is required to maintain a separate trust account for each principal.
    c. A broker must maintain a trust account.
    d. A broker must maintain true, sufficient, and proper records of deposits or funds belonging to clients and customers.

91. Which of the following describes the area of an acre?

    a. 15 square rods
    b. 4,840 square yards
    c. ½ section
    d. 43,580 square feet

92. Ms. Greystone owns a three-acre easement along the south side of a section. The width of the easement is approximately

    a. 25 feet.   c. 33 feet.
    b. 32 feet.   d. 36 feet.

93. Mr. Barry purchased a rectangular parcel of land that contained 1,263.6 square yards. One side of the parcel is 105.3 feet wide. What is the length of the other side?

    a. 15 feet   c. 108 feet
    b. 108 yards   d. 13 yards

94. Carter purchases a 50 ft. × 150 ft. lot on which she plans to build a home. The local building department requires a 20-foot setback on the front of the parcel and a 4-foot setback at the rear. There is also a 4-foot sideyard setback required. How many buildable square feet remain?

    a. 5,796 square feet
    b. 7,500 square feet
    c. 5,292 square feet
    d. 5,460 square feet

95. Mrs. Gordon wants to place a 6-foot wide cement sidewalk around the outside of a 100 ft. × 100 ft. corner lot. She was quoted $1.20 per square foot. The sidewalk would cost approximately

    a. $1,200.   c. $1,440.
    b. $1,397.   d. $1,485.

96. Jones purchases 9 acres of land for $78,000. His neighbor wants to buy a portion of it that measures 100 feet × 145.2 feet. If Jones sells the land at the price per square feet that he paid, the neighbor has to pay

    a. less than $2,500.
    b. more than $2,500 but less than $3,000.
    c. more than $3,000.
    d. 5 percent of Jones's price.

97. Baker purchases a home for $90,000. He had a down payment of one-fifth of the purchase price. The balance was paid $606 per month for 30 years. What was his cost of financing the purchase instead of paying all cash?

    a. 140 percent   c. 160 percent
    b. 142 percent   d. 162 percent

98. A building has a market value of $240,000. The net income before adjustment is $32,000. The anticipated economic life for the improvement is 50 years, and it has an 8 percent capitalization rate. What is the value that is attributable to the land?

    a. $50,000   c. $100,000
    b. $80,000   d. $300,000

99. Gwen has an $1,800 assessment lien on her property payable in equal payments over 10 years, beginning January 1, at 6 percent interest. She paid it for two years. On January 1 of the third year, she sold her home and stated that all liens would be paid by the close of escrow, which was scheduled for April 1. Approximately how much did she pay at the closing?

    a. $1,440   c. $1,526
    b. $1,462   d. $1,908

100. Abel sells a small farm. The purchaser assumes a $129,000 existing first trust deed, is credited $15,000 for a deposit, and must pay $52,750 into escrow to make up the difference in sales price in cash at the time of close of escrow. Abel is credited $67,750 and must pay a 9 percent commission on the sales price, $2,350 in delinquent property taxes, a 6 percent penalty on the property tax, $600 in attorney's fees, $290 for a survey, $400 for title insurance, $235 in assumption fees, and $48,000 for a lien on the irrigation equipment included in the sale. What transaction happened at the closing?

    a. Seller paid $1,973.50 to the settlement clerk.
    b. Seller paid $1,832.50 to the settlement clerk.
    c. Seller received $1,973.50 from the settlement clerk.
    d. Seller received $1,832.50 from the settlement clerk.

■ ANSWER KEY

1. b. The responsibility for developing zoning regulations rests with local government, typically the planning commission.

2. d. Statement of fact.

3. d. Statement of fact.

4. b. Statement of fact.

5. d. Statement of fact.

6. b. In the cost approach the land is appraised separately from the improvements using the sales comparison approach. The improvements are appraised, based on replacement or reproduction cost. The improvements are then depreciated based on the actual age of the improvements. As a last step in the cost approach, the depreciated value of the improvements and the land value are then combined to arrive at an estimate of value for the total property.

7. d. Statement of fact.

8. c. Statement of fact.

9. d. Depreciation as it is used in the appraisal process is not a concern with respect to either supply and demand forces or inflation.

10. a. Statement of fact.

11. b. Statement of fact.

12. d. Read the choices carefully. The "A" in FHA is for "Administration," not "Association."

13. d. If one specific item of the financing is issued in any advertising, all details must be given.

14. c. Statement of fact under current tax law.

15. b. An income-producing investment that will maintain its value is the best hedge against inflation. Historically, real estate investments tend to hold value over the long term, taking into consideration the economic impact of contraction and expansion forces.

16. c. Statement of fact.

17. d. Statement of fact.

18. d. Statement of fact.

19. b. Statement of fact.

20. b. Nonuse of an easement will not terminate it. An exception lies in nonuse of a prescriptive easement for five years (which takes five years to create).

21. d. Statement of fact.

22. c. Recall that in California, the first to record is first in right to the property, with the exception of possession of property. Because Green was the first to record, Green owns the property. Dale can take legal action against Jones.

23. a. Trade fixtures are the personal property of an individual. They are used for one's manufacture, ornamentation, trade, or domestic use.

24. a. A lease is a contract that runs with the land for its term.

25. c. A buyer in a community apartment project does not own the unit separately but receives an undivided interest in the land with a right of exclusive occupancy in a given apartment unit.

26. b. Amortization refers to the liquidation or extinguishment of debt. It is not considered a cost of ownership.

27. b. The Truth-in-Lending Act has strict guidelines governing the advertising of consumer credit.

28. c. Statement of fact.

29. c. Statement of fact.

30. b. Notaries can perform only in the state in which they are commissioned.

31. d. That land be for public use is not a required element for adverse possession.

32. a. Statement of fact.

33. a. A vendee (buyer) under a land contract receives equitable title to the property that conveys only equitable title and possession rights. Legal title does not pass until the terms of the land contract are met.

34. a. Statement of fact.

35. d. The extended coverage title insurance policy, among other items, covers unrecorded liens and off-record easements. Read the choices carefully. The word *obtain* in choice *d* is important. To be protected, one must actually obtain the policy, as opposed to merely requesting that the extended coverage policy be provided.

36. c. A subordination clause is a benefit to a trustor (borrower). It allows the existing loan to be lowered to a junior position so that a construction loan can be recorded as a first trust deed. Institutional lenders will not provide construction loans outside the first position.

37. b. Statement of fact.

38. b. Statement of fact.

39. d. Choices *a*, *b*, and *c* will not remove her fee simple ownership interest.

40. a. The deposit never belongs to the broker. At a certain point, the deposit could belong to the seller; until then, it belongs to the buyer. In any event, any change in the escrow process, including the matter of a deposit, requires the written agreement of both the buyer and the seller.

41. a. Statement of fact.

42. d. Both statements are incorrect.

43. c. The sale of community property requires the consent of both husband and wife.

44. b. Statement of fact.

45. c. *Economic rent* refers to the going market rent for comparable units.

46. a. Statement of fact.

47. d. The sales tax receipts whose total is to be reported to the State Board of Equalization would be a more reliable source for actual gross sales of a business.

48. a. While $10,000 a year for 10 years would total $100,000, future dollars are worth less than today's dollars. The closest choice is *a*.

49. c. Statement of fact.

50. d. Statement of fact.

51. a. Read the question carefully. If the depth of the lot decreases, the depth of the front footage also decreases, thereby causing a decrease in the front-foot value and an increase in the remaining square-foot value.

52. c. Statement of fact.

53. d. RESPA is concerned with proper advance disclosures of settlement costs to borrowers of consumer loans. It has many built-in protective devices for the borrower. Commission-split agreements between brokers are not under the jurisdiction of RESPA.

54. c. The question asks for the exception. Mortgage insurance rates for FHA loans are not necessarily lower than the rates charged for other loan insurance programs.

55. d. Statement of fact.

56. b. Statement of fact.

57. b. There are several levels of need or desire in the purchase of real property. The purpose could be for residential, commercial, industrial, or agricultural needs. The term *stratified* as used in this context refers to these various layers or levels of need.

58. b. Statement of fact.

59. b. The capitalization of income is an indirect way to estimate depreciation.

60. d. Statement of fact.

61. b. Statement of fact.

62. c. $18,000 × 2 lots = $36,000. $15,000 × 3 lots = $45,000 selling price. $45,000 selling price − $36,000 paid = $9,000 profit. $9,000 made ÷ $36,000 paid = 25 percent.

63. b. 750 width × 970 depth = 727,500 square feet. 727,500 square feet ÷ 2 triangular lots = 363,750 square feet in each lot. 363,750 ÷ 43,560 square feet to an acre = 8.3 acres.

64. c. Statement of fact.

65. b. Statement of fact.

66. c. Carry over the old basis, like you carry baggage when you move, to the new property. Add to it any boot paid. $207,000 + $20,000 = $227,000 new basis. Because Alex is trading "up" (for a more expensive property), there is no recognized (taxable in the year sold) gain.

67. d. Community property has a stepped-up basis to fair market value as of the date of the death of a spouse. At the time of the spouse's death the property was valued at $140,000. The surviving spouse sold the property for $140,000. For tax purposes, there is no gain.

68. b. Statement of fact.

69. c. There is no contract until the seller's acceptance is communicated to the buyer in the manner stated in the offer. In this case, because there was no communication of the acceptance, the offer was revoked due to the death of the offeror (buyer).

70. d. The term *tender* refers to an offer to perform.

71. c. The purpose of a specific performance lawsuit is to hope that the court will order a person to perform specifically as he or she had promised to perform. An example: A seller who has entered into a sales contract later refuses to sell. The buyer does not want the deposit back and insists that the seller sell. The buyer might choose to file a specific performance lawsuit as there may not be another property that could satisfy his or her needs as the subject property could.

72. d. Statement of fact.

73. d. Statement of fact.

74. a.   Statement 1 is in violation of the federal fair housing law. However, it is not a violation of this law to solicit prospective tenants from existing tenants and friends as long as there is no violation of fair housing laws.

75. a.   Statement of fact.

76. d.   It would be a mechanic's lien that the pool company might choose to file to ensure payment. A mechanic's lien is an involuntary specific lien.

77. b.   Statement of fact.

78. a.   Constructive notice is found through public information source, that is, a recorded instrument. Actual notice is determined by witnessing something (seeing it for yourself) or obtaining knowledge by some means other than public notices or public records.

79. c.   In a court probate sale, an offer must be at least 90 percent of the court-appraised value.

80. d.   The deed is void, as the element of capacity is missing. There are some instances where a person under 18 can contract. That is when the person is an emancipated minor. Nothing is said in the question about emancipation.

81. a.   The lessor holds the "reversionary interest" in property that has been leased out. This means that the control of the property reverts to the lessor (owner) when the lease terminates.

82. d.   Statement of fact.

83. a.   Statement of fact.

84. b.   An attachment lien is an involuntary specific lien against a piece of property. It is good for three years and continues even if the owner should die during the three-year period. An attachment is a prejudgment action whereby the court seizes the title to property to be used as security for the payment of a possible future judgment.

85. c.   Statement of fact.

86. a.   Moving out of state does not terminate a recorded homestead. In this case the homestead remains and is valid. The way to terminate the homestead is by recording a Declaration of Abandonment of Homestead or by the sale of the property.

87. b.   Statement of fact.

88. c. $187,500. Value of $250,000 × .06 = $15,000. The net operating income of $15,000 ÷ .08 = $187,500.

89. b. $250 × 12 months = $3,000. Annual income of $3,000 ÷ .04 = $75,000.

90. d.   Statement of fact.

91. b.   There are 43,560 square feet to an acre of land, not 43,580. Take 43,560 square feet and divide by 9 square feet (there are 9 square feet to 1 square yard), which equals 4,840 square yards to 1 acre.

92. a.   3 acres × 43,560 = 130,680 square feet in 3 acres. There are 5,280 linear feet to 1 mile, which is the distance on the side of a square section. 130,680 ÷ 5,280 = 24.75. Nearest answer is 25 feet.

93. c.   1,263.6 × 9 square feet to 1 yard = 11,372.40 square feet in the parcel. 11,372.40 square feet ÷ 105.3 width = 108 feet to the depth (not 108 yards).

94. c. 50 feet wide – 8 feet lost in the width (remember to take the sideyard setback off both sides) = 42 feet left for the width. 150 feet deep – 24 feet lost for setbacks (20 feet off the back and 4 feet off the front) = 126 feet left in the depth. Multiply 42 × 126, which equals 5,292 buildable square feet.

95. d. 6 feet × 100 feet = 600 square feet around one side of the corner lot. 6 feet × 100 feet = 600 square feet around the other side of the corner lot. Don't forget to add the corner piece of 6 feet × 6 feet, which equals 36 square feet. 600 + 600 + 36 = 1,236 square feet of sidewalk wrapped around the outside of the corner lot at $1.20 per square foot = $1,483.20. The closest answer is $1,485.

96. b. 9 × 43,560 = 392,040. $78,000 ÷ 392,040 = .20 per square feet. 100 × 145.2 (14,520 square feet) × .20 = $2,904.

97. d. $90,000 × 20% (one-fifth) = $18,000 down payment. $90,000 – $18,000 = $72,000 loan amount. $606 monthly payment × 12 months × 30 years = $218,160 – $72,000 loan amount = $146,160 interest. $146,160 ÷ $90,000 purchase price = 1.624 or 162%.

98. c. Building capitalization rate: 100 ÷ 50 years = 2%. 8% + 2% = 10% overall capitalization rate. $240,000 × 10% = $24,000 net operating income attributable to the building, which takes both rates, the "return on" (8 percent) and the "return of" (2 percent). From the net operating income to the total property— $32,000—subtract $24,000 to equal $8,000 net operating income attributable only to the land. $8,000 divided by .08 (land takes only one rate, the "return on") equals $100,000 for land value. This problem and answer is an example of the land residual technique used to appraise only the land portion of income property.

99. b. $1,800 ÷ 10 years = $180 per year. $180 × 2 years = $360. $1,800 – $360 = $1,440 × 6% = $86.40 annual interest. $86.40 ÷ 12 months = $7.20. $7.20 × 3 months = $21.60. $1,440 + $21.60 = $1,461.60.

100. a. Sales price is found by adding $129,000 + $15,000 + $52,750 = $196,750. Seller's credits total $67,750. Seller's charges are $17,707.50 (9% of $196,750) + $2,350 + $141 (6% penalty on taxes) + $600 + $290 + $400 + $235 + $48,000. These charges total $69,723.50. $69,723.50 minus $67,750 credit equals $1,973.50 that the seller still owes and has to pay to the settlement clerk.

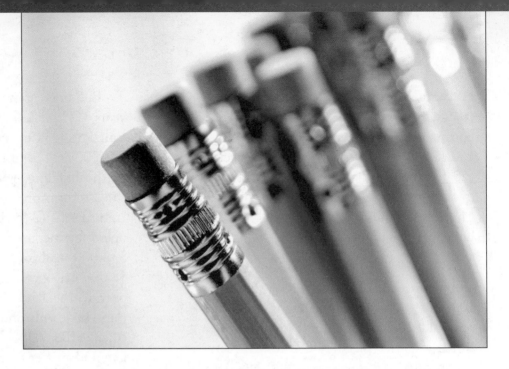

BROKER APPENDIX
Practice Examination II

1. Baker and Smith, single men, take title to their property as joint tenants, each with an undivided interest. Baker has a $100,000 individual mortgage on the property. Later Baker dies. Who owns the property?

   a. Smith and the mortgage company, as joint tenants
   b. Smith and the mortgage company, as tenants in common
   c. Smith owns the property free and clear
   d. Smith owns the property subject to the $100,000 mortgage

2. Consumption expenditure patterns directly influence the demand for housing

   a. by establishing the standard of living to which the residential neighborhood is accustomed.
   b. by determining the number of new construction projects that are devoted to apartments and single-family residences.
   c. because what members within a household do with their disposable income is a major consideration when determining how much income is available for housing.
   d. as spending habits and preferences of individuals are major factors when determining the well-being of a community.

3. Accepted methods of appraising land are all of the following, *EXCEPT* the _____ method.

   a. comparative   c. development
   b. economic   d. abstractive

4. Real estate investor Mary, who wishes to use the principle of leverage, would

   a. use her personal funds as much as possible.
   b. invest in real estate that is declining in value.
   c. use borrowed money to the maximum extent possible.
   d. use borrowed money and personal money on an equal basis.

5. The most detailed and accurate method of estimating the cost of an improvement is by which of the following?

   a. Quantity survey method
   b. Unit-in-place method
   c. Cubic-foot method
   d. Unit-of-comparison method

6. Which of the following is most difficult for appraisers to measure accurately?

   a. Capitalized income
   b. Replacement cost new
   c. The cost basis of the property
   d. The accrued depreciation

7. The unit-of-comparison method for estimating the cost new of a building involves

   a. lumping together the cost of all components of the structure on a unit basis.
   b. estimating the cost of materials or components of the building as installed.
   c. a sum of the cost of all labor and materials.
   d. estimating the unit cost of major functional parts of the structure as installed.

8. Which of the following is most important to be considered when appraising commercial sites?

   a. The proximity to shipping facilities and labor sources
   b. The community's purchasing power
   c. Zoning regulations including any building limitations or moratoriums
   d. Amenities

9. The seller, transferor, or his or her agent must deliver to the transferee (buyer) a copy of the structural pest control report before transfer of title, when the

   a. transferee requires it as a condition of purchase.
   b. transferee and/or the lender granting a purchase-money loan on the property require it as a condition for purchase or the granting of the loan.
   c. structural pest control report indicates infestation.
   d. lender requests it as a condition to granting the loan.

10. The activities and direction of the money market are very important to the real estate market. If interest rates increase, the capitalized value of income property subject to a long-term lease

   a. increases at a rate equal to the capitalization rate.
   b. become stable.
   c. decreases.
   d. is unaffected in the short term.

11. In appraising an apartment building, appraiser Johnson obtained a copy of the accountant's operating income and expense statement. The correct procedure for the appraiser to follow would be to

   a. deduct the same expenditures that the accountant did.
   b. use the net income that the accountant arrived at.
   c. adjust the accountant's figures to reflect the impact of value in the future.
   d. calculate depreciation of the improvements before arriving at a net income figure.

12. The number of townships contained in Mr. Greg's ranch measuring 28 miles square is most nearly

   a. 25.   c. 17.
   b. 22.   d. 11.

13. When offering a franchise for sale in California, one must either be identified in an application filed with the Commissioner of Corporations or be licensed by the

   a. State Board of Equalization.
   b. State Franchise Tax Board.
   c. Real Estate Commissioner or the Corporations Commissioner.
   d. Federal Trade Commission.

14. The division of a 150-acre farm into five or more parcels for use as smaller farms does not require the filing of a subdivision questionnaire with the Real Estate Commissioner if the parcels to be sold are

   a. more than 20 acres but less than 40 acres.
   b. 40 acres or more.
   c. not more than 20 acres.
   d. None of the above

15. The purpose of the assessment roll by the assessor's office is

   a. to determine the tax rates.
   b. to determine the actual tax to be paid by the owner.
   c. the equalization of the assessments among various types of properties.
   d. the establishment of the tax base.

16. Abel owns an apartment house and deducted $10,000 from the gross income for depreciation on his federal income tax return. For income tax purposes, the basis of the property is

   a. adjusted only when sold.
   b. unaffected.
   c. increased by $10,000.
   d. decreased by $10,000.

17. For income tax purposes, the owner of a duplex would most likely capitalize expenditures for

   a. landscaping.
   b. repainting the units.
   c. installing an air-conditioning system.
   d. real estate taxes.

18. When a real estate agent holds a nonexclusive listing, she should, after showing the property to a prospective buyer,

    a. note it in her office files.
    b. not accept a deposit from a buyer under a nonexclusive listing.
    c. send a memo to the prospect confirming the showing of the property.
    d. notify the seller as to the prospective buyer's name and relationship.

19. An exclusive authorization to sell generally

    a. requires the owner to convey the property at the listed price.
    b. compels the broker to effect a sale of the property.
    c. authorizes the broker to find a buyer for the property.
    d. becomes a legally binding contract if signed by a buyer.

20. The agent's commission for negotiating a real property lease is fixed by

    a. agreement, only if the term is over one year.
    b. real estate law.
    c. real estate law if the term is over one year.
    d. agreement.

21. An agency relationship may be created in the following ways, *EXCEPT* by

    a. necessity or emergency.
    b. ratification.
    c. verbal authority.
    d. subornation.

22. If a contract for the purchase of real property is to be enforceable, the consideration must be sufficient relative to value in order to enforce a suit for

    a. unlawful detainer.
    b. specific performance.
    c. damages.
    d. rescission.

23. A loan application for the purchase of a single-family home was received from borrower Smith. RESPA requires delivery of the uniform settlement statement to Smith not later than

    a. three business days prior to the close of the transaction.
    b. one calendar day before the close of the transaction.
    c. ten calendar days after the loan commitment is made.
    d. at or before the date of settlement.

24. If there is no agreement to the contrary, which of the following may not be assigned without the consent of the principal?

    a. The rights of a mortgagee
    b. The rights of an optionee
    c. The rights of a lessee
    d. The rights of an insured in a fire insurance policy.

25. Which of the following advertisements is correct under the federal Consumer Credit Protection Act?

    a. Assume a 6½ percent mortgage
    b. Take over a 6½ percent annual interest rate mortgage
    c. Assume a 6½ percent annual percentage rate mortgage
    d. All of the above are correct.

26. When analyzing the value of single-family homes, which of the following statements is *LEAST* correct?

    a. Demand for real estate depends on the availability and terms of financing.
    b. No two parcels are precisely alike due to the uniqueness of location.
    c. Because the supply of real estate is relatively fixed, effective demand is generally stable.
    d. Effective demand is a reflection of consumer incomes.

27. The secondary mortgage market is typified by

    a. lending on the security of second mortgages.
    b. the transfer of interest between mortgagees.
    c. lending on the basis of junior liens.
    d. the transfer of interest between mortgagors.

28. The tight money policies of the Federal Reserve Board seem to increase the

    a. volume of home sales.
    b. amount of money available for construction of a new homes.
    c. use of second trust deeds.
    d. use of new first trust deeds.

29. When negotiating a lease of commercial property, the broker's commission is usually a percentage of the

    a. deposit made by the lessee toward the advance payment of rent.
    b. total rent for the first year and the last year.
    c. total rent to be paid over the life of the lease.
    d. gross profit of the lessor.

30. The Subdivision Law treats all of the following as blanket encumbrances, *EXCEPT* a(n)

    a. mechanic's lien affecting more than one parcel in the subdivision.
    b. agreement affecting more than one lot by the subdivider who holds the lots under an option.
    c. trust deed affecting more than one lot in the subdivision.
    d. assessment lien levied by a public agency on more than one lot in the subdivision.

31. Private property restrictions on real property are usually enforced by a(n)

    a. indictment.
    b. desist and refrain order.
    c. injunction.
    d. None of the above

32. Which of the following restrictions that are to be inserted in a deed transferring title to property is enforceable?

    a. The leasing of this property to persons other than Caucasians shall not be permitted.
    b. Title to this property cannot be conveyed for a minimum of five years from the date of purchase.
    c. This property shall not be used for other than religious or educational purposes.
    d. Title to this property cannot be conveyed for more than $10.

33. The warranties within a warranty deed are specifically stated. In a grant deed there are implied warranties that the grantor

   a. owns the property in fee simple.
   b. owns the property and has not previously conveyed it to another person.
   c. has not previously conveyed the property.
   d. warrants all title he or she has in the property.

34. Which of the following instruments requires recording?

   a. A grant deed
   b. A Declaration of Abandonment of Homestead
   c. An assignment of a second trust deed
   d. All of the above

35. The voluntary alienation of real property would be manifested by

   a. a trustee's sale.
   b. dedication for public use.
   c. constructive eviction of the lessee.
   d. easement by judicial decree.

36. There is a legal process that can be used to clear title based on adverse possession, tax titles, or other defective titles. This action is called

   a. declaratory relief.
   b. specific performance.
   c. quiet title.
   d. None of the above

37. Brown and Williams hold title to farmland as tenants in common. Brown occupies and farms the land. He could be liable to Williams for all of the following, *EXCEPT*

   a. rental payments for Brown's use of the land.
   b. income received from oil and mineral rights.
   c. rent received from a third party who uses a portion of the land.
   d. payments of principal under a junior deed of trust.

38. Economic rent is the rent

   a. due under a written agreement.
   b. that the property would command in a perfectly informed market.
   c. necessary to produce a competitive return to the owner.
   d. received for comparable space in a competitive and open market.

39. In a lease agreement for an unfurnished apartment, the lessor may not take a security deposit that is great than

   a. $400.
   b. one month's additional rent.
   c. two months' rent.
   d. three months' rent.

40. A valid lease agreement must contain which of the following?

   a. Term, consideration, and description of the premises
   b. A landlord and tenant with the legal capacity to enter into a contract
   c. Agreement to let and take; delivery and acceptance
   d. All of the above

41. The holder of which of the following would have an estate in real property?

    a. The right to use the land of another
    b. An easement appurtenant
    c. A lease
    d. All of the above

42. Which of the following is correct concerning past and/or future depreciation?

    a. The cost-to-cure method is a way to estimate depreciation.
    b. The straight-line method may be used to measure past or future depreciation.
    c. The income approach provides for accrued depreciation in projecting net income into the future.
    d. The cost approach is concerned with accruals for past and/or future depreciation.

43. A real estate appraiser would use accrued depreciation in which of the following methods?

    a. Market data
    b. Income analysis
    c. Cost approach
    d. All of the above

44. The capitalization rate used in the valuation of income property would least likely make provision for

    a. a consistent return of the investment.
    b. a defensible return on the investment.
    c. depreciation.
    d. income taxes.

45. A woman pays $.50 per square foot for a one-quarter acre rectangular lot that is 90 feet deep. Later, she decides to sell the parcel at a price per front foot and wants to make a 25 percent profit on her investment after paying taxes of $50 and a broker's commission of 6 percent. The selling price per front foot would most nearly be

    a. $50.   c. $70.
    b. $60.   d. $75.

46. An owner had her rental property appraised by two appraisers. Appraiser Davis showed gross income as $8,000, expenses of $6,000, and net income of $2,000. Appraiser Altman showed the same expenses but predicted a gross income of $9,000. After appropriate capitalization, appraiser Altman's value of the property, when compared with appraiser Davis's value, was larger by

    a. 33⅓ percent.   c. 66⅔ percent.
    b. 50 percent.   d. 133⅓ percent.

47. Which of the following is correct?

    a. Ranges are numbered as they lie north and south of the base line.
    b. Ranges are numbered as they go from right to left.
    c. Townships are numbered as they lie east and west of the principal meridian.
    d. Townships are numbered in the same direction that meridian lines run.

48. Before advertising a land project, the sub-divider is required to file

    a. a copy of the proposed advertising with the Department of Real Estate.
    b. a copy of the subdivision public report with any media outlet carrying the advertising.
    c. any material changes to previously filed advertising with the Department of Real Estate.
    d. All of the above

49. Optimum development of urban areas would be concerned with all of the following, *EXCEPT*

    a. combined urban and rural use planning.
    b. design of environmental as well as social and economic policies.
    c. continuous long-range political planning.
    d. unvaried approaches in application of regional planning concerns.

50. Joseph is subdividing with the intent to create single-family residential lots that he intends to sell for cash. He needs maximum financing for the public improvements, such as streets, curbs, and sidewalks. He does not want assessment liens to appear as a matter of public record that would appear in the title insurance policies. Therefore, his best source of financing would probably be

    a. an installment land sales contract.
    b. corporate stock.
    c. improvement bonds.
    d. an interim loan from an institutional lender.

51. Salesperson Richards takes a listing that does not authorize the listing broker Abel to accept a deposit from an offeror toward the purchase of a home. The broker should advise Richards that

    a. the broker will not be able to accept a deposit from an offeror.
    b. it is an implied right of a broker to accept a deposit on behalf of the seller on any offer.
    c. a deposit will be accepted and retained by the broker from the offeror, but only as an agent for the offeror.
    d. None of the above

52. If a seller is required to execute a contract as agreed, this court decree is known as

    a. equitable performance.
    b. mandamus performance.
    c. specific performance.
    d. execution sale.

53. When a real estate sale requires new financing, which of the following advertisements would violate the Truth-in-Lending law?

    a. "Three bedrooms, two baths, owner will finance"
    b. "Two bedrooms, one bath, FHA and DVA financing available"
    c. "Two bedrooms, den, large lot, nothing down"
    d. "Three bedrooms, den, EZ terms"

54. A corporation decided to buy and manage a multitenant commercial building where it would also be a tenant. The equity investment capital for such a venture is usually created by

    a. borrowing from an insurance company.
    b. selling real estate securities.
    c. using retained earnings or selling common stock.
    d. pledging warrants as security for a loan.

55. The disclosure of the race, creed, or color of a prospective buyer by an agent to his principal is held to be a discriminatory act

    a. by opinion by the Attorney General, who states that race, creed, or color is not a material fact and should not be disclosed.
    b. unless it is claimed as a fiduciary responsibility by the principal.
    c. only under state law, not federal law.
    d. unless such fact is material to the transaction.

56. Ms. Roberts owns two personal residences. Regarding IRS tax gain deferral rules, which of the following is correct if she sells one of the residences and buys another?

    a. only the more expensive of the two residences is subject to tax gain deferral.
    b. only the principal residence is subject to tax gain deferral.
    c. both residences must be sold at the same time to qualify for the tax gain deferral.
    d. either residence may be sold to qualify for the tax gain deferral.

57. The subordination clause in a deed of trust would not do which of the following?

    a. Permit a buyer of the land to negotiate a construction loan in the first trust deed position
    b. Allow a senior encumbrance to maintain its priority on extension or renewal
    c. Create a hardship to a buyer by placing the lender of a larger sum in a favored position
    d. Create larger risks for the seller of the land and necessitate more stringent release clauses

58. Which of the following would cause a default under most deeds of trust?

    a. The borrower becomes delinquent in repaying the loan.
    b. The property is used for illegal business purposes.
    c. There has been failure to maintain the property.
    d. Any of the above

59. A person who endorses a note but does not wish to guarantee payment of the note would endorse it

    a. with recourse.
    b. with a restricted endorsement.
    c. without recourse.
    d. with a special endorsement.

60. The Bakers rent a beach home from the Smiths for the period of July 1, 2002, to September 5, 2003. The Bakers have a(n)

    a. periodic tenancy.
    b. tenancy at will.
    c. estate for years.
    d. estate at will.

61. All of the following are correct concerning a life estate, *EXCEPT* a

    a. life tenant does not hold a fee simple title.
    b. contract creating a life estate is required to be in writing.
    c. life estate is a form of a freehold estate.
    d. life estate may not extend beyond the life of the tenant.

62. Regarding the market data approach to value, any differences in the

    a. subject property are adjusted to the standard set by comparable sales.
    b. comparable sales are adjusted to the characteristics of the subject property.
    c. comparable sales are adjusted to the highest and best use of the property.
    d. subject property are adjusted to the market activity.

63. A change in the quality of the income received from an apartment house would be indicated by an adjustment to the

    a. interest rate used for capitalization of net income.
    b. amount of income that is to be capitalized.
    c. remaining economic life of the property.
    d. recapture rate as applied to the depreciable improvements.

64. A metes-and-bounds description of land could be used when the

    a. U.S. government survey system is used.
    b. land has not been surveyed by a licensed surveyor.
    c. streets bordering the land do not run north or south.
    d. property is not covered by an already recorded map and cannot be described by section, township, and range designations.

65. When the improvements have not yet been built on subdivision lots, the Real Estate Commissioner may require that a soils analysis be done. This is to estimate the cost necessary to prepare the soil for possible structural improvements. The commissioner's regulations require that the estimate of cost to prepare the soil be verified by

    a. the Bureau of Engineering Standards.
    b. the State Department of Architecture.
    c. a registered civil engineer.
    d. a registered architect.

66. Brokers sometimes make oral agreements among themselves regarding the division of commissions. These agreements are not required to be in writing to be enforceable, as

    a. each broker is the agent for the other.
    b. such agreements are not illegal and are not against public policy.
    c. such agreements between brokers are not covered by the statute of frauds.
    d. judicial notice can be taken of this practice.

67. The fiduciary relationship between a broker and the seller is comparable to the relationship between a

    a. trustor and trustee.
    b. trustee and beneficiary.
    c. trustor and beneficiary.
    d. mortagor and mortagee.

68. All of the following are essential to create a valid contract, *EXCEPT*

    a. legally competent parties.
    b. offer and acceptance.
    c. reciprocal consideration.
    d. reasonable performance.

69. When a contract buyer has received either possession or title to property, the Uniform Vendor and Purchaser Risk Act of 1947 states that if the property is destroyed by an earthquake, the buyer is

    a. relieved of the duty to make further payments.
    b. not relieved of the duty to pay.
    c. required to rebuild the improvements.
    d. bound to the agreement between the vendor and the vendee.

70. The amount of money available for real estate loans would be increased by all of the following, *EXCEPT*

    a. an increase in the real national income.
    b. a growing awareness of the need to provide for one's retirement years.
    c. an increased savings by individuals for retirement.
    d. the rate of return on government and corporate bonds.

71. An auctioneer offers property on behalf of the

    a. seller.
    b. buyer and seller.
    c. buyer.
    d. company who employs the auctioneer.

72. To set the period for a mechanic's lien, all of the following are considered equivalent to completion of improvements, *EXCEPT*

    a. the lapse of an 18-month period of construction on a single-family residence.
    b. cessation of labor for a continuous period of 60 days.
    c. acceptance of the project by the owner.
    d. occupancy by the owner with a cessation of labor.

73. The process leading up to a trustee's sale due to the delinquency in the repayment of a loan includes certain rights of reinstatement for the borrower. All of the following are correct, *EXCEPT*

    a. if the trustor does not reinstate, the trustee may publish and post a notice of intent to sell.
    b. the trustor's right of reinstatement exists only until the trustee's sale.
    c. when the trust deed provides for the sending of a copy of the notice of default to the trustor, publication of that notice is not required.
    d. the trustor has a right of reinstatement up to five business days before the trustee's sale.

74. Private restrictions on land are usually created by covenants or conditions. Regarding the two, a breach of condition usually provides for remedies that are

    a. less stringent.
    b. more stringent.
    c. the same.
    d. not comparable.

75. Which of the following would be considered a lien?

    a. An attachment
    b. An easement in gross
    d. An appurtenant easement
    d. Adverse zoning

76. When a tenant abandons a property before the lease expires, there are certain reasonable actions the lessor can take. The lessor can do all of the following, *EXCEPT*

    a. leave the property vacant and immediately sue for the entire balance due on the lease.
    b. relet the premises for the tenant's benefit after notifying the tenant of this intention.
    c. re-enter the property and take possession for his or her own benefit.
    d. leave the property unoccupied and sue for each installment of rent as it becomes due.

77. Sometimes there is an increase in the value of land that is not due to any effort on the part of the owner. This increase could be caused by inflation. Such an increase is described as

    a. highest and best use benefit.
    b. functional obsolescence.
    c. intrinsic value.
    d. unearned increment.

78. An appraiser would use the building residual technique to establish the value of the

    a. net operating income after depreciation.
    b. present value of the building.
    c. salvage value of the building at the end of its economic life.
    d. value of the land.

79. If a square one-quarter-acre parcel of land is measured, the length of each side would be

    a. ⅛ of a mile.
    b. ⅔ of a mile.
    c. ⅜ of a mile.
    d. ⅘ of a mile.

80. A planned unit development may be created for which of the following zoning usages?

    a. Residential
    b. Commercial
    b. Industrial
    d. All of the above

81. All of the following are found on a balance sheet, *EXCEPT*

    a. the value of goodwill.
    b. equipment used by the business for deliveries.
    c. sales.
    d. prepaid expenses.

82. When both local laws and federal minimum housing requirements apply to specific types of property, contractors must

    a. comply with the local building codes.
    b. comply with federal housing specifications.
    c. comply with the more stringent of the two.
    d. decide for themselves which one to use.

83. To hedge against the erosion of capital caused by inflation, an investor should consider placing funds into

    a. savings accounts.
    b. government bonds.
    c. equities.
    d. trust deeds.

84. A construction lender wants to make sure that its loan is adequately secured as a primary lien against the property. If the loan for the purchase of the land is already an encumbrance against it, a construction lender would be least protected by which of the follow?

    a. Ordering an ALTA policy of title insurance
    b. Recording, publishing, and posting a notice of nonresponsibility
    c. Recording a subordination agreement from the purchase money lender
    d. Ordering a physical inspection of the property

85. The grantor's signature on a deed is customarily obtained before a notary public. This is primarily for the purpose of

    a. giving validity to the deed.
    b. guaranteeing the legal delivery of the deed.
    c. enabling the deed to be recorded.
    d. All of the above

86. In the process of borrowing money, a person signs a promissory note for a purchase-money trust deed loan. In doing so, he or she creates

    a. a security device that hypothecates the property.
    b. a promise to pay with conditions.
    c. legally enforceable evidence of the debt.
    d. All of the above

87. Customarily, a percentage lease indicates that rent is based on a percentage of the

    a. income of the business that is subject to federal income tax.
    b. increased assets of the business.
    c. gross sales of the lessee's business.
    d. net sales of the lessee's business.

88. The most income that a given property is capable of producing, in terms of operating income, is called _____ income.

    a. gross scheduled
    b. effective gross
    c. net operating
    d. net spendable

89. In appraising a shopping center, select the one that would be given the most weight.

    a. Income—gross rent
    b. Gross rent multiplier
    c. Cost—income
    d. Comparison—income

90. When an Environment Review Board issues a negative declaration, it indicates that the subdivision

    a. has been approved, subject to compliance with additional requirements.
    b. has not been approved by the Real Estate Commissioner for the issuance of a public report.
    c. will have an insignificant effect upon the environment.
    d. has a public report containing information indicative of possible adverse environmental impacts.

91. The "basis of property plus improvement costs less any depreciation taken" refers to

    a. nontaxable gain.
    b. a recoverable loss.
    c. mortgage relief.
    d. adjusted basis.

92. As is sometimes used in real estate transactions, the terms *valuable*, *adequate*, *good*, and *sufficient* are most closely related to

    a. unilateral contracts.
    b. bilateral contracts.
    c. consideration.
    d. mutually.

93. An easement in gross

    a. creates an easement appurtenant.
    b. is attached to the dominant tenement.
    c. passes with transfer of the dominant tenement to another owner.
    d. must be expressly transferred.

94. Which one of the following deeds would be considered valid?

    a. A grant deed signed in blank
    b. A deed where the grantee is described as "Robert Jones or Bill Reed"
    c. A deed transferring title to John Smith, but using his fictitious name of Henry Wright
    d. A deed where the grantor has been declared mentally incompetent by a court of jurisdiction

95. Regarding an easement, the term *prescription* most nearly means the acquisition of the right of an easement by

    a. occupation or use of government lands for recreational purposes.
    b. condemnation proceedings.
    c. open and notorious use for the statutory period of time.
    d. undue influence hostile to the true owner.

96. Covered under police power, health and safety standards generally provide for control of

    a. residential densities.
    b. maximum occupancy requirements.
    c. water standards.
    d. All of the above

97. In a well-planned residential community, which of the following contributes most to the maintenance and preservation of value?

    a. Conformance to proper land-use objectives
    b. Variances to permit highest and best use of every parcel of land
    c. Deed restrictions
    d. Prevention of major thoroughfare construction throughout the neighborhoods

98. Retailer Sue sells her business and stock to buyer Jim. Jim must withhold sufficient funds from the purchase price to cover any sales tax liability of the business, or Jim, to the extent of the purchase price, will become

    a. personally liable for the entire tax amount.
    b. liable for 35 percent of the unpaid tax.
    c. secondarily liable if Sue fails to pay the tax.
    d. subject to disciplinary action by the Real Estate Commissioner.

99. The buyer of a parcel of land acted upon the fraudulent statement of the seller's agent and was injured. The seller, who did not know that the agent made a fraudulent statement, sought to enforce the agreement with the buyer. The buyer

    a. has grounds for rescinding the contract.
    b. can bring legal action against the seller's agent for fraud.
    c. can sue the seller for fraud.
    d. All of the above

100. Which of the following best describes the term *executed contract*?

    a. The contract is properly signed, notarized, and recorded.
    b. Both parties have completely performed.
    c. The first version of the contract is destroyed.
    d. The executor of the estate offers the property for sale.

■ ANSWER KEY

1. c. When Baker died, Smith took the property free and clear of any of Baker's liens against the property. Smith, as the surviving joint tenant, is not liable to the creditors of the deceased Baker (which is why lenders customarily require signatures of all joint tenants before they fund a loan).

2. c. Statement of fact.

3. b. Statement of fact.

4. c. Leverage refers to using little or none of one's own money for an investment.

5. a. Statement of fact.

6. d. Statement of fact.

7. a. Statement of fact.

8. b. Statement of fact.

9. b. A structural pest control report is not a requirement of law in the sale of real property. It is customary for a buyer and/or lender to require such a report, and if they do, it must be provided.

10. c. An interest rate is part of a capitalization rate. Therefore, if the interest rate increases, then so does the capitalization rate. If the capitalization rate (risk rate) increases, then value decreases.

11. c. One of the many jobs of an appraiser of income property is to estimate the present worth of future benefits (future income). Many appraisers will take the accountant's figures that are for taxation purposes and adjust them for what the appraiser projects is likely to occur in the future.

12. c. In 28 miles square (28 miles on each side), you could carve out 16 townships. Remember there are 6 miles on the side of a square township. 4 times 6 miles on the width and 4 times 6 miles on the depth equals 24 miles on each side and would allow the 16 townships. You would have 4 miles leftover on both the width and the depth of a 28-mile square parcel, and that is not enough to create additional square townships.

13. c. Statement of fact.

14. d. A 150-acre parcel for agricultural use divided by 5 or more parcels is regulated by the Real Estate Commissioner.

15. d. Statement of fact.

16. d. Statement of fact.

17. c. The cost of improvements of a permanent nature can be added to the cost basis of the property (capitalized).

18. d. In the event of a commission dispute, notifying the seller of a prospective buyer's identity helps the broker to prove he or she was the introductory factor of the buyer to this property.

19. c. A listing agreement is an employment contract between the owner and the broker and primarily authorizes the broker to find a buyer for the property.

20. d. Commissions are negotiable by law and are set by the agreement between the parties.

21. d. Subornation refers to an illegal act, such as a lie or some form of deceit. It is not a way to create an agency relationship.

22. b. Statement of fact.

23. d. Statement of fact.

24. d. An insurance company may not allow the assignment of the rights of an insured if it does not approve of the assignee.

25. c. Statement of fact.

26. c. Statement of fact.

27. b. The secondary mortgage market is made up of investors who buy and sell pools of mortgages from mortgagees (lenders).

28. c. A tight money policy of the Federal Reserve Board causes a shortage of money available to the general public. Therefore, in order to sell property, many sellers end up participating in the financing by carrying second trust deeds.

29. c. This is customary practice.

30. d. Statement of fact.

31. c. In a civil suit, a court order can be sought (injunction) that orders a person to stop a violation and comply with the proper deed restrictions.

32. c. Statement of fact.

33. c. A grant deed carries two implied warranties. One states that the property has not been previously conveyed, and the other states that there are not any undisclosed encumbrances.

34. b. A Declaration of Abandonment of Homestead requires recording, unlike the other choices that do not, for validity purposes.

35. b. Statement of fact.

36. c. Statement of fact.

37. a. Statement of fact.

38. d. Statement of fact.

39. c. In an unfurnished unit, no more than two months' rent can be taken as security deposit, in addition to the first month's rent.

40. d. Statement of fact.

41. c. Statement of fact.

42. b. Statement of fact.

43. c. Calculating an improvement's accrued depreciation is part of the cost approach.

44. d. Income taxes are not provided for in the selection of a capitalization rate. Income taxes are customarily deducted from a building's net operating income to determine the building's cash flow.

45. b. 43,560 ÷ 4 = 10,890 square feet to the parcel. 10,890 × \$.50 per square foot = \$5,445 × .25 = \$1,361.25 + \$50 tax + the cost of \$5,445 = \$6,856.25. 100% − 6% for the broker equals 94%. \$6,856.25 ÷ .94 = \$7,293.88. 10,890 square feet ÷ 90 = 121 front feet. \$7,293.88 ÷ 121 front feet = \$60.28 per front foot.

46. b. The income projection by Altman was \$1,000 higher (\$3,000 versus \$2,000). It was 50 percent higher.

47. d. Statement of fact.

48. d. Statement of fact.

49. d. Statement of fact.

50. d. Statement of fact.

51. c. Statement of fact.

52. c. Statement of fact.

53. c. This choice states a specific detail concerning financing, "nothing down." If one detail about the financing is stated in the advertising, then all of the financing details must be given.

54.   c.   Statement of fact.

55.   a.   Statement of fact.

56.   b.   Statement of fact.

57.   c.   Statement of fact.

58.   d.   Statement of fact.

59.   c.   Statement of fact.

60.   c.   An estate for years designates a specific time period for the leasing of a property (a beginning date and an ending date), regardless of whether it is for days, months, or years.

61.   d.   Statement of fact.

62.   b.   Comparable sales are always adjusted to subject property. A way to *remember*— C for comparable is before S for subject property in alphabetical order.

63.   a.   Statement of fact.

64.   d.   Statement of fact.

65.   c.   Statement of fact.

66.   d.   Statement of fact.

67.   b.   Statement of fact.

68.   d.   Statement of fact.

69.   b.   Statement of fact.

70.   d.   Statement of fact.

71.   a.   Statement of fact.

72.   a.   Statement of fact.

73.   b.   The trustor's right of reinstatement exists only up to five business days prior to the trustee's sale.

74.   b.   Remember that a condition is a qualification of ownership that runs with the land. A covenant is a promise of some type that may or may not run with the land. The breach of a condition could lead to loss of title to property. The breach of a covenant could result in court action for forced compliance and perhaps dollar damages.

75.   a.   Recall that a lien is a money encumbrance. An attachment is an example of a lien. But not all encumbrances are liens. There are encumbrances that have nothing to do with money and everything to do with how property is used, such as zoning, deed restrictions, and easements.

76.   a.   The lessor cannot *immediately* sue for the entire balance due, as the lessor is obligated to try to release the property.

77.   d.   Statement of fact.

78.   b.   The building residual technique is used to estimate just the value of the building. The land residual technique is used to estimate just the value of the land. The property residual technique is used to estimate the value of the property as a single unit (both the land and the building).

79.   d.   Four-eights of a mile is another way to say one-half mile. There is a one-half mile distance on the side of a square one-quarter section.

80.   d.   Statement of fact.

81.   c.   Sales would not appear on a balance sheet. They would appear on a profit and loss statement under "revenue."

82.   c.   Statement of fact.

83.   c.   There is a greater chance the equities would increase in value right along with inflation.

84.   b.   Statement of fact.

85. c. The acknowledgment of a deed is done merely to prepare it for recording. A valid title may or may not have passed. That is why obtaining a title insurance policy is so important.

86. c. The promissory note is the *evidence* of the debt. It is the deed of trust that is popularly used in California as a security device for a real estate loan. The question refers to the note.

87. c. Percentage leases are customarily based on a percentage of a business's monthly gross sales, in addition to a minimum amount of monthly rent agreed on.

88. a. Gross scheduled income is the greatest amount of income the building is capable of producing.

89. c. Statement of fact.

90. c. A negative declaration is good news to a developer. It means the proposed project will not have a negative impact on the environment. Therefore, the developer will not have to incur the expense or time delay of having to produce an environmental impact report.

91. d. Statement of fact.

92. c. Statement of fact.

93. d. An easement in gross only has a servient tenement. There is no dominant tenement. Further, it is given only to a specific entity or person, that is, the utility company, for a specific purpose. If the property owner wishes to transfer this right to another, it must be expressly transferred (in writing).

94. c. The deed has to state specifically who the intended grantee is; however, any name can be used.

95. c. Statement of fact.

96. d. Statement of fact.

97. a. Statement of fact.

98. c. The buyer has "successor's liability" if the seller fails to remit any sales or use tax due to the State Board of Equalization.

99. d. Statement of fact.

100. b. Statement of fact.

BROKER APPENDIX
Practice Examination III

1. Equity is best described as

   a. the initial down payment on a piece of property.
   b. interest an owner has in the real property in excess of the liens against it.
   c. the market value of a property less any loans against it.
   d. All of the above

2. If the interior side of an exterior wall is about the same temperature as an interior partition,

   a. the insulation is sufficient.
   b. the insulation is insufficient.
   c. there is no vapor barrier.
   d. None of the above

3. When an appraiser finds it necessary to use a higher capitalization rate while appraising income property, the aspect of future income he or she is most concerned with is

   a. quality.
   b. quantity.
   c. durability.
   d. None of the above

4. Neighbors who own homes in the flight path of a nearby noisy airport band together. They want the airport authority to purchase their properties before the noise causes any further loss in value. This is known as

   a. an involuntary severance.
   b. police power.
   c. eminent domain.
   d. an inverse condemnation action.

5. Which is the largest lot?

   a. A lot that measures 197 square feet
   b. A lot containing 4,040 square yards
   c. An acre
   d. A lot containing 41,580 square feet

6. The expression *R-value* refers to

   a. heat rating.
   b. wall thickness.
   c. temperature control.
   d. heat resistance.

7. The Structural Pest Control Board in Sacramento keeps files of pest control reports for

   a. one year. c. three years.
   b. two years. d. five years.

8. The term *potable* is used in conjunction with

   a. sewage. c. gas.
   b. land. d. water.

9. A person sold her house for $135,000, which was 12 percent more than she paid for it. Her gross profit was approximately

   a. $14,460. c. $16,200.
   b. $18,410. d. $15,000.

10. Under the Truth-in-Lending Act, all of the following must be disclosed to the borrower, *EXCEPT* the

    a. finance charge.
    b. annual percentage rate.
    c. name of the creditor providing the disclosures.
    d. maximum amount of interest that can be charged for this type of loan.

11. In the cost approach, the value of improvements such as sidewalks, landscaping, and concrete driveways is considered by the appraiser

    a. singly.
    b. jointly.
    c. as part of the land value.
    d. as part of the building value.

12. The primary concern of an appraiser in the analysis of residential property is

    a. marketability and acceptability.
    b. fixed and operating expenses.
    c. functional utility.
    d. total square footage.

13. Subleasing property is considered to be

    a. more than an assignment.
    b. less than an assignment.
    c. the same as an assignment.
    d. None of the above

14. Broker Daniel plans to do some promotional advertising for a new subdivision for which he will charge the subdivider an advance fee. Daniel must submit all contract forms, promotional brochures, and all radio and television advertising samples to the Real Estate Commissioner at least _____ days before use.

    a. 3 c. 10
    b. 7 d. 14

15. A licensed real estate salesperson negotiated the sale of a home on behalf of a buyer. The buyer could not make the required down payment; therefore the salesperson decided to personally loan the money to the buyer. The amount was for $2,000 as a second deed of trust with the note bearing 10 percent interest for three years. The maximum commission the salesperson could collect from the buyer for this loan is

    a. nothing. c. 10 percent.
    b. 5 percent. d. 15 percent.

16. An appraiser who does not use generally accepted appraisal guidelines and attempts to influence an insured lender has

    a. committed a misdemeanor.
    b. acted unethically.
    c. violated rules and regulations of the Real Estate Commissioner.
    d. committed a felony.

17. Under the Truth-in-Lending Act, the item that must be included in the finance charge is

    a. appraiser and credit report fees.
    b. title and recording fees.
    c. notary and reconveyance deed fees.
    d. assumption fees.

18. Which of the following activity buys and sells government securities to stabilize the economy?

    a. Federal Trade Commission
    b. Securities and Exchange Commission
    c. Federal Open Market Committee
    d. None of the above

19. The term *boot* is usually associated with the exchange of real property. Boot may be

    a. note and trust deeds.
    b. antiques.
    c. cash and other personal property.
    d. All of the above

20. A grant deed is invalid if it

    a. is not recorded.
    b. does not state the type of title the grantees selected.
    c. has no date.
    d. is not delivered.

21. Chung leases 160 acres from Abel to grow alfalfa. Abel sells the land to Baker. Chung's lease expires before he can harvest his alfalfa crop and Baker refuses to renew it. The right to the harvest belongs to

    a. Abel.
    b. Baker.
    c. Chung.
    d. They each must share in the crop.

22. A license differs from an easement in that a license

    a. can be revoked.
    b. can be assigned.
    c. must be in writing.
    d. All of the above

23. Under a nonexclusive listing agreement, the broker who is most likely to be paid a commission is the one who

    a. secures an acceptance to an offer.
    b. obtains a substantial deposit with an offer.
    c. produces a buyer who will purchase under the terms of the listing.
    d. has communicated the acceptance of the offer to the offeror.

24. Broker Carter is reviewing the income statement for an apartment building. Under which of the following categories would real estate taxes and fire insurance usually be listed?

    a. Capital expenses
    b. Operating expenses
    c. Fixed expenses
    d. Other expenses

25. All of the following are used by an appraiser to determine net operating income *EXCEPT*

    a. interest on the mortgage.
    b. replacement reserves.
    c. management fee.
    d. vacancy allowance.

26. If a broker neglects to include in any advertising that he or she is a licensed real estate broker when selling his or her own property, the broker would be in violation of

   a. the Real Estate Commissioner's Regulation 2785.
   b. the Real Estate Commissioner's regulations.
   c. real estate law.
   d. nothing, as the broker is acting as a principal.

27. Lance purchased a parcel of real property for $200,000, paid 25 percent cash down, and executed a note and deed of trust for the balance. During the next ten years, the property doubled in value. Disregarding the principal payments and other variables, the original cash invested is now worth

   a. $250,000.   c. $125,000.
   b. $200,000.   d. $100,000.

28. The owner of a standard title insurance policy receives protection against

   a. encroachments.
   b. eminent domain.
   c. lack of capacity of the grantor.
   d. off-record liens.

29. An appraiser values a building at $300,000 using a 6 percent capitalization rate. If the capitalization rate is increased to 8 percent, the building value would be

   a. $75,000.   c. $400,000.
   b. $350,000.   d. $225,000.

30. The UCC document that must be filed with the Secretary of State's office when a business is sold is called the

   a. bill of sale.
   b. financial statement.
   c. financing statement.
   d. security agreement.

31. The appreciation in unit value resulting from joining smaller parcels into one large single parcel and ownership is referred to as

   a. assemblage.
   b. progression.
   c. severance.
   d. plottage increment.

32. Investor Janus owns many promissory notes secured by deeds of trust. She wishes to have a broker handle the collection of the notes. A requirement of real estate law is that the broker needs to do which of the following before proceeding with the collections?

   a. Must post a bond
   b. Must obtain a special endorsement to his or her license
   c. Must obtain written authorization from the noteholder
   d. All of the above

33. Subdivider Washington purchased a nine-acre parcel of unimproved property and subdivided it into one-acre parcels. If he plans to sell three one-acre parcels each year for the next three years, he will have to comply with

   a. the State Subdivision Map Act.
   b. the State Subdivided Lands Law.
   c. Both *a* and *b*
   d. Neither *a* nor *b*

34. The process of developing hypothetical combinations of income and expense versus capital requirements for improvements refers to the principle of

   a. substitution.
   b. increasing and decreasing returns.
   c. supply and demand.
   d. surplus productivity.

35. Investor Charlene purchased $5,000 of 1911 Street Improvement tax-free municipal bonds that paid 6 percent interest. If she were in the 28 percent federal income tax bracket and the 5 percent state income tax bracket, the yield would be most nearly equal to which of the following?

    a. $9,000 savings account paying 5 percent interest
    b. $7,000 savings account paying 6 percent interest
    c. Income property paying $300 per month
    d. Preferred stock paying $300 per year

36. To an appraiser, the fact that some cities inflict a heavy burden of property tax is of interest because

    a. these cities tend to offer more public services and might attract more investors.
    b. these cities rarely have large bond indebtedness.
    c. new construction might move away from a city under these circumstances.
    d. these cities offer excellent locations for most types of urban development.

37. Broker Abel may legally refuse to show a piece of property to a prospective buyer who happens to be of a minority race if the

    a. licensee feels the home is not suitable.
    b. owners gave specific instructions against it.
    c. licensee seemed certain the home was not affordable.
    d. owners are away and left instructions that the home was not to be shown to anyone during their absence.

38. Which of the following statements is correct regarding encumbrances?

    a. Deed restrictions and zoning ordinances are examples of involuntary limitations of ownership.
    b. Leases and mortgages are examples of contractual limitations of ownership.
    c. Both a and b
    d. Neither a nor b

39. Which of the following would probably experience the *LEAST* return of investment?

    a. Personal residence
    b. Residential property
    c. Industrial property
    d. Commercial property

40. An 18-year-old student, who has a power of attorney from another student, enters into a contract for the sale of real property on behalf of the other student. The contract is

    a. valid.   c. voidable.
    b. void.   d. illegal.

41. A covenant differs from a condition in that

    a. a condition can be created only in the grant of an estate.
    b. a covenant cannot be created by the grant of an estate.
    c. only conditions run with the land.
    d. only covenants can restrict the use of land by the owner.

42. Productivity is dependent upon

    a. supply.   c. use.
    b. demand.   d. value.

43. Sales tax due on the fixtures in the sale of a business opportunity is

    a. paid by the buyer to the seller along with the purchase price.
    b. remitted be the seller to the State Board of Equalization.
    c. paid before the Certificate of Clearance is issued.
    d. All of the above

44. Upon the last payment and completion of the terms and conditions of a real property sales contract, a quitclaim deed would most likely be signed by the

    a. vendor.   c. trustor.
    b. vendee.   d. trustee.

45. The lender of a second deed of trust foreclosed on a property using a trustee's sale. The proceeds of the sale were enough to satisfy the demands of the first and second trust deedholders, costs, fees, and expenses, with a small surplus of cash remaining. In what manner would the cash proceeds from the sale usually be distributed?

    a. First trust deed; second trust deed; cost, fees, and expenses of the sale; trustor
    b. Costs, fees, and expenses of the sale; first trust deed; second trust deed; trustor
    c. Trustor; first trust deed; second trust deed; costs, fees, and expenses of the sale
    d. Second trust deed; first trust deed; costs, fees, and expenses of the sale; trustor

46. When mortgage money is borrowed at a rate less than that of the net return on a property that is not mortgaged, the borrowing of money raises the rate of return on the owner's investment. This principle is referred to as

    a. trading one equity.
    b. capital turnover.
    c. deficit financing.
    d. None of the above

47. Broker Smith arranged for a loan for borrower Johnson. Smith prepared his mortgage loan statement and had Johnson sign it. Smith then discovered that there was a lien on the property that Johnson had not disclosed to him during the negotiations. If the new loan cannot be consummated due to Johnson's failure to disclose the existing lien, Johnson would be liable to Smith for

    a. no costs, expenses, or commissions.
    b. paid or incurred costs and expenses of originating the loan plus the full commission.
    c. one-half of all costs, expenses, and commissions shown on the mortgage loan statement.
    d. all costs and expenses paid or incurred and one-half of the commission charges.

48. The Interstate Land Sales Disclosure Act is a federal law that protects buyers or lessees of subdivision properties that are located in the United States and are being offered for sale or lease in interstate commerce. The right of rescission available to purchasers is

    a. 5 days.   c. 14 days.
    b. 7 days.   d. 24 hours.

49. All of the following statements regarding an option are correct, *EXCEPT*

    a. the conditions of the option do not have to include specific terms to purchase within a specified or reasonable time.
    b. if the option is not exercised, the optionee forfeits the option money.
    c. unless prohibited, an option is assignable.
    d. the provisions of a lease option are sufficient consideration to support an option contained within the lease.

50. All of the following are demand sources for money, *EXCEPT*

    a. refinancing.
    b. Fannie Mae.
    c. construction.
    d. sales financing.

51. A seller of real property uses an installment sale and agrees to finance the transaction using an all-inclusive trust deed. For federal income tax purposes

    a. the buyer is presumed to have assumed the senior loan in the year of sale.
    b. the buyer is presumed to have not assumed the senior loan in the year of sale.
    c. it would be disallowed because the seller cannot use an all-inclusive trust deed with an installment sale.
    d. it would be disallowed.

52. A reconstructed operating statement would normally contain

    a. book depreciation.
    b. management costs.
    c. loan payments.
    d. expenditures for capital improvements.

53. An ambiguity in the legal description of the real property conveyed in a deed

    a. will require constructive affirmation.
    b. is curable by court action.
    c. will place a cloud on title.
    d. is curable by appropriate action of the parties involved, with or without court assistance.

54. If homeowner Carter intends to sell her home "as is," this

    a. means that Carter does not have to complete a Real Property Transfer Disclosure Statement.
    b. means that nothing will be warranted.
    c. indicates "buyer beware."
    d. requires that Carter complete a Real Property Transfer Disclosure Statement.

55. The following statements regarding special assessments and property taxes are incorrect, *EXCEPT*

    a. special assessments and property taxes are not on a parity with each other.
    b. special assessments are not superior to recorded trust deeds.
    c. both are levied to support the general functions of government.
    d. special assessments can be foreclosed in the same way as property taxes.

56. Tim sells his farm to George in the fall of the year. There is no mention in the sales agreement as to the existing unharvested corn crop. Based on these facts, which of the following statements is correct concerning the unharvested crop?

    a. It is part of the realty.
    b. Tim has a right to enter the farm and harvest the crop.
    c. Tim and George will share in the profits.
    d. Tim may enter George's farm and harvest the crop.

57. The secondary mortgage market refers to

   a. participation in real estate financing by out-of-state lenders.
   b. transfers of mortgages between mortgages.
   c. federal control over the savings and loan associations.
   d. junior financing.

58. Real property investments are funded by a combination of

   a. money market accounts and savings accounts.
   b. leverage and debt.
   c. lien funds and equity funds.
   d. chattel mortgages.

59. A method that can be used to stop a violation of private restrictions is a(n)

   a. desist and refrain order.
   b. injunction.
   c. junction.
   d. decree of partition.

60. Any fact that could affect one's decision in completing a transaction is known as a(n) _____ fact.

   a. evidential   c. legal
   b. material   d. unethical

61. An investor would be allowed to take a capital gain or loss for federal income taxation purposes if he or she

   a. received full payment of a short-term note that was purchased at a substantial discount.
   b. received less than the book value of an income property as the result of a sale.
   c. collected liquidated damages from a buyer who had defaulted under a land sale contract.
   d. received a substantial amount of cash as a result of refinancing an existing loan on an income property.

62. The difference between special assessments and property taxes is that special assessments

   a. are levied for specific local improvements.
   b. are levied by improvement districts only.
   c. and property taxes are both levied to support the general functions of government.
   d. have priority over property taxes and are on a parity with mechanics' liens.

63. In the preparation of a closing statement, the escrow holder would debit the seller of income property for which of the following?

   a. Prepaid taxes
   b. Prepaid rent
   c. Prepaid fire insurance premiums
   d. All of the above

64. Regarding property value and sales, the terms of the sale will affect the

   a. price of the property, but not the value.
   b. value of the property, but not the price.
   c. utility of the property.
   d. basis of the property.

65. The Federal Institutions Reform, Recovery and Enforcement Act of 1989 (FIRREA) provides that deposits in federally insured savings associations are insured by

   a. BIF.   c. FSLIC.
   b. SAIF.   d. RTC.

66. It is likely that the U.S. Attorney General would get involved in the federal fair housing laws if

    a. a person files a complaint with the Secretary of Housing and Urban Development.
    b. a conspiracy exists not to abide by the federal fair housing law.
    c. state laws are not being enforced by state officials.
    d. a complaint filed by an aggrieved party indicates a violation by an owner of more than four units.

67. Under federal regulations, the maximum amount a renegotiable rate mortgage can fluctuate is

    a. 5 percent.   c. 12 percent.
    b. 10 percent.   d. 15 percent.

68. The equity that a person has in his or her house can be found by calculating

    a. market value less the down payment.
    b. market value less all loans.
    c. market value less all liens.
    d. asking price less all loans.

69. If a piece of property is going to be changed to a higher and better use than its present use, an appraiser would refer to the current use as a(n) _____ use.

    a. interim   c. likely
    b. stable   d. temporary

70. A title insurance company conducts a very thorough search of the public records before issuing a title insurance policy. The records it would search would include those of the

    a. county recorder.
    b. county clerk.
    c. federal land office.
    d. All of the above

71. If a broker discovers that one of his or her salespersons participated in fraud, the broker should discharge the salesperson and

    a. return his or her license to the Department of Real Estate.
    b. immediately send a certified letter with a statement of facts to the Real Estate Commissioner.
    c. mail the salesperson's transfer form to the Department of Real Estate within five business days.
    d. immediately telephone the Real Estate Commissioner and present the details directly to the Commissioner.

72. An owner who sells a condominium must provide the buyer with

    a. CC&Rs.
    b. bylaws.
    c. the most recent financial statement of the homeowners' association.
    d. All of the above

73. An escrow transaction is termed *complete* when

    a. both agents deliver the signed deposit receipt into the hands of the escrow holder.
    b. all of the terms of the instructions are met.
    c. all documents are prepared and ready for execution.
    d. the buyer deposits all necessary funds into escrow.

74. Often, when the term *warehousing* is used in real estate financing, it refers to

    a. loans regulated under Article 7 of real estate law.
    b. a jumbo loan on an industrial storage facility.
    c. the underwriting of stock issues secured by real property.
    d. a mortgage banker holding loans prior to sale.

75. Numerous buyers and sellers with equal knowledge about products and prices describes a(n) _____ market.

    a. imperfect
    b. perfect
    c. blended
    d. real estate

76. There is a substantial difference in value between two properties that were built at the same time. They were built on adjoining lots of equal value, and construction and maintenance costs were the same. The difference in value is most likely due to

    a. nonconforming opposite the properties.
    b. economic obsolescence in the neighborhood.
    c. physical depreciation of one of the properties.
    d. functional obsolescence within one of the properties.

77. Which one of the following describes the occurrence of gross income being changed into value in one operation?

    a. Comparison
    b. Rent multiplier
    c. Cost
    d. Fixed factor

78. Which of the following is required to fill out a Transfer Disclosure Statement?

    a. Administrator, during a probate sale
    b. Trustee, in an REO sale
    c. Husband, to his ex-wife in a divorce settlement
    d. Transferor

79. Broker Hayes is acting as an agent but without a contract with the owner of the property. This is known as a(n) _____ agency.

    a. implied
    b. ratified
    c. actual
    d. intentional

80. The transfer of ownership of real property under the California Veterans Farm and Home Purchase Act is handled by a

    a. grant deed.
    b. reconveyance deed.
    c. real property sales contract.
    d. warranty deed.

81. Which of the following comes under the Uniform Building Code?

    a. Demolition and relocation
    b. New construction
    c. Properties taken under eminent domain
    d. Both *a* and *b*

82. Underground water that is not running in a well-defined channel is referred to as

    a. littoral rights.
    b. riparian rights.
    c. alluvium.
    d. percolating water.

83. Which of the following is a most likely benefit from an FHA loan?

    a. Mortgagee is insured against foreclosure
    b. Mortgagor is insured against fire
    c. Mortgagee pays insurance
    d. Mortgagor has a life insurance policy

84. If a developer sells a home in a tract that is subject to a blanket trust deed with a release clause, the

    a. developer executes a deed of reconveyance for the new homebuyer.
    b. beneficiary requests a partial reconveyance.
    c. beneficiary signs a deed of reconveyance.
    d. trustee request a deed of partial reconveyance.

85. Which of the following is mainly responsible for ensuring the availability of paved streets, sewers, sidewalks, gutters, and other improvements for the general public within a subdivision?

    a. Bonding company
    b. Developer/subdivider
    c. Improvement district for subdivisions within that community
    d. The city or county planning board

86. The role of Ginnie Mae when dealing with passthrough securities is to

    a. qualify the properties in the mortgage pool that are used as security for the loans.
    b. provide guaranteed, timely, monthly payments of principal and interest on its pool of mortgage-backed securities.
    c. pool the interest from mortgages into a central pool.
    d. act as a matchmaker bringing lenders and investors together.

87. All of the following are tests of the Law of Agency *EXCEPT*

    a. compensation.   c. election.
    b. disclosure.   d. confirmation.

88. Title insurance is effective as of the

    a. opening of escrow.
    b. closing of escrow.
    c. transferring of title.
    d. date of the receipt of the preliminary title report.

89. If an interior partition is the same temperature as the outer side of an exterior wall, the

    a. insulation is sufficient.
    b. wall outlets allow heat and air to escape to the outside.
    c. ventilation system is adequate.
    d. ceiling area around the ducts is leaking heat to the outside of the building.

90. A seller accepted a written offer from a buyer for the purchase of the seller's property. Three months later, the seller decided not to complete the transaction as she believed that property values were on the rise and she wanted to wait and sell later for a higher profit. Under the statute of limitations, the buyer should take action on this breach of contract within

    a. 90 days.   c. 3 years.
    b 2 years.   d. 4 years.

91. In the sale of a business, sales tax is paid on

    a. fixtures and furniture.
    b. the value of goodwill.
    c. leasehold improvements.
    d. stock in inventory.

92. Broker Abel wants to advertise property in a minority newspaper for a minority buyer. If Abel does not want to be discriminatory in his business practices he should advertise

    a. all of his listings in a newspaper directed toward minorities.
    b. the property in a newspaper of general circulation.
    c. properties located in minority areas in a newspaper directed to minority readership.
    d. All of the above

93. The down payment on FHA's most popularly used program is calculated as

    a. 5 percent of the appraised value of the property.
    b. 3 percent of the first $25,000 and 5 percent up to the appraised value and 100 percent of the excess over the appraised value.
    c. No down payment is required.
    d. None of the above

94. Select the order of words that correctly matches the order of the following definitions:

    I. Sudden perceptible loss of land by action of water
    II. Gradual accumulation of land deposited by the shifting of the river or ocean's action
    III. Wearing away of land by the action of water or wind
    IV. Land increased by the buildup of sediment

        a. Accretion, avulsion, alluvion, erosion
        b. Avulsion, accretion, erosion, alluvion
        c. Alluvion, accretion, erosion, avulsion
        d. Erosion, avulsion, alluvion, accretion

95. The maximum load factor that can be withstood by a roof has caused

    a. manufacturers to make stronger joists.
    b. builders to space roof rafters closer together.
    c. builders to extend eaves.
    d. None of the above

96. What is the maximum increase that a county tax assessor can apply to the base value of property annually?

    a. 1 percent
    b. 2 percent
    c. 25 percent
    d. An unlimited amount as determined by the assessor

97. The governmental agency that makes agricultural and large land loans is

    a. the federal land bank.
    b. Ginnie Mae.
    c. Fannie Mae.
    d. Freddie Mac.

98. A required disclosure under Civil Code Section 2079 became effective on January 1, 1988. It is the

    a. mortgage loan disclosure.
    b. good-faith estimate disclosure.
    c. agency relationship disclosure.
    d. property transfer disclosure.

99. The Alquist-Priolo Special Studies Zones Act requires a disclosure to buyers, if applicable, that the property is

    a. tainted with hazardous materials.
    b. near a flood hazard.
    c. on or near an earthquake fault.
    d. an environmental concern.

100. There is an acre of land that is divided into four equal lots that parallel each other. The depth of the parcels is 240 feet. The width of the lots is

    a. one-quarter acre.
    b. 180 feet.
    c. 45.4 feet.
    d. 5 rods.

■ ANSWER KEY

1. d. Statement of fact.

2. a. Statement of fact.

3. a. The quality of income refers to the creditworthiness of a tenant on the property. If a tenant is a poor credit risk, it could cause a slower flow of income. The higher the risk, the higher the capitalization rate.

4. d. Statement of fact.

5. c. An acre contains 43,560 square feet or 4,840 square yards.

6. d. The letter *R* stands for *resistance*.

7. b. Pest control reports are filed with the Structural Pest Control Board in Sacramento. It keeps its copies for two years. Anyone who requests a copy of a report may obtain one by paying a small fee.

8. d. The term *potable* refers to water that is suitable for drinking.

9. a. Use the cost rule, which says "add to 100 percent, and then divide into the sales price." 100% + 12% = 112%. $135,000 ÷ 1.12 = $120,535.71 (original cost). Profit = $14,464 ($135,000 − $120,536).

10. d. Statement of fact.

11. a. Sidewalks, special landscaping, and driveways are appraised separately or singly from the improvements. Later in the appraisal process, they are combined with the depreciated value of the improvements to arrive at the estimate of value of the total property.

12. c. The functional utility or "usefulness" of residential property will strongly influence the appraiser's estimate of value.

13. b. Subleasing is less than an assignment because the original leasee remains responsible for the lease contract. In an assignment, the assignee becomes responsible for the remainder of the lease contract.

14. c. Statement of fact.

15. a. Read the question carefully. A salesperson cannot collect a commission directly from a principal. The commission must be paid to the broker, who can then disburse a commission to a salesperson. In this instance, a *broker* can collect 15 percent commission.

16. d. Statement of fact.

17. d. Statement of fact.

18. c. The Federal Open Market Committee of the Federal Reserve System uses the buying and selling of government bonds as one of several ways to stabilize the flow of money in this country.

19. d. Boot is anything that is money or its equivalent used to equalize the value of the property that is being exchanged.

20. d. For validity, a grant deed does not require a date, method of ownership, or recording. It does, however, require delivery.

21. c. The tenant farmer has the right to harvest the crop even after the tenancy has ended.

22. a. A license is a personal and nonassignable right that can be revoked at any time. It is not an interest in the land like an easement. An example of a license—"You can cross my property to fish in the lake at the back until I say you can't."

23. d. An offer whose acceptance has been communicated to the offeror (buyer) creates a binding contract. It is the broker in a nonexclusive listing who brings together the above who is the one who earns a commission.

24. c. Statement of fact.

25. a. The appraiser does not consider financing costs in the appraisal process, as those costs can differ for each purchaser. The appraiser considers the operating expenses of the property itself.

26. c. Statement of fact.

27. a. $250,000 equity. The purchase price was $200,000. Twenty-five percent of $200,000 is $50,000 for the down payment. The mortgage was $150,000. $400,000 (increased value after ten years) minus $150,000 mortgage equals $250,000 equity after ten years.

28. c. Statement of fact.

29. d. $225,000 value. $300,000 × 6% = $18,000 net operating income. $18,000 ÷ .08 = $225,000. Remember that a higher capitalization rate typically indicates a higher risk. The higher the risk, the lower the value.

30. c. Read the choices carefully. It is the financing statement, not the financial statement, that is filed with the Secretary of State. It lists all of the items used as collateral for the credit extension in the sale of a business opportunity. On its filing, a lien is created against all of the personal property listed on the statement.

31. d. Plottage increment describes an anticipated higher value from the effect of combining small adjoining lots into one large parcel.

32. c. Statement of fact.

33. c. Statement of fact.

34. b. This defines the principle of increasing and decreasing returns.

35. a. $9,000 in savings × 5% interest = $450. $450 × 33% for taxation (28% federal and 5% state) = $148.50 for taxes. $450 − $148.50 = $301.50 after-tax yield. The return on municipal bonds is tax free. $5,000 invested in these bonds × 6% return = $300. Nearly equal to the $9,000 in the savings account whose taxable yield is at 5 percent.

36. c. Statement of fact.

37. d. Statement of fact.

38. c. Statement of fact.

39. a. The "return of investment" is part of what makes up a capitalization rate used to appraise income property. Of the choices offered, a personal residence is least likely to be treated as income property for its appraisal purpose.

40. a. The age of capacity for contracting in California is 18. An 18-year-old who holds a power of attorney may contract for another person.

41. a. Statement of fact.

42. a. A supply of raw material is needed before anything can be made, regardless of the demand of it.

43. d. Statement of fact.

44. a. Statement of fact.

45. b. Statement of fact.

46. a. Statement of fact.

47. d. Under Article 7 loans, if a borrower does not disclose all of the liens against the property being offered as security for a loan, and as a result, the broker cannot make the loan, the borrower may be liable for all costs and expenses incurred and one-half of the commission.

48. b. Statement of fact. The Interstate Land Sales Act involves 25 or more lots being sold or leased from state to state. The right

of rescission for borrowers is seven days. Think of 2 + 5 (25 lots) = 7 (seven days to rescind).

49. a. Statement of fact.

50. b. Statement of fact. Fannie Mae is a supply source for money. It is the largest investor in the secondary market.

51. b. The buyer under an all-inclusive trust deed is not presumed to have assumed the underlying loan (senior trust deed). The seller (beneficiary) of the AITD remains responsible for the senior loan and its payments.

52. b. Statement of fact.

53. d. Statement of fact.

54. d. Statement of fact.

55. d. Statement of fact.

56. a. Unharvested crops are still part of the earth and are classified as real property. They would pass to a buyer unless a seller reserves the right in the sales contract to harvest the existing crop. There is no reservation of crop rights in the question.

57. b. Statement of fact.

58. c. Lien funds refer to loans. Equity funds refer to down payments. Most real property is purchased by a combination of these.

59. b. Statement of fact.

60. b. Statement of fact.

61. b. Statement of fact.

62. a. Statement of fact.

63. b. When income property is sold, any prepaid rent and/or security deposits are to be either returned to the tenant, who then repays those amounts to the new buyer, or, more commonly, credited to the account of the buyer of the income property.

Therefore, prepaid rent would be a debit (charge) to the seller.

64. a. If a seller carries the financing, typically the purchase price of the property increase. Or if the sale is based on all cash, typically the purchase price decreases. Terms of the sale often affect the price, but not necessarily the value, of the property.

65. b. SAIF (Savings Association Insurance Fund) is the agency that insures accounts at savings associations. BIF (Banking Insurance Fund) insures accounts at commercial banks. Currently, both of these agencies are under the FDIC (Federal Deposit Insurance Corporation).

66. b. Statement of fact.

67. a. Statement of fact.

68. c. This is a better choice than the others. There could be other liens against the property in addition to a loan, for example, property taxes and recorded mechanics' liens.

69. a. When there is an expected change in the use of property, the current use is referred to as *interim use*. For example, sometimes you see commercially zoned undeveloped property being used to grow crops until such time as development is practical.

70. d. Statement of fact.

71. b. Statement of fact.

72. d. Statement of fact.

73. b. Statement of fact.

74. d. Statement of fact.

75. b. The question includes the definition of a perfect market. Real estate markets are historically imperfect markets.

76. d. Functional obsolescence refers to items that are obsolete, not desirable, or not currently useful, for example, out-of-date plumbing, poor floor plan, and old-fashioned appliances. The question states that maintenance costs are the same; therefore, physical depreciation is not a choice to select. Economic obsolescence occurs outside the property lines and would have the same effect on both properties.

77. b. The gross rent multiplier rule is sometimes used to estimate the value of income property. A number (multiplier) is selected from comparable sales data and is multiplied times gross rent to estimate the value of the total property. The formula for finding a gross rent multiplier is sales price of property divided by gross rent equals the gross rent multiplier.

78. d. The transferor or seller of residential property, one to four units, is required to complete a Real Property Transfer Disclosure Statement to be presented to a buyer. The broker cannot fill out the transferor's portion of the form.

79. a. Statement of fact.

80. c. A real property sales contract (land contract) is used by Cal-Vet as a way to transfer ownership of the house to the veteran. Legal title passes to the veteran buyer when the loan is paid in full.

81. d. Statement of fact.

82. d. Statement of fact.

83. a. FHA insures the lender against loss. There are two *e*'s in the word *lender*. There are two *e*'s in the words *mortgagee* and *beneficiary* (another term for lender). This should help to remember that the mortgagee is the lender.

84. b. The partial reconveyance is issued by a trustee at the request of the beneficiary. This allows the house to be released from the blanket trust deed. Now title to the house can pass to the buyer, who arranges for compensating financing for its purchase from the subdivider.

85. d. Local government, that is, city or county planning boards, is responsible for ensuring that areas dedicated for public use are properly improved initially by the sub-divider/developer.

86. b. Statement of fact.

87. a. Statement of fact. Compensation (consideration) is not essential to the creation of an agency. A gratuitous (no fee) agent will be held to the same standards of agency law as would the agent who acts for compensation.

88. b. Title insurance is effective at the close of escrow. This is a better choice than the "transfer of title." After all, there is a type of title policy that protects lenders for loan balances. The question does not specify the type of policy.

89. b. Statement of fact.

90. d. Under the statute of limitations, a written contract has a four-year period of pursuit. The question refers to a written contract.

91. a. Statement of fact.

92. b. Statement of fact.

93. b. Statement of fact.

94. b. Avulsion refers to a sudden violent loss. Accretion refers to the gradual depositing of soil. Erosion refers to the wearing away of land. Alluvion is the name given to the land that is added.

95. b. The rafters would be placed closer together to have a strong roof.

96. b. Assessed value can be adjusted by 2 percent annually.

97. a. Federal land banks make large land loans. A way to remember—*land banks make land loans*.

98. c. The agency Relationship Disclosure became effective on January 1, 1988. A way to remember the year and the subject of the disclosure—Agency—198Ate (1988).

99. c. Statement of fact.

100. c. There are 43,560 square feet to an acre. Use the formula Area ÷ Depth = Width. 43,560 ÷ 240 feet depth = 181.5 feet width. 181.5 ÷ four lots = 45.4 feet width.

BROKER APPENDIX
Practice Examination IV

1. The maximum fee that a lender can charge for the preparation and issuance of the Uniform Settlement Statement is

   a. nothing.
   b. 1 percent of the loan amount.
   c. a flat fee of $10.
   d. one-half of 1 percent of the loan amount.

2. The requirements under the Truth-in-Lending law apply in all of the following *EXCEPT* when

   a. a homeowner advertises to the general public that a person can buy the property subject to an existing loan.
   b. financial institutions advertise to promote consumer credit.
   c. a broker advertises that an existing loan can be assumed under certain terms.
   d. brokers advertise that loans can be assumed at certain annual percentage rates.

3. Construction loans that are granted by lending institutions are often released in a series of progress payments. The last disbursement by the lender usually occurs when the

   a. notice of completion is filed.
   b. building is completed.
   c. owner has approved the construction.
   d. period to file a lien has expired.

4. Zoning ordinances have a primary purpose. Their main function is to

   a. impose height limitations on buildings.
   b. maintain conformity within neighborhoods.
   c. provide for the safety and well-being of the general public.
   d. control growth.

5. Mary is considering the purchase of a hill-side lot in a new subdivision from a sub-divider who is not a real estate licensee. She prepared a list of questions concerning the maintenance of the hillside road, off-site improvements, public utilities, and assessments. She can obtain more information from the

   a. title company.
   b. Real Estate Commissioner.
   c. civil engineer on the job.
   d. county planning board.

6. The purchasing power of the dollar is usually measured by

   a. treasury bills.
   b. price indexes.
   c. the gold standard.
   d. interest rates.

7. The replacement cost method is usually more difficult to apply to older properties than to new properties because

   a. land values are difficult to estimate on older properties.
   b. historic costs are difficult to find.
   c. depreciation schedules are difficult to determine on older improvements.
   d. building codes and zoning are subject to routine change.

8. Which one of the following is correct concerning a real estate investment trust?

   a. At least 75 percent of its income must be from investments.
   b. Ninety percent or more of its ordinary income must be distributed annually.
   c. It must be owned by at least 50 investors.
   d. None of the above

9. For income tax purposes, on a 1031 exchange, the expression *tax free* usually means

   a. there was no gain.
   b. there will never be a gain.
   c. the properties exchanged were of equal value.
   d. deferred taxes.

10. A couple, each 63 years of age, own their home free and clear. Their total annual household income is $17,000. They are interested in postponing the payment of property tax on their home and are not sure where to inquire. They can obtain claim forms and information from the

    a. county tax assessor.
    b. county tax collector.
    c. state controller.
    d. Real Estate Commissioner.

11. There are delinquent property taxes on Smith's property. On June 30, the property will be sold to the state. This date is important, as it

    a. is a notice to the tenant or owner to vacate within six months.
    b. establishes the date for interest and penalty charges.
    c. sets the five-year redemption period running.
    d. All of the above

12. Which of the following deed restrictions found in the CC&Rs on property would not be enforceable?

    a. The use of this property is restricted for recreational use of the community.
    b. The use of this property is restricted for educational purposes.
    c. The use of this property is restricted for the construction of a Catholic church.
    d. The property may be sold only to members of the seller's church.

13. Adam gave John, who is not a property owner, the right to cross his ranch to fish in the lake that sits behind the ranch. John has a(n)

    a. easement in gross.
    b. license.
    c. easement appurtenant.
    d. easement by prescription.

14. A disadvantage of joint tenancy is that

    a. only the deceased joint tenant's interest in the property is given a stepped-up basis.
    b. terminating the joint tenancy by partition action is costly.
    c. it may be severed by the voluntary transfer of one joint tenant or by operation of law.
    d. All of the above

15. Which of the following is most often used as a standard for rent adjustments in commercial leases?

    a. Gross Domestic Product Index for all consumer (GDP-C)
    b. Consumer Price Index for urban wage earners and clerical workers (CPI-W)
    c. Consumer Price Index for all urban consumers (CPI-U)
    d. Consumer Price Index for urban workers in Los Angeles (CPI-LA)

16. As typically found in deed restrictions or by agreement, which of the following would be part of a condominium ownership?

    a. Central heat and air system
    b. Bearing walls
    c. The elevator in a three-story project
    d. None of the above

17. The term *turn-key project* refers to

    a. residential subdivisions.
    b. remodeled properties.
    c. low-income housing.
    d. a completed project, ready to move in.

18. In California, structural pest control companies are required to

    a. complete repair work no later than five days after escrow is closed.
    b. complete all repair work before escrow is closed.
    c. furnish a copy of the inspection report to the owner.
    d. furnish a free copy of the inspection report to anyone who requests it.

19. The Real Property Transfer Disclosure Act requires the broker to

    a. visually and physically inspect the home and disclose all defects.
    b. visually inspect all accessible and inaccessible areas and disclose.
    c. fill in the seller's portion of the disclosure.
    d. visually inspect the accessible areas of a home and disclose.

20. Salesperson Baker deliberately avoided showing property in certain neighborhoods to a minority buyer, even though the properties were in the buyer's price range. This action is known as

    a. redlining.
    b. blockbusting
    c. steering.
    d. All of the above

21. There is a statutory requirement that brokers and salespersons must enter in to an employment agreement. Regarding the agreement,

    a. the salesperson must keep a copy of three years from the date of employment.
    b. the broker must keep a copy for three years from the date of employment.
    c. both broker and salesperson must keep a copy for three years.
    d. both broker and salesperson must keep a copy for four years from the date of termination of the employment.

22. A prepaid rental listing broker decides to move the office to another location. Within how many days must he or she advise the client list of the change?

    a. By the next business day
    b. Within five business days
    c. As soon as is practicable
    d. Before the move

23. A salesperson with two years' experience within the last five years may

    a. initial real estate contracts on behalf of the broker.
    b. manage a real estate office.
    c. apply for a broker's license after completing the required course work.
    d. All of the above

24. Which of the following would constitute fraudulent misrepresentation on the part of the broker?

    a. Misrepresentation of a material and major fact
    b. Misrepresentation of a material and major fact that influenced the buyer to purchase the property and subsequently take a loss
    c. Misrepresentation of a material and major fact with full knowledge and intent of the broker
    d. All of the above

25. Broker Carter approaches a seller for the purpose of listing the seller's property for sale. The seller refuses to give Carter a listing but states that she will pay a 6 percent commission to Carter if he finds a buyer for the property. Carter finds a buyer whose offer is accepted by the seller, and the acceptance is communicated to the buyer. After the buyer takes possession of the property, he discovers several defects that the seller disclosed to Carter, but that were not disclosed to the buyer by Carter. The buyer proceeds to sue both the seller and the broker. Broker Carter states that because he did not have a formal written contract with the seller, he was not responsible to the buyer. Under these circumstances, Carter

    a. has no responsibility because the statute of frauds requires all employment contracts to be in writing.
    b. is subject to disciplinary action by the Real Estate Commissioner but has liability to the buyer.
    c. can be sued by both the seller and the buyer.
    d. can be sued by both the seller and the buyer and be subject to disciplinary action by the Real Estate Commissioner.

26. A properly executed and valid option agreement becomes a mutually binding contract

    a. at the time the optionor accepts the consideration.
    b. when the optionee pays the consideration.
    c. when the optionee exercises the option to purchase.
    d. All of the above

27. Jones enters into an offer to purchase a new strip mall contingent upon her ability to prelease 80 percent of the units. The type of contract that would be created is

    a. illusory.
    b. bilateral and executory.
    c. unilateral as to the lease and bilateral as to the purchase.
    d. enforceable.

28. Jensen lists a farm for sale with broker Laurel. Laurel locates buyer Smith, who offers $211,000 with a three-day period for the acceptance of the offer. Jensen counteroffered with $211,900 through broker Laurel, which Smith rejected. Prior to the expiration of the three-day period for acceptance. Jensen decided to accept the original offer of $211,000. Laurel notified Smith, but Smith said he was no longer interested. Under these circumstances,

    a. Jensen can sue for specific performance.
    b. there is no contract.
    c. Laurel has the right to a commission.
    d. the contract is void.

29. Tom purchased a home subject to the assumption of the seller's first trust deed. The beneficiary statement indicated that the existing loan was $4,000 more than either Tom or the seller was aware of. The excess of $4,000 will be

    a. paid by the seller.
    b. paid by the buyer.
    c. split 50/50 by the buyer and seller.
    d. paid according to whatever the buyer and seller agree on.

30. The acknowledgment of a signature on a grant deed is to

    a. verify the grant deed.
    b. record the grant deed.
    c. ensure that valid title is passed.
    d. All of the above

31. Allen purchased a title insurance policy, and six months later, he died. Allen left his property to his favorite niece, Mary. During Mary's possession of the property, she discovered a defect in the title. Allen's title insurance policy will

    a. not protect the niece because it was not issued to her.
    b. protect the niece, as it was an extended title insurance policy.
    c. protect the niece, as she is an heir to Allen.
    d. protect the niece, as the defect occurred during Allen's ownership.

32. Personal property cannot be acquired by

    a. occupancy.   c. accession.
    b. succession.   d. will.

33. Veteran John owns a home on which there is a conventional loan of $75,000 and a current market value of approximately $200,000. Using his DVA eligibility, John wishes to refinance and renovate the home. The lender with whom he is negotiating has agreed to make the loan, and there will be discount points charged. Which of the following is correct?

    a. He cannot refinance, as the DVA eligibility cannot be used for refinancing loans.
    b. He can refinance but legally cannot pay the discount points.
    c. He can refinance if the lender does not charge more than a 1½ percent origination fee.
    d. He can refinance using his DVA eligibility, and the DVA will allow a veteran to pay discount points.

34. The net effect of the Federal Housing Administration's participation in the financing of real estate loans has been to

    a. create uniform appraisals.
    b. ensure an ample real estate money supply.
    c. create a national market by investing in trust deeds.
    d. All of the above

35. When a trust deed is sold to an investor, the inclusion of an acceleration clause in the trust deed

    a. makes it nonnegotiable.
    b. does not affect its negotiability.
    c. does not affect its negotiability and increases its desirability.
    d. does not affect its desirability and increases its negotiability.

36. Builder Fran completed a house and sold it for $155,000, with a $25,000 down payment and a $130,000 note and first deed of trust. She contacted her banker and asked to borrow $100,000 to build another home on speculation and use the $130,000 first deed of trust as security. This transaction with the bank is referred to as a

    a. purchase-money transaction.
    b. chattel mortgage.
    c. smart move.
    d. pledge agreement.

37. A lender typically releases the last payment on a construction loan

    a. when the notice of completion is filed.
    b. after the filing of a mechanic's lien.
    c. when the building is accepted by the owner.
    d. when the mechanic's lien period has expired.

38. From a lender's viewpoint, a mortgage's highest yield is based on the

    a. total amount of dollars received less the cost of funds.
    b. total amount of dollars received less loan fees and cost of funds.
    c. term of the loan.
    d. interest rate named in the note.

39. Mortgage loan broker Abel has begun an advertising campaign. He advertised "megabucks" returns on trust deeds for sale. The facts and figures over the past six months and the yields stated are accurate. Abel

    a. can state the yield only if he believes that the information is true.
    b. cannot state the yield unless he includes the APR.
    c. can state the yield with the permission of the Department of Real Estate.
    d. can state the yield if he states the original balance, amount of discount, and contract rate.

40. Interest rates on trust deeds are determined by

    a. population.
    b. supply and demand of money.
    c. foreign exchange rate changes.
    d. None of the above

41. Ann is purchasing real property using a real property sales contract. If it is Ann's intention to sell her interest to Baker, Ann needs to execute a(n)

    a. grant deed.
    b. reconveyance deed.
    c. lease agreement.
    d. assignment.

42. Broker King offered to return part of his commission to buyer Mary Wong if she would increase her offer to the seller to the price that King knew would be acceptable to the seller. In this situation,

    a. this information must be disclosed to the seller prior to the seller's acceptance.
    b. this action violates licensing law and could lead to disciplinary action by the Real Estate Commissioner.
    c. King could be held liable for damages and sued, even if this is disclosed to the seller prior to acceptance.
    d. None of the above

43. An all-inclusive trust deed is sometimes referred to as an *overriding deed of trust.* Regarding this type of financing, which of the following is most correct?

    a. The trustor has the responsibility of discharging all prior loans.
    b. This type of financing is used to avoid the acceleration of the loan due to an alienation clause in the trust deed.
    c. The beneficiary, by instructions in the note, is required to make payments on any senior loans as they become due.
    d. The face amount of the note does not include the amounts of any senior loans.

44. In the appraisal of single-family residences, the appraiser uses listing prices to establish

    a. the lowest probable price.
    b. the ceiling of market value.
    c. market value.
    d. comparable values in the neighborhood.

45. Under the Uniform Commercial Code, a notice to creditors is required in the sale of a business that invoices the bulk transfer of goods. All of the following must be included in the notice EXCEPT the

    a. place and the date on or after which the bulk transfer is to be consummated.
    b. names and business addresses of the transferor and the transferee.
    c. names and addresses of the transferor's creditors.
    d. location and general description of the property to be transferred.

46. The following activities of a real estate licensee are in violation of the Real Estate Law EXCEPT

    a. the unauthorized use of the term REALTOR®.
    b. the demanding of a commission under an exclusive listing when the listing does not contain a definite termination date.
    c. failing to inform a prospective buyer that his or her principal will probably sell at a price lower than listed.
    d. using his or her access to confidential records, provided by employment with a government agency, to the licensee's advantage.

47. Owner Alvarez decided to use a dark color paint for one of her rooms. The use of the dark color will make her room

    a. larger.
    b. smaller
    c. more formal.
    d. None of the above

48. Although the Federal Housing Administration will, the VA will not provide loans on

    a. business properties.
    b. farm equipment.
    c. a duplex purchased for rental.
    d. agricultural property.

49. Baker hired broker Harry under the terms of an exclusive authorization and right-to-sell listing agreement to sell his home. The authority given to Harry

    a. is whatever Harry believes his duties to be even if they extend beyond the authority of the agreement.
    b. is whatever the buyer believes it to be.
    c. extends to whatever is necessary to create a sale, regardless of the terms of the listing.
    d. is that which has been agreed on between Baker and Harry and that which is necessary, proper, or usual for bringing about the sale of the property.

50. The statute of frauds requires that certain contracts be in writing for enforceability. All of the following require a proper writing under this statute, *EXCEPT* a(n)

    a. agreement that by its terms is not to be performed within one year of the making.
    b. agreement for the leasing of property for a period of more than one year, or for the sale of real property or of an interest thereof.
    c. general partnership agreement.
    d. agreement that authorizes an agent to represent the sale of real property for compensation.

51. In the appraisal process, it is essential for the appraiser to differentiate between the fundamental purpose of an appraisal and the

    a. forces that affect real property value.
    b. function that the appraisal will serve.
    c. amount of real estate activity.
    d. process followed in the appraisal.

52. Which of the following would be most acceptable to institutional lenders' loan policies regarding equities in the home of borrowers?

    a. Large equities are undesirable, as homeowners might choose to borrow against the home from other lending sources.
    b. Small equities are desirable.
    c. Substantial equities are desirable, as history shows that such property owners show a great sense of pride of ownership.
    d. Substantial equities are required by law to be preserved as a hedge against inflation.

53. An investor who was unlicensed purchased six promissory notes secured by second trust deeds at a substantial discount. She held them for five months and sold them at a profit. She then used the funds to purchase seven more notes secured by trust deeds, held them for a short duration of six weeks, and also sold them for a profit. Under these circumstances,

    a. a real estate broker with a securities dealer endorsement is required to handle this type of transaction.
    b. a real estate broker must handle this type of transaction.
    c. no real estate license is required.
    d. a bond is required for each transaction.

54. There is a process used in the analysis of investment property that includes the development of hypothetical combinations of income and expense versus the capital requirements necessary for improvements. This attempts to establish the combination that would return the greatest net yield to the investment. This concept refers to the principle of

   a. supply and demand.
   b. increasing and decreasing returns.
   c. surplus productivity.
   d. contribution.

55. Prospective purchaser Jones requests a copy of a condominium's conditions, covenants, restrictions, and the association's bylaws from the governing body. How many days does the association have in which to deliver them to Jones?

   a. 7 days   c. 14 days
   b. 10 days   d. 30 days

56. A valid grant deed, among other things, requires delivery. Which of the following is an example of a valid delivery of a deed?

   a. A grantee delivered the deed after the death of the grantor in accordance with the instructions left by the grantor.
   b. The escrow company delivered the deed to the buyer prior to the buyer's meeting all the terms of the escrow.
   c. The escrow company mailed the deed that was acknowledged by the grantor but was delivered after the grantor had died.
   d. The grantor handed the deed to the grantee but the grantee did not record the deed.

57. The principle of progression can be described in which of the following ways?

   a. The worth of a lesser property will be increased in value by its presence among the better properties.
   b. A property of greater value will decrease in value by its presence among the lesser properties.
   c. A property of greater value will increase in value by its presence among properties of lesser values.
   d. None of the above

58. Sam and Judy Smith obtained a loan for the purchase of a new home. The lender required an ALTA title insurance policy as one of the many conditions for the loan. Sam and Judy did receive a standard title insurance policy from the developer/seller of the home. Shortly after close of escrow and possession of the home, the Smiths decided to build a fence around their property. They made the proper application to the city for a permit. The city stated that a five-foot sideyard setback was required, and the Smiths discovered that their home was only three feet from the property line. They subsequently made a claim to their title insurance company based on this discrepancy. The title insurance company would pay for

   a. the cost to correct the misplaced improvement.
   b. the amount of damages to the neighbors for any injuries they might suffer.
   c. any difference in value for the home as valued in its present location versus its relocation.
   d. None of the above

59. A lessor and lessee negotiate a new three-year lease agreement. Which of the following is necessary for a valid lease?

    a. The lease must be acknowledged by the lessor.
    b. All leases require the signature of both the lessor and the lessee.
    c. The lease must include the description of the property.
    d. All of the above

60. Regarding depreciation in the appraisal process, all of the following are correct *EXCEPT*

    a. depreciation is a loss in value from any cause.
    b. depreciation is the difference between the current value of the improvements and the cost to replace them today.
    c. reserves for depreciation may be set aside for both past and future depreciation.
    d. depreciation results only from factors that are inherent to the property and not from extraneous factors.

61. The Federal Reserve Board would likely do which of the following to encourage construction in a tight money market?

    a. Increase the discount rate and sell government bonds
    b. Decrease the discount rate and sell government bonds
    c. Increase the discount rate and buy government bonds
    d. Decrease the discount rate and buy government bonds

62. Owner Jean listed her home with broker Butler for $225,000 and told Butler that to sell quickly, she would take less for her home if she had to. Broker Butler found a prospective buyer and suggested that he make an offer for only $210,000 because he knew Jean was anxious to sell. The buyer proceeded with the offer of $210,000, which Jean accepted. The way Butler handled this transaction was

    a. not unethical because Jean accepted the offer.
    b. unethical but did not violate his fiduciary duty to Jean.
    c. a violation of his fiduciary duty to Jean because he disclosed confidential information without obtaining her consent.
    d. not a violation because she was in a hurry to sell and he did what he thought was right.

63. Each county assessor gathers a roll of all private property owners of real estate within his or her jurisdiction. The purpose of this assessment roll is to

    a. determine the tax rate.
    b. establish the tax base for the county.
    c. set the amount of tax to be paid by property owners.
    d. None of the above

64. Johnson files a bankruptcy action. His claim is effective

    a. as of the day the notice is filed in the newspaper.
    b. as of the date of the filing for bankruptcy.
    c. for 10 years.
    d. when the judge hears the matter.

65. The California State Housing Law dictates minimum building standards throughout the state. Regarding unincorporated areas, which of the following is correct? State law

   a. applies only to city public housing projects.
   b. applies only when there is no county code.
   c. does not apply to unincorporated areas.
   d. applies even though a county may have its own building code.

66. A nonresident subdivider wishes to offer his out-of-state subdivisions for sale to California residents. To do so, the subdivider must file an irrevocable consent with a required questionnaire stating that if any action is brought against him in this state and personal service of process on him using due diligence cannot be made in California a valid service may be made upon him through

   a. the California Real Estate Commissioner.
   b. the Commissioner of Real Estate in his state.
   c. a relative or friend named in the application who resides in California.
   d. the California Secretary of State.

67. A basic contract requires all of the following for validity, *EXCEPT*

   a. a proper writing.
   b. legal object.
   c. capable parties.
   d. mutuality.

68. An easement held by a utility company is a(n)

   a. easement appurtenant.
   b. possessory right in the real property.
   c. nonpossessory interest in real property.
   d. license.

69. Which of the following is correct regarding the gross rent multiplier used in some instances to appraise income properties?

   a. This approach is based on gross income in relation to the property's net income.
   b. The estimate of value is based on the relationship between the total income and the sales price of the property.
   c. Gross income and effective gross income are used in this process.
   d. Current gross income and anticipated gross income are used in this process.

70. A buyer was successful in having a seller carry back a note secured by a trust deed for the financing of the purchase of property. This type of encumbrance creates a

   a. specific, voluntary lien.
   b. specific, involuntary lien.
   c. general, voluntary lien.
   d. general, involuntary lien.

71. When a person signs a contract without reading it, the contract is

   a. unenforceable.   c. illegal.
   b. void.   d. valid.

72. All of the following circumstances could cause a reappraisal of real property for property taxation *EXCEPT*

    a. a grant received as a gift due to inheritance.
    b. when new ownership is acquired.
    c. if Gordon and her daughter Smith change the method of title to their property to their property to read "Gordon and Smith, as joint tenants."
    d. the creation of a leasehold interest for a term of 35 years or more.

73. An exclusive-right-to-sell listing provides the principal with the right to

    a. revoke it, and could be liable for breach of contract.
    b. record a revocation if the agency relationship is from a recorded agreement.
    c. revoke it unless the real estate agent has an interest coupled with the agency relationship in subject property.
    d. All of the above

74. The term *market value* of real estate most nearly refers to the

    a. estimated value that was determined by considering the current prices of labor and materials needed to replace the improvements at the present time.
    b. estimate of value as determined by a fee appraiser or experienced real estate broker.
    c. expected price if a reasonable amount of time is given to find a ready, willing, and able buyer, with both buyer and seller knowledgeable about current market conditions.
    d. present value of the income that is expected to be produced over the remaining productive life of the property.

75. A prospective buyer has negotiated a six-month option on rental units by paying the owner a $700 deposit. Regarding option agreements, all of the following are correct *EXCEPT*

    a. the agreement carries no obligation on the part of the optionee to purchase the property.
    b. the optionee has the right to mortgage the property.
    c. a unilateral contract has been created between the optionor and the optionee.
    d. because the optionor has received valuable consideration, he cannot revoke the offer.

76. Regarding a second trust deed and its rights, it is

    a. usually in a highly secured position in the event of default.
    b. always protected, even if it includes a subordination clause.
    c. not a bar to a deficiency judgment.
    d. always in a junior position to a judgment lien.

77. The determining factor of a fixture is

    a. the degree of permanence of the annexation of the fixture.
    b. that it is inseparable from a chattel mortgage.
    c. that it is in an extraordinary relationship with the land.
    d. All of the above

78. Tenant Ray negotiates a lease with landlord Reese. The lease will extend for more than one year, and therefore,

    a. the lease must be signed by Ray.
    b. the lease must be acknowledged by Reese.
    c. a description of the property must be included in the lease agreement.
    d. the lease must be signed by both Ray and Reese.

79. Which of the following is a primary benefit of a net lease?

    a. Lessee receives net income.
    b. Lessor receives a percentage of the monthly gross income.
    c. Lessor receives net income.
    d. Lessor receives rent and then pays property taxes and insurance premiums.

80. Carter enters into an agreement to sell his community property. Mrs. Carter has not signed the sales agreement. This agreement is

    a. unenforceable.   c. valid.
    b. void.   d. illegal.

81. An example of police power is

    a. a judgment lien.
    b. a property tax lien.
    c. building codes.
    d. an assessment lien.

82. Which does not constitute a release or satisfaction of a judgment?

    a. Court order
    b. Order by the levying officer
    c. Release by the plaintiff
    d. Judgment in favor of the plaintiff

83. An attachment lien is valid for _____ years.

    a. two   c. four
    b. three   d. ten

84. A mechanic's lien filed today would take priority over a(n)

    a. tax lien.
    b. trust deed recorded yesterday.
    c. unrecorded trust deed executed last week.
    d. Both *a* and *b*

85. The way to create private restrictions on the use of land is by

    a. written agreement.
    b. private land use controls.
    c. general plan restrictions created in the sale of subdivisions.
    d. All of the above

86. Assess value on the real property tax rolls is shown as _____ percent of taxable values.

    a. 1   c. 25
    b. 2   d. 100

87. Smith purchases a piece of real property for $83,000 and agrees to assume $1,800 as a special assessment for new roads. The cost basis for the property is

    a. $81,200.
    b. $84,800.
    c. $83,000.
    d. the same as the purchase price, as special assessment bonds are not assumable by buyers.

88. The main reason a developer wishes to purchase six adjoining lots is for

    a. plottage in anticipation of assemblage increment.
    b. assemblage in anticipation of plottage increment.
    c. assemblage in anticipation of assessment.
    d. plottage in anticipation of highest and best use.

89. In the preparation of a corporation's tax return, which of the following is a description of a firm that has elected to be treated as an S corporation under the Internal Revenue Code?

    a. One whose profits are not taxable
    b. A corporation that cannot hold title to real property
    c. A corporation whose stockholders are allowed to report income and losses as ordinary income
    d. None of the above

90. The term *economic rent* as it is used in the valuation process refers to

    a. contract rent.
    b. the reasonable amount of rent that can be expected from a property at the time of the appraisal.
    c. market rent.
    d. None of the above

91. There are bad sewer lines in a given neighborhood. This is an example of

    a. physical deterioration/curable.
    b. functional obsolescence/curable.
    c. functional obsolescence/incurable.
    d. external obsolescence.

92. The appraised value of a long-term lease agreement is based on

    a. its original lease amount plus any rent adjustments to the lease over the term of the lease.
    b. the lessor's interest minus the lessee's interest.
    c. the creditworthiness of the lessee.
    d. None of the above

93. Gross income of property refers to

    a. total income from property before deducting a vacancy factor and operating expenses.
    b. income that remains after deducting a vacancy factor.
    c. income that remains after deducting a vacancy factor and operating expenses.
    d. income that remains after deducting a vacancy factor, operating expenses, and the mortgage payment.

94. Tracy owns income property and has deducted $10,000 for depreciation purposes. Which of the following is most correct?

    a. $10,000 will be added to the cost basis of the property.
    b. $10,000 will be subtracted from the cost basis of the property.
    c. The basis of the property will not be adjusted until the property is sold.
    d. None of the above

95. In urban areas, neighborhood analysis of property is required due to

    a. the number of transactions that will affect value stability.
    b. employment opportunities that affect the demand for properties in a given neighborhood.
    c. immobility of real property.
    d. All of the above

96. Regarding supplemental tax assessments for additional improvements made to a piece of property, a lien attaches

    a. when the improvements are completed.
    b. when the improvements are assessed.
    c. only if the cost of the improvement exceeds $400.
    d. on March 1 after improvements are completed.

97. Of the following, the only choice that contains general liens is

    a. decedent's debts, franchise taxes, inheritance taxes, and judgments.
    b. franchise taxes, mortgages, judgments, and assessments.
    c. property taxes, attachments, and judgments.
    d. blanket trust deeds, attachments, property taxes, and judgments.

98. Mrs. Ortega holds a life estate interest on a certain parcel in Los Angeles County. Mrs. Ortega's neighbor asks for an easement on the parcel. The easement

    a. can be granted by Mrs. Ortega.
    b. can be granted by Mrs. Ortega but only for the duration of the life estate.
    c. can be granted only by permission from the reversionary fee holder.
    d. cannot be granted by Mrs. Ortega.

99. Landlord Abel can evict tenant Baker

    a. after serving a three-day notice to pay or quit.
    b. after filing a notice of default against Baker.
    c. after serving Baker with a 30-day notice to vacate.
    d. On receiving a judgment against Baker.

100. Due to the curvature of the earth, the sections along the north and west boundaries of each township are about 50 feet shorter than one the south side. Due to this irregularity, additional lines called *guide meridians* and *standard parallels* are used to correct these differences. These correction lines run every _____ miles.

    a. 24   c. 18
    b. 22   d. 6

■ ANSWER KEY

1. a. No fee can be charged for the preparation and issuance of the Uniform Settlement Statement.

2. a. The Truth-in-Lending Act does not regulate advertisements by homeowners. It does, however, regulate advertising by businesses that offer consumer loans for personal or household purposes.

3. d. Statement of fact.

4. c. Statement of fact.

5. b. Statement of fact.

6. b. Statement of fact.

7. c. Statement of fact.

8. d. A real estate investment trust must be beneficially owned by a minimum of 100 investors. Ninety-five percent or more of its ordinary income must be disbursed annually to its shareholders. At least 75 percent of the income must be from *real estate* investments.

9. d. Statement of fact.

10. c. Statement of fact.

11. c. There are five years from June 30 to redeem tax-defaulted real property. If there is no redemption within this time period, the title to the property is deeded to the *state*, and the tax collector conducts the sale.

12. d. Restricting the sale of the property to only members of the seller's church is an example of a restraint of trade. Therefore, the restriction is unenforceable.

13. a. An easement in gross is a personal right given for a specific purpose. In this case, only John has the right to cross the property and only for the purpose of fishing. Therefore, John holds an easement in gross. If the question ended with "until I say you can't," or similar words that provide for the revocation of the right at the will of Adam, then the answer would have been "a license."

14. d. Statement of fact.

15. b. Statement of fact. This data is available on written request to the U.S. Department of Labor Statistics, San Francisco.

16. d. Statement of fact. Choices *a*, *b*, and *c* are items that belong to the common area, not to the condominium unit.

17. d. Statement of fact.

18. c. Statement of fact.

19. d. Statement of fact.

20. c. Statement of fact.

21. c. Statement of fact.

22. d. A prepaid rental listing service must present information to its clients on at least three actual rentals within five days of receipt of a fee. The requirement of a notice to the client list of an upcoming relocation *before* the move is to minimize the chance of a client not being given the information for which the fee was paid.

23. d. Statement of fact.

24. b. Statement of fact.

25. d. Statement of fact.

26. c. Statement of fact.

27. a. The terms of the offer cannot be illusory; they must be specific. The example in the question includes a contingency to "prelease 80 percent of the units," which is illusory.

28. b. There is no contract. A counteroffer terminates the original offer and is considered a new offer, which in this case was rejected by the prospective purchaser.

29. d. Statement of fact.

30. b. Acknowledgment (notarization) of a grant deed merely prepares the deed for recording. Acknowledgment does not ensure that a valid title has passed. Also, a deed must be acknowledged to be used as prima facie evidence in a court matter.

31. c. Heirs are covered by the title insurance policy on the property of the deceased until the property is sold.

32. a. Statement of fact. The question refers to personal property.

33. d. Currently, a veteran is allowed to pay a reasonable amount of discount points on a refinance or a purchase loan.

34. b. Statement of fact.

35. c. Statement of fact.

36. d. Statement of fact.

37. d. Most construction lenders will not release the final installment of loan funds until the mechanic's lien period has expired. Most will wait at least 90 days and not date the check for the final payment until the 91st or 92nd day.

38. a. Statement of fact.

39. d. Statement of fact.

40. b. Statement of fact.

41. d. A real property sales contract is another name for a land contract. The buyer, Ann, does not yet have legal title to the property and, therefore, cannot use a grant deed to transfer her interest to Baker. However, Ann can assign her vendee interest to Baker.

42. a. The agreement between the licensee and the buyer is not illegal as long as it is made known to the seller before the seller accepts the offer.

43. c. The beneficiary (seller) on an all-inclusive trust deed is the party responsible for continuing to make the payments to the lender on the underlying loan.

44. b. The listing price is considered the ceiling of market value. The offered price is considered to be the lowest probable value.

45. c. The names and addresses of the transferor's creditors are not required to appear in the bulk sale notice. However, the purpose of the public notice is to alert creditors of an upcoming transfer of the bulk of the inventory of a business.

46. c. Statement of fact.

47. d. The word *appear* is missing from the question. Colors do not alter room sizes, merely appearances.

48. c. Statement of fact.

49. d. Statement of fact.

50. c. A general partnership agreement does not come under the statute of frauds.

51. b. Statement of fact.

52. c. Statement of fact.

53. b. Because more than eight notes were bought and sold within a 12-month period, a real estate broker's license is required for the transactions.

54. b. Statement of fact.

55. b. Statement of fact.

56. d. Recall that a grant deed requires delivery, not recordation. Delivery is evidenced by the recordation of the deed *or* the possession of the deed by the grantee.

57. a. Statement of fact.

58. d. A standard title insurance policy, which Sam and Judy received, does not protect for loss of value due to a misplaced improvement, its costs to correct, or damages to neighbors. Typically, a standard policy protects against matters of public record, forgery in the chain of title, and lack of capacity of the parties to the transaction. The ALTA policy that was purchased by the buyers for the leader would cover more than the standard, but it only protects the lender and not the buyers.

59. c. Statement of fact.

60. d. The question asks for the exception. Recall that depreciation occurs from forces that are both inherent (inside) and extraneous (outside).

61. d. Statement of fact.

62. c. In a dual agency, the broker cannot reveal the seller's lowest price or the buyer's highest price without their consent.

63. b. Statement of fact.

64. b. Statement of fact.

65. d. The State Housing Law applies to *unincorporated* areas, even if the county has a building code.

66. d. Statement of fact.

67. a. A basic contract does not require a proper writing for the validity of the contract. However, under the statute of frauds, certain agreements, including real estate contracts, require a proper writing for the purpose of enforceability of the contracts.

68. c. An easement in gross held by a utility company is a nonpossessory interest; it conveys the right of use. A lease agreement is an example of a possessory interest in the land of another.

69. b. Statement of fact.

70. a. Statement of fact.

71. d. A contract is valid on signing it, even if one neglects to read it first.

72. c. Statement of fact.

73. d. Statement of fact.

74. c. Statement of fact.

75. b. The question asks for the exception. The optionee (prospective buyer) does not as yet have title to the property and cannot mortgage it.

76. c. In California, when a lender elects to foreclose under a power of sale clause (a public sale), there is a complete bar (prohibition) against a deficiency judgment. A deficiency judgment is a personal judgment against the debtor for the difference between the account owing on the debt and the net proceeds from a *court* foreclosure sale. Deficiency judgments are prohibited on purchase-money transactions (except for FHA and DVA loans, even if state law prohibits it, as they are federal programs). However, if a third-party lender provides funds to a buyer of residential property of more than four units, investment or commercial property, industrial property, raw land, or residential property of one to four units that are not owner-occupied, as in a junior trust deed, the lender under these circumstances may seek a deficiency judgment in a court foreclosure.

77. a.   Statement of fact.

78. c.   Statement of fact.

79. c.   Statement of fact.

80. a.   An agreement for the *sale* of community property that is signed by only one spouse is unenforceable. The signatures of both spouses are required for the *sale* of community property. However, a *listing* signed by one spouse alone is enforceable.

81. c.   The establishing of building codes is for the benefit of the general public and is one of the many examples of police power.

82. d.   A judgment in favor of a plaintiff creates a judgment. The question asks for a release or satisfaction of a judgment.

83. b.   Statement of fact.

84. c.   Statement of fact.

85. d.   Statement of fact.

86. d.   Statement of fact.

87. b.   The $1,800 special assessment can be added to the cost basis of the property.

88. b.   The combining of adjoining lots is done in anticipation of a higher value for the newly created large lot. The term *plottage increment* refers to an increased value.

89. c.   A main feature of an S corporation is no double taxation like that of a regular corporation. All profits and losses pass through to the stockholders. The stockholder reports his or her share of the ordinary income and/or losses and can deduct losses on the individual personal tax return.

90. b.   Statement of fact.

91. d.   Bad sewer lines in a neighborhood are an example of external or economic obsolescence, which occurs outside property lines and over which the owner has little or no control.

92. a.   Statement of fact.

93. a.   Statement of fact.

94. b.   Statement of fact.

95. d.   Statement of fact.

96. a.   Statement of fact.

97. a.   This choice includes only general liens that can affect all of a debtor's property. Property taxes, attachments, and mortgages are examples of specific liens that affect only a particular parcel.

98. b.   Statement of fact.

99. c.   Statement of fact.

100. a.   Statement of fact.

BROKER APPENDIX
Practice Examination V

1. On a commercial lease, HVAC stands for

   a. heating/ventilation/air-conditioning.
   b. high voltage/alternating current.
   c. housing/vacancy and controls.
   d. None of the above

2. Who customarily has the right to call for a loan payoff?

   a. Agent   c. Trustor
   b. Escrow officer   d. Seller

3. Andrew and his two brothers owned property as joint tenants. Andrew died and had willed his interest to a third party. Which of the following is correct?

   a. Andrew's interest expires.
   b. The other joint tenants who are brothers of Andrew become tenants in common with the new third party.
   c. There is a right of succession.
   d. The third party becomes a joint tenant with the two brothers.

4. Sales tax paid on the sale of a business opportunity applies to

   a. furniture and fixtures.
   b. stock on the shelves.
   c. the value of goodwill.
   d. accounts receivable.

5. In which of the following is a commission due to an agent?

   a. The buyer's agent takes the offer to the seller.
   b. The buyer's agent takes the offer to the selling agent and the seller.
   c. When the seller and buyer agree to the terms of the sale
   d. When the buyer himself takes the offer to the seller and his agent

6. Which of the following would be found in the elevation plan of the Smiths' home?

   a. Any backfill and excavation work
   b. The rooflines and exterior of the home
   c. The improvements, street, and sidewalks
   d. None of the above

7. What is most commonly called the company dollar?

   a. Gross income less office expenses
   b. Gross income less commissions
   c. Total gross income
   d. Gross income less commissions, office expenses, and insurance premiums

8. The best method to maintain the maximum value for a piece of property may be attained by

   a. conforming to the original land use plan.
   b. allowing a thoroughfare to be built through the neighborhood.
   c. allowing variances for the highest and best use.
   d. All of the above

9. The consumer price index is customarily used in which of the following?

   a. Single-family residences
   b. Apartment rental agreements
   c. Commercial properties
   d. Industrial properties

10. The formula for determining the volume of a gable roof is

   a. length × width × height.
   b. length × width × height ÷ 2.
   c. length × width × height ÷ 4.
   d. length × width × height × 2.

11. The Equal Dignities Rule states that to be enforceable,

   a. the authority to enter into a contract required by law to be in writing must also be written.
   b. the authority to enter into a contract need not be written.
   c. a real estate contract may be either written or verbal.
   d. None of the above

12. The Franchise Investment Law is designed to

   a. be just and provide fair treatment for all.
   b. protect franchisors whose offerings are under $50,000.
   c. protect prospective franchisees intending to purchase a franchise.
   d. None of the above

13. Crowell paid $100,000 cash for a vacant lot. She arranged to build an improvement on the lot that cost $500,000. She paid $100,000 down and executed a promissory note and first trust deed for $400,000 at 8 percent interest. On what amount is depreciation calculated?

   a. $100,000   c. $400,000
   b. $200,000   d. $500,000

14. The mixing of the principal's funds with the broker's money is known as

   a. conversion.
   b. commingling.
   c. good business practice.
   d. a requirement during the negotiation stages of an offer.

15. If a mortgage banker is involved initially in a real estate transaction, he or she does which of the following?

   a. Reviews credit and qualifies the buyer
   b. Physically transfers cash for the transaction from the bank to the seller
   c. Puts up the money for a short term initially and then sells the loan to investors
   d. Appraises the subject property and prepares all of the necessary paperwork for the lending agency

16. When brokering a loan, the amortization tables would most likely be used to determine the

   a. annual percentage rate.
   b. monthly payment.
   c. interest rate.
   d. length of the loan.

17. In general, a mechanic who is installing a hardwood floor may file a lien at

   a. the beginning or first date work was done at the building.
   b. the beginning of installation of the hardwood floor.
   c. completion of the building.
   d. completion of hardwood flooring.

18. Withdrawals from a broker's trust account can be made

   a. by a salesperson employed by and authorized in writing by the broker.
   b. by an unlicensed employee of the broker with a fidelity bond.
   c. from the trust account of a corporate broker upon the signature of an officer of a licensed corporation.
   d. All of the above

19. All of the following are secondary benefits from the National Housing Act of 1934 *EXCEPT*

   a. established maximum property requirements.
   b. a comprehensive valuation system.
   c. scientific subdivision planning.
   d. stimulation of mortgage investment on a national basis.

20. Which of the following is most correct concerning real estate loans granted by commercial banks?

   a. Interest must be paid in advance.
   b. These loans increase the bank's liquidity.
   c. The bank usually charges a discount when making a loan.
   d. The discount rate for the loans is in direct proportion to the amortization period.

21. Which of the following will terminate an offer to purchase?

   a. Rejection by the offeror
   b. Revocation by the offeree
   c. Requiring offeree to accept changes
   d. Revocation by the offeror

22. When filing an income tax return for a general partnership, which of the following is true?

   a. The partnership does not pay income taxes.
   b. The partners share in profits and will pay taxes on their share of the partnership income.
   c. The partnership must file an income tax return.
   d. All of the above

23. A valid deed must contain all of the following *EXCEPT*

   a. a granting clause.
   b. the signature of the grantor.
   c. an adequate description of the property.
   d. an acknowledgment of the grantor's signature.

24. Contracts made by a person with mental problems are automatically void when

   a. the person sees a psychiatrist twice a week and is unable to work.
   b. a person has mental problems but is able to work.
   c. a person admits himself into a mental institution.
   d. a conservatorship has been appointed over the person's estate.

25. An owner of land with nonriparian rights is granted use of water form a stream or lake by the state. This use was acquired by

   a. percolation.   c. allocation.
   b. prescription.   d. accretion.

26. Which of the following would appear as a credit on the seller's closing statement?

   a. Cash charge for the buyer's deed
   b. Proration for prepaid rents
   c. Proration for prepaid taxes
   d. Cash charge for recording a quitclaim deed

27. Failure to disclose a material fact is known as

   a. innocent misrepresentation.
   b. malicious misrepresentation.
   c. negligent misrepresentation.
   d. fraudulent misrepresentation.

28. A father placed property in the names of his three sons, Albert, Carl, and Bill, as joint tenants. Bill sold his interest to Wes. Then Albert died, leaving is son, Steve, as his sole heir. How is title held?

   a. Steve owns ⅓ interest with the others as tenants in common.
   b. Carl owns ⅔ interest with Wes, who has ⅓, and they are tenants in common.
   c. There is a newly formed joint tenancy between all parties.
   d. Ownership must be established by the probate process.

29. Which of the following is ordered after a judgment?

   a. A writ of execution
   b. An attachment
   c. A lis pendens
   d. None of the above

30. Escrow closes on May 1, 2002. Property taxes for the fiscal year 2002-2003 are a

   a. seller's personal responsibility.
   b. buyer's personal responsibility.
   c. lien on the property.
   d. None of the above

31. The party who holds equitable title in a real property sales contract is the

   a. vendee.   c. trustee.
   b. vendor.   d. beneficiary.

32. The balances on the buyer's and seller's settlement statements

   a. must be different.
   b. can be different.
   c. must be the same.
   d. None of the above

33. An acre of land measures

     a. 43,560 square feet.
     b. 4,840 square yards.
     c. 160 square rods.
     d. All of the above

34. The term *blockbusting* describes an illegal and discriminatory practice by speculators or real estate agents who induce the quick selling of property at prices below market value by exploiting the prejudices of property owners. Other terms used to describe this practice are

     a. panic selling.
     b. panic peddling.
     c. Both *a* and *b*
     d. Neither *a* nor *b*

35. When a subdivider submits an application to the Real Estate Commissioner concerning a new subdivision and requests a final public report, all of the following are required, EXCEPT

     a. copies of the sale contract to be used in the sale of the houses.
     b. floor plans of the proposed houses.
     c. a report on the condition of title.
     d. provisions made for the completion of utilities and recreational facilities.

36. A lender is in violation of the federal Equal Credit Opportunity Act when refusing to lend in all of the following situations EXCEPT

     a. when the applicant is of a minority race.
     b. if the applicant is older than 75 years of age.
     c. if the applicant has a poor credit history.
     d. when the applicant is divorced.

37. A licensee is found guilty of violating the Real Estate Commissioner's regulations concerning antidiscrimination. What legal action can the commissioner take against the licensee?

     a. Demand punitive damages to discourage any such violation in the future
     b. Sue for damages incurred
     c. Revoke or suspend the license of the agent
     d. All of the above

38. An encumbrance could include a

     a. homestead declaration.
     b. fee simple interest.
     c. lease agreement.
     d. None of the above

39. Title insurance policies will not protect against

     a. the signature of only one spouse in the sale of community real property.
     b. a forgery in the chain of title.
     c. city taxes that are unpaid and are not an exception from the policy coverage.
     d. a change in local zoning ordinances.

40. A developer who offers land found in Colorado for sale to California residents must comply with special filings with the

     a. Federal Trade Commission.
     b. Department of Real Estate.
     c. Secretary of State.
     d. Department of Corporations.

41. A legal description of property that uses monuments or markers to describe a certain parcel of land is not the most desirable nor accurate method and could be considered defective, as

    a. the monuments could be destroyed.
    b. it is difficult to find title companies that will insure title where descriptions are based on the use of monuments and markers.
    c. there is no apparent evidence of range lines.
    d. None of the above

42. A developer would be exempt from the Interstate Land Sales Disclosure Act if each parcel offered for sale in several different states contains

    a. 5 acres.
    b. 10 acres
    c. 20 acres.
    d. None of the above

43. There are houses found in certain areas of the state where woodframe construction is attacked by wood-destroying pests. As a result, a structural pest control report would be required

    a. for all woodframe construction.
    b. for FHA or DVA loans being used for the purchase by the buyer.
    c. if requested by the buyer.
    d. All of the above

44. In the event a licensee discriminates against a minority party, what action may the aggrieved party take?

    a. Collect punitive damages of not less than $250
    b. Actual and punitive damages
    c. Request revocation and suspension of the license of the agent
    d. None of the above

45. A lien is a(n)

    a. easement.
    b. restriction.
    c. trust deed.
    d. All of the above

46. Thomas owns a business opportunity and wants to know if sales tax is imposed on the sale of certain property within his business. He would contact which of the following state agencies?

    a. Franchise Tax Board
    b. Board of Equalization
    c. Department of Corporation
    d. Real Estate Commissioner

47. Who may not terminate an agreement for the purchase and sale of real property if such contract is not completed?

    a. Seller of residential property
    b. Buyer of an apartment building
    c. Attorney-in-fact representing a principal in a real estate transaction
    d. Broker representing a buyer

48. Riparian rights of an owner refer to

    a. rivers and streams.
    b. subterranean caves.
    c. bays and arms of the sea.
    d. lakes.

49. Standard title insurance policies protect the insured from

    a. defects known to the insured that are not disclosed to the insurance company.
    b. forgery in the chain of recorded title.
    c. zoning changes.
    d. rights of parties in possession.

50. Which one of the following parties may enter into a contract?

    a. Minors
    b. Aliens
    c. Convicts
    d. Children under the ward of the court

51. Successor's liability is set by the State

    a. Franchise Tax Board.
    b. Board of Equalization.
    c. Department of Corporations.
    d. Real Estate Commissioner.

52. The correct statement regarding an attachment and a judgment is that

    a. an abstract of judgment is recorded after the attachment.
    b. the attachment is a voluntary lien and so is the judgment.
    c. the attachment is a general lien and the judgment is a specific lien.
    d. both actions can be handled privately between the parties.

53. Which of the following has the authority to enforce local building codes?

    a. Planning commission
    b. State contractor's license agency
    c. Building inspector
    d. County assessor

54. What is the quickest and most efficient method for the estimation of building costs?

    a. Cubic feet
    b. Quantity survey
    c. Unit-in-place
    d. Comparative

55. In the valuation of a business opportunity, an appraiser would give the most weight to

    a. the value of goodwill.
    b. annual gross sales.
    c. monthly gross sales.
    d. annual net income.

56. Appraiser Jensen is assigned to estimate the value of land. He can use all of the following methods approach *EXCEPT* the

    a. market data approach.
    b. equity approach.
    c. development method.
    d. abstraction method.

57. Borrower Abel paid four points to ABC lender for a home loan. ABC then sold the loan to an insurance company for a 3.5 percent discount. The amount paid by the insurance company was $69,580. Based on this information, the face amount of the loan was

    a. $74,191.03.
    b. $72,103.63.
    c. $73,103.63.
    d. None of the above

58. All of the following are tests of a fixture *EXCEPT*

    a. the relationship of the parties.
    b. the method of annexation.
    c. the cost of the fixture.
    d. agreements.

59. Homeowner Baker is preparing her income tax return. For federal income tax filing purposes, she can deduct

    a. mortgage interest and any prepayment penalty.
    b. mortgage interest, property taxes, and any prepayment penalty.
    c. mortgage interest, principal and interest payments, and property taxes.
    d. mortgage interest, capital improvements, and property taxes.

60. In the appraisal process, the expression "the right to future benefits" relates to

    a. equity.   c. value.
    b. cost.   d. price paid.

61. Hawkins is seeking permission to use his property in a manner that deviates from the local building code requirements. It is possible that he will be granted a(n)

    a. variance.
    b. permit.
    c. exception to use.
    d. license.

62. Which of the following would not be grounds for an unlawful detailer action?

    a. Unlawful entry by the lessor
    b. Default in rental payments
    c. Violation of rental agreement conditions
    d. Holdover tenants

63. The party having legal title to property when its loan is in default is the

    a. beneficiary.   c. trustor.
    b. trustee.   d. court.

64. Loans for the following properties are regulated by the Truth-in-Lending Act, with the *EXCEPTION* of

    a. a business.
    b. duplexes that are owner-occupied.
    c. a mobile home as a primary residence.
    d. a single-family residence for owner-occupancy purposes.

65. The type of account where a bank would require a borrower to maintain an offsetting balance until a loan is paid in full is a(n)

    a. pledged savings account mortgage.
    b. adjustable rate mortgage.
    c. renegotiable rate mortgage.
    d. participation mortgage.

66. The term *liquidity* when used for a business is best described as

    a. total assets minus total liabilities.
    b. total capital minus total liabilities.
    c. current assets minus current liabilities.
    d. sales minus accounts payable.

67. The expression *after-acquired title* that goes with the use of a grant deed conveys

    a. improvements built on the land after title is acquired by the grantee.
    b. title to any personal property that will be affixed to the real property conveyed.
    c. additional land acquired later by the trustor that becomes part of the subject property.
    d. All of the above

68. Which of the following would be considered the original basis of property for federal income taxation purposes?

    a. Purchaser price plus current capital improvements
    b. Purchaser price
    c. Purchase price plus capital improvements minus depreciation
    d. Fair market value at the time of purchase

69. The legal due date for the second installment of property taxes and the last day for payment before delinquency are

    a. November 1 and December 10.
    b. March 1 and July 1.
    c. February 1 and March 1.
    d. February 1 and April 10.

70. Anderson completes a purchase contract and receipt for deposit and inserts in the financing clause that the offer for the home is "subject to" buyer Leon's obtaining a second trust deed. The seller accepts the offer and escrow is opened. During the escrow process, Leon was turned down for the second trust deed. In this case

    a. the seller may retain one-half of the deposit.
    b. Leon's deposit will be returned to him in full.
    c. the seller may use the liquidated damages clause and retain the entire deposit.
    d. the seller is entitled to file a specific performance lawsuit against Leon.

71. Stewart constructs a $500,000 home for his personal use in a neighborhood whose value range is between $200,000 and $250,000. Which of the following best describes this type of depreciation?

    a. Physical obsolescence
    b. Functional obsolescence
    c. Economic obsolescence
    d. Deferred maintenance

72. Broker Travis advertises a property for sale on television and says he will present a microwave oven worth $500 as a gift to the buyer of this property using his services. Travis may

    a. do this as long as the gift is actually given and there is a full disclosure made to all interested parties.
    b. not do this, as it is illegal, regardless of the number of disclosures made.
    c. do this if it is called a prize for a drawing.
    d. not do this, as the gift is more expensive than the law allows.

73. A mortgage broker

    a. is required to have a real estate broker's license.
    b. does not have to hold a real estate broker's license.
    c. does not have to hold a real estate broker's license because he or she does not lend money directly but acts as a matchmaker.
    d. is required to have a real estate broker's license due to the servicing of loans as a major part of the mortgage broker's work.

74. The home of Mr. Evans was appraised at $110,000. He wishes to refinance his home and borrow $25,000 against the equity. The lender that is least likely to refinance a home is a

a. savings and loan association.
b. commercial bank.
c. life insurance company.
d. private party.

75. Which of the following would be considered a trade fixture?

a. Underground gasoline tanks
b. A marble entry to an office building
c. Skylights in an apartment building
d. Display shelves attached to a wall

76. In a residential subdivision, the least desirable lot is the

a. corner lot.   c. middle lot.
b. key lot.   d. flag lot.

77. Johnson owns an apartment building and decided to add a swimming pool. Johnson should be concerned with the principle of

a. contribution.
b. regression.
c. progression.
d. increasing and decreasing returns.

78. The term *quiet title* describes

a. the quiet enjoyment and possession of property that tenants are entitled to.
b. a court action.
c. a promise to transfer title in the future.
d. a cloud on title.

79. Anyone who requests it is entitled to see a copy of a subdivision's final public report. Buyer Jones was asked to sign a receipt to evidence that she was given a copy of this report. The receipt for the final public report

a. is a duplicate form that was signed and dated by Jones.
b. is incorporated into the deposit receipt.
c. is on an approved form.
d. requires Jones' signature and date in a prenumbered receipt book.

80. The expression *megalopolis* refers to

a. retail centers.
b. very large cities.
c. industrial parks.
d. rural areas.

81. Chang gave an option for one year to Travis to purchase Chang's farm. This transaction is a(n)

a. offer to keep a contract open.
b. relationship of loyalty and trust.
c. contract to keep an offer open.
d. agency relationship.

82. Broker Peale has decided to open her own real estate company. The opening of a new office should be based on

a. familiarity with all of the surrounding neighborhoods.
b. Peale's objectives and goals.
c. her area of specialization.
d. the amount of disposable funds available.

83. The brother of a real estate broker bought a piece of property and paid the full price that was shown on the listing agreement. The broker represented his brother in the negotiations but failed to disclose their relationship to the seller. After the escrow closed, the seller became aware of the special relationship. The recourse available is

    a. to ask the Real Estate Commissioner to hear the anticipated dispute.
    b. for the seller to rescind the contract, take the property back and sue the broker.
    c. nothing as the contract was valid because there was a full price offer.
    d. for the seller to sue the broker.

84. If a broker intentionally withholds a material fact, the broker is guilty of

    a. fraud.
    b. misrepresentation.
    c. a misdemeanor.
    d. All of the above

85. Buyer Abel has presented an offer on a home that the seller has accepted. During the escrow period, Abel wants to begin making repairs on the property. The proper way to arrange this is

    a. for the buyer and the seller to execute an amendment to the escrow instructions.
    b. to ask the listing broker to allow Abel to enter the property.
    c. to have the seller agree to allow Abel to make the repairs.
    d. for the buyer to proceed with the repairs.

86. A Chicano buyer wishes to see homes for sale in his present neighborhood. If he does not indicate that he is interested in looking at homes in other neighborhoods, you as a licensee should show him homes

    a. that he specifically wants to see.
    b. only in his own neighborhood, as he does not appear to be interested in other areas.
    c. as you would when dealing with any other prospective buyer.
    d. only in the location that the buyer wants to see.

87. As an agent in a real estate transaction, a broker is required to follow the lawful instructions of his or her principal. Failure to do so by the broker could result in

    a. damages for failure to follow instructions.
    b. a fine or imprisonment.
    c. loss of licensing.
    d. All of the above

88. The buyer of real property waived his right to receive a settlement statement prior to the close of escrow. In this case, how long does the escrow holder have to send a copy of the statement to the buyer?

    a. Not later than three business days after the close of escrow
    b. As soon as is reasonably possible
    c. On or before the close of escrow
    d. None of the above

89. The Truth-in-Lending Act applies to all of the following *EXCEPT*

    a. a mortgage company making numerous consumer loans each year.
    b. on a loan with no finance charge that will be paid in full in four quarterly installments.
    c. on home loans made by savings and loan associations for refinancing purposes.
    d. on an assumption of a first trust deed.

90. Under the California Veterans Farm and Home Purchase Act, a transfer of ownership is made by

    a. grant deed.
    b. warranty deed.
    c. a real property sales contract.
    d. None of the above

91. A trustor is two months in arrears on her mortgage payments. A notice of default has been recorded. The trustor

    a. has the right to stall the foreclosure action by any means.
    b. has the right of replevin.
    c. is entitled to the right of reinstatement of the loan.
    d. None of the above

92. The primary difference between a mortgage broker and a mortgage banker is that a mortgage

    a. broker services loans.
    b. banker does not lend its own money.
    c. broker arranges loans between borrowers and lenders.
    d. broker does require a real estate broker's license but a mortgage banker does not.

93. In general, the smaller the down payment for the purchase of property, the longer the loan, the

    a. more total principal paid over the life of the loan.
    b. more total interest paid over the life of the loan.
    c. less total interest paid over the life of the loan.
    d. smaller the monthly mortgage payment.

94. The one similarity between trust deeds and mortgage contracts is the

    a. number of parties to the loan.
    b. redemption period.
    c. reinstatement period before foreclosure.
    d. security.

95. Private mortgage insurance companies are funded

    a. through insurance premiums and the issuing of debt and equity securities.
    b. by savings deposits.
    c. by money market accounts.
    d. All of the above

96. The importance of an environmental impact report is that it

    a. identifies adverse environmental effects.
    b. assesses possible alternatives to a project.
    c. further identifies any direct or indirect impact a project could have on the environment.
    d. All of the above

97. The sequence for the development of a residential property is

    a. planning, bonding, designing, mapping.
    b. bonding, mapping, planning, designing.
    c. planning, designing, bonding, mapping.
    d. planning, acquisition, mapping, designing.

98. Architect John has been hired to draw preliminary plans for a new project. These plans and drawings, which include preliminary building designs, elevations, and architectural renderings are also called

    a. foundation plans.
    b. subdivision maps.
    c. assemblage.
    d. schematics.

99. A common advantage for one who invests in real estate as compared with those who invest in stocks and bonds is the potential for

    a. a better treatment for capital gain.
    b. depreciation.
    c. appreciation.
    d. a favorable return during the period of ownership of the investment.

100. To arrive at the final estimate of value in the appraisal process, the appraiser

    a. combines the data from the estimates of value from the three appraisal approaches.
    b. averages the estimates of value from the market data, cost, and income approaches.
    c. reconciles the three estimates derived from the market data, cost, and income approaches.
    d. completes the report.

■ ANSWER KEY

1. a. Statement of fact.

2. b. Statement of fact.

3. a. Andrew's interest expires. Due to the right of survivorship in a joint tenancy, Andrew's interest would sift down to the two remaining brothers who continue as joint tenants. The will left by Andrew would not be valid. Remember, there is no right to will under a joint tenancy.

4. a. Statement of fact.

5. c. Statement of fact.

6. b. Statement of fact.

7. b. The company dollar refers to the dollars remaining after all commissions, including cooperative broker commission splits, are paid. The company dollar is then used to pay office expenses.

8. a. Statement of fact.

9. c. Consumer price indices are often used for rent adjustments in commercial leases, especially the CPI for urban wage earners and clerical workers.

10. b. A gable roof is an A-shaped roof. To find its volume, use this formula: length × width × height ÷ 2.

11. a. The equal dignities rule states that if a contract is required to be in writing, then the authorization to enter into it must also be in writing (there are certain exceptions). For example, under the statute of frauds real estate contracts must be in writing to be enforceable. Therefore, the listing agreement, which authorizes or employs a broker to represent the sale of the property, must also be in writing.

12. c. Statement of fact.

13. d. Depreciation is based only on the value of the improvements. The question states that an improvement valued at $500,000 is placed on the lot. For depreciation purposes, disregard the cost of the lot and the loan amount.

14. b. Statement of fact.

15. c. Most mortgage bankers package their loans for sale into the secondary mortgage market relatively quickly after making the loan.

16. b. Statement of fact.

17. a. Any mechanic's lien on a job takes the date the work of improvement commenced (the date work began on the project).

18. d. Statement of fact.

19. a. The National Housing Act established "minimums," not maximums.

20. c. Most often banks do not wish to deal with constant interest rate fluctuations. Therefore, they can adjust for the changes within the money market by charging discount points to equalize their desired yield.

21. d. Be alert to the wording. An offeror (buyer) may withdraw his or her offer by revoking it (revocation by offeror). An offeree (seller) may turn down the offer by rejecting it (rejection by offeree).

22. d. Statement of fact.

23. d. An acknowledgment (notarization) of the grantor's signature is not a requirement for a valid deed. If the deed is to be recorded, then the acknowledgment is required. Remember, a valid grant deed does not require recording; it requires delivery.

24. d. A conservator is appointed by the court to handle the matters for a person whom the court has declared to be mentally incompetent. If such a person entered into a contract without the conservator, the contract would be void.

25. c. This use granted by the state is under the Doctrine of Appropriations or Allocation.

26. c. If the seller prepaid the property taxes, the amount prepaid would be a credit on the seller's closing statement for the sale of property.

27. d. Failure to disclose a material fact is a form of fraud, whether it occurs in a real estate transaction or any other type of business transaction.

28. b. The interest of Albert passes to Carl under the right of survivorship. Albert's son Steve does not have a valid claim. Carl now owns two-thirds with Wes, who owns one-third, as tenants in common.

29. a. A "writ of execution" is a legal order, issued in the name of the people, sealed with the court seal and subscribed by the judge (or clerk of the court), directing the sheriff (or marshal) to satisfy the judgment out of the property of the judgment debtor. Real property belonging to the debtor and not exempt from execution is seized by the officer and sold at public auction.

30. c. Real property taxes become a lien on property on January 1 preceding each tax year. They are not considered the personal responsibility of a buyer or seller, but rather a lien against the property. The fiscal year for property taxes is from July 1 of any given year to June 30 of the following year.

31. a. The vendee (buyer) of property under a real property sales contract (a land contract) receives only equitable title. Legal title passes when the buyer meets the terms of the contract.

32. b. The balances on a settlement statement for a buyer and seller can be different, as the expenses to each party are not usually the same.

33. d. Statement of fact.

34. c. Statement of fact.

35. b. The question asks for the exception. The concern for "the floor plans of the proposed houses" is not under the jurisdiction of the Real Estate Commissioner under the Subdivided Lands Law (a consumer protection law). It would be a matter for local government under the Subdivision Map Act, which is concerned with the physical aspects of the subdivision.

36. c. Statement of fact.

37. c. Statement of fact.

38. c. A lease conveys the possessory rights and quiet enjoyment of property to the lessee. It precludes possession by the lessor (owner) and is considered to be an encumbrance on the title. An encumbrance is anything that affects or limits the fee simple title to property.

39. d. Statement of fact.

40. b. Because the sale is being made to residents of California, the out-of-state offering must be filed with the California Department of Real Estate.

41. a. Statement of fact.

42. c. Parcels of 20 or more acres are exempt from the Interstate Land Sales Full Disclosure Act.

43. b. Statement of fact.

44. b. Statement of fact.

45. c. A lien is a money encumbrance. A trust deed is a type of lien. Easements and restrictions are types of encumbrances that are concerned with physical matters and are not liens. *All liens are encumbrances, but not all encumbrances are liens.*

46. b. Statement of fact.

47. d. A broker may not terminate a sales agreement. Only the parties to the contract, that is, buyers and sellers, may terminate the agreement.

48. a. Statement of fact.

49. b. Statement of fact.

50. b. Aliens in California may enter into valid contracts in the state.

51. b. Statement of fact.

52. a. Statement of fact.

53. a. Statement of fact.

54. d. The comparative (or sales comparison) method is the fastest and easiest way to estimate building costs. The data needed is readily available through cost manuals, computer programs, and general building sources.

55. d. Statement of fact.

56. b. The question asks for the exception. Equity is not a way to estimate land value.

57. b. $72,103.63. Use the selling price rule to solve discounted note problems. Disregard any points paid. Start with 100 percent, representing the original amount of the mortgage. Deduct the 3.5 percent discount (100% − 3.5% = 96.5%). Now take the amount paid by the insurance company, $69,580, and divide it by .965, which equals $72,103.63.

58. c. Cost is not a test of fixtures. Use MARIA to remember the five tests of a fixture: M—method of attachments, A—adaptability, R—relationship of the parties, I—intention (most important test), A—agreement between the parties.

59. b. For federal income tax purposes, a homeowner can deduct mortgage interest, property taxes, and, don't forget, any prepayment penalty (treated like interest).

60. c. Statement of fact.

61. a. Statement of fact.

62. a. Statement of fact.

63. b. Statement of fact.

64. a. Statement of fact.

65. a. Statement of fact.

66. c. Statement of fact.

67. d. Statement of fact.

68. b. Statement of fact.

69. d. The question asks about the *second* installment of taxes. The legal due date for the second installment is February 1 with its grace period extending to April 10, delinquent on April 11. The legal due date for the first installment is November 1 with its grace period extending to December 10, delinquent on December 11.

70. b. Statement of fact.

71. c. Statement of fact.

72. a. It is legal for a *sales* brokerage to advertise a gift as long as the condition for earning the gift is in the advertisement, full disclosure is made, and the gift is actually given.

73. a. Both a mortgage broker and a mortgage banker are required to have a real estate broker's license of record for the firm. A mortgage broker does not lend its

own money but acts as a matchmaker between a borrower and a lender, for a fee. A mortgage banker lends its own money directly to a borrower. The loan is then sold into the secondary mortgage market. Most often, the mortgage banker is asked to service the loan, collecting service fees its main source of income.

74. c. The life insurance company is the least likely source for home loan refinancing. Life insurance companies prefer to make large commercial and industrial type loans.

75. a. Underground gasoline tanks can be considered trade fixtures. Some communities allow their removal so that they can be used elsewhere. Other communities require that they remain in place, fearing that removal might create a greater hazardous or toxic waste problem.

76. b. The key lot has several other lots on its side yard and is noisy. It is considered to be the least desirable residential lot. The preferred residential lot is the middle lot, as it has less noise and traffic than a corner lot. The preferred commercial lot is the corner lot due to its greater exposure.

77. a. Adding the swimming pool to the apartment building could contribute to an increase in the rent (principle of contribution). The increased income to the building will increase its overall value (value is a function of income on income-producing property). If the swimming pool were being added to a personal residence, the principle of regression would apply, i.e., one would ask, "Is the owner overbuilding for the neighborhood?"

78. b. Statement of fact.

79. c. The form used for the receipt must be approved by the Real Estate Commissioner.

80. b. Statement of fact.

81. c. An option is a unilateral *contract* to keep an *offer* open.

82. c. Statement of fact.

83. b. The broker is required to disclose when acting for a relative or for anyone with whom there is a special relationship. Failure to do so could lead to court action and rescission of the contract.

84. d. Statement of fact.

85. a. Statement of fact.

86. c. Statement of fact.

87. d. Statement of fact.

88. b. Statement of fact.

89. b. Statement of fact.

90. c. Statement of fact.

91. c. A trustor who is two months in arrears can still reinstate (cure) the loan. Currently, a defaulted loan under a trust deed can be reinstated up to five business days before the foreclosure sale is held.

92. c. Statement of fact.

93. b. Statement of fact.

94. d. The one similarity between trust deeds and mortgage contracts is that the property is used as *security* for the loan.

95. a. Statement of fact.

96. d. Statement of fact.

97. d. Statement of fact.

98. d. Statement of fact.

99. b. Statement of fact.

100. c. Statement of fact.

BROKER APPENDIX
Practice Examination VI

1. You are a California real estate broker. A prospect is referred to you by an out-of-state broker, and a sale is consummated by you. You want to split your commission with the cooperating broker. Under the California Real Estate Law you

   a. may pay a commission to a broker of another state.
   b. cannot divide a commission with a broker of another state.
   c. can pay a commission to a broker of another state only if he or she is also licensed in California.
   d. None of the above

2. The age of a house can be determined most accurately by inspecting the

   a. physical condition of the house.
   b. architectural style of the house.
   c. tax assessor's records.
   d. recorded subdivision map.

3. An apartment building cost $450,000. It brings in a net income of $3,000 per month. The owner is making what percentage of return on the investment?

   a. 7 percent   c. 11 percent
   b. 8 percent   d. 13 percent

4. A secured real property loan usually consists of

   a. a financing statement and trust deed.
   b. the debt and the lien.
   c. FHA or PMI insurance.
   d. a security agreement and a financing statement.

5. During the escrow process, if an unresolved dispute should arise between the seller and the buyer preventing the close of escrow, the escrow holder may legally

 a. arbitrate the dispute as a neutral party.
 b. rescind the escrow and return all documents and monies to the respective parties.
 c. file an interpleader action in court.
 d. All of the above

6. When a loan is fully amortized by equal monthly payments of principal and interest, the amount(s) applied to principal

 a. remains the same.
 b. decreases while the interest payment increases.
 c. increases while the interest payment decreases.
 d. increases by a constant amount.

7. The covenant of quiet enjoyment most directly relates to

 a. nuisances maintained on adjoining property.
 b. possession or real property.
 c. title to real property.
 d. All of the above

8. An interest in real property may be acquired by either prescription or by adverse possession. The interest resulting from prescription is

 a. the right to use another's land.
 b. a possessory title.
 c. an equitable interest.
 d. a private grant.

9. The term *highest and best use* would most likely include the

 a. net return.
 b. multiple units in place.
 c. capitalized income.
 d. ground rent.

10. Regarding past and future depreciation, it is true that the

 a. cost-to-cure method of estimating depreciation mainly focuses on future depreciation.
 b. straight-line method of depreciation may be used to measure past or future depreciation.
 c. cost approach deals with accruals for past and future depreciation.
 d. income approach provides for accrued depreciation in projecting net income into future income.

11. Many legal authorities state that a contract for the sale of land, in addition to the four essential elements of a contract, should have five additional specific items. These are a written agreement or memorandum or note, names and signatures of all parties, the designated purchase price, sufficient description of the land, and time and manner of payment. Which of the five may be substantiated by oral evidence?

 a. Designated purchase price
 b. Names and signatures of all parties
 c. Sufficient description of the land
 d. Time and manner of payment

12. Even when fully executed and performed, this contract is unenforceable. It is a(n)

    a. net listing where the broker did not disclose the amount of compensation to the principal.
    b. oral listing for the sale of a business opportunity.
    c. oral listing for the lease of a home for one year.
    d. signed open listing that did not contain a definite termination date.

13. Of the many requirements of an option agreement, it must specifically state

    a. that the offer will remain open for a specific time period.
    b. that the agreement is irrevocable.
    c. that the optionor can keep the price paid for the option if the optionee fails to purchase.
    d. the time for the optionee to purchase.

14. In which of the following is the appraiser estimating the value of the land by considering it as fully developed to its highest and best use, then deducting the cost of development?

    a. Land residual method
    b. Development method
    c. Comparative approach
    d. Building residual technique

15. A metes-and-bounds description typically uses degrees, minutes, and seconds to describe the angles of lines. These angles are a deflection from the _____ lines.

    a. east and west
    b. west and south
    c. north and east
    d. north and south

16. Subdivider Edwards divides a parcel of land into several lots. He uses real property sales contracts as the method of sale. In the contract, Edwards places an agreement that the purchaser agrees not to prepay the contract. With that consideration, it is true that the

    a. contract is void because of the clause.
    b. vendee can disregard the clause and can prepay.
    c. vendee cannot prepay the balance on the contract.
    d. clause is binding on all subsequent buyers.

17. Interest rates for real estate loans are influenced by many different factors, such as the

    a. amount and durability of the borrower's income.
    b. discounted stream of future interest and amortization payments.
    c. amount of the down payment and the length of the loan.
    d. All of the above

18. In the event of a lawsuit, this form of ownership would give the individual participant the least liability. It is a

    a. partnership.
    b. limited partnership.
    c. syndication.
    d. corporation.

19. The cost of owning property would include all of the following EXCEPT

    a. real estate taxes and assessments.
    b. depreciation of the improvements.
    c. amortization of the borrowed money.
    d. income lost on the equity.

20. Appraiser Wilson takes into consideration future deterioration of improvements when estimating value of property

    a. through extended future economic life.
    b. by providing accruals for depreciation.
    c. by allowing for accrued depreciation.
    d. All of the above

21. The federal open housing laws prohibit discrimination by parties in the sale of which of the following properties?

    a. A 25-unit apartment building
    b. A single-family residence purchased with government assistance
    c. A single-family residence sold by a real estate broker
    d. All of the above

22. The term *ethics* is synonymous with

    a. knowledge of the law.
    b. a science dealing with morals and conduct, and a broker's relations to customers, clients, and fellow agents.
    c. honesty.
    d. parties held in high esteem.

23. A real estate licensee is required to make quarterly reports to the Real Estate Commissioner in

    a. subdivision lot sales.
    b. condominium sales.
    c. real property syndicate securities.
    d. assisting others in filing an application for the purchase of government-owned land.

24. A Declaration of Homestead can be filed on a

    a. 25-unit apartment building in which the owner resides.
    b. home in which the occupant has a 30-year lease.
    c. cooperative apartment project in which the owner holds the unit in fee simple.
    d. All of the above

25. A subdivider wishes to place certain restrictions on the subdivision property. Accordingly, he should

    a. include the restrictions as covenants in the deed.
    b. post the restrictions in the subdivision sales office.
    c. record the restrictions and refer to them in each deed.
    d. publish the restrictions in a newspaper of general circulation.

26. The many ways to terminate an easement include all of the following *EXCEPT*

    a. the dominant tenement deeds the easement to the servient tenement.
    b. abandonment by the dominant tenement.
    c. the merger of the servient and dominant tenement.
    d. the revocation of the easement by the servient tenement.

27. All of the following concerning title to real property are incorrect *EXCEPT*

    a. it is proper for a deed to be delivered by an attorney after the death of a grantor.
    b. recording a deed may or may not convey title.
    c. title passes when the grantor delivers the deed to the escrow holder.
    d. a grant deed must be used to transfer title.

28. Lessor Baker and lessee Johnson enter into an oral agreement for the leasing of an apartment for a period of six months. Johnson decided not to occupy the premises and refused to honor the terms of the lease. The lease agreement is

    a. invalid, as Johnson did not take possession of the premises.
    b. void, as only written agreements will be upheld in court.
    c. valid, even though the terms of the lease are by oral agreement.
    d. valid, only if both Baker and Johnson can prove that the oral agreement exists.

29. A man owns a lot and wishes to build a home on it. He purchased lumber for $8,000 and it was delivered to the site on May 1st. On May 2nd, he obtained a construction loan and a first trust deed was recorded for $150,000. On June 25th, a painter did work in the amount of $3,000. Because the lumber company and the painter were not paid, they each filed a mechanic's lien. The borrower did not make the loan payments. On September 5th, the lender foreclosed and the property was ultimately sold at a foreclosure sale. How much did the lender receive?

    a. $150,000   c. $139,000
    b. $142,000   d. $147,000

30. Under real estate law an appraisal would be required

    a. in any sale of real property.
    b. in the sale of subdivided land located out-of-state being offered for sale in state.
    c. whenever land is subdivided in California.
    d. in the use of a land contract for the sale of property.

31. The evidence used to indicate a loan against personal property is a

    a. pledge agreement.
    b. security agreement.
    c. chattel mortgage.
    d. All of the above

32. When analyzing an area for a possible retail commercial site, an appraiser would be most concerned with

    a. government regulations.
    b. the purchasing power of the population within the surrounding community.
    c. amenities of the location.
    d. the labor pool.

33. In the income approach, the final estimate of value is least dependent on

    a. the net income experience.
    b. the net income expectancy.
    c. current interest rates.
    d. the recapture rate and the site value.

34. Franchisor Adams has a net worth of $5 million, with 25 franchisees operating for the last seven years in California. Adams wants to sell eight more franchises. To do so, she must register

    a. as a securities dealer.
    b. with no one.
    c. with the Commissioner of Corporations.
    d. with the Real Estate Commissioner.

35. The tearing down and rebuilding of urban neighborhoods under the jurisdiction of urban renewal programs is referred to as

    a. remodeling.
    b. rehabilitation.
    c. redevelopment.
    d. reclamation.

36. Buyer Grey signed a waiver regarding the delivery of a settlement disclosure statement that is required for loan transactions under RESPA. The settlement statement

    a. must be handed to Grey at the close of escrow.
    b. must be delivered to Grey as soon as is practical after the close of escrow.
    c. is a right Grey cannot waive.
    d. does not have to be given.

37. Gerald, a 17-year-old minor who is in the U.S. armed forces full time, wishes to purchase a home. This can be done legally when

    a. buying a home under the Cal-Vet program.
    b. buying a home only under FHA or DVA.
    c. seeking any type of conventional financing.
    d. None of the above

38. When one broker is authorized by another broker to act as a subagent for the principal, and the principal authorizes this, the broker becomes responsible to

    a. both the buyer and the principal.
    b. the principal.
    c. only the broker.
    d. neither the principal or the broker.

39. Often, there are comparisons made about different types of properties that lenders prefer as security for real estate loans. In comparing an apartment building with a motel, which of the following would reflect the attitude of many lenders?

    a. The loan-to-value ratio would probably be higher for a motel.
    b. An interest rate charged on a loan for a motel purchase would probably be higher than an interest rate charged for an apartment building loan.
    c. Government-backed lending programs tend to favor motels.
    d. All of the above

40. Title insurance companies examine various public records very carefully before issuing a policy of title insurance for a piece of property. It prepares a summary of pertinent information called

    a. an abstract of title.
    b. a certificate of title.
    c. a guarantee of title.
    d. the policy of title insurance.

41. The lender's right to foreclose on property in the event of loan default is for

    a. illegal use of property.
    b. delinquent payments.
    c. lack of maintenance of the property.
    d. All of the above

42. An appurtenant easement is best described as a(n)

    a. interest in the land that is capable of being transferred.
    b. license.
    c. possessory interest in the land of another.
    d. None of the above

43. Which of the following is a requirement by the county recorder before a deed will be accepted for recording?

    a. Acknowledgment by the grantee
    b. Legal description of the property being transferred
    c. A competent grantee
    d. Information indicating where the property tax statement is to be sent

44. The holder of a life estate, if not restricted by deed, can do all of the following *EXCEPT*

    a. sell the life estate.
    b. encumber it.
    c. rent it.
    d. will it.

45. A "hold harmless" clause in a listing agreement protects the broker from liability for

    a. incorrect information supplied by a seller.
    b. incorrect information supplied by a buyer.
    c. incorrect information given to the escrow holder.
    d. incorrect information given to the lender.

46. When an appraiser refers to a "neighborhood," he or she will typically give most weight to

    a. the geographic situs.
    b. income of the residents.
    c. ease of transportation.
    d. amenities within the area.

47. Fraud would be found if

    a. the buyer purchases property based on deceit by the seller, and the buyer loses a large sum of money.
    b. an intentional misrepresentation by the seller induces the buyer to purchase.
    c. material facts are incorrectly stated causing the buyer serious financial loss.
    d. All of the above

48. A house sold for $113,900, which was 11 percent more than the cost of the house. The cost was most nearly

    a. $99,960.   c. $101,370.
    b. $100,400.   d. $102,610.

49. Regarding limited partnerships, the limited partners

    a. are allowed to use their names in the partnership business.
    b. are equal to the general partners.
    c. are responsible for the debts of the partnership.
    d. do not have responsibility for the debts of the partnership beyond the amount of their investment.

50. When a note secured by a trust deed is sold through a real estate broker, the broker must record

    a. the trust deed.
    b. the assignment of trust deed.
    c. a reconveyance or satisfaction.
    d. a release.

51. The largest source of funds for farm loans is/are

    a. individual sellers.
    b. federal land banks.
    c. commercial banks.
    d. the Farmers Home Administration.

52. The federal fair housing law of 1968 was adopted to prohibit discrimination, as defined in law, in the sale or rental of housing. The federal agency responsible for administering this law is the

    a. U.S. Attorney General's office.
    b. Department of Health and Safety.
    c. Department of Housing and Urban Development.
    d. None of the above

53. In property management, the purpose of analyzing the market, setting a rental schedule, and estimating management expenses is to

    a. increase the net income from the property.
    b. protect the owner's invested capital.
    c. provide effective service for the owner.
    d. All of the above

54. When a final subdivision map is presented for recording by the subdivider, it must contain all of the following *EXCEPT*

    a. the lot, block, and tract data.
    b. the recorded mortgage information.
    c. easements for streets, public utilities.
    d. the subdivision name.

55. All of the following are encumbrances *EXCEPT*

    a. trust deeds.   c. liens.
    b. judgments.   d. claims.

56. Private property owner Abel discovered that his property was damaged by public works done in the area. Which of the following actions can he take to recover any financial loss?

    a. Police power
    b. Inverse escheat
    c. Inverse condemnation
    d. None of the above

57. David plans to build an improvement that is regulated by the State Housing Act and the local building codes. David must abide by

    a. only local regulations.
    b. the contractor's license law.
    c. the State Housing Law that prevails over local ordinances.
    d. the more stringent of the laws.

58. Which of the following is a violation of antitrust laws?

    a. Brokers agreeing to set commissions at a specific percentage rate
    b. Brokers paying referral fees to out-of-state brokers
    c. Brokers using cooperating broker contracts
    d. Brokers who discount their fees

59. Which of the following statements is least correct in analyzing the marketplace for single-family residences in a certain area?

    a. Effective demand for real property is a reflection of consumer incomes.
    b. Effective demand for real property is heavily dependent on the availability and terms of financing.
    c. Effective demand is generally stable, as the supply of real property is relatively fixed.
    d. Due to fixity of location, each parcel of real property is different.

60. Developer Stone is thinking of building a neighborhood shopping center. The population concentration needed for the area is

    a. 5,000 to 10,000.
    b. 20,000 to 30,000.
    c. 30,000 to 50,000.
    d. 75,000 to 100,000.

61. Broker Cooper solicited listings by canvassing a nonintegrated neighborhood that was adjacent to a minority neighborhood. He obtained many listings by telling homeowners that minorities were moving into the neighborhood and property values would drop. What he is doing is called

    a. steering.
    b. panic peddling.
    c. blockbusting.
    d. Both *b* and *c*

62. A developer wishes to sell lots to the public for cash only. She wants to install curbs and streets but does not want assessment bonds to appear on a title report. This can be done by

    a. a real estate sales contract.
    b. an improvement bond.
    c. an interim loan from an institutional lender.
    d. depositing funds into a neutral escrow account.

63. Mr. Lee entered into an oral contract with Mr. Leonard for the exchange of real property. This type of agreement is

    a. invalid.   c. void.
    b. unenforceable.   d. illegal.

64. The law that requires all real property transactions to be closed through escrow is

    a. California law.
    b. federal law.
    c. Both *a* and *b*
    d. Neither *a* nor *b*

65. The Truth-in-Lending Act requires that a disclosure statement be given to the consumer. This statement includes

    a. a description of the security interest retained and used for the loan.
    b. a listing of all items included in the finance charge.
    c. the annual percentage rate, fully spelled out.
    d. All of the above

66. The lowest loan-to-value ratio made by lending institutions on real property would probably be on

    a. industrial property.
    b. residential property.
    c. vacant land.
    d. commercial projects.

67. A real estate licensee must

    a. in the course of his or her business, act in the spirit of "do unto others as you would have them do unto you."
    b. be colorblind in all dealings with clients and customers.
    c. in no way encourage the violation of discrimination laws in the sale, lease, or rental of property.
    d. abide by all of the above.

68. Regarding Article 7 loans, the interest would begin when the

    a. mortgage loan disclosure statement is signed.
    b. funds are delivered to the borrower.
    c. money is placed into escrow.
    d. Either *b* or *c*

69. Which of the following is correct concerning an ALTA policy of title insurance?

    a. It protects a lessee who occupies the property after the date shown on the title insurance policy.
    b. It is limited to stated conditions of title as of the date of the issuance of the title policy.
    c. It protects against any encroachment that occurs after the date of issuance of the title policy.
    d. It protects against any easements created during the term of the title insurance policy.

70. Creating a valid mortgage debt requires a

    a. pledge of security and a power of sale clause.
    b. lien in favor of the mortgagor.
    c. pledge of security and a contract for repayment.
    d. note with a promise to pay.

71. Which of the following would receive the most favorable federal income taxation treatment?

    a. Real property held for production of income
    b. Real property held for sale to customers
    c. Investment property
    d. Real property held for use in a trade or business

72. After buyer Mathew purchases an interest in a stock cooperative he then

    a. obtains a grant deed from the seller.
    b. becomes a general partner.
    c. executes a lease agreement.
    d. purchases a share of stock in the corporation that owns the property.

73. Under the U.S. Government Survey method of land description, rows of townships that run north and south are called

    a. tiers.   c. meridians.
    b. ranges.   d. base lines.

74. The longest, most comprehensive and most detailed form of an appraisal report is called the

    a. form report.
    b. letter report.
    c. narrative report.
    d. comparative market analysis.

75. In performing an appraisal, what information may real estate broker Carter tell the property owner about a wood shingle roof on the owner's house?

    a. That the life expectancy of a wood shingle roof is 25 years
    b. That rafters are commonly spaced 24 inches apart
    c. That the life expectancy of a roof is dependent on the pitch of a roof
    d. That wood shingles are the best to use today

76. A bilateral contract is one that is a(n)

    a. promise for performance.
    b. promise for an act.
    c. act for a promise.
    d. promise for a promise.

77. For a real estate broker to be entitled to a commission if the property sells after the expiration of the listing, the broker should place into the listing agreement a

    a. liquidated damages clause.
    b. due diligence clause.
    c. safety clause.
    d. None of the above

78. A group of four persons forms a joint venture. To best protect each of his or her interests, each individual should

    a. prepare and record a partnership agreement.
    b. prepare and record separate certificates of ownership.
    c. record a deed showing the names of all owners and open a joint bank account in the names of all owners.
    d. obtain a title insurance policy.

79. The method used within the cost approach that tends to set the upper limit of value is _____ cost.

    a. historic   c. reproduction
    b. replacement   d. unit-in-place

80. The lender that tends to charge the greatest amount of points in a tight money market is

    a. the one who make DVA-guaranteed loans.
    b. a mortgage company.
    c. Cal-Vet.
    d. the one who makes FHA-insured loans.

81. Trust funds may be

    a. cash.
    b. a check used as a purchase deposit.
    c. a personal note made payable to the seller.
    d. All of the above

82. According to the Business and Professions Code, a real estate salesperson who accepts trust funds on behalf of the broker under whom he or she is licensed must immediately deliver the funds to the broker or, if directed by the broker, place the funds into

    a. the hands of the broker's principal.
    b. a neutral escrow depository.
    c. the broker's trust account.
    d. All of the above

83. To avoid a charge of commingling funds, any commissions, fees, and other incomes earned by a broker, collectible from trust funds and deposited into the broker's trust account, may remain there for a period not to exceed

    a. 30 days.   c. 60 days.
    b. 25 days.   d. 90 days.

84. Which of the following is correct regarding trust fund bank accounts?

    a. The broker may have a minimum of $100 of his or her own money in the trust account.
    b. The broker may have a maximum of $200 of his or her own money in the trust account.
    c. The broker may have a maximum of $500 of his or her own money in the trust account.
    d. There is no limit on the amount of the broker's own money in the trust account.

85. It is said that "good property management begins"

    a. before the property is acquired.
    b. after the property is acquired, but before expenditures are made.
    c. after the property is acquired.
    d. None of the above

86. An attachment lien can be discharged in all of the following methods EXCEPT

    a. by a release signed by the officer of the court who levied the writ.
    b. by a judgment in favor of the plaintiff.
    c. as a result of a court order.
    d. by a correctly acknowledged and recorded signed release by the plaintiff.

87. Hoover obtains permission from government authorities to build a structure and create a use that is currently prohibited by zoning laws. This is known as

    a. nonconforming use.
    b. spot zoning or a variance.
    c. revitalization.
    d. redlining.

88. All of the following do not require recording EXCEPT a

    a. lease agreement.
    b. quitclaim deed.
    c. declaration of abandonment of homestead.
    d. voluntary lien.

89. A grantee's name must appear in the grant deed as one of the deed's many essential elements. A deed would be construed as void from the beginning if the grantee is

    a. an unincorporated association.
    b. a fictitious person.
    c. not named in the deed, but adequately described or designated.
    d. described under an assumed name.

90. Which of the following parties is personally liable for unpaid business debts?

    a. Stockholders in a corporation
    b. All members of a general partnership
    c. Limited partners
    d. Investors in a real estate investment trust

91. Which of the following must be contained in a valid lease?

    a. A proper description of the property
    b. The signatures of the lessor and lessee
    c. The credit rating of the lessee
    d. All of the above

92. When a buyer of the bulk of inventory of a business fails to file a notice of intention to sell, the

    a. inventory could be attached by the seller's creditors.
    b. sale is still valid.
    c. sale is void.
    d. sale is illegal.

93. To determine the depreciation factor in the cost approach, the appraiser would use the _____ of the property.

    a. actual age
    b. effective age
    c. chronological age
    d. economic life

94. When acting as an agent, a real estate licensee is liable to third parties for

    a. only written contracts made in the name of his or her principal.
    b. actions of properly appointed sub-agents.
    c. his or her own torts.
    d. torts committed by his or her principal in the transaction.

95. All of the following statements concerning an option are correct *EXCEPT*

    a. unless prohibited in the contract, the option is assignable.
    b. the optionee has the first right to purchase the property.
    c. the optionee has the legal right to enter and use the property right after the option has been entered into.
    d. performance of the terms found in the lease option is sufficient consideration for the option agreement.

96. Buyer Smith agrees to pay $25,000 down for the purchase of seller Jones's home. Smith also agrees to assume the existing note and first trust deed of $120,000. The assumed loan on Jones's closing statement would appear as a

    a. debit to Smith.
    b. debit to Jones.
    c. credit to Smith.
    d. credit to Jones.

97. A VA loan is guaranteed to protect the

    a. trustee.
    b. veteran borrower.
    c. seller.
    d. lender.

98. A Caucasian person would have recourse to fair housing provisions under the Civil Rights Act of 1968 if denied the right to

    a. have minority neighbors.
    b. attend the church of his or her choice.
    c. meet neighbors.
    d. choose neighbors.

99. A collection service is trying to collect a note at the insistence of a holder in due course. The maker of the note could use as a real defense that

    a. there was fraud in the inducement of the note.
    b. there was no consideration to the maker.
    c. the face of the note was materially altered.
    d. None of the above

100. Regarding the California Real Estate Broker's License Examination,

    a. I will pass.   c. I will pass.
    b. I will pass.   d. I will pass.

■ ANSWER KEY

1. a.   Statement of fact.

2. c.   Statement of fact.

3. b. $3,000 per month × 12 months = $36,000 per year (always convert monthly rent to annual rent in the income approach). Net income $36,000 ÷ $450,000 cost (or value) = 8% return on the investment.

4. b.   The debt is evidenced by a note. The lien is created by a deed of trust, which is a security device.

5. c.   Statement of fact.

6. c.   Statement of fact.

7. b.   One example of possession or real property occurs when a lessee (tenant) moves in. There is an implied covenant (promise) with every lease agreement that the lessee is entitled to the quiet enjoyment and possession of property.

8. a.   Prescription (easement by prescription) conveys only the right to use another's land.

9. a.   The principle of highest and best use refers to that use which at the time of an appraisal is most likely to produce the greatest net return to the land and/or buildings over a given period of time.

10. b.   Statement of fact.

11. c.   You could substantiate the description of property by oral evidence, that is, by agreeing that the street address is a sufficient description.

12. a.   The broker must disclose the amount of his or her compensation on a net listing prior to or at the time the principal binds the broker to the agreement.

13. a.   The option must state that the offer remains open for a certain period of time. In effect, when the buyer pays consideration to the seller for the option, the buyer is purchasing an agreed amount of time in which to accept or reject the offer to purchase the property.

14. b.   Statement of fact.

15. d.   In the metes-and-bounds form of land description, angles are a deflection from the north and south lines. Parties move easterly or westerly so many degrees (a degree is divided into 60 minutes) from the north and south lines. An easy way to remember is that there are five letters in the word *metes*. There are also five letters each in the words *north* and *south*.

16. b.   The vendee can disregard the clause that prohibits early payment. In a real property sales contract, a vendor cannot prevent the prepayment of the contract on subdivided residential lots that contain a dwelling of not more than four units. The vendee cannot waive the right to prepay. (However, a seller and buyer may enter into a written agreement to not prepay the contract for the first 12 months following the sale.)

17. d.   Statement of fact.

18. d.   Statement of fact.

19. c.   Statement of fact.

20. b.   Accruals for depreciation refer to dollars being put aside to provide for the effects of future deterioration or depreciation.

21. d.   Statement of fact.

22. b.   Statement of fact.

23. d. Statement of fact.

24. d. Statement of fact.

25. c. Recording the restrictions (commonly on a "declaration of restrictions") and referring to them in each subsequent transfer of title is a usual and efficient method of imposing and disclosing restrictions on a subdivision.

26. d. Revocation by the servient tenement is not a way to terminate an easement. There are many ways to terminate an easement, including express release, legal proceedings, nonuse of a prescriptive easement for five years, abandonment, merger of the servient tenement and the easement in the same person, destruction of the servient tenement, and adverse possession by the owner of the servient tenement.

27. b. Recording the deed may or may not convey title. Recording is one way to evidence *delivery* of the deed and to give public notice of the transfer. Valid title may or may not have passed (the deed could have been forged), which is why title insurance has become so important.

28. c. Leases for one year or less may be by oral agreement; such agreements are considered to be valid.

29. c. Recall the date of a mechanic's lien is the date any work of improvement commenced on the property. Therefore, the date of both the lumber company and the painter's liens will be May 1st. As a result, they take priority over the trust deed that was recorded later. They will be paid a total of $11,000 from the proceeds of the sale, and the lender will receive $139,000.

30. b. The requirement of an appraisal is to try to minimize the potential for fraud or misrepresentation in the sale of property located out-of-state being offered to Californians.

31. d. Statement of fact.

32. b. The purchasing power of the area is a good indicator of the potential for the success of retail development.

33. a. The income approach is based on future expected income. Past and present income is used only as a guide in the appraisal process. Net income expectancy and not "net income experience" would be of greater concern to the appraiser, along with the recapture rate, site value, and current interest rates.

34. b. A franchisor with a net worth of $5 million who has had 25 franchises operating continuously for five years preceding the offer or sale is exempt from registration with the California Department of Corporations.

35. c. Statement of fact.

36. b. Statement of fact.

37. a. Cal-Vet allows minors who are on active duty with any of the armed forces of the United States to purchase a home using the Cal-Vet program, if otherwise qualified.

38. b. Statement of fact (old law was five days; current law is 10 days).

39. b. A loan for a motel, whose occupants by nature of their purpose are transitory, is a higher risk loan for the lending institution than a loan for an apartment building. In lending, the higher the risk, the higher the interest rate.

40. a. Statement of fact.

41. d. Statement of fact.

42. a. Statement of fact.

43. d. Statement of fact.

44. d. Unless restricted in the deed, the holder of a life estate can do many things with the property, such as rent, lease, sell, or encumber it (although such transactions are rare). However, the holder cannot will the interest, as the life estate interest terminates when the person on whose life the estate depends expires. The property would then revert to the original grantor (estate in reversion) or continue on to a third party (estate in remainder).

45. a. Statement of fact.

46. a. The term *neighborhood* describes a certain geographic area.

47. d. All of the above.

48. d. Use the cost rule: Cost equals 100 percent. Add the 11 percent profit to 100 percent to equal 111 percent. Divide the sales price of $113,900 by 1.11 to equal $102,613 cost. The closest choice is $102,610.

49. d. Statement of fact.

50. b. Statement of fact. Broker has one week after close of escrow to record.

51. c. In rural areas, commercial banks actively make farm loans.

52. c. Statement of fact.

53. d. Statement of fact.

54. b. The question asks for the exception. Mortgage data is not shown on a final map.

55. d. The one that is not an encumbrance is a claim. The other choices are all examples of encumbrances.

56. c. Inverse condemnation is the reverse of a governmental condemnation action. In this instance, it is the property owner who wants a government agency to take his other property to avoid further financial loss caused by a public entity.

57. d. Statement of fact.

58. a. Statement of fact.

59. c. Statement of fact.

60. a. Statement of fact.

61. d. Choices *b* and *c*. *Panic peddling* and *blockbusting* are terms used to describe the same illegal activity.

62. d. Statement of fact.

63. b. The oral agreement for the sale or exchange of real property is unenforceable. Contracts for the sale or exchange of real property require a proper writing under the statute of frauds for enforceability of the agreement.

64. d. Using the escrow process to close real estate transactions is not a legal requirement (with some exceptions), but rather a well-established practice.

65. d. Statement of fact.

66. a. Statement of fact.

67. d. Statement of fact.

68. d. Statement of fact.

69. b. Statement of fact.

70. c. Statement of fact.

71. d. Statement of fact.

72. d. Statement of fact.

73. b. Range lines run north and south and are six miles apart. (*Range* has five letters and *north* and *south* each have five letters.)

74. c. Statement of fact.

75. c. The life of the roof depends upon its pitch. The steeper the pitch, the less the exposure to the sun and rainwater collection, and the longer it will last.

76. d. A bilateral (two-sided) agreement contains a promise for a promise. For example, an exclusive authorization and right-to-sell listing (a bilateral agreement) contains the owner's promise to pay a commission if the property sells during the listing period. In exchange for this promise, the broker promises to use due diligence in procuring a buyer for the property.

77. c. Statement of fact.

78. c. Statement of fact.

79. c. Reproduction cost refers to the cost of an exact replica or duplicate of subject property. This is too costly to estimate and reproduce, as some component parts of the building might no longer be made.

80. b. Statement of fact.

81. d. Statement of fact.

82. d. Statement of fact.

83. b. If a broker maintains a trust fund account, the broker must remove any of his or her own funds from the account within 25 days of deposit (under current law—old law was 30 days) to avoid a charge of commingling funds.

84. b. A *maximum*, not a minimum, of $200 of the broker's own money can remain in the account (to cover bank service fees, etc.)

85. a. Statement of fact.

86. b. Statement of fact.

87. b. Statement of fact.

88. c. Statement of fact.

89. b. The term *fictitious person* implies that no such person exists. A deed to such a person would be void. Do not confuse this term with *fictitious or assumed name*, which could be a business name. A deed to a fictitious or assumed *name* would be valid.

90. b. Statement of fact.

91. a. Statement of fact.

92. a. Statement of fact.

93. b. The term *effective age* refers to the physical condition of the property. Depending on how well an owner maintains property, it could appear to be older or newer than its actual age. Appraisers base a depreciation factor on the physical condition (effective age) of the property.

94. c. A tort is any wrongful act (not involving a breach of contract) for which a civil action is available to the person who is wronged.

95. c. The question asks for the exception. The optionee does not have the legal right to use the property covered by the option until the option to purchase is exercised and the sale occurs.

96. b. The question asks about the *seller's* closing statement. A loan assumption is a debit to a seller (deducted from sale proceeds).

97. d. The federal DVA program guarantees a lender against loss in the event a veteran defaults on the loan.

98. a. Statement of fact.

99. c. A material alteration of a note (e.g., the face of the note is changed from $500 to $5,000) is an example of a real defense for a maker (borrower) of a note. The maker can refuse to pay the holder in due course (investor and owner of the note) for this reason.

100. All choices are correct. Congratulations on completing the practice testing and best wishes on your exam.

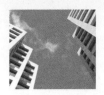

1. How did you use this book? (Please select one of the following choices.)

   ◯ I took a review course at _____ and completed the course in _____.
   Name of School month/year

   ◯ I studied on my own using this book.

   ◯ I studied on my own using this book and [please list other materials used]

   _____

2. Please rate the **usefulness** of each feature in this book by circling a number on a scale from one to five, with **one** being **very useful** and **five** being **not at all useful:**

	Very Useful			Not at all Useful	
Hot Notes	1	2	3	4	5
Hot Notes Categories *(Real Property Law, Property Ownership,* *and Land Use Controls and Regulations, etc.)*	1	2	3	4	5
Number of Questions	1	2	3	4	5
Content of Questions	1	2	3	4	5
Broker's Appendix	1	2	3	4	5
Overall	1	2	3	4	5

3. If you could choose a format, how would you prefer the Hot Notes to be presented?

   ◯ Outline   ◯ Numbered List (the current format)   ◯ Other _____

4. The Hot Notes were also organized by category. Did this feature help you to be more prepared or less prepared? Please check one.

   ◯ More Prepared   ◯ Less Prepared   ◯ It didn't make a difference

5. If all of the answer keys for each section were in one place (at the back of the section), would the book's organization be better or worse? Please check one.

   ◯ Significantly Better   ◯ Better   ◯ Doesn't Matter   ◯ Worse   ◯ Significantly Worse

6. Did this book do a good job of preparing you for the exam? Please explain.

   _____

   _____

7. Please add any additional comments about your favorite and least favorite features of the book, and any suggestions you have for improving it.

   _____

NOTE: This page, when folded over and taped, becomes a postage-free envelope that has been approved by the United States Postal Service. It has been provided for your convenience.

Important—Please Fold Page and Tape Before Mailing

- -

Important—Please Fold Page and Tape Before Mailing

- -

Return Address:

_____

_____

_____

BUSINESS REPLY MAIL
FIRST CLASS MAIL   PERMIT NO. 88176   CHICAGO, IL

POSTAGE WILL BE PAID BY ADDRESSEE:

Dearborn
Real Estate Education
30 South Wacker Drive
Suite 2500
Chicago, Illinois 60606-7481

Attn: Editorial Department